DARK BLACK AND BLUE

THE SOUNDGARDEN STORY

DARK BLACK AND BLUE

THE SOUNDGARDEN STORY

BY GREG PRATO

Written by Greg Prato
Printed and distributed by Greg Prato Writer, Corp
Published by Greg Prato Writer, Corp
Front cover photo by Karen Mason-Blair
Back cover photo by Kurt Christensen
Front cover design by Mary Prato
Copyright © 2019, Greg Prato Writer, Corp. All rights reserved.
First Edition, September 2019

ISBN: 9781691086139

INTRO

To those who were not cognizant of what was going on in rock music during the mid to late '80s (or in some cases, weren't even living nor breathing yet), it is probably tempting to say that it was all jolly good fun. After all, this was an era that saw the emergence of Metallica, Slayer, Guns N' Roses, Beastie Boys, Run-DMC, Public Enemy, Red Hot Chili Peppers, Pixies, REM, Fugazi, Jane's Addiction, and Faith No More, right? *Wrong*. Coming from the view of a bystander who actually witnessed music and pop culture during this time period, by and large, it was a steaming pile of feces.

If you were to switch on mainstream radio or MTV, chances are you would be assaulted by squeaky clean, cookie cutter, soulless-sounding rubbish, that often times, resulted in it being darn difficult to differentiate one fooler from another. But...the underground rock scene was an entirely different story— Bad Brains, Meat Puppets, Sonic Youth, Dinosaur Jr., Ministry, Jane's Addiction, Primus, Nirvana, Mudhoney, and Nine Inch Nails all offered up outstanding music during this period. And of course, Soundgarden.

As I mentioned a while back in the intro to my earlier book, *Grunge Is Dead: The Oral History of Seattle Rock Music*, I was first introduced to Soundgarden via an airing or two of the "Hands All Over" music video on MTV's *Headbangers Ball,* probably in late '89 (to their credit, we should give MTV props for launching two shows that would help provide first glimpses of Soundgarden and some of the aforementioned underground bands to many—the metal-based *Headbangers Ball* and the alt-based *120 Minutes*).

But when I first saw Soundgarden live, they were *not* the real reason why I attended a show at a Brooklyn metal club, L'Amour, on Saturday, March 17, 1990. The main attraction for yours truly was the first band that went on that night, Faith No More, and to a lesser degree, the last one, Voivod. It also served as my first ever "club show"—after spending the previous few years strictly attending arena concerts. To say I was blown away by FNM's set was an understatement, as it served as one of those life-changing moments where I seemingly listened to rock music differently (as well as what I expected from subsequent rock shows) immediately afterwards.

As I retreated to the back of the general admission section for Soundgarden (after being smushed up front for FNM), I didn't have high hopes, but was curious to see them, regardless. From the first note, Soundgarden demanded your attention, and particularly, their already shirtless, long-haired singer—who entered the stage by immediately climbing out over the audience via a ceiling pipe, and dropping down below (sounds familiar to the stage antics of a certain other daredevil rock singer a year or two down the road, eh?).

Like Faith No More, what grabbed my attention the most about Soundgarden was how *real* the band not only sounded, but looked on stage. Instead of getting all dolled up in outfits (like most of the bands I had previously seen in concert), they were wearing the same clothes as if it was a rehearsal—t-shirts, well-worn jeans, and long-hair devoid of any primping or spray. By the end of their set, I was thoroughly impressed—so much so, that I made a personal promise to myself that I would indeed purchase their latest album, *Louder Than Love,* on compact disc as soon as possible (and in case you were wondering, Voivod also offered an inspired set...but for me personally, not in the same league as their bill mates).

In the ensuing months, I became a major Soundgarden fan (purchasing *Ultramega OK* and the just-released comp, *Screaming Life/Fopp*), as myself and some pals made it a point to travel to NYC to catch a follow-up performance on August 17th, when SG were the middle men on a bill at the Beacon Theater, sandwiched between Warrior Soul and Danzig. By far the best performers that night, it only solidified that the band that hailed quite a long way from my home state of New York—Seattle, Washington—was fast becoming one of my favorites. *Without question.*

But it would be Soundgarden's next two studio albums that made them one of my all-time favorite bands— *Badmotorfinger* and *Superunknown.* There are few albums that I have listened to as consistently as these two over the years—never going too long of a distance without a sonic re-examination, and never getting tired of what I heard. As a result, there have been few rock bands that I connected with as greatly and whose music meant as much to me as Soundgarden. In fact, there are probably few rock bands I have made such an effort of exposing their music to as many friends as I did with Soundgarden—making countless tape copies back in the good old cassette days, to help spread the word (just so you know, *Badmotorfinger* fits perfectly on a single side of a 90-minute cassette...if you delete "Searching with My Good Eye Closed" and "New Damage").

I've stuck with Soundgarden through it all—disappointed by their break-up in 1997, honored to have interviewed the members for either articles and/or for my aforementioned book, *Grunge Is Dead,* and overjoyed by their reunion in 2010. And then of course, the shock, disbelief, and sadness I experienced upon learning of Chris' death in 2017 (which, truth be told, I still feel the unsettling tremors of even as I type this intro—two years later).

I have contemplated the idea of doing a book about Soundgarden's history going as far back as to when I penned a feature about the band's history for *Classic Rock Magazine* (that appeared in their "Summer 2005" issue under the title *Black Hole Sons*...no, I didn't title it). However, with the arrival of *Grunge Is Dead,* I figured that would serve as "my Soundgarden book," since at the time, the band was still kaput—with no signs of life— and *GID* covered most of the bases concerning their career.

But after their reunion and Chris' passing, there was a whole other part of the Soundgarden story to document, and their earlier history to explore in greater detail. Which ultimately led to me deciding to finally put fingertips to keyboard, open my memory bank, do research/interviews, embark on an extreme Soundgarden listening spree, and construct this book.

But honestly, my main decision to do this book was because I was—and remain—so affected by Chris's death, and find myself now listening to Soundgarden's music and reading into Chris' lyrics differently (and admittedly, having experienced trouble listening to it *at all* immediately after his passing). I figured doing a book may help me make sense of it all...or at least, come to terms with it.

I've been deaf now I want noise,
Greg Prato

p.s. Wonder what this book's title is in reference to? Read on...and remain alert—it lurks somewhere within this book!

p.p.s. Questions? Comments? Feel free to email me at gregprato@yahoo.com.

DEDICATION
To the memory and music of Christopher John Cornell
July 20, 1964-May 18, 2017

INDEX

CHAPTER 01: MASS POPULAR THING................................1
CHAPTER 02: CHRIS..4
CHAPTER 03: KIM...9
CHAPTER 04: THE GARDEN GROWS................................14
CHAPTER 05: MATT..25
CHAPTER 06: SCREAMING LIFE...................................30
CHAPTER 07: FOPP..39
CHAPTER 08: ULTRAMEGA OK.....................................44
CHAPTER 09: LOUDER THAN LOVE................................56
CHAPTER 10: BEN...69
CHAPTER 11: TEMPLE OF THE DOG................................90
CHAPTER 12: BADMOTORFINGER I.................................97
CHAPTER 13: SEATTLE GRUNGE FLANNEL....................111
CHAPTER 14: BADMOTORFINGER II.............................123
CHAPTER 15: 93...149
CHAPTER 16: SUPERUNKNOWN I................................165
CHAPTER 17: SUPERUNKNOWN II...............................189
CHAPTER 18: 95...211
CHAPTER 19: DOWN ON THE UPSIDE...........................223
CHAPTER 20: 97 09...246
CHAPTER 21: 10 11...266
CHAPTER 22: KING ANIMAL.....................................279
CHAPTER 23: CHRIS..308
CHAPTER 24: IF YOU LIKE THE SOUND........................318
PHIL ANSELMO INTERVIEW....................................333
DAVE WYNDORF INTERVIEW...................................337
JIM ROSE INTERVIEW..348
GILLIAN GAAR INTERVIEW.....................................362
THE REVEREND HORTON HEAT INTERVIEW.................368
TRAVIS STEVER INTERVIEW....................................374
KAREN MASON-BLAIR INTERVIEW............................379
MARKY RAMONE INTERVIEW...................................383
MATT PINFIELD INTERVIEW....................................390
SOURCES..399
PHOTO CREDITS..424

CHAPTER 01
MASS POPULAR THING

If you were to switch on MTV or flip through a rock music magazine any time in 1992, chances are, you would either see, read, or hear about something to do with grunge or Seattle. The reason? Rock music fans were being fed the same cookie-cutter-esque music from the mainstream for so long, they were starved for something real and truly rockin'. From roughly the late '80s through the early '90s, the three most popular styles of music being championed by MTV and radio were rock, pop, and hip-hop. And in each of those styles, things had largely grown stale.

Case in point, within the realm of rock, fourth-wave hair metallists and bands cloning Led Zeppelin were constantly detected, and even one of the more original rock styles, thrash metal, was becoming same-sounding/predictable. Within pop, artists "singing" to an electronic/programmed backing track became the norm (the reason singing is in quotes is because who knows who was really singing or not...i.e., "the Milli Vanilli syndrome"). And when it came to hip-hop, the lyrical topics often lacked substance and mostly just reflected what was going on in the pop world.

I'm sure if you asked most music fans where they thought the next rock movement was going to hail from, probably the usual suspects would have been listed—New York City, Chicago, Los Angeles, etc. In other words, *not* Seattle. Especially Seattle before Starbucks, Microsoft, and Amazon became globally-recognized brand names (both Starbucks and Amazon were founded in Seattle, while Microsoft relocated to the city in the '80s). In fact, you could make a valid argument that at this time, the town was probably best known for the Mariners, Seahawks, and the SuperSonics, as well as for fishing, logging, and Boeing...plus the burial place of Bruce Lee (and in nearby Renton, Jimi Hendrix). In other words, *not* for its music.

But getting back to the musical side of things, something had to change at the time, and change it did, with Seattle's "Big 4" (Nirvana, Soundgarden, Pearl Jam, and Alice in Chains) not only leading the charge, but also, an additional wave of alternative rock acts that had already either broken through, or were in the process of doing so, right along with them. However, of the quartet of popular Seattle bands, Soundgarden—whose line-up at the time (and their best-known one) was comprised of singer/guitarist Chris Cornell, guitarist Kim Thayil, bassist Ben Shepherd, and drummer Matt Cameron—had been at it the longest.

"It was bound to happen," explained Cornell at the time. "Bands like Nirvana and Nine Inch Nails have been embraced by either TV or radio because younger people have moved into positions of power. And as far as Guns N' Roses are concerned, there were people who wanted more than just another corporate rock band. I'm sure the industry is surprised that any of these bands are successful. The only issue was how many times you had to hit the music business here over the head before they finally realize they were marketing the wrong groups to the wrong audience."

"From Metallica to Jane's Addiction, gradually the walls are getting kicked down," added Thayil. "I take great pleasure in the fact that an awful lot of big-budget corporate rock acts have been failing to sell any tickets, because it means that the industry has failed in its conception of what the audience wants." And Cornell wasn't finished with his assessment. "And believe me, this industry needed a slap in the face, because it should never have been allowed to produce so much commercially contrived music in the first place. Music driven by money deserves to fail. Somehow, people have managed to create a production standard that makes everything sound inhuman and horrible. The bands that are now bustin' through have records that sound like they've been made by human beings. I believe anything formulaic will eventually be recognized as that, which is good news for the likes of Perry Farrell and Kurt Cobain, who despite their success, refuse to allow people to put anchors around them."

Even the newest member at the time, Shepherd, had seen the uprising emerging on the distance for some time. "I always saw it as all of America. When I went on that tour with Nirvana [as a roadie, in 1989], you could see everybody was 'on music' at that point. Music was suddenly alive again and doing something. Sometimes it's film and writing that does that culturally. That time, it was music." And speaking of Nirvana, some unenlightened newcomers may have assumed that Cobain and co. were the originators of the grunge style, since they were the first band to strike big. And while there was no denying that they led the charge—they knocked bloody *Michael Jackson* out of the #1 spot on *Billboard* with their surprise blockbuster, *Nevermind*— Soundgarden had already been at it for nearly a decade, which Cameron was not shy to point out. "We've worked very hard to get where we are. And it's been a very gradual thing. Once we get past that to where it might be a mass popular thing, we might hate it. And I'm not really in any hurry to get into that situation."

Little did the drummer know at the time, the "mass popular thing" would come soon enough, but also, would spin out of control for Seattle's top bands...and eventually, contribute to Soundgarden's ruin.

CHAPTER 02
CHRIS

From the very beginning to the very end of Soundgarden's existence (and throughout various line-up changes), you could always count on two gentlemen to be present through it all—one of which was Chris Cornell. Born on July 20, 1964, in Seattle, Cornell early on went by the name Christopher John Boyle. The youngest of six children ("I'm Bobby in *The Brady Bunch*," he once mused), Chris' father was a pharmacist and his mother an accountant and psychic. He once described the location of his upbringing as "Very Seattle-ish. For lack of a better word, it was white. Urban but not really urban, suburban, but not really suburbia. It was lower-middle-class white. At the time I was growing up, it was the tail end of the baby boom, so there were tons of kids in the neighborhood. Tons of boys, young and old. So there was tons of drugs. The definitive Seattle neighborhood."

And by adding in little-to-no adult supervision ("I would just get up in the morning, go outside and disappear for the whole day"), this ultimately served as the perfect recipe for juvenile delinquency. "We all got in trouble for years. Somebody stealing a car, somebody selling drugs. We were all selling drugs by the time we were twelve, or doing them. Pot or pills or anything that was easily available. My neighbors to the south had two boys who were probably in their late teens when I was about eleven, and they were just huge into drugs. I remember walking by the basement window one time, and this one dude who had like huge, poofy Lynyrd Skynyrd hair and a goatee and a mustache was shooting something at me from a syringe out the window. I don't even know what it was, but it was shooting 15 feet, and I'm walking by, trying to dodge this thing. Those were the kind of people who lived near me."

"From eleven to fourteen, I did drugs every single day," Chris once admitted. "I grew up with the guys that had the nervous twitches and half their brains dead because of the shit they did. In Seattle, when I was young, the drug culture wasn't the same as in San Francisco in the '60s. It wasn't really a philosophy of, 'Free your mind with drugs.' It was more like, 'Fuck up your mind with drugs'." And it sounds like Chris was not too selective when it came to troublemaking—"From auto theft to burglary to selling drugs to beating other kids up and burning down buildings."

Despite being seemingly up to no good, Chris' look at the time did not sound comparable to his cronies. "I was a teeny-tiny baby-faced guy who looked like I was about eleven and who chain-smoked cigarettes and would do drugs! People thought I was cute 'cause I was this tiny guy who could out-drink the other guys. So, I was a mascot, but it wasn't as if people necessarily cared about me or were true friends." But it was also as a youngster that Chris developed a love of music—after hearing the Beatles classic, "Hey Jude." "It made me feel like I hadn't felt before. Sort of a strange euphoria. I remember having the single. I was probably six or seven...rifling through my neighbor's older brother's records was a common thing, and listening to Lynyrd Skynyrd and Alice Cooper and the Beatles."

"I remember stealing a stack of Beatles records from my neighbors' basement. They had thrown them on the ground and the basement flooded and all the sleeves were warped. And I took out all the records and put them in between paper towels and brought them home and started listening to them. I sat in my room for weeks on end listening to these records." Other rock bands were examined, too. "Most of my friends had pretty weird tastes, always drawn towards lyrics that were between intellectual and drug-taking. We were the slacker generation before it existed. Tastes would go from AC/DC, through more fucked up Yes records, to Captain Beefheart and Frank Zappa. It was stoner music, man. You could smoke pot and listen to Black Sabbath."

But ultimately, there was a price to pay with all of his early drug experimentation—Chris later admitted that he would suffer from depression and agoraphobia, possibly due to his drug experiences. "I had a bad PCP [angel dust] experience when I was fourteen and I got panic disorder. And of course, I wasn't telling anyone the truth. It's not like you go to your dad or your doctor and say, 'Yeah, I smoked PCP and I'm having a bad time.' So I became more or less agoraphobic because I'd have flashbacks. From 14 to 16, I didn't have any friends. I stayed home most of the time. Up 'til then life was pretty great. The world was big and I felt I could do anything I wanted. Suddenly, I felt like I couldn't do anything. But in the isolation, my imagination really had time to run."

And as it turns out, his home life wasn't much better— Chris' parents split up when he was fourteen (he adopted his mother's maiden name after his parents' divorce), and soon after, dropped out of school. "I never went to high school. I never really finished eighth grade. I was kicked out of seventh grade once and eighth grade twice. Mainly for not showing up and not doing it. Then I went to an alternative high school [North End alternative high school] for what would have been ninth grade and part of what would have been tenth grade. It was mainly for degenerate young people. It was the last ditch for kids that couldn't go anywhere else. The concept for me was entirely wrong because it was sort of learn at your own pace, do your own thing, and my thing was not school. So I'd go there and not do anything at all. It was just a waste of time."

Years later, he expressed disappointment concerning his decision to not complete his education. "I still regret dropping out, especially being a guy that writes words for a living. I pretty much have a seventh-grade Catholic school education; it would have been helpful if I had continued." But out of all the gloom came something that would eventually give the barely-teenaged Cornell a new direction. "I started playing drums. They didn't seem to require lessons, and music started changing too. With punk bands, you didn't have to be as good as Eddie Van Halen to do it." However, it was not an automatic realization that he had finally found the right path. "There was no decisive moment when I thought, 'Wow, I want to do this.' That wasn't there at all. It just made me feel good."

Almost as soon as he began pounding on a drum set, Cornell found himself part of the local music scene. "I was in a band after only a few months of playing the drums and was fairly involved in it. I got into a lot of other groups really quickly and was sought after by a lot of people locally really quickly. It seemed like I got the rewards really fast without having to really do anything. And then, once I got the rewards, it seemed like I got the taste for it, and started to crave that side of it. It sort of allowed me to mellow out and actually work at [drumming], and concentrate on something—whereas, before that point, I never really could. I couldn't concentrate on anything. I didn't have the patience to do anything."

His first band was called the Jones Street Band (since he lived on a street called...Jones Street). "We rehearsed in my garage. We'd play everything from contemporary-rock shit like Rush and AC/DC to whatever punk music was at the time—the Ramones and the Sex Pistols. There were some local punk bands we would mimic. A band called the Fartz—we'd listen to their records and try to mimic them. And as a drummer I was really into the Police." And immediately upon playing in bands, he recognized newfound attention from the opposite sex. "The first time I was on stage in a band, the opinion of girls toward me changed *in seconds.* And really, it has absolutely nothing to do with how you look—you can look like anything, and that's going to happen."

By the age of 17, Cornell was living on his own with a roommate—a chap by the name of Kevin Tissot, who he had met while briefly attending North End alternative high school—first at a house located on Lake City Way, and then another house in Ballard, with additional roommates. And Chris and Kevin supported themselves by working at a well-known Seattle seafood restaurant, Ray's Boathouse. "I always liked working with food," Chris once remembered about this time in the early '80s. "It's not that different from music. Unless you're a short-order cook or something—there's no poetry in fried food."

And as it turned out, there was no "poetry" in the dead-end cover bands he was playing with at the time. "When I was 15 or 16, I didn't even think in terms of the future. I would play with guys who would also try to do top-40 tavern gigs to make enough money to buy guitar strings and cigarettes, and that never made any sense to me. They weren't musicians at all—they were just dishwashers with guitars. So I learned early on that I wasn't going to allow music to be this thing I used to pay the rent. It was mine, and more sacred than that." Soon after, he realized pursuing original music rather than remaining stuck in the covers circuit would prove far more satisfying creatively, and looked to form a group that "Didn't allow its inability to support itself to dictate what it did creatively."

Luckily, the drummer eventually crossed paths with a pair of Illinois transplants who he would musically connect with far better than the "guitar strings and cigarettes" specialists he had played up to this point.

CHAPTER 03
KIM

The other member of Soundgarden besides Chris that was present throughout all of their line-up switcheroos was Kim Thayil. Born on September 4, 1960, in Seattle, both of his parents hailed from Bombay, India (Kim also has a younger sister)—resulting in Kim being East Indian. "My dad was an engineer and my mother was a teacher—and they were pretty strong opposites," is how Kim once described his parents. "My dad was real stoic and rational, my mom was more cosmic and romantic. I've probably exhibited both traits in my upbringing as far as being romantic, arty, a politically sensitive idealist—with definite tendencies towards stoicism!"

Thayil's mother was musically talented, as well. "She's classically trained, she went to the Royal Academy in London, and graduated when she was 18. She was either going to be a concert pianist or a teacher; she ended up teaching music and English." Despite being born in Seattle, Thayil did not grow up there. When he was five years old, they relocated to a town about 40 miles southwest of Chicago—Park Forest, Illinois, which the eventual guitar player described as "A somewhat suburban sort of community, educated but not wealthy. Young families, generally. Somewhat integrated...there were a lot of young professional families, Asian, black, Hispanic, white, Jewish."

As a youngster, comic books and baseball (namely the Chicago Cubs) piqued Kim's interest...until like most people his age during the mid-late '70s, he fell under the spell of a certain make-up clad rock band and a classic concert recording. "Kiss: *Alive!* That was special in that I was using my own money, so it was a big deal. That record got me hooked into Kiss as a band—but not metal as a genre."

And ultimately, it was via Kiss that Kim ventured outside mainstream rock. "In reading interviews about Kiss and reviews of their records, I uncovered references to the MC5, New York Dolls, and stuff like that. I read a little bit about the MC5 and started hearing about the Stooges and then went to a used record store near where I grew up in Park Forest, Illinois, and found a couple of Stooges and MC5 records. The original things, you know? The original MC5 records with 'Kick Out the Jams Motherfuckers.' I got those and thought, 'This is even more of what I'm looking for. This is heavy, chaotic, it's wild, and dangerous.' So around 1976-1977, I was pretty into the MC5, the Stooges, and New York Dolls. It was perfect timing because all of the sudden, the Sex Pistols and the Ramones came out, and I was like, 'OK, this is the music I was meant to play'."

And by the age of 16, Kim began playing the guitar himself. "I would say early on I was really into Ace Frehley, and as I was learning how to play guitar during that period of time, I was turning on the MC5, the Stooges, and the Ramones. People like Wayne Kramer, 'Sonic' Smith, and Johnny Ramone became my big influences. My first electric guitar was an Encore Strat copy—bright red. I had that from about age sixteen to eighteen. When I was eighteen I bought a Guild S-100 [built in 1974, in white]. It was affordable, light, and I liked the action on the neck. The stock pickups are really hot and the tuning keys that came with it were very easy to tune and keep in tune, which is good for beginning guitarists. If you have a shitty guitar when you're starting out, it's very frustrating having the thing slip all the time, and not having chords sound like they should." Kim would eventually become synonymous with the S-100 (which resembled a Gibson SG—y'know, the guitar shape that Tony Iommi and Angus Young made famous), and played a variety of colors of the model throughout the years.

Having mastered the art of the power chord, Thayil soon made his live debut at his school, Rich East High. "It was 1978 and I was in a band that I started, Bozo and His Vast Army of Pinheads. We played in front of about five hundred people at a year-end fundraiser/talent show, held by the alternative school I went to. I played the Encore Stratocaster copy, and we did the Ramones' 'Pinhead,' the Sex Pistols' 'God Save the Queen' and 'Submission,' and 'Mongoloid' by Devo. We also did some originals, including 'Bureaucracy in the US,' 'If I Were A Bomb, I'd Explode In Your Face,' 'Plastic Love,' and 'TV Clones'. I was very nervous because there were teachers and parents, and my friends from the school. The audience response was, 'You guys are pretty good for that kind of music, punk rock and all.' But our band didn't seem to like it. We played well, but the band was comprised of people who weren't into punk rock—except for me. I had long hair like a Ramone. I wore sunglasses and a black derby bowler. And I wore a blue jean jacket. I was a fucking Ramone!"

But similar to his eventual bandmate, Thayil was not satisfied merely replicating covers of other artists. "I started playing guitar to write songs. I didn't learn other people's songs. I started jerking around with it, and came up with things that sounded cool to me. The craft for me was working on a song, working on arrangements that I felt would have some power. I've never taken a guitar lesson in my life. I would see how fast I could play, like everyone does, right? I kept trying to play faster and faster. It didn't help, 'cause I didn't know all the scales. I could do it with one scale. That was about the extent of my interest in playing guitar—how fast I could play."

While attending Rich East High School, Thayil crossed paths with three other gentlemen that would prove significant in the world of rock music throughout the '80s and beyond—Tom Zutaut, Bruce Pavitt, and Hiro Yamamoto. Zutaut would later relocate to California and earn fame and fortune as the A&R scout that helped sign Mötley Crüe to Elektra and Guns N' Roses to Geffen (and in 2019, was portrayed by actor Pete Davidson in the Crüe biopic, *The Dirt*), Pavitt would relocate to Washington and cofound Sub Pop Records (more on that later), while Yamamoto and Thayil would strike up a friendship—that would eventually lead to the formation of Soundgarden.

Born on April 13, 1961, the Japanese-American Yamamoto did not initially share Thayil's fondness for blaring hard rock. "I listened to 'Have You Seen Her' by the Chi-Lites daily before school in fifth grade," he once recalled. However, around the time that he and Kim crossed paths in high school, the more rockin' *Everybody Knows This Is Nowhere* by Neil Young was closer to the style of music that most other rock-loving teenaged males in the area favored. "It affirmed the futility I felt. Still, it had a powerfully intangible quality that overcame my depressiveness. The Butthole Surfers' debut is so freaky, fucked-up, and wild that it made my head spin. It has the same qualities Neil Young has that make me go, 'Yeah'!"

And what were Hiro's initial impressions of his new friend (who was a year ahead of him, grade-wise)? "Back then Kim even seemed argumentative. [Laughs] He liked to talk and was introspective. He's really into philosophy. You could tell he was thinking about where he fit in the world and what it all meant, all the time." At the time, Hiro's main instrument was the quite un-rock n' roll mandolin. Eventually, Kim convinced him to move over to bass guitar—"I said, 'Hey, it's almost the same stringing as a mandolin, it's backwards, and you're more likely to get in a band playing bass than mandolin.' We wanted to play together, so he got a bass. I showed him all his initial scales and stuff. He'd insist on using his fingers instead of a pick, saying, 'The good bass players use their fingers.' He ended up being really good with his fingers."

Although no longer based in Park Forest, Pavitt continued to keep in touch with Thayil. While attending Evergreen State College in Olympia, Pavitt became interested in the local music scene, due to a radio station that specialized in independent music, KAOS, and also, a magazine that reviewed independent records, *Op*. As a result, Pavitt would send Thayil tapes of some "KAOS bands" (namely the Beakers and the Blackouts) and copies of *Op* to inspect. Eventually, this led to Kim and Hiro hatching a plan— the pair should head out to the Northwest, as well.

"It seemed like a romantic, accessible scene for a high school or early college teenager/musician," recalled Kim. "Eventually, I think Hiro was 20 and I was 21. We packed up Hiro's Datsun b210—with clothes, amps, and whatever money we had, and drove out on I-90. Hiro and I at the time simultaneously had our bands break up and our girlfriends leave us. [Laughs] We moved out in '81. That's a big move when you're broke, a college dropout, and have nothing going on."

Upon their arrival in Washington (located at the most Northwest point of the United States—above Oregon, and below British Columbia), Thayil and Yamamoto followed their friend's

13 KIM

lead, and enrolled at Evergreen State College. Little did they know, they were also relocating to an area that in ten years' time, would touch off a rock revolution.

CHAPTER 04
THE GARDEN GROWS

A misconception from the unenlightened was that Seattle was devoid of notable rock music until the grunge movement. *Hogwash*. In fact, Washington has been rich with musical talent for decades. The best known of the pre-1991 bunch being guitar legend Jimi Hendrix (born in Seattle), classic rockers Heart (although the Wilson sisters were not born in Seattle, they were raised there), prog metallists Queensrÿche (hailing from Bellevue), and thrash metallists Metal Church (whose founder, Kurdt Vanderhoof, hailed from Aberdeen).

But Washington's rock music lineage reaches back even further, to the late '50s/early '60s with such garage rock bands as the Sonics and the Wailers. And by the early '80s, a whole wave of punk bands had sprouted up, including the Beakers, the Blackouts, the Accüsed, the Melvins, the Fastbacks, the U-Men, Mr. Epp and the Calculations, the Fartz, and Ten Minute Warning (the latter two featuring a pre-Guns N' Roses Duff McKagan), plus such metal acts as Sanctuary and Malfunkshun (the latter featuring a rather flamboyant chap by the name of Andy Wood, on vocals/bass).

"Initially, when I came to Seattle, there was more of a new wave, jangly, quirky type of sound here," Kim once recalled. "It was the same thing that was happening all over the country, except that Seattle was stuck in it a little longer. But there were plenty of guys playing some progressive stuff, and there was a hardcore scene, so these things naturally developed. Seattle is divided into two regions. There's the east side, which is across Lake Washington, and most of the metal bands are from there, groups like Queensrÿche, Sanctuary, and Fifth Angel. Here on our side, there was a lot more hardcore and punk, and these bands started to add more leads and double bass and just more of a speed metal sound. The more progressive, hardcore bands added different, artier elements."

However, the guitarist recognized a noticeable absence concerning touring underground bands from outside of the area. "Not too many bands came out to Seattle. The bands that played

15 THE GARDEN GROWS

Seattle back then, in the early '80s, were mostly from the SST label—they would send the bands up the coast. Seattle is quite a bit out of the way—it's three hours from Portland, and like, fourteen hours from San Francisco. And if you're a band from Washington, DC, and you never had a lot of financial resources—including food, gas, and hotel—that's a big jump from Minneapolis to Seattle, or Denver to Seattle. So, not a lot of bands made it up to the Northwest, except for the California bands."

As Kim just mentioned, the indie label, SST—founded by Black Flag guitarist Greg Ginn in Long Beach, California—was quickly leaving their mark on the Northwest, and particularly, with Mr. Thayil. "Around '83/'84, a lot of the records I liked were produced by Spot. I heard Hüsker Dü, the EP with "Real World" and "Diane" on it [*Metal Circus*] was produced by Spot, the Minutemen records I picked up were produced by Spot. I noticed that a lot of the records I was getting were either on SST or produced by Spot. I got *Lullabies Help the Brain Grow* by the Big Boys, which is a great fucking album. That is one of the most underrated/underappreciated punk/post-punk albums ever. I think it was on Moment Records, and it was produced by Spot. I'm thinking, "Why the fuck aren't these guys on SST?"

It was also around this time that Hiro and Kim first met Chris. And it turned out that another Illinois transplant helped facilitate their fateful introduction. "A friend of ours was in a cover band," explained Yamamoto. "This guy, Matt Dentino, was from Park Forest like we were. When he was in high school, he was a great guitarist—he played better than any of us. He was playing rock n' roll and put an ad in *The Rocket* looking for a singer."

Kim also remembered this transitional period—which led to the formation of an oddly-named band. "Matt Dentino was a fan of *The Three Stooges*, and nobody else was a fucking *Three Stooges* fan, or gave a shit about it. But Matt called it the Shemps because he thought it was funny. Hiro had no interest in the music, other than it was a learning experience for him—he would learn how to play bass in a working situation. So he did that for a couple of months, got sick of it, and quit. When Hiro quit, Matt had his hands tied because he had booked a few gigs in advance. I never played bass in any situation other than jamming—I'm a guitarist. So he was crashing on our couch, and says, 'Kim, if I get you a bass, would you learn these songs?' I was like, 'Eh, I don't know man.' As much as I love Hendrix, I just had no fucking interest in Hendrix, Stones, or Doors songs at that point in my life. But, he needed the help. Somehow, I ended up with a bass for a period of time."

And how does the introduction to Mr. Cornell figure into the equation? Via *The Rocket* ad that Hiro previously mentioned. "I always figured I would just end up being such a good drummer that the best band in the world would ask me to be in it," Chris once reminisced. "I guess I lost that attitude pretty quick." So, despite being a drummer first and foremost, Chris answered the ad. Thayil's initial assessment of Cornell was not exactly what you would expect.

"When I met Chris, my first impression was that he was some guy who just got out of the navy or something. He had real short hair and was dressed real slick. He had a great voice—even though we were doing shitty material." And Dentino's evaluation of the young Cornell didn't differ much from Thayil's. "When he came in that little apartment—I was living in Kim's three by six closet for a year—he just knocked it out of the ballpark. I think the first tune we tried was 'White Wedding,' and that was it. He also did a scary Jim Morrison—his timing and phrasing on everything was just powerful and raw, the way it's supposed to be sung."

Although impressed by Chris' voice, it did not initially result in a "thunderbolt moment" for Kim—concerning what the future held for both he and Chris musically. "Chris at some point knew it was a waste of time, but he also knew it was an opportunity to not play drums and practice singing in front of twenty or thirty people. Chris had a really good voice—but I had no interest in doing anything musical with the guy, because it seemed to me that Chris really wanted to be in a fucking bar band. If I pictured my 'dream Stooges or MC5 band,' none of these guys fit in this picture."

17 THE GARDEN GROWS

Interestingly, at some of the Shemps' performances, two chaps that would figure mightily in the "grunge story" were in fact members of the audience. Meet Matt Cameron: "They were playing Morning Town Pizza—it was a hippie pizza place in the University District of Seattle. I was playing with another band at the time—Feedback—that played before the Shemps. I remember Chris being a really strong presence—Chris' singing back then was still incredible." Kim: "I was friends with Mark Arm, and I did talk Mark into coming to see us. It was pretty hilarious—a bunch of drunk blues-rock losers...and then Mark and me."

Over the years, it has been erroneously reported that the Shemps were an important building block in the creation of grunge, where in fact, it was merely a bar band that lasted several months, before being laid to rest. But—and this is a mighty "but"—the seeds of Soundgarden had unknowingly been sown, as Cornell and Yamamoto had struck up a friendship as a result of their brief affiliation together in the Shemps.

"Chris was living at my house and we started jamming," recalled Hiro. "We used to go upstairs—I'd play bass, he'd play drums, and we'd just jam out for hours at a time. So that's kind of how it started. Chris was younger than us—he was just a kid. He was young and quiet—he really liked to keep to himself. Me and Kim would sit around, drink beer, and watch *David Letterman*. He was more private—he liked to disappear in his room and think. Kim didn't live at that house; he lived in a different place. It was Eightieth and Roosevelt. That's when Soundgarden started—in that house."

So, with Chris on drums and Hiro on bass, the next step was to find a suitable guitarist. After some prodding, Kim agreed to a jam with the duo. "Immediately everything clicked—the first day we jammed, we wrote two songs. Stylistically, it didn't sound like anything any of us had heard—it wasn't the heavy stuff we ended up doing. Everybody was interested in their contribution— everyone liked the material we came up with and how it supported their interest in their instrument. And Chris—at this time—we didn't realize yet that he had lyrical ideas. So we had these songs that were entirely arranged instrumentally that were very interesting."

"So we said, 'Let's do it again tomorrow.' We were very happy, very satisfied—we were all smiling, it was so much fun. The next day, we wrote three songs. So in two days and a case of beer, we wrote five songs. They're all songs that we ended up playing live and recorded, but none of them we released on vinyl. But that's where it ended—those two days and those five songs. I still had to finish my last quarter at the University of Washington, I still had this new relationship, and I was still working full-time at this Native American Cultural Center. I was also working at the radio station, at the University of Washington."

Because of so much going on in his personal life at the time, Thayil was slow to commit 100% to this new musical project—with the group's "birth" often being cited as sometime in September 1984. Eventually, he wisely relented...but it came with a price to pay. "They wanted me to commit. I was able to practice with them three nights a week eventually. I lost my fucking job because I was spread too thin. Now I had no money, but I was able to go rehearse with these jerks." [Laughs]

Soon, the trio got serious—initially focusing on penning mostly instrumental material, before lyrics began being added, and Chris and Hiro splitting vocal duties 50/50. Eventually, they came to the sensible realization that Chris possessed an extraordinary voice...so he was appointed the group's main vocalist, but also retained drum duties—joining a small fraternity of "singing drummers" (a la Don Henley, Phil Collins, and Karen Carpenter, among a scant few). And since the house that Chris and Hiro lived in was located on a busy street corner, it could double as a rehearsal space (with rehearsals sometimes lasting into the wee hours of the morning).

Up next...selecting a band name. "At one point, Hiro wanted to call us the Stone Age Alliance," Kim once remembered. "But New Age started up and we didn't want anything to do with it." Fair enough. But it turned out that the trio didn't have to search far for a suitable name. In nearby Magnuson Park, a sculpture had recently been designed and constructed by a gent by the name of

19 THE GARDEN GROWS

Douglas Hollis—which looked like several mini weather vanes, that when wind passed through its nooks and crannies, created sounds. Its name? *A Sound Garden*—which would eventually be streamlined to simply "Soundgarden," and adopted by the fledgling band as their name.

And it turns out that the new group's playlist leaned more on the SST punk bands than it did anything that resembled headbanging fare. "Just a few months from when *Meat Puppets II* came out [April 1984], Soundgarden formed. So here's [Hüsker Dü's] *Zen Arcade*, here's *Meat Puppets II*, I had this new girlfriend at the time. I had met the love of my life—I thought then—and started the band of my life. And here was the soundtrack to it—*Meat Puppets II*, *Zen Arcade*, and [Black Flag's] *My War*. It was an unbelievable time. So needless to say, when Soundgarden formed, these records are getting heavy airplay after practice, after jamming, when we have enough beers in us that we have to go down to the store to get more and listen to records for another hour or two, and then head home."

Wasting little time, two months after their formation, the band had already recorded fifteen original tunes via a four-track cassette recording device, entitled *The First 15*. Unlike other notable rock band's early demo tapes that eventually made the rounds in cassette trading circles (Metallica's *No Life 'Til Leather,* the Pixies' *The Purple Tape,* the pre-Nirvana band/recording Fecal Matter's *Illiteracy Will Prevail*, etc.), not even a morsel of material has ever surfaced from *The First 15*—nor even its tracklisting—as of this book's release.

However, when I spoke to Kim in 2009, he did discuss several early Soundgarden tunes that are quite possibly included on this first demo. "'Ocean Fronts,' 'Open Up,' 'Summation'— that was a pretty heavy song, in 5/4 time. 'Ocean Fronts' is a little bit more of a trippy, arpeggiated song. A song called 'Beast,' which is going to sound exactly like the title. 'Beast' and 'Summation' were really strong songs live—from the mid-late '80s. I cannot believe those two songs have never been released. 'No Shame' is another title."

Years later, Thayil reflected upon SG's first four-track demos, and also, some unique terminology the group came up with around this time. "In our early rehearsals, when we were writing songs and would practice, we'd write a new song, and by the end of the week, we'd say, 'OK, we've got a bunch of new songs, let's whip out the four-track and try to play them.' We weren't really good at punching in or whatever. We didn't have much in the way of isolation—we just put a mic on the drums, a mic on the guitar amp, a mic on the bass amp, and we'd play live into this four-track recorder. And we'd have a mic for the vocals. We didn't do overdubs, we didn't have that ability. We were shoved off at first in an attic and then in a basement."

"So we'd run through our song, and then it's like, 'Oh, I totally fucked this part up. OK, let's do it again. Everyone ready? One, two, three.' And we'd get near the end of the song, and Chris would make a clam on drums, and then on the third time we'd go through it, I'd fuck it up again or Hiro would fuck it up. We'd listen back, and go, 'You know, that's not bad, that's cool! That gives personality to the performance and the song. Yeah, dude...that's *a Meat Puppets fuck up*.' And that word became part of Soundgarden jargon, it was part of our lexicon—'Meat Puppets fuck up'."

"If we had our own dictionary, we'd have dozens—if not hundreds—of terms in it. From 'beer o'clock' to 'soft-on' to 'Meat Puppets fuck up.' If the chick was alright, you know, 'She's kind of giving me a 'soft-on'.' 'Beer o'clock' was we'd pulled into town, it's after dinner or it's 6:00, it's OK to start drinking. As you get older, 'beer o'clock' starts moving further back...or further up, depending on your degree of alcoholism. But 'Meat Puppets fuck up' meant that you missed your part or your fingers kind of slipped on the strings or on the sticks, but it augmented the performance or the song. 'Meat Puppets fuck up' meant you fucked up, but it was for the better—it was cool. 'Let's don't record over that, because you'll never be able to fuck it up in that cool way again'."

And a short while after *The First 15* reared its head, the trio played their first-ever show—opening for an obscure New York band, Three Teens Kill Four. And wouldn't ya know it—old pal Dentino was in the audience. "I saw their first show. [They opened] for some band, and I thought they blew them away. Their first show was upstairs...I don't even know the place. There was Astroturf—it was like a club, but the rest of the building was for golfing or baseball." In February of 1985, Soundgarden landed an opening spot for Hüsker Dü and the Melvins at a local punk rock venue, the Gorilla Gardens. And it turns out that once again, several audience members who attended these early shows would later figure prominently in grunge's eventual uprising—including Green River/Mother Love Bone/Pearl Jam bassist Jeff Ament.

"I remember seeing them open up for Hüsker Dü at the Gorilla Gardens. They were a three-piece at the time. Chris was playing drums and singing. Kim's amp was way louder than anybody else's onstage—he played through a phaser the whole time, and a chorus pedal. That was their predominant sound. But I thought they were pretty frickin' cool." Also present was *Bleach*-era Nirvana drummer Chad Channing. "I went to their second show—I put a tape in the board and recorded it. Unfortunately, that recording is long since gone." And none other than Ben Shepherd was probably there, too! "The very first show I saw they blew some national act away. I have the set list from that show somewhere. They sounded huge, and their riffs weren't stupid or anything—something more to them. Something disturbing and huge."

But if you're figuring that Soundgarden automatically sounded as monolithically heavy as they would by the early to mid '90s, you would be dead wrong—some who were lucky to witness early Soundgarden performances described their sound at this point as more "post-punk." And while just a few years down the road, most members of the rock press would be listing Led Zeppelin and Black Sabbath as the bands that Soundgarden reminded them most of sound-wise, by this early stage, Keith Levene-era Public Image Limited, Joy Division, and Bauhaus proved to be better comparisons.

And it was this more post-punk style that was reflected on the group's second-ever demo, *6 Songs for Bruce* (the "Bruce" being Mr. Pavitt), which was recorded on April 24, 1985, by the eventual "numero uno producer of grunge," Jack Endino. Unlike *The First 15,* the tracklisting of *6 Songs for Bruce* has been leaked to the public, featuring such mostly-never-heard selections as "I Think I'm Sinking," "Bury My Head in Sand," "Tears to Forget," "The Storm," "Incessant Mace," "In Vention," and "Out of My Skin." Of the seven selections, three would be re-recorded for subsequent SG recordings ("Tears to Forget," "The Storm," and "Incessant Mace"). Similar to *The First 15,* the actual sonic contents of *6 Songs for Bruce* have not found its way to the public as of this book's release. But, at least one tune has surfaced—the version of "Incessant Mace" here was lent a year later to an obscure compilation issued by C/Z Records, *Pyrrhic Victory,* and this version (yes, with Cornell on vocals *and* drums) is YouTube-able.

Something else that also made Soundgarden's original three-piece line-up unique—its members' ethnic backgrounds. Hard rock and heavy metal from the United States was almost 100% Caucasian circa the mid-80's (the Bad Brains, Fishbone, and Los Lobos being a few notable exceptions, while Living Colour was still a few years away from issuing *Vivid*), whereas—as stated earlier—Soundgarden was comprised of a Caucasian (Cornell), an Indian (Thayil), and a Japanese-American (Yamamoto). Despite Soundgarden slowly building a following and a buzz locally, the band experienced their first line-up flutter in '85—when it was decided that Cornell would put down the sticks and solely become a frontman. And while he would eventually become widely known as one of rock's all-time great vocalists, funny enough at the time, his bandmates did not exactly recognize this.

"Believe it or not, Hiro and I actually thought he was more valuable to us as a drummer," recalled Kim. "Because of his songwriting ability, we would work out arrangements on the drums. Hiro had really established his musical relationship with Chris as a rhythm section. We didn't want to lose that—the instrumental part was what we felt was strong. So we thought, 'Let's get a guy to sing,' some guy who has some dynamic personality and voice. Somebody with some theatrical skills, charisma...a monkey, y'know? [Laughs] We knew he could sing, but I guess we didn't actually think, 'Well, here's this great-looking, statuesque front man.' We just thought he was more reserved—he didn't seem like 'a presence.' But we knew he could sing. We did that for a good half-year to a year, before we got Scott [Sundquist] as our drummer. Scott worked with Chris at the restaurant, Ray's Boathouse."

Jack Endino once described how SG sounded with Sundquist on the drums. "Scott was an older guy, he had kind of a Ginger Baker touch on the drums. A rolling, jazzy sort of feel, that was really dynamic, and very fluid. It wasn't so 'conventional heavy rock' as they became later. It was a slightly psychedelic kind of vibe. And at times, it was really pretty amazing." There is early concert footage (single camera shot) from around this time—of Soundgarden performing at a KCMU benefit at the Central Tavern. The drummer appears to indeed be Mr. Sundquist, while Cornell is playing a Gibson ES-347 guitar, and Hiro is sporting a white Fender Jazz...while Thayil barely appears one iota in this footage (only at the end). The band is seen playing one and a half songs (whose titles have never been confirmed, as they never appeared on any SG release, and the audio is quite rough) during this near five and a half minutes' worth of rare video (in front of a white banner that says "KCMU: ALTERNATIVE RADIO").

Although Sundquist would only remain a SG member for a year (he'd exit in '86, citing family obligations as the primary reason), he did stick around long enough to keep the beat on three songs recorded for another comp featuring local talent (Melvins, Malfunkshun, U-Men, etc.), *Deep Six*, issued by C/Z Records on March 21, 1986. And those tracks would include..."Heretic," "Tears to Forget," and "All Your Lies" (all co-produced by the pair who founded C/Z—Chris Hanzsek and Tina Casale).

"That's basically the only [recording] that has Scott on drums," remembered Hiro. "The thing about Scott—he was ten years older than me. Scott was really cohesive—he made sure we were all getting together. So those times with the band were really fun, because Scott was more of a fatherly figure—he made sure as a band we were *a band*. To me, those were the best days of

Soundgarden. After Scott left, we were more of 'individuals' that played in a band. When we played with Scott, we were all kind of a family. We wanted to go on tour, and Scott had a young kid. So he wasn't up for it. It was the saddest times of Soundgarden."

But truth be told, when all three songs would be re-recorded with Sundquist's replacement over the next few years for later Soundgarden releases, they sounded far superior. Which is quite understandable—after all, Sundquist's replacement was none other than *Matt Bloody Cameron*.

CHAPTER 05
MATT

The phrase "taking it to the next level" is quite fitting to describe what occurred within Soundgarden when Matt Cameron joined in 1986. Born Matthew David Cameron on November 28, 1962, in San Diego, California, he began drumming at the age of eleven and played in local bands by the time he was thirteen—including a Kiss tribute band. Cameron was lucky to have caught most of the top names of '70s rock in their prime in concert (Queen, Kiss, Thin Lizzy, etc.), and has listed the varied likes of Buddy Rich, Count Basie, and David Bowie as early influences/inspirations.

And in 1978, Matt made his *somewhat* professional music debut, when he sang the song "Puberty Love" in the b-movie/cult classic, *Attack of the Killer Tomatoes* (if you're wondering, the storyline revolves around humongous mutant tomatoes wreaking havoc, until a certain song is played that shrinks these buggers back down to size). Credited as "Foo Cameron" (supposedly because his older brother, Pete, used to pronounce "Matthew" as "Ma Foo"), the eventual world renowned drummer once explained how he got involved in such a peculiar project.

"My neighbors up the street were making a low-budget comedy/horror movie called *Attack of the Killer Tomatoes*. So they recruited a lot of kids from the neighborhood to make these big papier-mâché tomatoes and play bit parts in the movie. They knew that I was a musician, so they asked if I knew how to sing. I sort of knew how to sing, but I wasn't that good. I think that was part of the charm of the song. It sounds like a prepubescent voice that is cracking and can't sing that well. So I fit perfectly for the role."

Cameron decided to relocate from San Diego to Seattle in 1983, and almost immediately, became a sought-after drummer, playing in such bands as Feedback (an instrumental trio featuring C/Z Records co-head Daniel House), and Skin Yard (a prog-punk outfit featuring well-liked producer Jack Endino on guitar)...in addition to holding down a job at Kinko's. "I was playing [in] Feedback, and we eventually became Skin Yard," recalled he drummer. "Kim came to some of our shows—we started talking.

We figured out that we lived pretty close to each other. Then he told me to check out his band at the Rainbow Tavern—I did, and I was completely blown away. I loved it instantly—they were my favorite band in Seattle. I heard that Scott left, and I called Kim. I said, 'I'd like to try out.' I knew a few of their songs—'Heretic,' 'Incessant Mace,' and a few of their other earlier songs."

The band obeyed Cameron's command, and a tryout was arranged in the middle of February of 1986. Years later, Cameron still had vivid memories of this career/life-changing day for all parties involved. "I auditioned for Soundgarden in Chris' living room, sat behind his rusty Tama kit and counted in 'Ocean Fronts,' my all-time favorite SG tune. The tune had kind of a long intro, it sounded great and then all of a sudden Chris starts singing the verse. I was instantly blown away by the impact of his voice and I felt myself settling into the band on my first try. It was all because of that mind blowing voice. When the song was over Chris turned to me with a big smile on his face and said 'You played it perfectly, we have a gig at the Central in one week, want to do it?' 'Yes, I want to do it,' I replied." And just like that, the dazzling Cornell-Thayil-Yamamoto-Cameron line-up was in effect.

Although Cameron listed a performance at the Central as being his first with Soundgarden in his previous quote, he would also at least one other time say his first show was at the Ditto Tavern. Either way, it was definitely memorable. "My first Soundgarden show in 1986 at the Ditto Tavern was a baptism by fire. I had joined the group one week prior to the gig and I wanted to impress. The drummer I had replaced, Scott Sundquist, was in the front row critiquing my every move. I remember him saying from the front of the stage, 'Kick drum too loud!' 'Too fast!' etcetera." Despite the distraction, Matt did indeed pass the test, and shortly thereafter, experienced another standout onstage moment with the band, which confirmed that he had found himself in a very special musical situation.

"Opening for Love and Rockets in 1986 [on October 18th] was a big moment for me. We had never played a show in a theater before, just local bars and such, so we were a little nervous. Our opening song, 'Entering,' sounded a lot like 'Bela Lugosi's Dead' from their previous band, Bauhaus. Both songs have a very similar drum intro, so when I got the cue, I laid into the beat, and I remember the first two rows looking at each other with mild confusion. Once Hiro Yamamoto and Kim Thayil hit the first gnarly guitar notes, there was no more confusion. It was the first big stage the band had played—the Moore Theatre in Seattle— and after the show, I realized we had a sound that could fill any size venue, and we could hold our own with anyone."

"It got a lot crisper, tighter," recalled Thayil about how SG's sound changed after the arrival of Cameron. "We were looking for something in terms of more minimalism—trying to hold down a beat, and a strong repetitiveness in the beat. But at the same time, Matt was obviously a great improv drummer. We certainly jammed a lot, and a number of songs had an extended solo section—not necessarily guitar solos, it might be drums, bass, or just feedback. And Matt had that ability—Matt could play a minimal, tight jazz kit. He was also available to tour, as well as contributing to the songwriting."

Jack Endino considers the arrival of his former Skin Yard bandmate into SG's ranks as the birth of the sound that eventually became their trademark. "After they got Matt in the band, they became more focused, and narrowed down to, 'We're just going to play these big rock riffs.' They zeroed in on the sound they became known for later. When he joined Soundgarden, they became something to be reckoned with." And while the group would eventually be tagged with not being the most cheery of bands (earning the nickname "Frowngarden" a few years later by the road crew of Guns N' Roses), Cameron's personality did not reflect this, according to Thayil. "I think he likes life. I think we're all helpful to each other. I think Matt's kind of easygoing and perhaps a little better adjusted socially in terms of temperament. He's a good balance to the volatility to the other personalities in the band."

It was also around this time that Soundgarden first crossed paths with another group they would befriend and tour with several times throughout the years—Faith No More. And Thayil still remembered specifics about the first time the two soon-to-be-mighty bands played together. "We didn't even have a record out yet, so it may have been in '85/'86. I know we knew [FNM drummer] Mike Bordin—Mike had heard some demo of ours, doing the song 'Nothing to Say,' and he loved it. He's a great guy—he's the guy that Chris and I initially took to. He was hugely into us and spoke highly about us. We played three shows in the Northwest."

"Now, we hadn't really toured yet—that was sort of our first tour. We played in Seattle, then we played in Ellensburg, and then we played Vancouver—out of the country. Chuck [Mosley] was singing with them, and he sang at the gigs in Seattle and in Ellensburg. I do not believe he sang in Vancouver—I do not think he could get into the country because of a previous DWI arrest, and his DWI was either in the US so they wouldn't let him into Canada, or the DWI might have been in Canada so he was expelled. I can't really remember the details. He couldn't make it up to Vancouver. So [keyboardist] Roddy Bottum did the vocals."

"We did the gig opening for them in an area of Vancouver called Gastown, at a small bar. A couple of things I remember about that was some time during the middle of the set, Chris said he heard someone say, *'Fucking Led Zeppelin crap,'* and then threw a glass ashtray that shattered on Matt Cameron's kick drum. I remember hearing the thud and the crack. Which is kind of fucked up, and whoever did that, could have seriously gotten their fucking ass kicked by the band. But we weren't really the kind of band that would cower, so what we did was we just moved to the front of the stage and played even louder and more aggressively. That kind of shit got us more aggressive and combative. And almost always, we won them over."

"But then Faith No More came out and did this set that they had done with us on two previous shows, playing it without Chuck. They were so friendly. They almost seemed like big brothers. And I immediately got the sense—especially with Mike Bordin—that he was kind of taking us under his wing. And we got that feeling from [bassist] Billy Gould, too. Those guys are just great guys. And it was very important to us." And while we're on the subject of Faith No More, somewhere around this time, they even supposedly tried to poach Chris—to replace Chuck! "Soundgarden opened up for us a few times in Seattle," Gould once explained. "I think one day, Mike and I went to [Cornell's] house to jam, but I don't think that we had a musical connection."

Video footage does exist of this era—June 7, 1986 at the Rainbow Tavern. Although the four minutes and 25 seconds worth of tape suffers from horribly distorted sound, whoever filmed it was right up front—so at least we have close shots, which include a guitar-less Chris sporting a white tank top that exposes his belly and a Jim Morrison-esque belt, a somewhat short-haired Kim *not* playing his Guild (looks like a Strat), Hiro playing with a pick (even though he was primarily a finger man), while Matt is out of view. And the song performed? A trusty inside source once confirmed to me...it's the mysterious "Ocean Fronts."

Also around this era, Cornell indulged in something that he and his fellow Soundgarden mates would continue doing off and on throughout their career—a side project. As a member of the interestingly-titled Center for Disease Control Boys (providing drums and serving as one of six vocalists), little info exists about the band, except that it sounds like it was a "country joke band," issuing a single comprised of an a-side, "CDC Boys Theme," and the very '80s-punk-titled b-side, "Who We Hatin' Now, Mr. Reagan?" With several members singing in a faux country twang, it's difficult to tell who is singing what on the two tunes, but Cornell can be detected going by the alias of "Jake" on "CDC Boys Theme" (as each singer announces their name before their vocal bit)—at the 3:14 mark.

All in all, '86 was an efficient year for Soundgarden—they solidified their line-up *and* began spreading the word outside of Washington State via shows. But that wasn't all—a great local music scene was forming around SG, an old pal was starting up a local indie record label, and a member of the scene would soon take on the fledgling group as their manager.

CHAPTER 06
SCREAMING LIFE

If you think about most great rock bands, it is their talent and uniqueness that made them stand the test of time and endure. But at some point early in their career, there were certain variables out of their control that made the stars align for them—namely, luck and being in the right place at the right time. And all of the above neatly summed up Soundgarden circa 1987. First off, there was an organic music scene on the upswing in the Seattle area and nearby regions in addition to Soundgarden—including Green River (which would soon splinter off into two bands, Mudhoney and Mother Love Bone), Screaming Trees, Nirvana, Alice in Chains, Tad, and Skin Yard (the Melvins had relocated to San Francisco by this time, in case you were wondering). And the abundance of great bands in one state not only solidified their scene, but also, would soon begin to garner national—and eventually, global—attention.

But unlike certain scenes that were overly competitive, it sounds like Seattle bands at the time were mostly friends who supported one another—as it's been said that if you were to catch a show at such then-popular local venues as the Vogue or the Central Tavern, the audience would be comprised of familiar faces of friends and/or members of other bands. Which sounds like quite a different vibe than say, what was going on at the time in Los Angeles, where hair metal hopefuls were trying to out-do one another and achieve that seemingly elusive big break by any means necessary.

And in 1986, Sub Pop Records was founded—by KCMU DJ Jonathan Poneman (who hosted a show of local music, *Audioasis*) and Kim's old pal from Park Forest, Bruce Pavitt (who at one point was doing a cassette fanzine entitled *Subterranean Pop*, which later turned into a column for *The Rocket* streamlined to *Sub Pop USA,* and a compilation entitled *Sub Pop 100*). In fact, while writing for the local paper *The Rocket,* Pavitt offered a phrase to describe Soundgarden that would become linked to the band—"Total fucking Godhead." And it turns out that Thayil helped get the ball rolling concerning the formation of the label.

31 SCREAMING LIFE

"Both Jonathan and Bruce wanted to put out a Soundgarden record. They had different resources—Jon had the financial resources, Bruce had established a network of magazines and record labels. So he was tied in with any national or international indie music scene. That was an important resource for us. He couldn't afford to make a record at that point in time, and I thought, 'Well, both of you guys are interested in making this record, and you guys have two different capacities which could be useful to us. So why don't you work together'?"

And work together they did—as Jack Endino once explained, "They borrowed a bunch of money from various gullible people and somehow set the wheels in motion to start an indie label. I was already working in this eight-track studio from the middle of '86 [Reciprocal Recording, in Seattle], and I had been working with Soundgarden almost from the moment the studio opened its doors. So some of the recordings we had been making anyway, wound up on the first Sub Pop record— Soundgarden's 'Nothing to Say'/'Hunted Down'."

"And that became the *Screaming Life* EP, those two songs plus four others. Sub Pop had a strange rationale when they started—'Let's just do EP's at first. They're cheaper to record and you can put a lower list price on them, which means more people will take a chance on buying them.' The other side of the equation is you make less money on it. [Laughs] So Sub Pop did a lot of seven-inches and EP's in their first few years." Soon after, Sub Pop opened their first office at the Terminal Sales Building on First and Virginia in Seattle, with their warehouse located in the basement, and their office not entirely reachable by the elevator in the building (you would have to get out on the tenth floor, and then walk up another flight-and-a-half of stairs!).

Concerning Mr. Endino's quote, he certainly speaks the truth about Soundgarden's first-ever single...except that "Hunted Down" was the a-side and "Nothing to Say" was the b-side— issued on June 1, 1987, and as the catalog number "SP12" (the reason why it was not "SP1" is because the numeration started with issues of the Sub Pop fanzine). Sensing that they could create further buzz with record buyers by putting a "collectors" spin on it, Sub Pop's "Singles Club" was launched—with "HD"/"NtS" being issued on blue vinyl as an exceedingly limited 500 copy pressing. The single's cover featured a black and white action shot of the band playing live at a "Sub Pop Sunday" at the Vogue (with Chris shirtless)—courtesy of now-renowned photographer Charles Peterson, whose images featuring the "flash and drag shutter effect" (which would create streaks, and perfectly captured the spontaneity and energy of the grunge bands live) would become a trademark of Sub Pop recording artists.

Regarding the single's actual musical content, "Hunted Down" perfectly captured the group's early "Bauhaus Sabbath" sound—with the atmospheric production representing the first part of the sonic equation, and a sinister, repetitive riff representing the latter. Lyrically, the song faithfully represents its title—and years later, would be regurgitated as the basis for the music video for the song "Rusty Cage" (a gentleman on the run through a woodsy area, dogs on his trail, an escape, etc.). "I had the main riff and came up with some chord changes," recalled Kim about the song's creation. "That song was originally played slower, so it had this heavy riff. And the focus went from that to this noisy, chaotic, kind of jazzy solo. And that was the song, and then we filled it in with these chords and stuff. At the end, we needed an ending, and I thought, 'Well, maybe when we record it, we'll just have it fade out on the groove.' And Matt came up with the idea of ending that in the way it does, in kind of a rhythmic fashion, to complete it."

"For some reason, growing up I kind of loved the idea of songs fading out. There's probably periods of my life where if it was up to me, every song on an album would fade out. Which, of course, would be a bad idea. It's something that I might have leaned towards. Drummers don't necessarily like that, because they have the ability to conclude things and resolve melodic pieces. In this case, Matt came up with one. He's like, 'Hey, why don't we do this...' And he tapped out a rhythm or groove and he kind of hummed it. And I go, 'OK.' So I figured out what the chords were. He tapped out the groove, and I go, 'Like this'. And then Chris wrote the lyrics. I think he might have had lyrics laying around, and he just got in front of the mic and tried them out. It felt great, it was dynamic, and that's how that worked."

"Nothing to Say" was another strong composition, and while it may not hit you as immediately as the a-side, it offers a more murky/moody vibe, and also showcases Cornell's vocals more throughout. Looking back, two very strong tracks to launch the SP era of SG. Also of importance, "Nothing to Say" was one of the first times Kim utilized drop-D tuning—which would eventually become a Soundgarden trademark. "It was the song 'Nothing to Say' from *Screaming Life*. I had been talking to Buzz of the Melvins, and he was telling me about a tuning he was getting into. He showed me how you could play a single-finger power chord and move it around real easily, and I showed it to Chris and Hiro. Drop-D tuning also made the notes below the bridge ring out differently on the S-100."

And just four months later (October 1st, to be exact), Soundgarden's first-ever EP, *Screaming Life,* was unleashed via Sub Pop (which was promoted on local TV by a 30-second ad featuring live footage, with the bold message, "Soundgarden...you've heard of them, you've seen them, now you can own a little piece of them"). Six tracks total—with Cornell penning all the lyrics and Thayil handling composing all the music (save for a pair of tracks)—the aforementioned "Hunted Down" kicks things off (the same exact version issued a few months earlier on the single). The second track, "Entering," contains at the beginning what Cameron mentioned earlier—a very "Bela Lugosi's Dead" vibe—before abruptly transforming into a noise rocker. The band's punk rock roots are displayed on the mere two-minute long "Tears to Forget," which sounds like Cornell is pushing his vocals to the max (sung almost in a "possessed witch" voice) and also, features the line "I scream for life," which would be altered slightly for the EP's title (with music co-penned between Hiro and Kim).

We've already covered "Nothing to Say" (again, a duplicate version as the single), before "Little Joe," a mid-paced rocker that features slightly funky bass by Hiro, and Chris' vocals altered to make it sound like he's singing through a telephone or some mono-sounding device. Lyrically, the tune is a departure from your normal S. Garden subject matter, as it deals with a character (that the song is titled after), who decides to leave the safety of his home for "the border" where "reptiles roam." And it turns out that many years later (2011, to be precise), Chris still could recall the guitar he played on the song's recording. "The first guitar I ever had was a Gibson ES-347, which is a 335 with a fine-tuning tailpiece on it. It was a little heavier than a 335, but I loved it. I used it on 'Little Joe' on the *Screaming Life* EP. It was so nice that I was afraid to use it onstage, because the shows were so crazy. I ended up trading it for a used Twin Reverb amp and a Mexican Strat, but I really missed those tones."

Closing things is one of the EP's top tunes, "Hand of God" (the only song on the release with no input from Thayil, as Yamamoto is solely credited as the author of the music) which focused on a subject that many metal bands seemed obsessed with at the time—evangelists and religion (in fact, Cornell was not finished exploring this topic, as he would return to it again on Temple of the Dog's "Wooden Jesus" and Soundgarden's "Holy Water"). The song also showed that even at this early stage, Cornell certainly had a talent for lyric-writing—as evidenced by the memorable line (or as I like to refer to them, "Cornell-isms"), "The hand of God has got a ring about the size of Texas."

"I got some really old rolls of quarter-inch [tape] at a garage sale, and turns out some of them were recordings of some guy giving sermons from the early fifties," recollects Endino about a speech that was inserted into the tune. "They were dated in a near-illegible pencil scrawl but the name of the preacher was unreadable. I had them at the studio, and Chris said, we should have a preacher on this, and I said, 'Hey, I've got just the thing.' We got one out and just listened a bit until we heard a part that seemed right, then just synced it up to the eight-track machine and copied it over onto an empty track. Pretty amazing how the guy's rhythm is so intrinsically heavy rock. I guess God smiled upon us, it was weird how it just worked out perfectly. Still don't know who the guy was or where it was recorded! By the way, the lyrics were written first. One of the things Chris says in the bridge is fake preacher-talk, 'Let it be known today that if you've got two hands you're supposed to pray.' All it needed was a bit of the real thing..."

Looking back on the recording of *Screaming Life,* Cameron remembered, "We only had three or four days to get the rhythm tracks done—me and Hiro—because we had day jobs. I remember that being a very quick recording session—we recorded everything live, other than the vocals. At the time, we were a pretty ferocious live act—that record really captures our live sound at the time. It's holding up wonderfully. I remember listening back to the mix of 'Nothing to Say,' and I just couldn't believe that I was playing in a band so good—at such an early stage of development." Thayil also offered his recollections. "'Tears to Forget' was a very popular song—that was the one song on the album that was a regular part of our set. All the other songs we back-burnered, to hear what these new ones sounded like. It was not entirely representative of what we were doing live then. 'Entering' was a song we had been playing for a few years— 'Entering' and 'Tears to Forget' were certainly part of our live thing. And then we'd come up with 'Nothing to Say,' 'Hunted Down,' and 'Little Joe'."

Listening today, *Screaming Life* holds up extremely well—even remaining a favorite of a certain fan at the time, who would later play a large role in the band. "*Screaming Life* is still my favorite record of theirs," said Ben Shepherd. "That's what Soundgarden sounds like to me—dark, black, and blue. Like the overcast days of Seattle." Thayil, on the other hand, agrees *and* disagrees with Shepherd's assessment. "I think it was—up until Ben joined the band—[the recording] that captured our spirit and sound best. Even though the music is somewhat dark, it seems sunshiny to me." In addition to the quality of the material, what has made *Screaming Life* endure and not sound dated is the production. Whereas countless hard rock/heavy metal bands were utilizing canon-like and/or electronic-sounding drums, Soundgarden's debut EP sounds like a glorified demo...but in a *good* way. So, kudos should be given to Mr. Endino for keeping things raw and straight-ahead. Once more, photographer Charles

Peterson got the go-ahead to supply the cover image (and again, it was a shot of Chris shirtless).

And how was it for Kim to finally have more than just a Soundgarden single in his hands? "Oh it was fantastic, because it seemed real then. As opposed to a cassette, it seemed like it had now been published and manufactured in a form that I was used to and that I'd appreciated since I was a young kid. I used to wake up in the middle of the night and just take it out and stare at it. Wow!" In the ensuing months (and in some cases, *years*), quite a few now-classic recordings would be offered up via Sub Pop— Green River's *Dry as a Bone* and *Rehab Doll,* Mudhoney's *Superfuzz Bigmuff* and "Touch Me I'm Sick" single, Nirvana's "Love Buzz" single and *Bleach,* Tad's *God's Balls*, etc. And with these releases came the first known citing of the word "grunge" to describe this music. In fact, it can be pinpointed to a phrase that Sub Pop utilized to promote Green River—"Gritty vocals, roaring Marshall amps, ultra-loose GRUNGE that destroyed the morals of a generation."

Along with this flurry of activity in '87, it was also around this time that Soundgarden began being managed by Susan Silver. How one can judge a manager and their importance is via several examples—by their roster, the quality of their artists' music when they were managing them, how many top tours the artist that they represent landed, how long they were able to remain successful, etc. If you were to take this all into account, then Silver is one of rock's best from this era, as she not only managed Soundgarden during their ascent and peak, but also, Alice In Chains. Yet, she is not as well-known as say, Sharon Osbourne, Peter Grant, or Brian Epstein. The main reason is that unlike those other rather flamboyant characters, Susan opted to remain out of the spotlight.

"It was just before we put out the Sub Pop record," Chris recalled about when Susan began managing the band. "We asked Jonathan to manage us, and he declined. I was dating Susan at about the same time. But it was, like, three years into the group. Before then there was no need, really. It went from us being a local band trying to do our first indie record to major labels calling us before the first Sub Pop record even came out." Susan also once recalled how she came to manage the band. "I'd met Chris at a vintage clothing store that I'd worked in, and we started going out. They'd been a band already for about a year. A friend, Faith Henschell, who worked at KCMU, was sending these compilation tapes out to people. And someone from a record company heard it and called. In the meantime, Bruce Pavitt had been introduced to Jonathan Poneman through Kim. I had no intention of managing Soundgarden—I'd been managing the U-Men and a pop group, the First Thought. One thing led to another, and I started doing their business—just to help them out."

But since Chris and Susan were dating, was it a case of mixing business with pleasure? And did the other members voice concern? "Initially, I didn't think her being our manager was a good idea," admitted Cornell. "But everyone agreed to keep a levelheaded attitude about it. And she's so protective as a manager that I don't think anyone's felt they weren't being taken care of. There have been situations where I get caught in the middle because Susan will be angry with the band, and I come out championing the band and getting angry with her. And there's been situations where it's the complete turnaround."

As it turns out, Susan herself even had some apprehensions at first. "I didn't want to manage Soundgarden in the beginning—it was by default. It was just too 'Spinal Tap' at that point. But nobody else was there to help them—no regrets about that whatsoever. The thing that I really tried to keep conscious of at all times was their feelings—I tried to keep a field of neutrality, and let everyone know that I was there for all of them, and not just as 'the singer's girlfriend.' [Laughs] I guess the fact that I'm still really close to the other three guys says how that worked out."

"We were generating interest," adds Kim, concerning the time that Susan began managing SG. "We knew we needed someone for no other reason than this—to answer the phone and make phone calls while we were at our jobs. We needed someone to help us get the gigs—especially when some bigger band was coming to play at the Paramount or Moore Theatre. We wanted to be able to get those shows, and Susan was a local promoter we thought could help us out in getting these gigs, maybe booking tours. And we were starting to get interest from labels. We knew we might have lawyers get involved, we anticipated somewhere down the road we might need an accountant. These were decisions that were going to take up a lot of our time, and we needed someone to do that with us—so that was going to be Susan."

CHAPTER 07
FOPP

What is one to do when they have already issued an EP? Issue another one, of course! Instead of following up *Screaming Life* with a full-length, the even shorter *Fopp* (containing only a scant four tracks) appeared little less than a year later—on August 1, 1988, once again via Sub Pop—featuring another black and white Charles Peterson photo of Chris on the cover (of course, shirtless again)...as well as the album credits (?!). But this time, instead of re-enlisting producer Jack Endino and revisiting Reciprocal Recording, the quartet hooked up with Steve Fisk (who either had already worked with or would soon work with the likes of Nirvana, Mudhoney, and the Screaming Trees), and set up shop at the Moore Theatre, to satisfy their recording needs.

However, unlike *Screaming Life,* which was comprised solely of original material and rocked fiercely from start to finish, *Fopp* was a throwaway release—two cover tunes, a remix of one of the covers, and one so-so original. Perhaps SG got the idea to issue an EP primarily of covers from Metallica and their 1987 offering, *The $5.98 E.P.: Garage Days Re-Revisited*...or, maybe not. Anyway, by the late '80s, several alt-rock bands were showing off their admiration of '70s funk—tops being Fishbone, Red Hot Chili Peppers, Faith No More, Living Colour, and Primus—and it turns out that SG wasn't afraid of the funk, either, by covering the Ohio Players' classic, "Fopp." Which admittedly, pales in comparison to the original version—as does its blah remix (titled the "Fucked Up Heavy Dub Mix"). But that said, via Soundgarden's cover, a whole new audience discovered the veteran funk band—and I speak from experience, as it would serve as my intro to the Ohio Players when I heard SG's cover a few years down the road.

"That's an Ohio Players song off of *Honey*—I've had that album since I was in high school," explained Kim. "We thought we could take the song and make it AC/DC or something. We'd take the power chords, turn up the volume and make it heavy. 'Fopp' is a good song that needed to be given its due as a 'kick-ass rock song'!" And rounding out the brief set was the sole original, "Kingdom of Come," followed by a cover of the recently-split-up Green River, "Swallow My Pride"—which is by far the best tune of the four. "It was Bruce Pavitt's idea," Fisk remembered about how he got involved in producing the EP. "They played in Ellensburg—Faith No More played an under-attended show, and they opened. They closed with 'Iron Man,' and Faith No More opened with 'War Pigs.' This is before anybody knew who the fuck they were. Cornell had the best sense of humor—it was really wicked. Kind of vicious but also funny at the same time."

And as stated earlier, Soundgarden opted to bypass recording in a traditional studio. Cameron: "We were playing in this big empty theater—it was kind of cool to me, but I didn't really understand how we were going to get a record out of it. But lo and behold, we did. That was like a one day session, and Steve did a remix at his studio." Fisk: "At one point, a jackhammer crew went to work on pavement, and we couldn't hear anything in the truck. We got the crew to come back later in the day—they knew Seattle bands were starting to get some attention. So they did it to be cool." [Laughs]

Years later, Thayil admitted that the *Fopp EP* is not in the same league as *Screaming Life*—and never was intended to be. "The *Fopp* EP is not a piece of serious or creative work by Soundgarden. It has a novelty component. It's definitely for humor's sake." Regardless, both EP's are still held in high regard by many—including Alice in Chains' Jerry Cantrell. "Those early EP's, and going to see them, the way that Chris sounded, and the way that the band sounded together was an amazing thing. It was very inspiring."

To celebrate the release of the *Fopp EP,* Soundgarden performed as part of the "Capitol Lake Jam" at Capitol Lake Park in Olympia, on August 20th—with none other than Nirvana opening up (unbelievably, the only time both bands would ever appear on the same bill). "They [Nirvana] had no damn stage presence—at the time," remembered Kim. "They seemed a little bit nervous. They were opening for us outside in this park in

Olympia. We really liked the songs, but Kurt just stood there—his hair was in his face. He didn't move."

Soundman/Avast! studio owner Stuart Hallerman recalled the ending of Soundgarden's performance that day. "I stepped away from the mixing board to hear what's it like for the audience. I happened to find myself between the Park Department guy and the DARE Olympia Police Representative. The police officer is like, 'There's no cussing coming off stage; it's really good music!' They were playing 'Fopp,' their encore. We all wistfully look up at the stage into the sunset there, and Chris is bending over, yelling, 'SUCK MY COCK! SUCK MY COCK!' into the microphone. We looked at each and shrugged, like, 'Eh—so much for being nice'." And once again, none other than Ben Shepherd was in the audience. "They were playing a show down in Olympia—one of those daylight shows. Seattle was totally cool back then—the music scene was happening, people were fun, life was cool as fuck, and there they were. Chris was just singing, and Hiro and Kim—that was the true Soundgarden."

As a result of the performance, SG wound up enlisting Hallerman as their soundman. "After the show, the band pointed out that they were about to hit the road for a west coast tour and Europe in the spring. They're like, "Hey Stuart, you've got a PA, and you got your old Dodge van. You sounded good tonight—do you want to come on the road with us?" I'm thinking, drag my PA to all these beer-soaked, smoky, nasty punk rock clubs? Sure, I'll go! [Laughs] Hiro I'd known for almost my whole life by that point, and Kim I'd known for nine years or something. Chris I'd known for about three or four years. I was struck by how much of a kid he was at that point—he had these little rubber birds and GI Joe-ish kind of things that he would fly around the van. He'd be the cassette jockey—playing Aerosmith, Butthole Surfers, and Fugazi. [And] weird mainstream things I'd never think he'd be into."

But not everyone who was part of the local music scene was entirely pleased with Soundgarden—and namely, the antics of their "sex god" lead singer. "They were pretty cool, but Chris' antics got a little annoying," points out Mark Arm, who would have just co-formed Mudhoney at this time. "I'm all for somebody flailing around onstage and engaging the audience—but he would wear a tearaway shirt. It's one thing to take off your shirt, but it's another thing to pre-rip the seams. He'd grab the front of his shirt and pull straight off in a forward motion. It was a preplanned part of the act designed to show off his good body."

"Y'know, maybe there was some jealousy there, because my body was not nearly as hot. [Laughs] But it just seemed so contrived—it didn't seem like a genuine reaction to the music. To be fair, I did some fairly contrived things in Green River. I played most of one show with a fish down my pants, the joke being that my huge bulge was actually a perch, which I pulled out and split open—spilling fish guts on the crowd. This was a punk rock gross-out act—not an act of narcissism." Then-Screaming Trees drummer Mark Pickerel had some concerns, as well. "It was hard to figure out at what point did they cross the line from rock n' roll parody with actual inspired rock n' roll."

One less controversial development in Soundgarden's "looks department" was contributed by Kim around this time—"I didn't have a beard until two years ago [1988]. I decided to grow my hair on my face and my head at the same time." And it turned out that almost immediately, Kim's new look struck a chord with their local following. "Before Ben joined our band, when he was a bit younger, he and his friends would come see Soundgarden play. And he said his friends called me the Zig-Zag man [after the logo for Zig-Zag rolling paper]."

And to add to all the "are they serious or not?" confusion, the band offered a semi-tip of the cap to one of arena rock's most bombastic bands on the next tune they would offer—"Sub Pop Rock City," for the *Sub Pop 200* compilation. Released on December 1, 1988, the 20-track/double vinyl set was first issued as a limited edition run of 5,000 copies, and as its title alludes to, showcased most of Sub Pop's stable of artists, including tracks that were exclusive only to this comp—"Spank Thru" by Nirvana, a cover of Bette Midler's "The Rose" by Mudhoney, and Soundgarden's "Sub Pop Rock City." While not the most sterling tune S. Garden ever offered, it managed to serve its purpose—a throwaway that doesn't take itself too seriously (which turned out to be a collaboration between Chris and Kim).

"We wrote that song with [Kiss'] 'Detroit Rock City' in mind," Kim once explained. "I wrote the riffs and jammed a bunch of grooves together. I thought we'd make it a little 'butt rock.' It's the only time you'll hear a boogie riff in a Soundgarden song; we threw it in mostly for humor. While we were in the studio recording Bruce Pavitt and Jonathan Poneman from Sub Pop were very concerned about what we were doing. They'd call the studio and we wouldn't answer. Jack Endino, who produced the track, just left the answering machine on. We took the messages from Bruce and Jonathan and sampled sections of them to come up with the fake conversation that's on 'Sub Pop Rock City'."

Now having released a single and two EP's (plus a comp appearance) via Sub Pop, an important decision was made concerning Soundgarden's future around the time of *Fopp*. Susan: "There was a really exciting memory—standing on the corner of First and Pine downtown with Jonathan. *Screaming Life* had already come out, *Fopp* was about to come out. The guys—even though lots of major labels had called by that time and we'd gone to LA and had meetings—still wanted to be on SST, that was the goal. I remember standing on the corner, with Jonathan saying, 'Soundgarden should stay on Sub Pop.' They hadn't really formalized their business enough to where they had an office yet or people helping them. I remember looking at Jonathan and saying, 'Soundgarden is a juggernaut, and it's taking off. It's got to go—I've got to move as fast as I can to keep up with it'."

CHAPTER 08
ULTRAMEGA OK

In the '80s, it seemed like the dream of most up-and-coming rock bands was to get signed to a major label—which would then, hopefully, lead to fame and fortune. But in the case of Soundgarden, their strategy was quite uncommon—*not so fast.*

"By the time of their second record, they were already talking with A&M," remembered Endino. "Well before anyone else. Their [third] record came out on SST, and A&M said, 'Why do you want to do this?' And they said, 'We don't want our career to stop for a year while we're negotiating with you. So we're going to continue and release this other record on an indie label—to have something out.' Because most bands would start negotiating with a major label, and it would take six to eight months. Then they would record, and the label would sit on it for three or four months, and then a year goes by. Suddenly, the band lost all its momentum. Soundgarden, very cleverly, said, 'We're going to release one more indie record'."

"When it came to switching labels it was an easy decision to make," explained Kim. "I love the Sub Pop label but we just couldn't make another record with them. They had no real distribution and very little money, and when our record went out of stock they had no way of re-pressing it. We were talking to SST at the time, and they had Saint Vitus, Screaming Trees, and Das Damen, who were all doing well, so it was an easy decision. They had the money and the distribution..."

Perhaps more so than any decade, the '80s were rich with outstanding indie labels—Dischord, Touch and Go, Epitaph, 4AD, Alternative Tentacles, Enigma, Homestead, Creation, Twin/Tone, Slash, IRS, and of course, Sub Pop, all thrived and issued now-classic recordings throughout the decade. But one of the very best was undoubtedly SST—the label that would release Soundgarden's full-length debut, *Ultramega OK*. As previously mentioned, SST Records originally formed in 1978 by Black Flag guitarist Greg Ginn, and would go on to issue classic recordings throughout the '80s by not only Ginn's band (including *Damaged*), but also, the Minutemen (*Double Nickels on the*

Dime), Hüsker Dü (*Zen Arcade*), the Meat Puppets (*Meat Puppets II*), Bad Brains (*I Against I*), Sonic Youth (*Sister*), and Dinosaur Jr. (*You're Living All Over Me*), among others. And it just so happened, Soundgarden thoroughly enjoyed all of these artists.

"The cool thing about SST Records in the mid-to-late '80s—there were a number of bands where the sound was so unique that it could only be the Bad Brains, Hüsker Dü, the Minutemen, the Meat Puppets," explained Kim. "These are very unique, distinct bands. The Meat Puppets are doing this kind of country/Grateful Dead/hardcore crossover, the Minutemen are doing this kind of beatnik jazz/hardcore crossover, Black Flag is doing this kind of metal and hardcore crossover, and the Bad Brains are this hardcore/reggae crossover. There was an interesting post-hardcore/progressive movement of the mid '80s, which was best captured by SST Records."

And it turned out that a member of the local scene was the one who put band and label in touch. "I was instrumental in getting Soundgarden signed to SST," admits Mark Pickerel. "They came out and played a show in Ellensburg in about 1987, and the Screaming Trees' soundman, Rob Doak, recorded the show on his soundboard and made me a tape of it. I was so impressed that I sent it to Greg Ginn. A couple of months later, SST signed them."

"Initially, when Soundgarden formed, we thought it would be great to be on SST, but most of those bands were friends of friends or something, so we resigned ourselves to the fact that it wouldn't happen," recalled Chris. "The strange thing was that Soundgarden was kind of the hype band; I mean, we were getting worried about being talked about too much. It was the first time a band out of the scene was getting that much attention. Like *The Rocket* mentioning that someone from Warner Bros and A&M had come to our show—that was huge news because we hadn't really released anything yet. We were just putting out *Screaming Life* and I think that level of attention was really good for us. Then other bands took some of the focus, which was good as far as we were concerned. I mean, when we put out *Ultramega OK*, it was at the time when a lot of the other bands were starting to do really well. That was around the time Mudhoneymania happened and the very first demos of Nirvana were heard."

So, rather than going with a major, SST got the nod to release *Ultramega OK* (whose title means "absolutely, amazingly not bad")—on Halloween 1988. Album cover image-wise, a black and white photograph featuring Kim's left hand on a guitar neck and Chris strumming a Les Paul with his hair covering his face was utilized—taken by another talented Seattle photographer who would soon make quite a name for himself via his work with grunge acts—Lance Mercer. The inside of the CD booklet also debuted a single "S" design which would turn up from time to time as a logo for the band.

Music-wise, for any fan who may have been misled into believing that *Fopp* was the follow-up to *Screaming Life,* it quickly became clear that this thirteen-track offering was Soundgarden's *true* follow-up—unlike the lighthearted *Fopp,* it showed that the band was back into "serious and focused" mode. And while SG's previous recordings were done entirely nearby, *UOK* saw the band record tracks in Seattle, but also, in Newberg, Oregon, with producer Drew Canulette (with the group earning a co-production credit). And when it came to songwriting credits, there was a major change detected—Cornell still handled writing the majority of the lyrics, but now, all four members took turns contributing music.

Kicking things off is one of SG's all-time great album-openers, "Flower," which Cornell once explained the lyrical meaning of. "It's about a girl. About a girl who becomes a woman and basically invests everything in vanity and then burns out quick." The song also featured an odd guitar technique, which may have been trailblazed by Thayil (who also penned the song's music). "This song marks the first time I ever blew on a guitar. I put the guitar down on the ground near the amp to get a humming feedback, as opposed to a squealy one, and blew across the strings in rhythm with the drums. There's probably some obscure Mississippi blues guitarist like 'Blind Lemon Pledge' who's done that before, but 'Flower' is the first time any rock band had recorded the sound of someone blowing across the strings. It sounds like a sitar." The song would also get the music video treatment, and while not SG's most stellar clip (filmed entirely in black and white, and featuring scenes of a woman running through a graveyard, the members' faces, and performance footage), at least the band now had something to service to such outlets as MTV.

Up next was one of Soundgarden's more underrated tracks, "All Your Lies," a rollicking rocker co-penned by Kim and Hiro, that stops dead in its tracks at several points for Cornell to "rap" (no need to be fret, however—it never approaches treacherous Vanilla Ice nor Limp Bizkit territory). "That chorus part, Hiro wrote that," Thayil once told me about the song's composition. "But basically I had the main riff, the A part, the verse section. And then the transition bridges, which are very guitar-y. They're kind of quick, fast guitar runs. I wrote all those things. And then we needed kind of a break, and Hiro's like, 'Well, how about this? Let's take this groove.' And he came up with the bass riff, which he thought was a good counterpoint to the sort of quick, fast gallop of that riff. When he brought it down, it had a groove, it had a dynamic thing."

"Chris came up with lyrics and introduced them at rehearsal. Back in those days we wrote a lot of songs in practice and then songs would be introduced live. Later on, songs would be introduced on record, then we'd have to learn them to perform them live. But our first three albums, many of those songs existed for years in some cases live before they ever got recorded." Up next, some of the spookiest moments Soundgarden ever committed to tape—"Beyond the Wheel," sandwiched between two instrumental bits, "665" and "667." Concerning the two numerical musical numbers composed by Yamamoto, way back when in the '80s, various religious groups were obsessed with supposed "Satanic messages in rock music lyrics" (remember the good ol' PMRC?)—whether they be detected traditionally, or, discovered by listening to a record backwards.

The S. Garden boys decided to have some fun with these doofuses that had far too much time on their hands—by recording various backwards messages within both tunes. And when listened to backwards, you hear Cornell screaming not about Satan, but rather, about another similarly-named larger-than-life fellow—"Santa is King," "Hail Santa," "I love you Santa baby...got what I need." "The alternative is to see 665 and 667 as the neighbors of the beast," Chris once joked. "The two pieces were originally one song but we split it because it sounded better that way." And what about Kim's opinion? "Some people might think we're really thrashy because we're so evil that we go *beyond* 666."

And concerning the mysteriously-titled/slow-building "Beyond the Wheel" (written entirely by Cornell, and would go on to become a concert highlight throughout the years, and even a sometime set-opener), Chris once set the record straight about its lyrical meaning. "It was about people—small groups of people— with lots of money, who don't give a shit about me, and they don't give a shit about you." Thayil's thoughts? "That song is very industrial sounding. I love the solo; it's wild and loose. We did a backward guitar intro, which gives the song a nice sweep. Chris wrote 'Beyond the Wheel,' recorded it on a four-track, and brought us the demo. We thought it was a great, trippy, heavy song. But Chris thought there was something missing from the middle section. He asked me if there was some kind of drone thing I could do to fill it up. I came up with that part that goes beeoop beeoop, which gives the song great dynamics. That solo is one of my favorite things I've ever done, and one of the best Soundgarden solos."

Up next is the debut of an acoustic guitar on a Soundgarden album (albeit brief, and only detected in its intro), "Mood for Trouble"—a rocker composed completely by Cornell, that is broken up by trippy, psychedelic sections (in the middle and ending). And just when you thought the band was getting all hippy-dippy, we are met head-on with one of the fiercest SG rockers ever, "Circle of Power." The only Soundgarden tune to ever feature Hiro on lead vocals (who also penned the lyrics, with Kim supplying the music), it features a tip of the cap to the late/great Jimi Hendrix, with the line "Not necessarily dumb but beautiful" (compared to Jimi's "Not necessarily stoned but beautiful" from the title track off *Are You Experienced?*). And when the song was performed live, Chris would borrow Hiro's bass, while Hiro would borrow Chris' microphone.

Up next is "He Didn't," which starts off with some Sonic Youth-esque harmonic/feedback squeals, before leading into a repetitive/chromatic riff—composed by Cameron—who also provides some great drumming throughout the tune, as well (including some tricky off-time beat maneuvering during the guitar solo). Up next was a cover of bluesman's Howlin' Wolf's "Smokestack Lightning." It's been said that rock music was formed a top a blues basis, but after hearing Soundgarden's reworking, "the blues" had been wiped completely clean and then promptly dirtied up by "the grunge." And one tiny tidbit—the song's ending included bits of Sonic Youth's "Death Valley 69." It also turns out that although the tune had been covered to death since its original release in 1956 (the Who, the Grateful Dead, Aerosmith, CCR, and the Gun Club all have taken turns over the years), Soundgarden had no idea. Chris: "We learnt the Howlin' Wolf version. We didn't know it had been covered a lot." Hiro: "I did and I told you not to put it on the record. It's a bit crass, a bit like getting BB King to sit up on stage with you."

Then comes another one of the album's more curiously-titled tunes, "Nazi Driver." Featuring a somewhat mutated "Bo Diddley drum beat," the tune also features a jackhammer-like guitar riff from Kim (although the music is courtesy of Hiro). When asked by *Sounds* around the time of the album's release, "Surely Soundgarden aren't foisting any Slayer-esque Nazi controversy on us here?", Chris replied, "We couldn't do that— half of this band are non-teutonic, non-aryan." Kim on the other hand, was willing to dig a bit deeper concerning the song title's meaning. "The song is about cutting up Nazis and making stew out of them—we used driver because it made a cool name. It sounds better than Nazi Stew, Nazi Soupmaker, Nazi Cup-O-Soup, or indeed Cup-O-Nazi. A title can be a poster sometimes. It can be a slogan. Hey, it can be an anthem!"

And then...we arrive upon the album's home stretch. The entirely Cornell-composed "Head Injury" is not necessarily a throwaway, but when you have an album that features the lofty likes of "Flower," "All Your Lies," and "Far Beyond the Wheel," it gets lost in the shuffle. But the heavy "Incessant Mace" makes up for this—serving as another one of the album's top highlights. With music written by Thayil, the song is based around a Sabbath-y slow guitar groove, although the descending riff itself brings to mind Zeppelin's "Dazed and Confused."

"We wrote one song called 'Incessant Mace' pretty early on that sounded blues-based," explained Chris. "It was very slow. Lyrically and vocally, it was very European Gothic. But I guess because we're American and because of our influences as kids, it sounded to people more like Sabbath or Zeppelin, and people would hate it. That was the first reaction, really: that this was the most uncool thing anyone could do at this point in music in this city. That was a turning point in our career as a band. Because we could play atonal, post-punk, ridiculous, quirky shit, and everyone thought it was great. But we'd play that song, and it would create more of a reaction. So we started doing that more."

"By the time it was on the record, it was the sixth time we recorded it," adds Kim about the tune. "We'd always recorded it, we'd never released it. It's like our favorite song, but it's always too long, or it's four-track, or I don't like the four-track, let's do an eight-track. So it was released on the SST record, and it was our least favorite version. Another time we recorded it, then we got rid of the drummer we did it with, so we decided not to use that session."

And just when you thought the "Soundgarden humor quota per album" was satisfied with the album's earlier "665"/"667," a cover of John Lennon's "One Minute of Silence" (which truth be told, isn't a *true* minute of silence, as you hear what sounds like an amp or two being clicked off around the 30-second mark). Chris: "We were trying real hard to shut up, but Kim couldn't possibly shut up for a whole minute." Kim: "No, it's the heavy metal version—we had the silence switched up to eleven."

Concerning the recording of *Ultramega OK,* Cameron recalled, "We went down to record in this kind of homemade studio that was pretty good. It was in Newberg, Oregon. Again, we didn't have a lot of time—I think we had two weeks to do it all. We recorded some up here in Seattle, in an abandoned warehouse; we got a mobile truck. Recorded some drums there, then we finished the rest in Newberg." "Production-wise we left Seattle and it showed," adds Thayil. "It wasn't exactly what we were after. Material-wise we went through the process that we always do, but the producer wasn't used to the sound we wanted and didn't know what was happening in Seattle."

Like Thayil, Cameron also voices reservations about the album—when comparing it to the others that came in its wake. "I think some of the music on our past records is a little more show-offy. Everyone was trying to make their individual part stand out more than it should have—not all the time, but enough to notice it. We listen back to some of our earlier records and cringe because it sounds like we were just showing off. Personally, on the *Ultramega OK* album, I feel there are some songs with bad approaches to drumming. 'Nazi Driver' is a song that comes to mind. I totally missed a drum on 'Flower,' but we left it in there."

Additionally, you can add Cornell to the list of SG bandmembers that was critical of *UOK,* in hindsight. "I think we made a huge mistake with *Ultramega OK*, because we left our home surroundings and people we'd been involved with and used this producer that really did affect our album in a kind of negative way. The producer was suggested by SST because they could get a good deal. I regret it, because in terms of material, it should have been one of the best records we ever did. It actually slowed down our momentum a little bit because it didn't really sound like us." The singer also once offered a witty spin on the album's title—"It was *Ultramega Alright."*

In 2017 (March 10th, to be exact), the band's objections about *Ultramega OK* would be squashed once and for all, as the man who produced the demos for the album, Jack Endino, remixed the entire recording from its original tapes, and also included several eight-track demos as bonuses. But let's travel back to the timeframe surrounding *UOK*'s original release, shall we? 1988 would see Soundgarden's first shows *far* outside of

Washington, including performances in Los Angeles (Club Lingerie, of which great single camera-shot footage exists) on February 11, New York City (CBGB's) on July 19, and San Francisco (I-Beam) on October 24. And then in early 1989, Soundgarden launched not only their first extensive US tour that took them from coast to coast, but also, throughout Europe.

"That was exciting—going around the whole country," reflects Hiro. "What an adventure. I remember [being] crammed in the van, getting hotel rooms—someone would always sleep in the van to watch the gear, and it was four or five of us crowded in the room. It was always like, 'Man, I need a break from these guys.' [Laughs] We went all the way down to Florida, touring the South, and up to New York. The thing with the South I remember is that they weren't as into us—they didn't know as much about us. But the big cities, like New York and Los Angeles, we were pretty well-known. There was the whole Los Angeles/music industry deal, because every time we went towards Los Angeles, the wining and dining started."

"We'd do ten-week tours—we'd be gone for two and a half months," adds Kim about SG's early road jaunts. "I was in Pioneer Square—I went to see some band, I don't know if it was the Melvins. Kurt [Cobain] was there—I think Kurt was by himself and I was by myself. I went over to tell him how much I loved *Bleach*. He was very quiet and subdued. He said, 'Thanks—that means a lot coming from you. Consider yourself our biggest influence.' I was like, '*Whoa!*' We'd always been a 'younger band'—we'd always been an 'up-and-coming band.' Now, we'd made a record on SST and were playing nationally, and to have a guy you consider a peer put out a record that you absolutely love, and to have him say, 'You're a big influence,' was head-spinning for me at the time. It was one of the many things that gave us a new perspective about ourselves." And it turns out that Mr. Thayil has an impeccable memory, as he was able to recall what the band was listening to in the van during this tour. "The stuff in heavy rotation was Fugazi's first [self-titled] EP, Nirvana's *Bleach*, Neil Young's *Everybody Knows This Is Nowhere*, and *Meat Puppets II*. That's the '88/'89 tour—'the SST tour'."

It was also around this time that a Seattle native now based in Los Angeles caught a SG performance—in his new adopted hometown. "I remember hearing a lot about Soundgarden," recalled Guns N' Roses bassist Duff McKagan. "They finally came down and played LA—I want to say '88. Maybe they played while we were on tour for *Appetite*, but the first time I saw them was at the Scream in downtown LA. *That* was a rock band. There wasn't many gigs of bands I wanted to go see at that point. '88 was a pretty shitty time for music—a lot of White Lion, Whitesnake, and Warrant. It was terrible. So when I heard Soundgarden was coming down to play, I went, and I was really hoping that it would still be the Soundgarden that I remembered and heard such great things about. And they just fucking blew my mind. For some reason I always look at the drummer—if the drummer is good, the rest will follow. And Matt was just insane; playing all those different meters. And Kim Thayil, wow—what the fuck is that? And Cornell's voice was fucking Robert Plant on acid. They were menacing, beautiful, musical—the whole thing."

Looking back on these early tours in 1994, Cornell recalled making an interesting observation. "When we first started touring, we were really excited to go to places like New York, San Francisco, Austin, and Athens. But we'd get there and check it out and think, this is OK, but things are so much cooler and the scene is so much more vibrant in Seattle where you could go to any club—and there were only a few then—but there'd always be someone playing. Even though a good show was only 200 people, it was still a pretty amazing scene. There wasn't the audience at the time to create a larger scene, but there was a consistent audience and we supported each other heavily. Maybe that lack of attention allowed it to germinate more. Maybe that was a good thing."

But Matt did once remember an on-tour hassle that occurred during this era. "On one of our first van tours, we got pulled over as soon as we crossed into Louisiana by these undercover DEA cowboy dudes. They searched the van, and our soundman had a smidgen of pot. They took all of our money, all the stuff they thought was evidence—vitamins and stuff. They thought we were selling pot. So they left us pretty much high and dry for a gram of pot."

And right in the middle of the Euro tour, SST issued what would be their last full-on Soundgarden release—a three-song single for "Flower" (SG would also donate two tunes, "All Your Lies" and "Head Injury," to the SST comp, *Program: Annihilator II*, in October of 1989). Released on May 14th, in addition to the headlining track, the EP also included "Head Injury," as well as a non-LP tune, "Toy Box," which was an outtake from the *Screaming Life* sessions. Why the song did not make the cut in the first place remains a mystery, as it was a strong one—moody and slow, and twisting and turning for nearly six minutes. Also of note—the single's cover shot. A color shot of the band standing in the bright shining sun on what appears to be a rooftop is not anything out of the ordinary...until you realize that it was taken by Charles Peterson, who seemed to work exclusively in black and white at the time (and sans his trademark "flash and drag shutter effect," either).

On the same day as the release of the "Flower" single, Soundgarden made the most of their time of being on tour in England by recording their first-ever session for John Peel, at the Hippodrome in Golders Green, London (which would be broadcast on June 7th). In addition to an accurate reading of their latest single's featured tune, the band also offered up a pair of covers—Sly and the Family Stone's "Thank You (Falettinme Be Mice Elf Agin)" and the Beatles' "Everybody's Got Something to Hide (Except Me and My Monkey)." Concerning the Sly cover, the tempo is taken down a notch or two, as is the funk (the only thing funky about it is Hiro's bass), while the Beatles tune proves to be a faithful cover.

Which for me, personally, Beatles covers are always a waste of time, 'cause you're never gonna top the original that just about every living, breathing human being is already familiar with...unless if you're going to completely rework it and put an entirely new spin on it (which by that point, why not just change the lyrics and make it one of your own original songs!). However,

Soundgarden would correct this missed opportunity concerning selecting covers the next time they would indulge in a BBC session (in 1992).

After the tour in support of *UOK* wrapped up in the summer of '88, it was clear that Soundgarden was making great strides in not only building a Statewide following, but also, *a global one*. "We'd sold like 3,000 records in Italy on the SST label," said Kim. "That was impressive...kind of a surprise...we sold more records in Italy than we did in Washington State!" But the greatest sign that Soundgarden was making major progress was when it was announced (albeit a year later) that the album had earned a Grammy nomination in the "Best Metal Performance" category—when they went up against the likes of Dokken (*Beast from the East*), Faith No More (*The Real Thing*), Queensrÿche ("I Don't Believe in Love"), and Metallica ("One").

Perhaps feeling badly about the blunder that the Grammy folks committed a year earlier (awarding Jethro Tull over Metallica), Metallica wound up taking home the little golden gramophone statue on February 21, 1990, at the Shrine Auditorium in Los Angeles (why several recordings issued back in '88 would be up for the prize in '90 still remains a bit befuddling, but anyway...).

It didn't take a mastermind to realize that Soundgarden was more than ready to sign on the dotted line with a major label. But little did most people know, *a deal was already struck.*

CHAPTER 09
LOUDER THAN LOVE

It turns out that circa *Fopp,* A&M Records began being interested in signing Soundgarden. Yet, in a not-so-common twist, the band signed with A&M *two months* before the release of *Ultramega OK* for SST. Co-founded in 1962 by trumpeter Herb Alpert and executive Jerry Moss (hence the A&M name), the label had success throughout the years with a variety of popular musical styles—including such artists as Cat Stevens, Cheech and Chong, Peter Frampton, the Police, Joe Jackson, and Janet Jackson. But as far as a heavy metal band with punk and indie rock leanings go, there hadn't yet been any on the A&M roster—which looking back, makes their interest in such a unique band quite curious. In any case, A&M deserve props for seeing the potential in Soundgarden —especially at the time, when within the realm of hard rock/heavy metal, most majors were content to sign only glam or thrash bands.

"Actually, we'd been talking to people at A&M almost a year before we went with SST, but we weren't interested in a major label deal that early in our career," explained Chris in 1989. "We wanted to do more independent stuff first, get to design our own packaging and know the industry before people were in a position to tell us what to do. As far as our choice of A&M goes, they've stuck with us for two years and they've allowed us to maintain our ideas and originality, as well as providing major distribution."

Looking back years later, Susan had nothing but positive memories. "A&M—as its reputation—was a really artist friendly place. People were genuine and cared. There was no bullshit. They had a way of hiring people there that were genuine and music fans—that had a history of doing cool things in the music business. Everybody was really supportive. We met with Geffen several times, and then negotiated with Epic for quite a while— but nobody felt the same as they did about A&M. There were days where we thought Epic would be the way to go—and I probably wouldn't be here today telling you the story if that had been the case, because I'm sure they would have knocked me out for a bigger manager somewhere in the early days. Whereas A&M was really supportive of young bands and managers."

But according to Hiro, it was a certain band that may have helped facilitate the conversation between the major labels and Soundgarden in the first place. "Faith No More was one of the big reasons we got signed. Those guys had just gotten signed, and they were really into us. I think they were in their record label's office, saw a demo of ours, and were like, 'You should check this out.' And then once that started, everybody was interested." [Laughs]

Getting back to the earlier point of A&M's lack of a hard rock or heavy metal roster, according to Kim, it actually played into their favor. "A&M haven't worked with much hard rock but they are a label that takes risks. They've taken risks with the Police, Squeeze, and even Budgie in the past, and that was something that attracted us to them. At least we know we don't have to compete with anyone for the company's affection."

And how did Chris liken working with A&M early on compared to their previous two labels? "You gotta keep more on top of what's going on. SST just said, 'Deliver a record and packaging and we'll put it out.' We just did it. Sub Pop, on the other hand, is really involved in the mix of the songs, the song choices, the packaging, just like a major. The advantage with labels like Sub Pop is that you're dealing with creativity from your friends, people on the same wavelength...whereas with a major, sometimes that doesn't happen. Fortunately with A&M, they have a progressive staff. It's not like dudes in suits all worried about something."

So with the deal in place, sessions finally got underway for Soundgarden's sophomore full-length, *Louder Than Love*. And as it turns out, the sessions occurred *before* the band had even launched their tour in support of *Ultramega OK*. "We recorded *Louder Than Love* over a year ago," recalled Kim. "It was recorded in November and December of '88, and January '89; and mixed in the spring of '89. By that time, I was like, 'I'm really sick of hearing this thing a million times, even though there are certain songs that still give me the creeps at night'."

Louder Than Love would be recorded at London Bridge Studios in Seattle—a studio founded by brothers Rick and Raj Parashar, and would serve as the location for the recording of such subsequent classics as Mother Love Bone's *Apple,* Alice in Chains' *Facelift, Sap, Dirt,* and *Jar of Flies,* Temple of the Dog's self-titled debut, and Blind Melon's self-titled debut. And it turns out Thayil found the surroundings quite comfortable. "The people there are Indian and they're the first I've met in the music business besides myself. Most Indian people I know have short hair, wear glasses, and are engineering students."

Louder Than Love would also be the first of two albums that the group would co-produce with Terry Date. Best known up to that point for his work with such metal acts as Metal Church, Sanctuary, and Dream Theater, Date would become one of rock's top producers in the '90s—working on classic albums by the likes of Pantera (all of their studio albums in the '90s, including such classics as 1990's *Cowboys from Hell* and 1992's *Vulgar Display of Power*), White Zombie (1995's *Astro Creep: 2000*), and the Deftones (1995's *Adrenaline* and 1997's *Around the Fur*), as well as Mother Love Bone's one-and-only full-length (1990's *Apple*). "It was a good experience, probably our first time in a professional studio—a real big-time studio with a 24-track machine," remembered Matt. "We didn't want to fuck up—we were well-rehearsed. We knew what songs we were going to do. So we treated every recording session as a chance to bust it out quick, and try to get our live sound down as much as possible. I think later on we tried to use the studio more as a composition tool."

"There's a lot of quirky little memories—convincing Kim to buy a second guitar, which was difficult," recalled Terry Date. "Trying to decide if we were going to go with the equipment he was using, or if we were going to buy some new stuff. As far as my production memories, we experimented with layering guitars. I think the band felt like it led to too smooth of a sound. We were also doing that record at a time when Metallica's *...And Justice for All* was coming out. So there was a very different sound in 'heavy metal.' Soundgarden, Metallica, and Mother Love Bone were all being lumped into heavy metal—they're about as different as I can imagine." And the producer remembered nothing but positive vibes between the four band members. Well, *almost*. "They all got along great. I think the only argument I can remember is when I finally did get Kim to get a new guitar, and somebody picked it up to play it in the morning, after they'd been eating powdered donuts. They got white powder all over the guitar. Kim kinda got pissed off."

"Terry Date could make things...things just shimmered," Hiro explained. "It boomed and it shimmered at the same time. I remember being skeptical about Terry, because his big thing was metal bands, and I was always like, 'Are we a metal band'?" Chris at the time was quick to set the record straight concerning Hiro's last concern. "It's not a metal record. If you look at what's on the market today, it's all pretty defined—Metallica, Megadeth, Anthrax. And there's all those silly LA bands like Great White. We're heavy enough for anyone into speed metal, but we're heavy rock, like you say. Neo-metal maybe."

Interestingly, although in his last quote Hiro sounded impressed with how *Louder Than Love* came out sonically, others did not share his opinion—including the producer of *Screaming Life,* Jack Endino. "I was pretty disappointed with everybody's first major label record, to be honest. I don't think *Louder Than Love* is a very good record—it's not produced well, it's not mixed well. The later records blow it away. The problem with all the indie bands—they had come up making records in a week, two weeks. Suddenly, you're presented with two months to make a record. What you wind up doing—if you're not familiar with the process and have never done it before—is basically instead of using the technology, *the technology uses you*. You wind up making a record with all the rough edges removed. You wind up making everything perfect. That's alright if you're making a Radiohead or Police record, but not if you're trying to make a rock n' roll album. So you ended up with *Louder Than Love*—a fairly safe-sounding, not very exciting-sounding record."

But at the time however, Soundgarden seemed quite pleased with how the album turned out. Cornell went as far as calling the recording "Magic, it was cosmic, it really worked, the sound is definitely what we want." Thayil was also pleased, by gushing, "Yeah it's heavy. The sound is a lot thicker and wider than *Ultramega OK*; bigger guitar, bigger drums, bigger everything." And you could count Cameron in, too, concerning the lovefest surrounding *Louder Than Love*—"The songs are a lot better, the arrangements work better as music, they're less choppy, more hypnotic."

Some members of the rock press circa '89 felt like the sound of the album had more in common with yesteryear, rather than what was popular at the time. Case in point, when Cornell was told at the time by an interviewer that he felt that *Louder Than Love* had more in common with Aerosmith's 1976 classic, *Rocks,* rather than what Tyler and co's then-current album, *Pump,* had in common with *Rocks*. "I heard the whole new Aerosmith record but it didn't sound any different to *Rocks*. We tried to get away from the Def Leppard production technique, the exploding gunshot snare drum. Our production sounds like a band rather than thousands and thousands of dollars. It's not so much '70s as not very late '80s."

While Endino's main gripe with *LTL* is the sonics, from your humble narrator's "2019 perspective," it was *the quality of the material* that was its main problem—more so than the sonics. If you were to parallel *Louder Than Love* to *Ultramega OK,* there is simply no comparison—*UOK* is an extremely consistent listen from front to back, with not a single stinker in the bunch—whereas although *LTL* does contain a few gems, it is padded with filler or material simply not as strong as the album's standouts. The ultimate proof of this being that once the tour in support of *Louder Than Love* wrapped up, quite a few of the songs would never be heard from again in a SG setlist (or at least were performed infrequently).

And...if you were to compare renditions of the songs that would be played in concert to the studio versions, in most cases, the former usually proves to be a major improvement over the later. Also, as you will soon learn by reading the ensuing song-by-song study of the album, the majority of the first four songs on the album are by-and-large similarly mid-paced, whereas most

Soundgarden albums past and present tend to break things up tempo-wise from the get-go—resulting in not exactly the most exhilarating start to a SG record. Lastly, what proved to be truly puzzling is that two non-album b-sides recorded circa the *LTL* era, "Fresh Deadly Roses" and "Heretic," were actually *stronger* than some of the tracks included on the album—so whoever had final say in the album's tracklisting most certainly fumbled the ball.

As with *Ultramega OK,* Cornell handled nearly all of the lyric writing duties on *Louder Than Love* (except for a single track, which has an interesting story, which we will get to...*patience, patience*!), and also penned the music for the album-opener, "Ugly Truth." Lyrically, the tune seems like it's a distant cousin of "Beyond the Wheel," since judging from such lines as "You share but money can't give what the truth takes away, Throw it away," it appears to be about finances. And instead of walloping you over the coconut with an explosive number right off the bat, Soundgarden opts to go with a hypnotic Zep-like groove, instead (with an interesting middle section, where the bass and drums drop out entirely).

Up next would be one of the album's undisputed great tracks (and the one that served as my and quite a few other *Headbangers Ball* viewing fans' intro to the band), "Hands All Over." With music supplied by Kim, "Hands All Over" is built upon a simple, repeating, and ascending guitar riff (that sounds a kin to a siren or horn), and this is what appealed to Thayil the most about it. "What I liked about the song was that it was just one simple riff—one note, one chord—but with a lot of dynamics. In some ways it's simple and basic; in other ways, it's very sophisticated in how it was layered. We don't really have many songs that are like 'Hands All Over'."

That said, at the time, the tune received a bit of criticism concerning its lyrics and people misunderstanding its message. "We're having problems with some of the lyrics on the new album," admitted Chris. "Some of the radio stations and stores got advance copies with no lyrics; we have some songs where if you just listen to it without paying attention you might get the wrong idea. Like 'Hands All Over,' I'm singing, 'Put your hands away, you're going to kill your mother,' but all people hear is the 'Kill your mother' part. Then they think, 'He's saying 'kill your mother!' 'We can't play this in the store'!"

"It can be interpreted either way though," added Kim. "The 'Kill your mother' part is about the third world situation...we're all at home, eating tortillas, and the contras come barging in and they're gonna kill our mother because we are with the resistance." However, when I broached the subject to Kim in 2010, he had a different view. "I think there was a minor protest about [the lyric "You're gonna kill your mother"]—of course, 'your mother' being a metaphor for the environment or the Earth. People flipped out about that. But I am going to go on the record now to tell everyone, 'Kill your fucking mother'!" [Laughs]

Another highlight, "Gun," comes up third on the album— a rocker (composed entirely by Chris) whose tempo slowly gains speed as it goes along featuring a simple three-note guitar line...which eventually collapses into a cacophonic solo. "The thing about this song that's so distinct is that the tempo starts off slow and gradually speeds up, but it doesn't walk up steps or come to sections that are faster. It just speeds up until it culminates in a big jack-off guitar solo. Then it slows down again. It's a fun song to do live because Matt always speeds up way too fast. Faster than we can play." [Laughs]

Lyrically, Cornell once introduced "Gun" on stage as being about "If you believe in something, getting off your ass to make it happen." But with such lyrics as, "I got an idea of something we can do with a gun, Sink load and fire 'til the empire reaps what they've sown, Shoot, shoot, shoot 'til their minds are open, Shoot, shoot 'til their eyes are closed," the lyrics could be construed as advocating taking violence into your own hands— via a firearm. Which at the time that the song was released, wasn't all that big of a deal. However, in subsequent years, the amount of mass shootings and the whole gun law debate have cast the song's lyrics in a whole new light. And another personal favorite Cornell- ism is included—"Regret must weigh a ton" (this hefty unit of weight must have intrigued the singer, as it would reappear on the song "Mind Riot," with "I was tight rope walking in two ton shoes").

Cornell explained at the time about balancing political-minded lyrics with other subjects in their songs. "We're not a party band and we're not all gloom and hate. We have angry lyrics, we have political lyrics, cerebral lyrics, and poetry. Our last record was more in that vein but our new record is more political, more straight-ahead fist-in-the-face kind of anger. Not like 'fuck you' for no reason but 'fuck you' for this reason and this reason and this reason."

Up next, the first bit of "filler," in the form of "Power Trip"—a tune whose music was penned by Hiro, that well...doesn't really seem to go anywhere or leave much of an impression. But the lull doesn't last long thankfully, as another standout immediately follows—in the form of one of the album's truly upbeat numbers, "Get on the Snake." And the chap who penned the song's music, Kim, once discussed the song musically—"In 'Get on the Snake,' we developed a great riff, but it turned out to be in 9/4 time. You can't dance to it, but it sort of sneaks up on you anyway." Lyrically, I would venture to guess it deals with environmental abuse (especially such lines as "Get on the snake under the cola colored sky" and "Get on the snake where the metal river bleeds").

Another forgettable ditty lurks around the corner, "Full on Kevin's Mom"—entirely penned by Cornell, the song seems to be about a romantic encounter between a friend of the singer's and another friend's mother...hence its daring title. But all is forgiven by the next tune (again, entirely penned by Chris), "Loud Love," which challenges "Hands All Over" for the album's very best. "The intro was a feedback melody," recalled Thayil. "Many people think we used an E-bow. I've seen transcriptions that have said to use an E-bow. The truth is, I've never even seen an E-bow. I simply stood in front of the amp, got the note ringing until it was feeding back, and slid my finger up the fret on the string and dragged the feedback with it." And once the intro subsides, we are treated to one of Soundgarden's all-time best guitar riffs—showing that one-time drummer Cornell was quickly becoming a master of constructing riffs. Lyrically, another gem of a Cornell-ism is included—"I've been deaf now I want noise."

What follows are three songs in a row—"I Awake," "No Wrong No Right," and "Uncovered"—that for some reason, I always link together as a "trilogy." Not because there is a lyrical theme that runs through the trio, but rather concerning where they are located on the album, all have similar sleepy tempos, and all were rarely played in concert after the *LTL* tour. The first track of the bunch, "I Awake," is the best, with music by Hiro, but lyrics penned by his then-girlfriend/future-wife, Kate McDonald. As journalist Grant Alden once explained, "Yamamoto came in one day with a lyric sheet to 'I Awake,' but Cornell read the other side of the paper, a note from Yamamoto's girlfriend, and so Kate McDonald ended up with a songwriting credit." With that in mind now, when examining the lyrics, it does indeed read like a letter! And the simple/common phrase, "I love you," is emphasized by Cornell, singing it repeatedly throughout—in both screechingly-high and lower-than-low registers.

Another tune with music courtesy of Yamamoto, "No Wrong No Right," is the second tune off the album to begin with an extended drum bit by Cameron ("Ugly Truth" being the other), followed by "Uncovered," with Cornell providing the musical composition, and built around a sturdy guitar riff. And then...another one of the album's most memorable tunes—the magnificently titled "Big Dumb Sex." Thinking back to the time, MTV was one big glut of unbearable hair metal bands, all of which were bragging about their success in the romance department. But instead of just coming out and saying it, they would hide behind juvenile phrases and/or double entendre lyrics—straight out of a high school locker room (for example, Whitesnake's "Slide It In," Mötley Crüe's "Ten Seconds to Love," Warrant's "Cherry Pie," Kiss' "Let's Put the X in Sex," the Poison album title *Open Up and Say...Ahh!*, etc.).

Cornell decided to knock off all the pussyfooting and get straight to the point—"The lyrics don't specify whether it's a man talking about a woman or a woman talking about a man. We're surprised it got such a bad reaction, particularly because people like Poison and Madonna say pretty much the same thing every time they use the word love. We just replaced the word love with the word fuck and the world went crazy. It's hypocrisy." And to the singer's credit, he has always been able to slip in a few words that your average hair metal band would never think to incorporate. Can you really picture Pretty Boy Floyd or Danger Danger using a word like "discretion" in one of their filthier tunes?

"Hiro, our bass player at the time, hated that song," recalled Kim. "He thought it was obnoxious butt rock, a total rock n' roll cliché. We tried to explain to him that the song was making fun of butt rock." And while the chorus of "I know what to do, I'm gonna fuck, fuck, fuck, fuck you" prevented the tune from receiving any airplay, musically, the song proved to be one of Soundgarden's most melodic and easiest-to-digest yet. However, including the song on the album still proved to be controversial, as Thayil once explained that it "Irritated Jerry Moss, the 'M' in A&M Records. But eventually the whole label got behind the song because I think they realized what we were up to."

And let's have its author have the final word on this delightfully smutty rocker, shall we? "'Big Dumb Sex' was, to me, one of the hookiest songs I ever wrote, but I don't know whether I would have written a song like that for Soundgarden if it hadn't said 'fuck' 35 times in it, because it was making fun of that kind of music, really." But as a result of the song's inclusion, *Louder Than Love* was the recipient of a "PARENTAL ADVISORY EXPLICIT CONTENT" sticker slapped on its CD case. "I think it was done to appease one of those watchdog groups like the PMRC (the Parents Music Resource Center)," Thayil said. "We're not interested in appeasing anyone, but the label has its interests to protect and Soundgarden has theirs." And closing out the album is the tune "Full on (Reprise)," which as its title suggests, contains elements of "Full on Kevin's Mom" at a much slower tempo.

Released on September 5, 1989 (and eventually peaking at #108 on the *Billboard 200*), *Louder Than Love* would feature an album cover image provided once more by Charles Peterson— a now classic live shot of Chris (yep, again shirtless), holding a mic, and his mop of hair completely covering his face, although not blurred like the majority of the photographer's other work with grunge acts. And concerning the album title, it turns out that the album cover's designer had something to do with that—a chap by the name of Art Chantry.

"They didn't have a name for the record. We were talking about it and joking—I said, 'You should really call this record *Louder Than Shit.*' They go, 'That's a great name!' I go, 'No...call it *Louder Than Fuck.*' 'Oh, that's great!' And Susan Silver goes, 'My band isn't putting out a record with 'Fuck' in the title.' That's where *Louder Than Love* came from." Cornell also offered *his* thoughts concerning the album's curious title. "It's sort of making fun of heavy metal bravado. Metal bands would say *Louder Than Thunder* or something. So *Louder Than Love*, what is *Louder Than Love*?"

Upon its arrival, *Louder Than Love* seemed to receive an impressive amount of positive praise, including the *Chicago Tribune's* Greg Kot stating, "Even Soundgarden's hardest, loudest workouts have a subtle, sensual underpinning, an unlikely mix that makes *Louder Than Love* one of the most innovative hard rock records to come skateboarding down the pike since Metallica's *Master of Puppets* (Elektra) in 1986." Additionally, *Rip's* Don Kaye stated—"I've been championing this Seattle juggernaut for some time now, starting with praise for that first album, and now that the band is graduating to the big leagues via a deal with A&M Records, I see no reason to discontinue my campaign, especially in light of the magnificence of their recent major-label debut, *Louder Than Love*." But perhaps the most impressive praise that the band received was via W. Axl Rose— during a cover story interview for *Rolling Stone* in 1989, when asked, "What kind of music and bands do you enjoy?", one of his replies was "I enjoy Sound Garden [sic]. The singer just buries me. The guy sings so great."

However, just five years after the album's release, Chris expressed some concern about the band's coverage in metal mags around this time. "When we released *Louder Than Love*, everyone wanted us to be heavy metal, because that's what was big. The record company, the publicists...the heavy metal magazines especially, who were having a pretty serious time trying to find something worthy to write about because all the bands sound exactly the fucking same, sing about the same shit and have nothing to say. It's a totally lacking genre. Part of that categorization was our fault because *Louder Than Love* was a metal record and, being our debut for a major, was the one that made the impression."

At the time I first discovered it, I certainly did enjoy *Louder Than Love*—in fact, along with Faith No More's *The Real Thing,* it was one of my most listened to CD's of the year 1990. But like the Faith No More album, in the ensuing years, if I am to be brutally honest, it has become my least-listened to SG recording (and interestingly, the same could be said about *The Real Thing*—I much prefer most of FNM's other albums). I have to agree with both Endino's earlier harsh-yet-honest evaluation, as well as Cornell's concern about it being a bit too "heavy metal" (and quite one-dimensional)—especially if you are to compare it to Soundgarden's following studio offerings. And something else that became glaring when comparing *LTL* to even the band's following album two years later—Matt Cameron's drumming is not properly showcased. *At all.* In fact, if you were to judge his playing solely from this album, he sounds like your average/ordinary metal drummer that lacks pizzazz or anything separating him from the rest of the pack. And as we all know by now, was certainly not the case—Soundgarden had one of rock's top drummers in their ranks...yet his talents were mysteriously muted here.

And the performances themselves are rather workmanlike throughout the record. The proof is if you are to view/hear live renditions of these songs post-1991 (for example, "Gun" filmed during a Lollapalooza tour stop in Bremerton on July 22, 1992, "Hands All Over" filmed while opening for Guns N' Roses in Vincennes, France on June 6, 1992, "Ugly Truth" from Irving Plaza, NYC on November 13, 2012, etc.), a whole new groove, vibe, and swagger is detected—showing what the material *could have been.* In fact, I would be bold enough to say that *Ultramega*

OK is the superior album when compared to *Louder Than Love*—
from both a quality of the material and performance perspective.
Which leads to one of those "woulda/coulda/shoulda"
thoughts/scenarios—what if it was *UOK* that was issued in place
of *LTL,* as Soundgarden's major label debut?

Regardless, Soundgarden at least now had a major label
release under their belt, and with material to choose from two full-
lengths and two EP's, the time couldn't have been better for the
band to embark on their most extensive and longest tour yet.
Unfortunately, one band member was preparing his exit.

CHAPTER 10
BEN

In the last chapter, you may have remembered Hiro admitted thinking, "Man, I need a break from these guys," during the group's first substantial US tour. It turns out that it was not just a brief break he needed, but rather, *a permanent one*. "He got tired of being a musician," explained Chris. "He didn't like touring. He began contributing to the band less and less. He didn't like the tension level. He wanted to go back to school and continue a degree in physics. It seems an odd time to quit. We're doing real well. We've got a touring budget now. We don't haul amps or do such long van rides anymore."

"He left about a month before the *Louder Than Love* tour," adds Kim. "It was a combination of a lot of things...he was not at all eager to go on the road again. In other respects, he's a smart guy and there's other things he could do. He decided to go back to college and study physics. It had been five years for Hiro and Chris, and I think he was just getting burnt out. Everything was getting more demanding, plus he quit drinking and smoking. And if you have the strength to stand by those kind of decisions, it's very difficult to be on the road and deal with these kinds of temptations."

"He was losing confidence," continues Chris. "In himself, in the band, in his own songs." In fact, in an *Alternative Press* article from 1994, writer Dave Thompson claimed that at the time, "Several latter-day Yamamoto compositions went unrecorded, not because the band disliked them (Cornell: 'They were actually among the best he'd ever done'), but because Hiro had no faith in them."

"I guess the reason why I left was the whole deal about metal—'I don't want to be in a metal band'," explained Hiro. "To me, that's still the most embarrassing thing in my life. We were a hard rock band, but I don't know if we were ever a metal band. We got bigger than I ever imagined we could have—I wasn't really ready for that at the time. That wasn't what I wanted out of music. I guess promotion scared me—advertising and promotion are things to me that seem very foreign. Mixing music and the two

of them was something that was hard for me to grasp at that point.
I was unhappy before we left for Europe. And then halfway
through Europe, I was like, 'I can't keep doing this.' A&M was
telling us to tour 350 days a year, and I was like, 'I'm not doing
this, you can't make me!' [Laughs] I remember being in Italy
somewhere—that was pretty much near the end of the tour. That
was it. [*Louder Than Love*] had been recorded, it just hadn't been
released yet."

"It was certainly heartbreaking for us, because he was a
founding member, and such a significant creative part of the
band—in our sound," Kim admitted two decades later. "What we
were about, and the style that all our peers and friends had come
to love was founded on certainly a creative interaction between
Hiro and I. And definitely the three of us working together—not
leaving Matt out of that. With four people in the band, there are
six different two-man relationships, there are four different three-
man relationships, and there's one four-man relationship. So that's
eleven relationships, I guess. Having Hiro leaving the band, you
have now changed the nature of seven relationships."

After exiting Soundgarden, Hiro kept in touch with Kim
the most, but not so much with the others. After completing a
master's degree in physical chemistry, he would go on to help
form one of grunge's most underrated bands, Truly. Also
consisting of singer/guitarist Robert Roth and original Screaming
Trees drummer Mark Pickerel, the band would go on to issue a
handful of albums—including the exceptional 1995 effort, *Fast
Stories...from Kid Coma* (picture a "grunge-psychedelic-
Radiohead," and you're not far off). "Some of the songs and lyrics
[on *Fast Stories*] still put a chill down my spine when I hear
them," Hiro would later say. "Certain parts of songs just have this
feel, and to me, that's the reason why I always played music—to
make that kind of sound." In addition to playing in the on-
again/off-again Truly, at the time of this book's release, he also
plays in an instrumental "surf-inspired trio," Stereo Donkey,
including guitarist Pat Wickline and drummer Mike Bajuk.

So...with Hiro now out of the picture, a replacement
needed to be located, and rather quickly—as a lengthy tour was to

be launched in September 1989 (and as it turns out, would keep them on the road until October 1990!). And in a great "what if?" moment, a certain individual considered inquiring about the bass vacancy—but ultimately chose not to. "[Kurt Cobain] loved Soundgarden," Kurt's then-girlfriend (and photographer of the *Bleach* album cover), Tracy Marander, once recounted. "At one point, when they were looking for another [bassist], he actually thought about quitting Nirvana. He wanted to try out for them, because he liked them that much."

But when the process of trying out potential replacements actually got underway, one turned out to be ex-U-Men member, Jim Tillman. "I played with them several times—trying to figure out if it would work," remembered the former U-Man. "They had a tendency to tune everything down—*way down*. They'd take an E string and tune it down to a C. I promptly blew up Hiro's bass cabinet. So we went bowling instead."

Up next...the younger brother of Kim's friend/one-time roommate Henry Shepherd—Ben Shepherd. "They were crunched for time, they had deadlines—they had these make up tours they had to do. Once we got to the rehearsal room, I didn't say anything; I just walked over to the amp, turned it up, and started playing. Then we jammed for three hours, we didn't play any of their songs. They went, 'The next time we get together, we've got to work on the songs.' And they took Jason [Everman] because he knew the songs. He was more connected and on-beat with it."

So, it was former Nirvana guitarist Everman that got the gig. Born on October 16, 1967 in Ouzinkie, Alaska, Everman's prior claim to fame was being included on the album cover image of Nirvana's full-length debut, *Bleach*...despite not playing a single note of music on the album (although he *did* pay the bill of $606.17 to cover producer Jack Endino's recording fee). His tenure in the band was brief, however—only touring in support of *Bleach* and recording two songs with the band, a cover of Kiss' "Do You Love Me?" and an alternate version of the b-side "Dive." Shortly after exiting Nirvana, a tryout with Soundgarden was arranged. "Jason knew the material already," Cornell once said.

"And we sort of took that to mean he would be more into what we were doing." With Jason now onboard, the promotion machine behind *Louder Than Love* was about to kick into high gear.

Despite not playing on *LTL*, it was Jason who was spotted in two music videos from the album—"Loud Love" and "Hands All Over." And even though both clips were overseen by a bloke who would become one of rock's most in-demand music video directors of the '90s, Kevin Kerslake (who would go on to direct such now-classic clips as Nirvana's "Come as You Are," Smashing Pumpkins' "Cherub Rock," and Stone Temple Pilots' "Interstate Love Song"), to be frank, his work with SG is *not* his best. Reflecting your average/blah metal videos of the era, both clips are similar-looking, with the band miming to the songs, while standing a top two comparable sets, with lotsa flashing lights. For "LL," black and white clips of car crashes are spotted (and there is one striking scene—albeit brief—at the beginning, in which Cornell is crouched down and a single white light beam oscillates back and forth, showing his silhouette), while for "HAO," scenes of a female model wearing a white body suit poses in front of a screen that shows images of planet earth and the abuse of nature, while the singer takes a ride on what appears to be a conveyor belt at one point.

Speaking to VJ Riki Rachtman about the "HAO" video during an interview segment on MTV's *Headbangers Ball* in 1990, Cornell explained, "Making this video was fun because we were in a steel foundry. And there was like a black cancer dust all over everything. We're all gonna get cancer from it and die. So, I hope you enjoy it. This will be the video that killed Soundgarden." However, years after both clips were filmed, Thayil had harsh criticism for the clip. "The video for that song was one of the lamest ever made. It really sucked." Well said, Kim.

And while we're on the subject of *Headbangers Ball,* the band's presence on the program seemed to confirm once and for all that Soundgarden was now a full-on *metal band...*or were they? "I remember talking to Kim at one point back then, and they made a conscious turn toward going for more of a metal thing," recalled Mark Arm. "This was before *Nevermind* broke. And his argument was, 'Well, would you rather be on *Headbangers Ball* or would you rather be on *120 Minutes*?' And I was just like, 'I don't know if it's an 'either/or' thing.' Because I wouldn't want to be just lumped into like, 'We're totally one of these guys or we're totally one of these guys.' Because there's plenty of irritating shit about both camps."

But getting back to the line-up adjustment, Everman's mug would also be spotted on the cover of the album's first single, "Loud Love." Issued on August 30th, the UK version would be comprised of four tracks—"LL," a "dub version" of "Big Dumb Sex" (a remix that inserts dialogue from what sounds like a talk show about the supposed dangers of rock music, as well as moans and groans from a porno), "Get on the Snake," and "Fresh Deadly Roses." The 100% Chris Cornell composition (let's refer to these as a "CCC" from now on, as in "complete Cornell composition," capeesh?), "Fresh Deadly Roses" is the main attraction here, however—a strong tune that begins with a ringing guitar bit, with quite a few words that have probably never been spotted in a heavy metal song before or since—"concertina" and "congeal." And as a special bonus, the cover photo includes Mr. Thayil making quite an intense "possessed" stare, while also forming a fist with his hand.

The group also found some time to enter a recording studio and record a b-side for the "Hands All Over" single (released October 12th and featuring two of the four band members holding cigarettes on the cover), which included a cover of the Beatles' classic, "Come Together"—serving as Jason's debut on a Soundgarden studio recording. Similar to their earlier cover of another Beatles classic, "Everybody's Got Something to Hide," this version is rather pointless, as it doesn't come close to topping the original (which contained one of the greatest bass lines of all-time).

Perhaps to make up for this misfire, when a four-track CD single of "HAO" was released, a killer retake of the early track (first appearing on the *Deep Six* comp), "Heretic," was included. Co-penned by Kim and Hiro and recorded during the sessions for *Louder Than Love,* this version of "Heretic" is superior to some of the songs included on the eventual album—which makes the inclusion of such throwaways as "Full On (Reprise)" instead of this gem quite perplexing.

"'Heretic' was the first song we wrote where we thought, 'Why can't the main riff be built entirely on harmonics?', remembered Kim. "The harmonics weren't as loud as the regular low-string stuff, but the chorus gave it the boost it needed to be as present as the picked notes." And lyrically, Hiro once explained the thought behind it—"The only 'demonic' song we have is 'Heretic,' and that talks about how ridiculous it is that scientists were persecuted in their times and appreciated years later. It's not about witches or Satan—even though it refers to them." And in case you were wondering, the fourth track rounding out the "HAO" CD single was "Big Dumb Sex."

A year later (October 21, 1990, to be exact), both the "Loud Love" and "Hands All Over" singles—and all five of their collected b-sides—would be compiled together as a Japanese release, entitled *Loudest Love,* that featured the same exact cover photo as the "Loud Love" single. It was also around this time that Soundgarden's music proved to be quite popular in motion pictures, as SG tunes were detected in such films as *Say Anything...* ("Flower" and "Toy Box"), *Lost Angels* ("Get on the Snake"), and *Pump Up the Volume* ("Heretic"). And the same year, Soundgarden would find tracks of theirs included on three separate multi-artist compilations—*Fuck Me I'm Rich* ("Hunted Down" and "Nothing to Say"), *1989 New Music Awards* (a live recording of "Ugly Truth"), and *Pave the Earth* ("Fresh Deadly Roses").

With *Louder Than Love* in the record store racks, gaining favorable press, and *Headbangers Ball* spinning their videos, a supporting tour was finally launched. In the fall, Soundgarden commenced a headlining tour of clubs and smaller venues (quite a bit of stellar video footage exists of this era, including performances at Rhino Records, Concrete Foundations Forum, and New York University—the latter of which includes a stellar Cornell audience request/dare, "Let's all take our shirts off and make this place smell as bad as I do"). Various supporting bands were enlisted—with at least a few of the dates seeing a teaming of two of alt-rock's soon-to-be finest acts. Let's let Kim explain, shall we?

"The first time I met the guys in Primus, they opened for us—or we opened for them, I can't remember—in St. Louis, at a venue called Mississippi Nights. [Note: This is incorrect, as it's been confirmed that Soundgarden and Primus played at least two shows together—October 23 and 24, at Staches in Columbus, Ohio and the Phantasy Nightclub in Cleveland, Ohio] I remember talking with Les [Claypool] and Larry [LaLonde] afterward—I don't think it was a tour bus, but they had an RV or a Winnebago. And specifically, I talked to them about Captain Beefheart and the Butthole Surfers. And they didn't seem to be well acquainted with either band. But they were very much into Tom Waits. Which surprised me—sometimes I thought of Tom Waits as the acoustic Butthole Surfers. Or the Butthole Surfers being the acid-drenched-electric-psychedelic Tom Waits. We played a few shows with Primus around then, but that was the one that I remember, because we got to sit down and watch them, and we went to go talk to them."

And in early December, Soundgarden headlined four nights at Los Angeles' famed Whisky A Go Go, which was filmed, and a handful of highlights eventually included on the home video, *Louder Than Live* (released on May 22, 1990). Directed by the same chap who worked with the band on their two promo videos, Kevin Kerslake, the 50-minute VHS release featured five live tracks ("Gun," "Big Dumb Sex," "I Awake," "Get on the Snake," and a medley comprised of Spinal Tap's "Big Bottom" and Cheech and Chong's "Earache My Eye") and the album's two promo videos ("Loud Love" and "Hands All Over").

Concerning the concert footage (which was shot entirely in black and white), it tends to get too artsy fartsy for its own good. Case in point, a somewhat irritating effect is used throughout, in which a scene will be repeated again...and again...and again—so you do not see a few seconds of what was actually occurring at that precise part of the song. Of the live performances, the closing medley is the best, which features Jason smashing his bass at the beginning (and an offer was included in early pressings of VHS copies, that if you filled out the card and mailed it in, one lucky fan would win the remnants of the battered bass!) and Chris falling into the audience and crowd surfing...while continuing to strum his electric guitar. A&M would also issue a promo-only CD and vinyl of the audio of the video in the summer of '90, with two additional live performances—"Beyond the Wheel" and "Hunted Down."

It was also around this time that Cornell began sporting a look comprised of cargo shorts (including one pair that he covered entirely in what appeared to be silver electrical tape), Dr. Martens boots, and as expected, bare chested...which would not only become his fashion trademark, but soon, one associated with the fast-approaching grunge movement. Also, he was now playing more guitar live (allowing Kim more fretboard freedom)—preferring a sunburst Gibson Les Paul. And it just so happens that shortly after the dawn of the new decade, Soundgarden was able to hook up with a killer three-band bill, which also included Faith No More (who had issued *The Real Thing* the previous June) and Canadian sci-fi prog-metallers Voivod (having released one of their best recordings, *Nothingface,* in October), with Prong replacing FNM on select dates. The tour—which was sometimes referred to in the press at the time as the "Munsters of Rock" (a play on words of Van Halen's 1988 stadium jaunt, "Monsters of Rock")—ran from January through March, playing clubs and theaters.

And shortly after the tour wrapped, Kim discussed being pleasantly surprised about the crowds' reaction to SG. "We played three shows in Canada, and it was kind of different for us. We didn't have people yelling for us...well, we did, [but] not in Montreal. In Ottawa we had a lot of fans there. But Voivod would come on and it was like [simulated crowd noise] 'Yeah!'' We played Detroit and there was 800 people in St. Andrews. People just went crazy, stage diving all over the place. We get done and 200-300 people leave. Then they [Voivod] start, and people start walking out. It's been that way for the past five weeks."

Chris also explained at the time the type of crowd reaction Soundgarden was getting on this tour. "Detroit is always good for us, I don't know why but most Seattle bands seem to do well there. We get the same sort of feel in Chicago, that's always very exciting, but in a more violent way. [Laughs] One night I got all my clothes and jewelry ripped off and there was like this ongoing battle between the audience and security!" Years after the "Munsters tour" wrapped up, Thayil expressed disappointment that one of the bands on the bill never managed to break through commercially. "That tour was great. Faith No More were getting big success from 'Epic,' and Voivod is a great band. I think what really hurt [Voivod] was the lack of promotion from Mechanix/MCA, their label."

Interestingly, in a feature for *The Rocket,* writer Jeff Gilbert not only wrote about how well all three bands got along, but also, was willing to spill the beans concerning certain tour expenditures. "Voivod play 'Loud Love' at their soundcheck, and Mike Patton sits in with Soundgarden. Chris gargles apple vinegar and stays at the hotel until showtime, not wanting his flu to get worse. On the last tour, due to lack of sleep and stress, an unchecked cold cost the band $5,000 in lost gigs. This time, he says, the band literally can't afford him getting sick. The bus still costs them $400 a day whether the band plays or not."

Years after the tour, Matt still had great memories—especially concerning two of the singers. "I think Patton and Chris...the two singers were egging each other on each night, who could sing the highest or who could do the craziest acrobatics. I remember once, Patton played before us and he threw the mic cable over the lighting rig, and he said, 'I predict Chris Cornell will do this tonight!' And he started to crawl up the mic cable and dangle from the lights."

When writing the 2013 book, *The Faith No More & Mr. Bungle Companion,* I interviewed Kim for it, and he had several vivid and amusing stories/memories of the FNM/SG/VV bill. First, he discussed how then-recently-joined FNM singer Patton was still trying to find his comfort zone as a vocalist and performer. "When we started that tour, Mike Patton was trying to figure out his stage persona. He kind of seemed to be working on his identity—trying to figure out who he was. After a while, he was kind of imitating Chris. He wasn't mocking Chris, because he definitely seemed a little bit like 'a freshman'—he seemed a little bit nervous. Here he was, joining a band that was already up and running for a few years—a band that had a history with Chuck Mosley and a number of albums. Mike seemed a little like a fish out of water, trying to get 'land legs'."

"He was kind of awkward for the first few shows—his stage presence wasn't that great—but eventually, he started jumping around stage like Chris did. And Chris would take his shirt off...and then Mike started taking his shirt off. But we didn't think he was mocking, because he seemed so nervous and insecure. He is an athletic guy, he is in shape, he has a great voice, he had this long beautiful hair—like Chris did. First he started flailing his hair around like Chris did, he started jumping around on stage. But he has a great voice—amazingly versatile and powerful voice. It's funny, because he was very 'rock star-ish' then, which is very different from his Mr. Bungle thing and the other stuff he's done."

Kim also recalled an oft-overlooked stage prop that both Patton and Cornell took full advantage of during these dates. "If there was any plumbing [in the venue], Chris would climb it or treat it like monkeybars. And eventually, Mike Patton started doing that, as well! And later, in 1992 on Lollapalooza, [Pearl Jam's] Eddie Vedder started doing that as well. So Chris definitely had a 'stage antics influence' on at least Mike Patton then, and Eddie later. But Mike started stomping around and climbing things, and jumping off the stage, and Chris would jump from the stage and stagedive, and do the crowd surfing. When Mike started jumping from the stage and crowd surfing, we were like, 'Fuck dude. We're going to go on after them, and Mike's already doing stuff that Chris does. Is he mocking us?' Because we got wind that he had a smartass, prankster element to him. But he seemed sort of insecure and nervous about his new gig, so we thought he was trying to figure out how to be a rock star in his band that he just joined, that already had a history."

And also, Kim shared a memory from the tour, that literally, must have stunk. "I think we were playing the Aragon Ballroom with Faith No More. I remember going to the bathroom and Faith No More was on stage. I was taking a piss, and all of a sudden, Mike ran into the bathroom—he was all sweaty. He ran into the shower, and I was laughing. I go, 'What the fuck are you doing? Aren't you guys on stage?' I can still hear the band, but there's no vocals—maybe a guitar solo. He's in the shower, he ran out, he smiled at me, and then ran back onstage. Then, after the show, our tour manager comes up, and he's like, 'Someone took a dump in the fucking shower. Some of the employees say they saw you in the bathroom.' I go, 'Yeah, I took a piss! Mike Patton ran down off the stage! It must have been Patton—that's what he was doing in the shower'!"

"We ended up learning that was his 'thing.' I think Mike Patton influenced Matt Cameron into doing some similar things. This is all shit that Mike Patton and Matt Cameron did—they'd take dumps into a bowl or a plate, and then undo the vents in a hotel room, then put the plate or bowl into the vent, then re-screw the vent screen back on, so that the room I guess would be inundated with a certain 'perfume,' and the employees would have a hard time figuring out what the origination point was for that foul odor. They'd eventually take off the vent screen and find Mike Patton's 'prize.' And I know Matt Cameron did that a couple of times because he learned that from Patton."

As I mentioned in the book's intro, it was right at this point in the story that I was lucky to catch my first-ever Soundgarden show on March 17th at L'Amour in Brooklyn, New York. Rather than reiterate my experience, feel free at this point to return to the beginning of the book to re-read my memories. If not, let's continue on with the story, shall we? Little did I know that right around the time of the L'Amour show, news was broken to the band that a close friend of Chris' (and a one-time roommate of his) had overdosed on heroin, and was on life support—Mother Love Bone singer Andy Wood.

MLB was set to be the second grunge band (yes, Soundgarden being the first) from Seattle to release an album on a major label—their full-length debut, *Apple*—via Mercury. The group was comprised of veterans of the Seattle music scene, including former members of Green River (guitarists Stone Gossard and Bruce Fairweather, plus bassist Jeff Ament) and 10 Minute Warning (drummer Greg Gilmore), while Wood was previously a member of Malfunkshun. With a style that merged grunge with '70s style glam (not feeble '80s style glam), it definitely appeared as though the quintet was headed for stardom, before tragically, it all came to a sudden end.

"We were in this crappy apartment-hotel place that we stayed at, because it was eighty bucks a night and had a kitchen," recalled Susan Silver, who was on tour with Soundgarden in New York at the time. "A bunch of people lived in it—you always smelled liver cooking and heard people practicing instruments. It was by the Beacon Theater. I got a call, and it was Kelly [Curtis, Mother Love Bone's manager], and he said that Andy was in a coma, and they weren't sure if he was going to make it. We were all in a daze. It was scary—everybody was in shock. I remember after soundcheck, sitting at this table and there was a TV playing—waiting for the doors to open. It was during that period that Sinead O'Connor had done 'Nothing Compares 2 U.' For some reason it seems like that was playing over and over—that stark video with her face taking up the whole screen."

Knowing that Chris and Andy were close, Andy's family opted to wait for the Soundgarden singer to return home from tour before taking the Mother Love Bone frontman off life support, so that he and Susan could say goodbye. "We came back the next day, dropped our bags at home, and went right to the hospital. All the band was around, and his girlfriend. They told us when we got there that they were going to take him off life support. His family was there—his parents, his brothers, and his little two-year-old nephew. I remember holding his hand, giving him a kiss on the forehead, and saying that he was an angel. None of us will ever meet another human being that looks more like an angel—a cherub. Gorgeous, cherub, porcelain skinned face, with long blond hair. A really surreal moment. I said, *'Goodbye angel,'* stepped outside the curtain, and they turned off the machines."

"I felt really alone when Andy died," Chris once admitted. "I spent a lot of time with him and tried to work out his pain creatively. Most of the time I really didn't know Andy was using. I offered to have him live with me, because he had just gotten out of treatment. He was going to live on the island with his parents, where he grew up. I thought that would be harder for him. Most of the time it was me watching him struggle not to shoot up, not to drink. It wasn't like observing Andy's high; it was more like experiencing him squirming."

Kim was also affected by Andy's death, admitting two years later that he cried for an entire week afterwards, and explaining, "Bruce Fairweather is one of my closest friends now. When we put on *Apple*, we make jokes, we drink, we laugh. We remember the good times. There was no one like Andy, and regardless of when in his life he died, he did live all of his life. That's the way he lived it. There are a lot of people acting as if Andy has taken something away from them. When I cried for Andy, was I weeping for his loss or mine? Maybe both. We were on tour last year, listening to Love Bone, and I was silent for an hour. Then, all of a sudden, I punched out this glass globe on the bus. I just sat there afterwards, shaking. And periodically I hear Andy's voice. It gives me this rush. It really hits me, especially when I'm sitting there with Bruce. [Pause] God, I was just thinking about him now. It's weird. Shit, I've known too many people who have died now. One thing that really bugs me is the list keeps growing."

Chris also once recalled what it was like attending Andy's funeral. "When I went to his funeral...there were tons of people there who didn't know him, who were just, like, fans, and that were coming up to me and saying that they knew how I felt and how awful it was. It was really ridiculous. I mean, they didn't know how I felt, they didn't know anything. They were just rock fans, basically, going to a show. And the idea that Andy was perfect, you know, is pretty laughable. I mean, he had a lot of serious problems, like we all do. But something about a person dying, especially someone in the entertainment industry, always elevates who they were and what they did into this other space."

Years later, Chris was asked pointblank how he reacted to the death of his friends (sadly, the number would rise in the coming years). "The same as anyone else, I guess. I was confused. Like all these crazy things go through your head, the same crazy stuff that goes through anybody else's. I thought, 'I shoulda seen it coming', I thought, 'Too bad someone with that much talent had to die', I thought, 'Too bad he had a drug problem'. Then I guess I just thought about all the other kids that had died that I'd never hear about. You try to rationalize this shit, but there are no rational ways of looking at stuff like that. People ask me if I learnt anything from it, I don't really think I did because all the lessons that could be learnt, I had already learnt. I knew dope killed, that's why I didn't do it." Soon, Chris would turn to songwriting to mourn the loss of his friend...but we will get to that in a bit.

Unfortunately, there wasn't much time to reflect or get their heads around the loss of their friend, as a European tour was already booked and set to get underway two weeks later. And judging from a glowing review by Phil Wilding in *Kerrang!* about one of the Euro tour's first shows (at Riverside in Newcastle, England), the band was able to block out what was going on in their personal lives—and focus on the task at hand. "'Loud Love' is uglier than incest, more commanding than religion. Struck out in filthy hammer blows, the first stage-diver flops off awkwardly to it. Cornell takes his cue, standing momentarily on his monitor then toppling quickly into the crowd. He's instantly swamped, then dragged back to the stage, only to jump straight back off as soon as he reaches it. Oh, the place was simply jumping."

It was also during this Euro jaunt that Soundgarden was filmed for an episode of the long-running German music television show, *Rockpalast*—on April 16th in Dusseldorf, West Germany. As far as pro-shot/recorded *LTL* era performances go (and filmed on a large stage), this is mighty hard to top—and proves to be superior in a lot of ways to *Louder Than Live,* since it is filmed in full color and features a longer setlist (including great renditions of such early classics as "Flower" and "Beyond the Wheel"—the latter of which features some truly super-humanly sung vocals courtesy of Mr. Cornell). And it must be noted—this Soundgarden edition of *Rockpalast* is probably one of the few shows from the late '80s/early '90s that Chris does not take off his shirt!

Even more impressive was that Soundgarden was able to continue putting on inspired shows when it had become obvious by now that it was not working out with their newest member. "He certainly could do the musical thing, but it wasn't keeping the band together," remembered Kim. "We were at a point where Chris and I realized, 'I don't think we're going to be able to be on the road all the time.' We really weren't identifying or behaving as a band. We had our moments where everything was great. But we weren't like four fingers curled up into one fist. We realized we had to make a decision. Chris' suggestion was Ben. He'd been thinking of Ben's ability and personality, and thought that could be the thing that gets us back to where we were—personally and creatively."

After exiting Soundgarden after the Euro tour wrapped in the spring, Everman would go on to continue playing music in such bands as Mind Funk and OLD, before joining the United States Army, and serving with the Army's 2nd Ranger Battalion and later with the Special Forces, during which time he served tours in both Afghanistan and Iraq. In 2013, *The New York Times* published a revealing article about Everman, entitled *The Rock n' Roll Casualty Who Became a War Hero* (penned by Bullet LaVolta guitarist Clay Tarver), and a year later, attended Nirvana's induction into the Rock and Roll Hall of Fame.

So, just prior to the summer of 1990, Soundgarden welcomed their third bassist in a mere one year span. Born Hunter Benedict Shepherd on September 20, 1968, in Okinawa, Japan...well, let's just let Ben explain. "I was born in Japan, then we moved to Texas. When I was three, we moved up here—I've lived across the water from Seattle my whole life. Never really lived in Seattle until [recently]. My dad used to play guitar—the first song I ever heard was 'Big River' by Johnny Cash. When I was eight, I heard [Iggy & the Stooges' 1973 release] *Raw Power*. That was it—I was doomed. I had older brothers and sisters, so I'd go all the way from Earth Wind & Fire and Eartha Kitt to Syd

Barrett and Captain Beefheart. Even though we were poorer than hell, they always had music going."

"Ben's mom has a huge book collection and his father was in the military," Kim once explained about Ben. "One thing we all have in common is that we're all products of divorces within suburban families and grew up with our moms." And similar to Chris, Ben came from a family of six children. "My brothers were in a pretty progressive crowd," he recalled. "Especially for where we lived, in a small redneck town. Once people found out we listened to punk, they totally disregarded us as human beings. They thought I was a faggot 'cause I read too many books, but I knew they were full of shit. I had my friends, and we had bands off and on all the time. Everyone hung out at my house and when kids ran away from home they'd come to my house, 'cause my parents were cool. Our family were the freak family! Very rarely you'd come across another punker at school—most often with a black eye. I wonder if a lot of these kids even know how much shit punk rockers used to get. I don't think they do; they don't get it the same way."

Eventually, Shepherd began playing guitar in local punk bands, including one called March of Crimes (which briefly also featured none other than eventual Green River/Mother Love Bone/Pearl Jam/Brad guitarist Stone Gossard), and as mentioned earlier, attended quite a few early Soundgarden performances— including their live debut. In fact, out of everything he saw at those shows, it sounded like Ben was most impressed with their bassist—"Hiro Yamamoto was the king. There's only a few I've seen that I think are good, and he's one." Paying bills by the late '80s via construction work, Shepherd initially auditioned for Nirvana (as a second guitarist) and Soundgarden (as a bassist) around the same time in 1989, but didn't get either gig. At least, initially—admits Matt. "So after Jason didn't work out, we all figured, 'We chose the wrong guy! Let's see if Ben is still interested.' Luckily, he was."

So, on June 15, 1990 at the Lake City Concert Hall in Seattle, Ben made his debut as the bassist for Soundgarden. And exactly two weeks later, he was on tour with the band. The last go-round of dates in support of *Louder Than Love* would see the group spend the entire summer on the road—first hitting Europe (including a performance at the Roskilde Festival on June 29), followed by yet another set of dates Stateside, including a tour that saw Soundgarden sandwiched in the middle of a bill between Danzig and Warrior Soul. And somehow/someway this same month, Chris found the time to earn a production credit on the Screaming Trees' major label debut, *Uncle Anesthesia* (on Epic, which was also co-produced by the band and...Terry Date)— which would eventually be released on January 29, 1991.

And on August 17th, I attended a show on this tour—at the Beacon Theater, in NYC. It just so happens that the Beacon is one of NYC's best venues to see a show (fully seated and extremely picturesque inside), and a capacity or near-capacity crowd turned out. Although my seat was high up in the balcony, the seats are on an incline, so I was able to get a good, clear view of the stage. Now remember, in the days before the internet, news concerning line-up changes in rock bands was very slow coming if you were not, say, Guns N' Roses or Mötley Crüe (*MTV News* was quite selective with who they would report about, and unlike weekly UK publications like *Kerrang!* that were quick to report news, US publications were *slooooow*). So, imagine my surprise when Soundgarden took the stage with one of best renditions I've ever heard of "Beyond the Wheel"...and a new bass player was present?!

Also, keep in mind, Shepherd's look was the complete opposite of Everman's—short hair, tall and lanky, incredibly low slung bass, and at this performance at least, he was walking a bit spastically, as if his knees could not bend properly. And Ben just happened to once explain how his trademark "low slung bass" came to pass—due in part to the instrument he used quite often, a 1972 Fender Jazz. "It belonged to the Wood brothers. I bought it to try out for Soundgarden, and I played it on every Soundgarden record and every tour. I called it 'Tree' because it was so heavy. At that time it felt like it weighed more than I did because I was scrawny as hell."

"Then my bass tech said, 'Man, you're too tall. This bass looks tiny on you.' I lowered the strap so it would look cooler, and I wanted to straighten out my arms so I could just use my fingers. The ergonomic advantage is you don't get tennis elbow or sore wrists or anything else because you're not doing anything your body wasn't designed to do. That's why I always wore it long, and I'm tall enough to get away with it looking exaggeratedly long. I can still touch all the strings where I want. You have to contour your body, and be willing to throw your whole body into it. Always spread your legs to get closer to the neck."

I also recall spotting that Cornell's image had changed a bit at the Beacon—gone was the freshly shaven look, as he now sported facial hair that was a cross between Zorro and a goatee (a look he would embrace for much of the rest of his life). Another memory of the show included a brave fan leaving his seat to stand as close to the stage as possible, and Cornell "high-fiving" him. But one of the most memorable events for yours truly was when my friends and I made a pilgrimage to the men's restroom after Soundgarden's set, and on the way through the hallway, we were treated to a trail of vomit on the ground. Once inside the restroom, we did not actually see the culprit, but we certainly could hear him behind a stall...not only continuing to spew his evening's culinary contents into a commode, but most startlingly, also crying aloud for his mother!

Returning to our seats, we only stayed for a smidge of Danzig's set—after all, we had a train to catch back to Long Island...but most importantly, it was clear that Soundgarden was the best band that night, and could not be topped. "[The Beacon show] was one of the best times we ever played 'Beyond the Wheel'," recalled Ben. "I met the guys from Queensrÿche and flipped them shit after. 'Whoa, I've never seen anybody play bass like that before!' I was like, "'Well, you've never seen us then. *Why are you talking to me?*' Then I went and hid in this room in the dark and smoked cigarettes."

Less than two weeks later (September 1st), Soundgarden issued a surprise single via their old chums, Sub Pop, as part of their *Sub Pop Single of the Month*, "Room a Thousand Years

Wide" b/w "HIV Baby"—serving as Shepherd's first appearance on a Soundgarden recording. With another old pal, Stuart Hallerman, serving as producer, it was an obvious step away from *LTL* sonically—as it was much more lo-fi sounding, which put it more in league with *Screaming Life* and *Ultramega OK* (which most certainly was *not* a bad thing). While the a-side would be re-recorded (admittedly as a better/definitive version) on *Badmotorfinger,* the version of "Room a Thousand Years Wide" here is almost demo-like, but you can still make out that it is indeed a winner. The song chugs along in an odd time signature (6/4 time), and features the first appearance of horns on a SG record (saxophonist Scott Granlund and trumpeter Ernst Long)—whose freeform squawks and squeals at the end definitely evoke a Stooges/*Funhouse* vibe.

A collaboration between Thayil (the lyricist) and Cameron (musical composer), it also happens to feature one of my favorite SG phrases of all-time, "Tomorrow begat tomorrow," which I later asked the song's lyricist about. "Actually, that lyric Steve Fisk referred to me from some weird movie. God, which movie was it? I wonder if it's the movie *Häxan* [a 1922 film subtitled *Witchcraft Through the Ages*]. But there's some movie, there's a line...we were just talking about this. There's a line where a witch is chanting that or some witches are saying some spell, 'Tomorrow begat tomorrow.' Like an infinite regress, 'Tomorrow begat tomorrow begat,' meaning it just keeps going. And so I thought, 'Oh, man, that'd be fucking cool in a song'."

And its b-side, "HIV Baby," is well...let's say it's a prime example of a track that should be delegated to a single's b-side, as it's not necessarily the most memorable or strongest SG track—but certainly not a stinker, either. And Kim once explained the story behind the song—"I wrote the middle and ending riff, but Chris wrote the lyrics and Ben came up with the title, which was based on me, because I don't like sharing other people's silverware, drinking out of other people's bottles or sharing cigarettes. I'm pretty uptight about that. Ben said to me, 'Wow, Kim, you're a total HIV baby'!" Fair enough.

Two days after the single dropped (September 3rd), Soundgarden would play their largest headlining show yet, when they got the nod to top the bill at the Bumbershoot Festival at the Seattle Center Coliseum (supposedly after the planned headliners, the Psychedelic Furs, failed to turn up). Inserting in a few golden oldies into the setlist for the hometown crowd ("All Your Lies," "Nothing to Say," etc.), an undisputed highlight was when they performed Spinal Tap's "Big Bottom," a substantially-sized skull was lowered onto the stage—a prop left at the venue from when Tap themselves actually played the venue, years earlier! And on a side note, it was also around this time that Chris and Susan wed.

The *Louder Than Love* tour would finally grind to a halt after Soundgarden got the nod to perform a pair of shows as part of a multi-band festival, A Gathering of the Tribes (which was organized by Cult frontman Ian Astbury and legendary promoter Bill Graham). A clear precursor to the following year's Lollapalooza—AGotT featuring such diverse artists as Iggy Pop, Joan Baez, Public Enemy, London Quireboys, Ice-T, the Mission UK, the Cramps, and Michelle Shocked, among others—with the shows taking place on October 6th and 7th (at the Shoreline Amphitheatre in Mountain View and the Pacific Amphitheatre in Costa Mesa, respectively), and like Lolla, tents with info about various causes and organizations were spotted on site. But unlike Lolla which would be ongoing, AGotT would only last for one more year, before being put out to pasture.

Also around this time, Matt provided drums for the debut recording by Tone Dogs, *Ankety Low Day,* issued on November 15th via C/Z Records. A short-lived trio that was comprised of a pair of multi-instrumentalists—Amy Denio (who was also the lead singer) and Fred Chalenor, in addition to Cameron—the band's sound was certainly more funky, jazzy, and arty than SG. And unlike *Louder Than Love,* definitely does a better job of showcasing the drummer's exceptional percussive skills, and being able to handle odd meters. However, this would be the sole T. Dogs album that Matt would appear on—when the band issued their second (and final) studio album in 1991, *The Early Middle*

Years, the drum throne would be occupied by a chap named Will Dowd.

Despite all the non-stop touring, press accolades, and MTV exposure circa 1989-90, *Louder Than Love* did not serve as the big commercial breakthrough that for instance, their buddies in Faith No More had secured at the time—with *The Real Thing,* and its surprise hit single/video, "Epic." In fact, as of this book's writing, *LTL* has never even received a single bloody certification for units sold by the Recording Industry Association of America. "Our major label debut didn't do that well initially," explained Thayil a few years later. "I don't think the label knew what to do with us. They were more used to handling Peter Frampton or Sting. We were something really different. A lot of the people they approached about us thought we were just another metal band. Those, of course, were the same people who were dying to speak to us a year or so later. But that's part of the fun. In rock n' roll, I've learned you never can know exactly what to expect."

But that said, *LTL* did inspire others, including Pantera, who was about to work on what was their first classic album, *Cowboys from Hell.* "They had their influence of metal," recalled Pantera bassist Rex Brown. "One of the reasons that we used the producer Terry Date was because of *Louder Than Love.* That record changed a lot of what was going on before." And most significantly, the album inspired Metallica guitarist Kirk Hammett to compose one of the most instantly recognizable metal riffs of all-time—"Enter Sandman." "It was about two or three o'clock in the morning. I had just been listening to *Louder Than Love,* the Soundgarden album. It was when Soundgarden [was] still somewhat underground and [was] on an independent label. [Not exactly, but please, do continue...] I just love that album; it's a great Soundgarden album. And I heard that album, I was inspired, I picked up my guitar, and out came that riff."

So, with the *LTL* chapter now in the books—both figuratively and literally—the group's sights began being set on their third full-length overall. But before work commenced, Chris found himself writing songs that were inspired by the passing of Andy Wood—and not intended for Soundgarden.

CHAPTER 11
TEMPLE OF THE DOG

"Not long after Andy died, Susan and Kelly shared offices, and she mentioned that Chris had recorded a couple of songs that pertained to Andy, and wanted us to hear them," remembered Jeff Ament. "I hooked up with Chris, and he gave me a tape—I was blown away. I thought initially that he could just release them like that and they would have been great. The demos of 'Reach Down' and 'Say Hello 2 Heaven' are really not that much different than what ended up on the record. Chris had all these songs together, and there were a couple that Stone had—we knocked them out in five or six days. We were down and out, and those guys picked us up for a minute, and helped us out. It was pure music, it wasn't anything else."

And it just so happens that around the same time, Jeff and Stone had begun jamming on new material with guitarist Mike McCready and drummer Dave Krusen. And at the suggestion of former Red Hot Chili Peppers drummer Jack Irons, the new group was put in touch with then-San Diego resident Eddie Vedder, who soon signed on and relocated to Seattle—eventually leading to the formation of Mookie Blaylock...and later, changing their name to Pearl Jam. And two of the new recruits, McCready and Vedder, would contribute along with Ament and Gossard to the aforementioned Wood-inspired material that Cornell had penned. And none other than Matt Cameron would serve as the drummer for the project, which would eventually be dubbed Temple of the Dog (after a lyric Wood penned for the Mother Love Bone song, "Man of Golden Words"—"I want to show you something like joy inside my heart, Seems I been living in the temple of the dog").

It turned out that the material was more in a "70's classic rock style" than what Cornell usually offered up with Soundgarden (I always thought that Robin Trower's 1974 classic LP, *Bridge of Sighs,* sounded similar to TotD—especially in both McCready and Trower's Hendrix-y guitar work, and also, the late James Dewar's soulful vocals were comparable to Cornell's). Before recording the material, TotD played one full show at the Off Ramp in Seattle, on November 13th (without Vedder, however), to help fine-tune the tracks. Once again entering London Bridge Studios in Seattle (which was where *Louder Than Love* was recorded), the album would be co-produced by one of the studio's co-owners, Rick Parashar, as well as the band— recorded from November-December 1990. "They went in the studio, and eleven days later, came out with that entire album," remembered Silver. "It was just an unbelievable, cathartic experience. An amazing record—a big, powerful record."

The first two songs that Cornell penned for the project— "Say Hello 2 Heaven" and "Reach Down"—also start off the album. And "SH2H" was one of the album's very best—a slow burning rocker that never quite retreats to ballad territory, but comes awfully close, and contains more than a few obvious references to Wood (including "He came from an island, Then he died from the street, And he hurt so bad like a soul breaking, But he never said nothing to me"). Up next, "RD" is the longest track on the album (clocking in at a whopping 11 minutes and 11 seconds)—thanks to a super-duper extended guitar solo courtesy of McCready.

Out of the album's ten tracks, the best-known of the bunch is "Hunger Strike." Issued as the album's first single, the song is built upon a memorable guitar chord picked string by string rather than strummed (for guitar geeks, that would be a G major chord, followed by a A7sus4, back to G, and then a Cadd9), which lyrically, seems to contain a Robin Hood-esque or even a "meek shall inherit the earth" message (including the memorable line in the chorus, "I'm going hungry," which stood out so much that it's understandable for the casual fan to assume that was also the song's title). The song was also one of four that featured vocal contributions from Vedder—but the only song on the album that featured his vocals up front, as both vocalists duet together.

"It was during that same week that I was up there," recalled Vedder about the day that he became involved with the project (which was also the first week he had made the pilgrimage to jam with Pearl Jam). "Day four maybe, or day five, they did a Temple rehearsal after our afternoon rehearsal. I got to watch these songs, and watch how Chris was working, and watch Matt play drums. It got to 'Hunger Strike'—I was sitting in the corner, putting duct tape on a little African drum. About two-thirds of the way through, he was having to cut off the one line, and start the other."

"I'm not now, and certainly wasn't then, self-assured or cocky, but I could hear what he was trying to do, so I walked up to the mic—which I'm really surprised I did—and sang that other part, 'Going hungry, going hungry.' The next time I was up, he asked if I'd record it—so it was just me and Chris in the same studio that we made [Pearl Jam's] *Ten* record. I really like hearing that song. I feel like I could be real proud of it—because one, I didn't write it, and two, it was such a nice way to be ushered onto vinyl for the first time. I'm indebted to Chris time eternal for being invited onto that track."

The song would also be the only track from the ensuing album that a music video would be filmed for—directed by Paul Rachman, who had worked with Alice in Chains on their classic "Man in the Box" clip. Rachman recalled meeting Cornell up in Seattle a week before filming was to begin, to discuss ideas. "I'd been to Seattle once before, but I'd never really spent time in Seattle, so I was quizzing him. I said, 'This is a Seattle thing. Why don't we integrate Seattle into the imagery, keep it outdoors and find some great locations.' That clicked with Chris and he became my location scout, in a way. He said, 'I know just the place. Let me take you there,' and he brought me to Discovery Park. He wasn't as arrogant or bold as to say, 'Let's shoot here,' but he chose these locations in this park that were just perfect. When he brought me to them, we were just hanging out and walking around, and during the scout, I was picking out my setups. So it was a great collaboration in terms of solving the riddle of the creative on that video."

"The crux of it was that the Soundgarden guys, Chris and Matt, didn't necessarily want to be in the video—they wanted to make a little film to Andrew. Whereas the Pearl Jam guys wanted to be in the video because they wanted the exposure. A Pearl Jam record was going to come out within six months or something. So it was truly inspiring to collaborate with him on the creative, and then when we went out to shoot, as you can tell in the video, he was a pro. I told him, 'Use your guitar and go stand here. I'm going to shoot from the back of you and just look out towards this great vista'."

"It's not the most comfortable thing to do, to kind of fake it with a guitar as a rock star out on a sand dune, and he just nailed it every time. He really was able to let the music transcend his actions in those moments, and in the playback he becomes Chris Cornell. In all those shots, he's giving it, he's putting out. It was amazing footage to work with. The Pearl Jam guys were in there, too, but you could tell in the video that they were less experienced at music videos and in terms of being big rock stars. Chris was solid. He was really great, too. He was kind, he was collaborative. He was a pleasure to collaborate with."

Up next on the album was one of only three compositions that were not entirely penned by Cornell, "Pushin' Forward Back," which contained music co-written by Ament and Gossard, which honestly, is probably the weakest tune of the lot (but is another track that includes backing vocals from Vedder). The piano-heavy "Call Me a Dog" follows, and is a pleasant enough ditty (including another standout Cornell-ism, "I call you beautiful, If I call at all"), before another one of the album's top tracks, "Times of Trouble." Musically, the tune is a carbon copy of the Pearl Jam b-side, "Footsteps" (hence Gossard earning a sole music writing credit), but lyrically, pulls no punches right off the bat, as the opening line, "When the spoon is hot, And the needle's sharp, And you drift away" is an obvious reference to Wood's addiction. Also, the song features a great, wailing harmonica solo—surprisingly supplied by none other than Cornell (to the best of my knowledge, the only time he ever played the instrument on a recording).

Cornell's interest in the dark side of organized religion is reflected in "Wooden Jesus" ("Coat hanger halos don't come cheap, From television shepherds with living room sheep") which features the singer plucking away at a banjo (another instrument I don't think he was ever heard playing again—or at least not frequently). However, the singer was quick to shoot down any assumptions that his friend's passing affected his thoughts concerning religion.

"It didn't affect the way I felt about religious topics or the way I thought about my own life at all, but it did affect the way I felt about other people in my life. Because of the loss of somebody that I thought was brilliant, it sort of directed me towards worrying about relationships that I have with people who I feel are important, as opposed to wasting my time with people who don't seem to be, who are just sort of trying to be energy vampires sucking whatever they can out of you. It helped me define differences between the two, and definitely made me a little more aggressive towards avoiding that kind of person."

One of the album's hardest rockers follows—and most underrated—"Your Saviour," which contains a very Pearl Jam-y guitar riff, but surprisingly, was penned by Cornell and not Gossard (again, another one of the four tracks featuring Vedder on backing vocals). But Gossard *did* pen the music to the following tune, "Four Walled World," which contains another wailing McCready solo at the end (and serves as Vedder's last vocal appearance). Before finally, things are brought to a close with another gem, the sleepy "All Night Thing," which contains some of Cornell's best vocals and lyrics, and some nifty organ work from producer Parashar.

It turns out that two additional tunes were demoed for the project that were never recorded full-on by the band, "Angel of Fire" and "Black Cat," which would surface in fan tape trading circles and on at least one bootleg CD (1994's *Stolen Prayers*). After hearing both tunes, it's easily understandable why they did not make the cut—neither were as strong as the lucky selections that made it past the finish line (however, both would finally receive an official release in 2016, when the album would be issued as "deluxe" and "super deluxe editions").

Released to little fanfare on April 16, 1991 via A&M, the album caught the attention of diehard Soundgarden fans—thanks to a spin or two of the "Hunger Strike" clip on *Headbangers Ball* (I recall being lucky to snag a used promo copy at my favorite record store shortly after its release...hey, I was on a budget!). "I remember when that record was coming out," Ament once said, "we had just picked our name, and we said, 'Can you put Pearl Jam on the sticker because it'll be a good thing for us?' We didn't want it to say Mother Love Bone, and they refused."

"A lot of people were surprised by the idea that I would do something so different, you know, than how Soundgarden are," Cornell once said about Temple of the Dog. "People were more surprised when it first came out, because no one knew who Pearl Jam were, no one knew any of those guys really, so it seemed more like the Chris Cornell solo project." And with Soundgarden plotting a return to the studio around this time as well, was there any tricky schedule juggling? "Not really," recalled Chris. "Most of the arrangements were written when I was on tour with Soundgarden and the recordings were just done on spare weekends so it never crossed over. A&M were also very helpful and made every effort to support both projects."

Right around the time of TotD, Pearl Jam—again, then going by the name of Mookie Blaylock—began performing their first shows. And it turns out that Chris attended at least one of these shows, and played a role in the introduction and acceptance of Vedder, with local fans. "After the show, I was getting some positive reinforcement from a few folks that I knew were part of the family and scene. Cornell coming up to me, and he just happened to be standing under a black light. He was talking to me, and his eyes and his teeth were glowing—he absolutely looked like Satan. He was saying he thought it was great, and was happy for Jeff and Stone. Andy was a friend of his and this felt like a good thing. To hear it from Chris, especially from his connection with Andy...but to hear it from Satan at the same time, it left a really strong impression."

Susan also remembered Chris supporting the new band and their singer. "[Alice in Chains] filmed the show [at the Moore Theatre, on December 22, 1990], and that was the show that this new band opened for them. Everyone was still reeling from Andy's death—it had been nine months, but it was such a shock. They hadn't really played out yet. The band came on, and Chris carried Eddie onto the stage—he was on his shoulders or something. It was another one of those super powerful moments, where it was a big healing for everybody. He came out as this guy who had all the credibility in the world—in terms of people in Seattle—and Malfunkshun and Mother Love Bone were loved bands. Andy was such an endearing personality. It's a hard thing to do—to show up after people die. And Chris bringing Eddie out, and pointing at him, as much to say, *'This is your guy now'."*

CHAPTER 12
BADMOTORFINGER I

Certainly, there was a fair amount of pressure on Soundgarden to deliver with their third full-length overall—which would be titled *Badmotorfinger*. Especially taking into consideration that their last album (and first for A&M) did not exactly set the charts alight—and major labels were going to be patient for only so long concerning artists on their roster who may be considered "underperforming." Undeterred, the band went to working up new material—in fact, this would be the first SG album comprised solely of no holdovers from the past. And it turns out that Cornell was obsessing so much over the creative process—that he had to enlist the aid of some "outside assistance."

"There was a point during the writing for *Badmotorfinger* where I just spent every single day for a couple of months working on it and working on it and working on it, and it got to the point where I didn't have any objectivity over any of the shit we were doing. One day I just took off and bought a bottle of Jim Beam and drank it all myself. I got really drunk. It really kind of spun my perspective around, and I was just looking at it through different eyes. But the thing is, the next day I remembered every different thing I had thought. I don't drink on a regular basis, so that isn't my reality. That's an alternative, and...uh, for a lot of musicians, an alternative would be not drinking and not taking drugs. That would help change their perspective."

But one thing that A&M—wisely—never did was try and make the band compromise artistically. "In almost every interview I do, people ask us if we've had to compromise," Chris explained. "If A&M Records have tried to impose anything on us. And every time I answer the question the same way—no, they've let us do whatever we've wanted to. We've made two records now without any kind of influence whatsoever." But with Cornell seemingly going straight from the end of the *Louder Than Love* tour to the preparation/recording of Temple of the Dog, it boggles the mind as to where the heck he found the time to write worthy material for another Soundgarden record. "Most all the material is actually new," he explained. "Some of it I wrote on tour, and the rest of it the band sort of collaborated on after the Danzig tour was over. During the time when Matt and I did Temple of the Dog, we were writing then. We pretty much wrote all the way up to the time that we started recording it."

And according to Cameron, there was a more "one for all" feel concerning the writing—as all four members (including new member Shepherd) contributed. "There's definitely more a band vibe on this one. The last record was mostly contributions by Chris and Kim, and to a lesser degree Hiro, and I didn't write anything. On this one, I wrote music for two songs, and collaborated on two songs." Even Jeff Ament could hear the difference. "You could see a little bit with *Badmotorfinger* that Chris was starting to stretch out songwriting-wise. I think with Temple of the Dog, too, that gave you a sense that he could go a lot of different ways and he wasn't just gonna be locked into doing a heavy, odd-time-signatured rock thing. He had a pop element to him, and then he also had kind of weirdo Syd Barrett melodies going on. I think once Matt and Ben got their influence on the record, that pulled it apart even more."

Despite *Louder Than Love* not necessarily representing Soundgarden the best sonically, the band did opt to bring back Terry Date as the album's co-producer (with the band once again serving as the other side of the "co"). "We'd developed a good relationship working on the first record and he knew what we were looking for as a band," explained Cornell. "We felt it would be easier going back with him rather than going through the labor of figuring out someone else's personality."

"We rehearsed our asses off," Cameron adds. "We did a lot of [*Badmotorfinger*] at our friend's studio, Avast! Our old soundman, Stuart Hallerman, let us hole up in his new studio for what seemed like months—at least three or four months—rehearsing these songs, working on music. So by the time we got down to Sausalito, California, we recorded at this place called Studio D—that was suggested to us by Faith No More. We never really went into the city—we were very workman-like. I think we recorded the bass and drums down there for two weeks, then we came up to Seattle again, and overdubbed the guitars and vocals at Bear Creek Studios in Woodinville, Washington. They had a really cool Jack Russell Terrier there. [Note: The studio owner had three dogs on the premises—two Jack Russell Terriers named Little and Robbie, plus a German Shepherd named Frida, while a Pomeranian named Howdy that belonged to Chris and Susan was also a visitor!] The sessions were pretty quick and efficient."

Although hard at work laying down tracks, the producer recalled an outdoor game the band would indulge in. "It was spring or summer—we were playing some game with a Frisbee. It wasn't normal Frisbee; it was some sort of full contact Frisbee. Two guys would get on either end of the field, someone would throw the Frisbee up in the air, and the other guy would throw the Nerf football at the guy trying to catch the Frisbee. I think you had to catch them both, or if you dropped them both—there were points involved. I have video of it. I remember Eddie Vedder came up, with the first test mixes of the first Pearl Jam record—being pretty concerned if it was any good or not."

Despite the hijinks, Date recalled paying attention to creating a different sound than what they had obtained on *LTL*. "They felt *Louder Than Love* was a little too smooth—they wanted more of an edge. At the time, most of the stuff I was doing and what they were doing wasn't getting a whole lot of radio play. Nobody took it very seriously. Which gave us a lot of freedom to do whatever we wanted to do. I had no expectations—I knew it was a good record." Cameron remembered another contributing factor concerning the album's sound. "[*Badmotorfinger*] was a lot darker sounding. We got a heavier guitar sound, and we used Ron St. Germain to mix it. He did a lot of records we liked—*I Against I* by the Bad Brains. So he mixed the drums dry, and the bass is really loud—it was a cool sound. It's certainly different than *Louder Than Love*."

"It's the heavy metal *White Album*!" Kim joked at the time. "There's the same trippiness and quirkiness that was on the first coupla records. There's the heavy grind of *Louder*. It's twelve different ways of approaching the idea of heaviness." And the guitarist also pointed out another sonic "differentiator" (is there really such a word?). "It sounds more live. There are a lot more noises, that's the only way I can put it. Noises! That's a lot cooler than reverb. Little squawks, feedbacks, little unplanned performance things that just kinda happen when you turn up loud and play it on 11!"

As it turns out, the guitarist knew exactly how he wanted his instrument to sound on the record. "I was trying to get a low, heavy sound while at the same time getting it to cut through. I was into Metallica's sound back then, the Melvins, too, and wanted to achieve that same overwhelming heaviness." Equipped with his trusty old Guild S-1 plus Peavey VTM amplifiers, the guitarist found a winning sonic combo—discovering that the amp wouldn't flounder when he detuned his instrument to subsonic levels. "The VTM's have this circuitry where you can boost the lows. I had it cranked. That sound has a good feel to it and good boom, which is great for muting. It also has a nice full lead tone and a warm low end that is good for vibrato."

"I think you go through periods where you learn to get that kind of aggression out of you," said Chris concerning going for a more live sound on *Badmotorfinger*. "If you really think about it, it's not that tough to do. On *Louder Than Love* it didn't really come out in what we did, so we decided we wanted to hear more of it. The new album is very close to us as a live band, but the main problem with most bands is capturing that live sound on record. Listen to the Stooges though...they did it, no problem! When you're in the studio, you can be in trouble if your producer does his job on the basis of technology as opposed to trying to capture you. But we're pretty hands-on as far as that goes. Although, in the past, we have had situations where a producer has tried to push things like that on us."

Released on September 24, 1991, the cover art for *Badmotorfinger* was designed by Mark Dancey (who was the guitarist of an overlooked Sub Pop recording artist at the time, Big Chief)—which features gold colored blades (that seem to resemble an "S" or an "M," depending on how you gaze at it), a mini sparkplug in the middle (a *motorfinger*, geddit?), with a blurred black and white photo of the band behind it (looks like it's Ben and Matt), with a new band logo in red on top (which would reappear from time to time in the future). And as far as the album's title—it had nothing to do with the similarly-titled power pop band from the early '70s, who had close ties with the Fab Four and were struck by multiple tragedies. "It was sort of off the top of my head," Kim once said about the album title. "I simply like it because it was colorful. It was kinda aggressive, too. It conjures up a lot of different kinds of images. We like the ambiguity in it, the way it sounded and the way it looked."

And for the collectors out there, there was an extremely rare version of the CD (only 1,000 printed), which was housed in a package comprised of two half-oval pieces of wood painted white, with the booklet and CD inside—and a gold metal plate in the upper right, including a # out of 1,000. And the cover on the outside of the white wood is not the *Badmotorfinger* album art, but rather, a sparkplug on top of a red chainsaw shape. But with no extra tracks included, only the most complete of completists will want to pay top dollar to acquire a copy.

I remember purchasing *Badmotorfinger* on compact disc shortly after its release. And like most albums released around this era that would go on to become my all-time favorites (Primus' *Frizzle Fry*, Faith No More's *Angel Dust,* Blind Melon's *Soup*, etc.), I was unsure of what I thought of *Badmotorfinger* at first. But after spin upon spin upon spin, it found the right receptors in my brain, and eventually, I couldn't stop listening to it. And as I explained in the book's intro, I soon made it a mission to turn as many associates on to this wonderful recording as possible.

You could hear that this was a more ferocious and focused Soundgarden from the get-go—with their greatest album-opener of all-time, "Rusty Cage." Starting with a guitar riff played through a wah pedal that was turned on but kept in a "set" position (veteran metal listeners may have sensed this as a bit of a familiar sound, as it was a trick that Michael Schenker often utilized on his classic '70s recordings with UFO), before the entire band joins in—adding a splendid swirling/spinning element to the riff, which sucks you in like a whirlpool!

Although entirely penned by Chris, Kim offered some insight behind the song's unique riff. "The tuning on that song was pretty nutty. It's recorded with a wah wah in the low position used as a filter. That was the first time we did anything like that. It was Chris' idea; he wanted to get that weird tone that you can't really dial in on an amp. But if you use the wah wah as a filter, it gets an incredibly weird sound. And if you listen to that riff, especially if you've heard the original demos of it, it almost sounds backward."

Speaking to me nearly two decades after the song's original release, Kim offered additional thoughts—"What I love about that song is the arrangement—it has this one kind of 'A' section, then it goes to a 'B' section, and then culminates in this slower, heavy 'C' section. I love the way it starts out kind of fast, and ends in a heavy, undanceable riff." And the ultimate proof concerning the song's greatness was that the legendary Johnny Cash would offer up an excellent, deconstructed cover of the tune (with Tom Petty and the Heartbreakers backing him) on his 1996 Rick Rubin-produced album, *Unchained*. Lyrically about escaping an unpleasant situation (as in, "I'm going to break my rusty cage...and run"), the song also contains another personal favorite Cornell-ism—"Hit like a Phillips head into my brain, It's gonna be too dark to sleep again)."

Up next is the tune that would soon serve as Soundgarden's breakthrough—"Outshined." Another CCC, from a lyrical standpoint, it's another track which makes little sense if each line was studied separately. However, the song is best known for what has gone on to become one of Cornell's most recognizable—yet mysterious—lyrics, "I'm looking California and feeling Minnesota." And once upon a time, the singer was willing to explain the line's creation and meaning. "One of the first times I remember writing something personal was on tour. I was feeling really freaky and down, and I looked in the mirror and I was wearing a red t-shirt and some baggy tennis shorts. I remember thinking that as bummed as I felt, I looked like some beach kid. And then I came up with that line—'I'm looking California and feeling Minnesota,' from the song 'Outshined'— and as soon as I wrote it down, I thought it was the dumbest thing."

"But after the record came out and we went on tour, everybody would be screaming along with that particular line when it came up in the song. That was a shock. How could anyone know that that was one of the most personally specific things I had ever written? It was just a tiny line. But somehow, maybe because it was personal, it just pushed that button." Just how popular did this line prove? Part of it was re-utilized in the title of a film starring Keanu Reeves and Cameron Diaz (1996's crime-drama-comedy, *Feeling Minnesota*).

And according to Chris, the late Andy Wood would once again serve as his lyrical inspiration for the tune. "After Andy had died and Temple of the Dog had already been written and recorded, the period I was writing the lyrics was literally two days before Desert Shield turned into Desert Storm. And personally too, I was getting a little bit sick of avoiding certain aspects of lyric writing. Some of which was maybe I didn't want to get too personal, because I didn't think anybody would care, because it would annoy me sometimes—when I would hear other people sing about their lives too personally, I would be like, 'Why would I care? Fuck off.' And the other aspect was there were three other members in my band that had to get up here and play this, and it has to somehow kind of relate to them. In 'Outshined,' it was almost like I imagined myself singing that song to this guy who is my friend who is now in heaven, kind of looking down on me, and being like, 'What the hell am I going to do now?' And just opening up that much in that lyric and letting it go was the beginning of that feeling."

Up next is quite possibly the most celebrated track of Soundgarden's entire discography that was never issued as a single, "Slaves & Bulldozers"—as it has made its way into most Soundgarden headlining performances ever since its release (and was often utilized as a set-closer, complete with a never-ending feedback jam at the end). More astute listeners will recognize several topics or phrases that have appeared time and time again in Chris' lyric writing, and "slaves" is probably at the top of the list (as exemplified by this song's title, as well as the line "While the slaves are all working" from "Hunger Strike," and perhaps most obviously, the name of his future project, Audioslave).

The song also features some of Chris' most intense singing ever—where he pushes his vocals further than he ever has before (or after), when he sings the repeated line, "Now I know why you've been shaking." Years later, Kim would select the tune as his favorite Chris Cornell vocal performance. "It captures everything that Chris was able to do in the one track. He's screaming like a reptile one minute, then crooning in a high pitch the next, and so soulful during the verses."

Guitar-wise, Kim once pointed out, "That's the second song we did where I blow on the guitar. [Friendly reminder: "Flower" being the first] I'd do it live and people would think I was playing with my tongue or my teeth or my beard. 'Hey look, he's playing guitar with his beard!' No, I was blowing on it—making a wish!" It also features one of Kim's best guitar solos ever captured on tape (yes, they were still recording on tape at that point)—which would also take on a life of its own when performed on stage.

"Every solo of 'Slaves And Bulldozers' when we play it live can be of different length and incorporate different elements, and I've played it with different feels emotively, on different parts of the neck. I'm having a hard time recalling the studio version, because we've done so many dozens—if not hundreds—of different versions. The way the song has developed over the past twenty years, it's in a very different place now than where it was on the record. But it was the same thing there. The song was slow and creeping, and it creeped up on you. And the guitar solo, you want things to unravel and explode at the same time. And that was the goal there."

And then...quite possibly the baddest tune off *Badmotorfinger*—"Jesus Christ Pose." While it is understandable to assume that the tune focuses on the topic of nefarious preachers and televangelists (a subject previously explored on "Hand of God" and Temple of the Dog's "Wooden Jesus"), it's actually about...well, let's let the author of the song's lyrics—Cornell—explain.

"The idea of the song was based on seeing fashion models and rock stars being filmed and photographed in that pose. It just seemed that in the past year or so, I'd seen that so much that it started annoying me. It's just another way of emulating a rock star. I mean, Christ is pretty much the most famous rock star out [there]. So Christ has an influence on rock stars and fashion models. That's fine, it's just the way they exploit that symbol, as if they're putting themselves into the light of assuming their self-persecution, which is irritating, especially when it comes to fashion models. They sold their souls for rock and roll, they sold their souls for really expensive shoes that hurt when they walk but look really good."

While the top rock star at that point known to utilize a Jesus Christ pose or two would be Axl Rose (although it harkened all the way back to the '60s with a famous pic of the Doors' Jim Morrison), one can't help but think that Cornell himself was calling the kettle black, as he not only was modeling a Christ-like look around this time, but also, was known to pose with his arms outstretched for photoshoots.

I once discussed with Kim his memories of writing the music to the tune—which he happened to co-pen with all his fellow bandmembers. "We were at the original Avast! Studios. They had a cement-floored recording room, and we'd go there and rehearse during the day, then at night we'd push our amps in the back and he'd have clients come in and record. I think we were jamming, whacking that out on bass. That was definitely one of Ben's riffs—the main riff. And then Matt started drumming on it. It was very quick."

"It was hard to discern exactly what the notes and the rhythm were from what Ben was playing, because it was very loud, blurry and quick. So while I was trying to figure out that groove, I came up with that weird 'pterodactyl on crack' guitar line. It was easier for me to hear that odd melody. That was my contribution. So we took that riff and recorded it. Chris took the tape home, listened to it and tried to learn the guitar part himself. And then he came up with the bridge and turnaround...I still love that song. I'm pretty sick of hearing a lot of Soundgarden songs, but not 'Jesus Christ Pose'."

If you figured that SG would give the listener a break from all the brutality, think again—the Cornell/Shepherd collaboration (the former handling the lyrics, the latter the music), "Face Pollution," is an explosive punk rocker clocking in at a mere 2:23 (the shortest composition on the entire album), with some of the most offbeat lyrics Cornell ever offered ("Scared by monkey faces, drowned in shark fins" and "Now I've made a mask, it looks like fish heads"). Up next is probably one of the most underrated selections of Soundgarden's entire recording career, the enormously melodic "Somewhere." Penned entirely by Shepherd, the song absolutely shoulda/coulda been a single, but mysteriously never was selected—and shows that although Cornell (rightfully) was an incredibly gifted lyricist, Shepherd could also put pen to paper and provide passionate prose.

And then...the album's first hard left turn, the amusingly titled "Searching with My Good Eye Closed." Another CCC, it features the most peculiar beginning to a SG song (what sounds like robotic phrases from a children's teaching toy—actually spoken by Seattle DJ Damon Stewart—before it leads to a demonic shriek), as well as one of Kim's most wailing guitar solos at the end, the song was used to great effect as the set opener on the album's supporting tour, and would often find its way into their setlist subsequently. Just don't expect to find any deep lyrical meaning here. "A lot of times, there's no particular intent to my songs lyrically," Chris explained. "A lot of times, like on 'Searching with My Good Eye Closed,' I'll sort of let the music write the lyric. What I enjoy doing is making paintings with lyrics—creating colorful images. I think that's more entertaining and what music should be."

A re-recording of "Room a Thousand Years Wide" follows, which as stated previously, is a far superior rendition when compared to the earlier single version. Saxophonist Scott Granlund and trumpeter Ernst Long lend a hand once more, while a single guitar note feeding back is heard throughout most of the song (which was not included on the single version). And whereas the single version fades out, the *BMF* version actually has an honest-to-goodness ending. The album's only ballad-y type tune,

"Mind Riot," follows, which due to such lyrics as "Candle's burning yesterday, Somebody's best friend died, I've been caught in a mind riot" leads one to believe that it may have been inspired by the passing of Andy Wood.

Another tune featuring horns is up next, "Drawing Flies" (featuring lyrics by Cornell and music by Cameron) —sounding like a not-too-distant-cousin of the earlier "Face Pollution," as it certainly musters up quite a bit o' punk rock attitude. Only three seconds longer than the aforementioned speedy little ditty, "DF" features another one of my favorite Cornell-isms—"Sitting here like uninvited company, Wallowing in my own obscenities, I share a cigarette with negativity."

The entirely Cornell-penned "Holy Water" is to the best of my knowledge the only song on *BMF* that was never performed live (or if it was, was done so very infrequently), and seems to be about a topic that its composer would visit several times— religion. But this didn't exactly prove to be its inspiration, according to its composer. "In America, they seem to be trying to tell the average person what to think. 'Holy Water' from the album is mainly about that, about people trying to force what they believe on you. It's pretty strange for album stickering to be going on so much, the anti-abortion movement to be so strong and for laws being passed that make freedom of speech even harder, but at the same time a band like NWA get to number one! They're obviously saying something more challenging than the chart fodder, so it must be what people want now they're getting pushed."

Closing *BMF* is another ditty that was never a regular addition to the setlist (but did enjoy at least a few on-stage airings over the years), "New Damage," which turns out to be quite a cacophonic composition, courtesy of Cornell (lyrics) and Thayil/Cameron (music). Lyrically, "ND" sounds like an attack on the right wing government of the US, and contains (you guessed it!) another killer Cornell-ism—"The wreck is going down, Get out before you drown." "The beauty of something like 'New Damage' is that if you can say something like that with the smallest amount of words possible, it has more impact and it becomes less of a sermon," its lyricist once explained. "The first time I read 'New Damage,' I was like, politically it totally speaks for me," adds Matt. "I think it speaks for the whole band—as do most of the other songs. We totally trust Chris' instincts as a lyricist and we don't even have to think twice about them."

So...how does *Badmotorfinger* stack up to the other SG albums offered thus far? I would be so bold to declare not only was it their greatest offering up this point...but has gone on to become one of the greatest rock recordings *ever*—judging from the high quality of the songwriting and performance (sonically it still wasn't all that exceptional, but unquestionably a mighty improvement over *Louder Than Love*). In fact, I'm sure many reading this will agree with the following statement—there's no comparison between *Badmotorfinger* and most of the copycat/unimaginative rock and metal stinking up the scene at the time of this book's release. Also, now is as good a time as any to mention that it was with *BMF* that I noticed the amusing publishing names that each SG member had chosen to mark their tunes—You Make Me Sick I Make Music (which was Chris), In One Ear and Out Your Mother Music (Kim), Noyes Music (Ben), and Walpurgis Night Music (Matt).

However, reviewing the album at the time for the ultra-mainstream mag, *People,* Craig Tomashoff warned, "It isn't for everyone. You don't get the catchy melodies of a more mainstream metal band like Guns N' Roses, so there will be no hit single. Chris Cornell's lead scream, while perfectly suited to this musical style, would probably give Casey Kasem a heart attack. Still, a song like 'Jesus Christ Pose' has enough raw energy to command your attention. And keep you from ramming your car into the guy in front of you."

JD Considine on the other hand was quicker to offer praise, in his review for *Musician.* "Don't make the mistake of calling this music 'metal.' Heavy, sure; few bands can push a riff to the speaker-shredding extremes these guys achieve on any given chorus. Instead of the rigid rhythms and monolithic structures most metal bands seem locked into, however, songs like 'Outshined' or the constantly churning 'Somewhere' are as rich in texture and dynamics and prime Led Zep (to cite another heavy non-metal band) and every bit as stunning. Hear and believe."

And right around the time that *BMF* dropped, a video for "Jesus Christ Pose" began being aired on *Headbangers Ball,* but not on MTV during daytime hours (a popular rumor is that the video was outright banned by the channel, but I can confirm first-hand this was not the case, as I remember seeing it with my own peepers late at night). And compared to the lackluster videos from *LTL,* the "JCP" clip (directed by Eric Zimmerman) was a major improvement—featuring images of crosses, a female Jesus impersonator, the band walking through a sandy location, the band hung upside down, and an effect that saw Chris hammering a spike through your TV screen. Also, the "JCP" vid is one of the few by the band that does not feature its members playing their respective instruments.

"I liked the video, but one thing that stood out was that we used a lot of provocative images of the cross," Kim told me years later. "We had a few images of an upside-down cross, and of a burning cross. The reference of a burning cross had been used in lyrics that Hiro had written in earlier songs. Generally we used a visual image or a burning cross. And MTV didn't want to [play it]. They held back showing it in their regular prime-time rotation."

"And then shortly before, Madonna did that video for 'Like a Prayer' with a burning cross! It's like, a 'dancer/actress' can put a burning cross in her video, but a rock band—an *integrated* rock band, by the way—has a far briefer image of a burning cross and MTV worries about it. Well, that was the excuse they used. And we specifically wanted a woman of color to be on the cross—we didn't want a white guy to be on the cross. We ended up using a woman who I think was part East Indian, but you couldn't really tell. It would have been better if she was more Indian or African-American. We wanted representation with minorities in our videos—and girls who weren't dancing on the hood of a car. It was always an uphill battle for some reason."

And to coincide with the video, a "Jesus Christ Pose" single was issued in Europe during October (which would eventually peak at #30 on the UK singles chart). Featuring an image from the video on its cover (of a chrome skeleton-like figure on a cross, who looks similar to the Terminator after he was stripped of his synthetic skin in the first *Terminator* flick), and pix of the band hung upside down on the back, the 12" version included four tracks, two of which were plucked off *BMF* ("JCP" and "Somewhere"), plus two non-LP cuts ("Stray Cat Blues" and "Into the Void (Sealth)").

"Stray Cat Blues" is a cover of an obscurity from the Rolling Stones (off their classic 1968 offering, *Beggars Banquet*), while "Into the Void (Sealth)" is a cover of one of the heaviest tunes Black Sabbath ever offered (from what I feel was their greatest album, 1971's *Master of Reality*). Both versions stick close to the originals musically, but when it came to the Sab number, the lyrics were completely overhauled, and replaced by lyrics about the white man's destruction of the environment, written by Chief Sealth, the same gentleman that Seattle was supposedly named after (there has been some debate over what his actual last name was—Sealth, Seattle, Seathl, or See-ahth).

"That was our bass player's idea, Ben Shepherd," Kim explained about their take of "Into the Void." "He noticed a similarity in the meter of the lyrics. And Chris made them fit. It was just such a Seattle thing to cover a Sabbath song, and then use the lyrics of the man whom our town was named after. Kinda funny. Born of sincerity, but it also had its humor." And it turns out the same fella was responsible for suggesting "Stray Cat Blues," to boot. "That was Ben's idea, too. He just played it for us and we liked it. I didn't use any of Keith's tunings. My E string is firmly in place. Our version is more threatening, like we're going to kill ourselves."

As it turned out, Soundgarden couldn't have picked a better time to issue their best studio offering yet—as all eyes were about to turn to the Northwest of the US.

CHAPTER 13
SEATTLE GRUNGE FLANNEL

There have only been a handful of times throughout history that you can pinpoint when a rock music movement reached beyond just music, but also, affected society (fashion, art, advertising, politics, etc.). For example, the psychedelic/hippie movement of the mid '60s, the punk rock movement of the mid '70s, and most certainly, the early '90s grunge movement.

As stated in this book's intro, some documentaries, books, and articles would like you to believe that from out of nowhere, grunge took over the charts, and killed hair metal and mainstream rock. Not entirely the case. It's not like fans of rock music automatically forgot about or stopped embracing the old guard. Case in point, two gargantuan-selling albums were issued during this time that were chart mainstays for *years*—Metallica's *Black Album* (released on August 12, 1991) and Guns N' Roses *Use Your Illusion I & II* (September 17th). Heck, *Queen and Meat Loaf* even made comebacks during this era!

But you could see on the horizon that something was a-brewin'—and not just in Seattle, but alternative rock in general from throughout the world was beginning to infiltrate the charts and the mainstream. And it just so happened that the majority of Seattle's Big 4 were about to issue classic/landmark recordings all within the span of a little over a month in 1991—Pearl Jam's *Ten* dropped on August 27th, and both *Badmotorfinger* and Nirvana's *Nevermind* on September 24th (interesting fact—another alt-rock classic was issued on the same day...the Red Hot Chili Peppers' *Bloodsugarsexmagik*). And although it was already out for almost a year, Alice in Chains' *Facelift* hit just a few months before the aforementioned trio of releases, so for most rock fans just discovering the band via "Man in the Box," it certainly *felt* like a new release, as well.

"We were the horse to bet on for a few years before that," remembered Kim. "Then all of a sudden, there was a whole bunch of us. We hadn't even gone gold yet, and Nirvana was going multi-platinum. We went gold around the same time as Pearl Jam, and then they just skyrocketed. Alice in Chains...there was so much going on." And with the shift in rock music during the fall of '91, soon came grunge's influence elsewhere—suddenly, flannel shirts (Kurt), brown corduroy denim jackets (Eddie), and Dr. Martens boots (Chris) were in high demand, and spotted on the runways and in department stores. Additionally, a much more liberal point of view seemed to be sweeping the nation (especially when Cobain and Vedder publicly voiced their pro-feminist and pro-choice stances).

"We're not these pick-up driving, beer-guzzling, 'Hey look at the pussy on her!' guys," Kim once explained. "Our maleness comes a lot from our creativity, our aggression, our intelligence. When I was younger, I had a real problem with maleness. Between the ages of 18 and 25, I thought that was the thing that sucked most. I was so offended by male behavior. And I was very protective towards the women I came into contact with." Quite a different mindset from the "fast cars and fast women" obsessed hair metallists that MTV was flaunting just a few months earlier, eh?

As a result of grunge's global success, there were good things that came as a byproduct...but also, sour things (in fact, you will soon discover that throughout this chapter, it seems like a positive outcome of grunge's massive success is often followed by a negative one). But one definite plus was that *the sound* of rock music switched back to a much more live sound of a band playing together in a room—a la the '60s and '70s. So, at this moment, let's turn our attention to a man who knows a thing about grunge production—Jack Endino—who will give us a thorough examination of how grunge's sound was created...and what inspired it.

"Those ['80s era metal] albums were meticulously crafted—they would spend months and months in the studio making these records. Everything was on a click-track, all the drums were replaced by samples, all the reverb was kind of a crazy gated cannonball sound. You can go back and basically blame Def Leppard—the latter Def Leppard records seem to be the blueprint for a lot of this stuff. And you have to give Mutt Lange some credit for that—as well as David Bowie, with 'Let's Dance' basically starting that whole early '80s giant drum sound phenomenon, which the pop metal bands totally took it over-the-top. You could go back to [Simon & Garfunkel's] 'Bridge Over Troubled Water' if you really want to know where it comes from, but nobody thinks of that."

"To me, the mainstream metal recordings all shared one thing—they did not sound like *a band*. They sounded like *a production*. Which is fine, because the Beach Boys sounded like a production, but fundamentally, you could hear that there were actual voices and actual instruments. Even the Beatles at their most produced sounded like human beings singing and playing instruments. And that, to me, was what I was trying to do with everything I did. It's like, 'I want it to sound like a band playing songs and singing songs. Let's make it sound as good as we can make it sound, but there's a fine line between making something sound really, really good, and making it sound artificial and phony. Like, completely constructed and sculpted out of artificial sounds'."

"So, the grunge thing was basically going back to the basics of, 'This is what a band sounds like in a room.' Now, in order to sound good, without all that production trickery, the band needs to be a really good band. What you've got is just something that sounds like a band playing in a garage, so it needs to be a really, really good band playing really, really good songs in a really, really good sounding garage—what can we do with that concept? And that's what I was going for. I shouldn't even say that, because I wasn't thinking 'garage,' I was thinking, 'How can we make records that sound like '70s hard rock records, instead of '80s hard rock records'?"

Yet, not everything was rosy as a result of grunge's emergence—case in point, a wave of "carpetbagger bands" soon crashed the scene, mimicking grunge for a recording contract...even though probably just a few weeks before, some (most?) were primping up their mile-high hair, squeezing into spandex, and shredding away on their high-priced/pointy guitars (some even actually relocating to Seattle—knowing that record labels were homing in on the location).

"There's always someone who is the trendsetter or who establishes a style that other people run with," explained Kim. "But there is absolutely no reason for us to complain, especially when you see a band like Stone Temple Pilots achieving success while bands like Mudhoney and Tad, who are far more deserving because of the work they've put in and the quality of the material they churn out, haven't. Yet, as much as I might have a lack of affection for the Stone Temple Pilots, they are part and parcel of this whole alternative sound and I'm happy to see them having success instead of some of the goofy, cowboy-booted, hair farmer, strip club-frequenting rock bands that used to dominate the music scene."

"You see, I think that's a good thing," countered Chris. "It's like, OK, here's this other band that's trying to do this thing that was categorized as grunge, and they seem to have elements of almost every Seattle band there is in one song or another, but they're not from Seattle. And they've already sold a million-plus records in the US. In one way, it is the commercialization of grunge, but in another it takes the emphasis away from Seattle, which is good. See, I'm not really worried about the title 'grunge', because I don't think it applies to any of the bands it was put on. It applies more to bands that are gonna come out now, like Stone Temple Pilots, 'cause they've been influenced by the media perception of grunge."

"We get a lot of people asking what we think of Alice in Chains, Tool or Kyuss, Nirvana, 'cause people say they were obviously influenced by us," adds Kim. "I know Nirvana were but that's 'cause they said so! And I know Alice in Chains were because I know what sort of band they were before they came to see us play. They used to be more glam, a sorta Poison-type band. Then I told Jerry about dropped D tuning 'cause he wanted to cover one of our songs. Next time I saw them, everything was tuned down! But that's OK, 'cause I haven't been playing this music for all my life either. But I think you can tell the bands who've taken our influence. We should really hate 'em all though, 'cause they're all making more money than us!"

But that said, quite a few veteran underground artists that had been slogging it out for years finally experienced commercial success (Soul Asylum, Meat Puppets, Butthole Surfers, Henry Rollins, Ministry, etc.). Additionally, many artists became fearless in discussing sensitive and real topics in their lyrics or in interviews, and the barrier between artist and audience seemed to be demolished. In other words, it was now difficult to differentiate members of grunge bands on stage and members of the audience (as opposed to previous arena rock acts...where it was *clear* where the division lay). And MTV was right there, covering it all—proving once and for all what a powerful influence the channel had over its viewership. Case in point, MTV's portrayal of Bill Clinton as a "young/hip presidential hopeful" and George Bush as a then-president that was old and out of touch in their news segments concerning the 1992 US presidential election—which undoubtedly gave Clinton a boost (as he would go on to win the election).

And speaking of MTV, not only were such specialty shows as *Headbangers Ball* and *120 Minutes* regularly spinning videos of grunge bands, clips from all four were also often spotted during non-vampire friendly hours, as well. But as a result, newcomers to not only the bands—but to alt-rock in general—were missing the plot, especially at shows, where moshing and crowd-surfing was getting dangerously out of hand. And I speak from experience—I remember having to put one hand atop my head while I tried to tough it out close to the stage during a Faith No More show in 1992 at Roseland to try and soften the blow of taking a Dr. Marten to the noggin, while a few months later, witnessing Blind Melon's Shannon Hoon resorting to punching an overzealous crowd surfer in the face, after numerous requests to knock off the silliness.

As Eddie Vedder remembered, "I think with the advent of MTV and us putting stage diving in 'Alive,' [it] was regretful, because then it was like training videos for how to jump in the crowd—like that was the mode of expression. It wasn't the same version that was happening at early Social D or X shows. It got to be a distorted MTV version, and now it was like every frat boy buying a pair of spikes from the corner novelty shop, putting spikes on their big white gym shoes, and doing it. And guys that were way too big to have any business landing on people. It got out of control real quick."

And for a span of a year or two beginning in '91, rock fans were getting spoiled, as seemingly every month, a now-classic album was being issued (or in a few cases, was out for a while but was finally receiving recognition)—Nine Inch Nails' *Pretty Hate Machine,* Smashing Pumpkins' *Gish,* Primus' *Sailing the Seas of Cheese,* My Bloody Valentine's *Loveless,* Beastie Boys' *Check Your Head,* etc. In fact, this was one of the few eras that I can recall that you could make a valid argument that it seemed as if good music actually *outweighed* bad music in the mainstream (which is an extremely uncommon occurrence).

Getting back to Kim's earlier quote concerning the Stone Temple Pilots, there was an incredible uproar at the time concerning the Scott Weiland-led band's authenticity. Sure, their first album (1992's *Core*) was at times a bit too close for comfort to Pearl Jam and Alice in Chains. But their subsequent albums saw the band from San Diego branch out stylistically, and showcased what expert songsmiths they were. And the reason I bring this up is if you are to compare STP to what came afterward in the mainstream (blatant and highly forgettable copycat one-hit wonders, mining the grunge goldmine), it's pretty laughable.

As a result of his strong songwriting skills with both Soundgarden and Temple of the Dog, several established rock acts reached out to Chris around this time to see if he would pen or co-pen a song for them. But when asked at the time if such hair metallists as Bon Jovi or Poison had inquired yet, it turned out not to be the case. "I've already had calls like that, but not from those guys. I'm not really sure that I can even remember who they were, but there have been quite a few. I've never gone and sat in a hotel room with someone I've never met before and tried to write songs. It doesn't seem a very natural way of coming up with something you'd like." Eventually however, Chris would relent and offer his songwriting skills to other artists, including veteran thrash metallists Flotsam and Jetsam ("The Message" from 1992's

Cuatro) and theatrical rock icon Alice Cooper ("Stolen Prayer" and "Unholy War" from 1994's *The Last Temptation*).

Something else that tends to get overlooked—how such a small, concentrated region of the US gave us some of the greatest rock singers of all-time—Cobain, Cornell, Staley, Vedder, and the Screaming Trees' Mark Lanegan—with each possessing their own unique vocal style, and all singing in a soulful manner. And "soulful" was certainly not a fitting description for most hard rock vocalists throughout the '80s—I bet you'd be hard pressed to find a hair metal admirer who would honestly describe the vocals of Vince Neil, Stephen Pearcy, or Bret Michaels as such.

But again, there was another downer concerning "grunge mania," as Cornell explained just a few years after its initial eruption. "It's hard not to be a little bitter about it. We lost good friends in the process. And all of a sudden you realize that it's turned into something that's considered a fashion statement. It's like mining. It's like somebody came into your city with bulldozers and water compressors and mined your own perfect mountain and excavated it and threw out what they didn't want and left the rest to rot. It's that bad."

"Yes, things have changed," admitted Kim. "It's kind of funny, the attitude of people towards you is different, even old friends, how they speak to you, or treat you. My life has changed in many senses—you're too busy doing things around that it gets hard to maintain personal relationships, keep your identity, you know. Sometimes it gets kinda confusing, how your life has changed, but sooner or later you learn how to adapt in it."

Ben also could sense that a large part of Soundgarden's following that appeared to share the same interests may have been wolves in sheep's clothing, who suddenly adapted to the times—especially the whole "Lollapalooza crowd." "A lot of those 'freaks' are the same fucking assholes who used to give you shit in high school for liking what you liked, and now it's 'cool,' now they're there, way after the fact, 'cause now the whole alternative underground thing is out of the closet. In a way, it's kinda cool to see people getting into new music, but all those fans, I'd suspect, are more close-minded than the '70s rock fans! The more people you get together the stupider they are."

Unlike others who had trouble coming to grips with their sudden fame, according to Kim, Soundgarden was ready. "To begin with, we were pretty well prepared in that we avoided all the rock star pathways. We weren't womanizers or druggies or anything. So I think that was probably a big buffer to that, and I think we had a good understanding of ourselves. There's a way that you see yourself and there's a way that hundreds and thousands of people see you. As long as you don't value yourself in the way they see you, you'll keep your head screwed on. Your closest friends don't think you change that much, so they're not affected by it, which is good."

However, Chris' viewpoint differed a bit—concerning all the sudden attention. "Celebrity is odd. The fans find out where you're staying, I don't know how. Say it's 7am and you've been on the bus all night, and you've gotten drunk and fallen asleep. You wake up and all of a sudden you're surrounded by people, and you can't figure out what they're doing there, because you're just a normal jerk. They're not necessarily that polite and they give you some shit sometimes. You feel obligated in a way. I don't handle that well, we all have the ability to be rude or abusive in that situation. A lot of bands like it. You see clips of Trixter or Slaughter mixing it up with the fans. Just because we don't enjoy that kind of attention doesn't mean that we think we're better than the fans or they don't deserve appreciation. There's no member of our band that doesn't appreciate them. We're just socially awkward. I've always been a bit reclusive, and I've always thought that was a bit unhealthy and have tried to be around people. Now I have an easy excuse to be on my own. It affects Kim a lot; he's a real social guy and a real recognizable guy. He can't go anywhere, and it bugs him."

Chris also had an idea of what it would be like for out-of-towners who arrived in Seattle circa '91/'92—in search of fame and fortune. "The fantasy is that you're going to run into Mark Arm on the street, and you're going to see Tad one night, Mudhoney the next night, Soundgarden the next night, then

Nirvana after that. That's not really the case. But I have to admit the first time we ever went to Austin, we were under the impression that maybe we could see the Big Boys or the Butthole Surfers. So I can't really blame people for thinking that."

That said, Kim does recall Chris' last quote coming true on at least one occasion. "Chris was walking downtown. He was going to a music store, and a bus had just come in from out of town. This kid gets off the bus, just coming out of Kansas or something, and the first thing he sees is Chris Cornell walking by him. So unfortunately, all his stereotypes about Seattle are reinforced: He thinks that's what Seattle is about and that he's now arrived!"

Interestingly, it was something totally different about all the success that rubbed Matt the wrong way. "The only time I get real miffed is when people think of all the Seattle bands out of chronological order. We were one of the first ones to sign a major label deal to come out of that amazingly fertile scene that peaked around '86, '87. And we were kind of the guinea pigs for what was going to happen with a lot of the other bands. And here we are—we're still doing it. But they think that Nirvana's the first band from Seattle."

And speaking of Nirvana, it was actually a member of Soundgarden that played *Nevermind* for one of their former members. "My first impression was I loved it," Chad Channing once admitted to me. "I was totally into it. I remember my friend Ben [Shepherd] had a recording of it on cassette. I think this was right around the time of its release or maybe shortly after. He was like, 'Chad, you've got to check this out.' I listened to it, and I was like, 'God, this is fantastic. This is a killer record.' I was pretty stoked."

But as it turns out, it was not exactly a "one for all/all for one" feeling amongst all the bands in Seattle. According to the press, there was a faction formed between one group of bands, "the purists" (Nirvana, Mudhoney, Tad, etc.), and another, "the careerists" (Soundgarden, Pearl Jam, Alice in Chains, etc.). But according to Chris, these feuds were largely a media creation. "When we were starting out and playing shows with Green River and Skin Yard, there was always a certain amount of talking behind other people's backs, you know, like 'That song sucks' or 'Those guys are totally lame.' And we would say things about people who were obviously our friends and are still our friends. And people would say things about us."

"The only thing is now, when somebody says anything, it becomes national or international press. I think a lot of it is getting sucked into the whirlwind press thing. When the *Rolling Stone* article came out, the interviewer wanted my feelings and my rebuttals to the point of saying, 'Well, Mark Arm said such and such a thing about your band,' and I said, 'Well, that's fine with me.' Mark Arm isn't the sole Soundgarden fan and whatever he thinks of my music doesn't really have a lot to do with the people who appreciate it. And his answer to that was, 'Well, who's going to give Mark Arm a check?' Who gives a shit? My point is that it's more often a situation created by the press that it is created by actual animosity between bands." Although once, Chris did admit a comical comparison Mark once bestowed upon Soundgarden— "Mark Arm once called us the Rush of Seattle."

Even members of "the old guard" had thoughts and observations considering the movement that had usurped them, such as Cinderella's Tom Keifer. "That look, which was dressing down and rebelling against the flash or the glam or the glitz of the '80s, ultimately, was what the rebellion was about. It was more of a visual thing than the music. Nirvana and Soundgarden—which were two of my favorites from that era—were screaming rock singers with loud guitars. Musically, it wasn't that different. But ultimately, that image was the thing that was the rebellion, because it became probably more mainstream than the glam look—to be honest. It really did. Which is ironic. [Laughs] That's why I always say people should really just listen to music with their ears and not their eyes."

And according to Trouble guitarist Rick Wartell, it all came down to advertising and marketing. "Grunge is just a marketing name that industry people put on music to sell it and make it a cool thing. But if you listen to Soundgarden's riffs, man, they're not different than Trouble riffs—just marketed differently.

I listen to some of their songs and it's like, 'There are identical riffs here and there. That could be a Trouble song.' And vice versa. To me, they're just metal."

Even the stadium rock bands that were lucky to successfully navigate through the treacherous grunge/alt-rock waters noticed the change. "I remember in the mid '90s, an event that happened," remembered former Guns N' Roses guitarist Gilby Clarke. "Slash and I were at the Rainbow, and I had the car and I was waiting for him, to get in the car. He came in, and he just had this sad look on his face. I was like, 'What the fuck? What's going on? Did something bad happen?' He goes, 'Some guys just pointed at me, and said, 'Hey look, there's Slash,' and they were laughing. *How come we're not cool anymore?*' And I remember that event, when he said that. It's twenty-something years later, and I still remember that. And that was the period where it was not cool to be in Guns N' Roses anymore. It was cool to be in Soundgarden and Nirvana and Alice in Chains."

Also, photographer Ross Halfin offered an interesting perspective about this era of rock n' roll. "Pearl Jam, with all their anti-everything, still very much liked the trappings of being rock stars. The bodyguards, the this, the that. Whereas Soundgarden were very accessible, Pearl Jam was 'Keep everyone away.' In a sense, Nirvana was accessible. Soundgarden always had women around them, which is probably because of Susan Silver working for them. And the women would always wipe their asses—they were always pampered. Everyone around them was fussing and panicking—when you actually got them, they were totally fine."

And lastly, perhaps the biggest negative consequence after the Big 4 hit was heroin addiction—publicly affecting Kurt Cobain and Layne Staley the most (and of course, Andrew Wood, shortly before). When asked if any Soundgarden members ever had a problem with the drug, Chris replied, "It's never been a problem for us—except we've had friends who've died from it. But Seattle's not the heroin capital of America—that's bullshit. Per capita, in New York or LA there's a lot more people doing heroin. Seattle's a port city, so I'm not gonna lie and say heroin's not easy to get. But it's just as easy in LA or San Francisco."

But back at the time when Soundgarden and the other grunge leaders were still in business and in the eye of the storm, it seemed like the band had no idea how the movement would be viewed by future generations, as Ben was quoted in 1992 as saying, "In the same way that people hear a certain guitar sound and equate it with surf music, they'll do the same thing with Seattle in 15 years' time. I really hope that Seattle will mean as much to future generations of bands as the surf music scene of the 60's does to this one."

Looking back on the grunge boom in 2014, Chris said, "I can't look at it as anything but positive. My view of rock history now includes grunge as a major genre shift in the history of rock, the same as you would look at punk rock or the British Invasion. And we're clearly pioneers of that genre and are recognized as being that. When the story is told—which it will get told over and over and over and over—we will be there as opposed to maybe not being there. And that comparison could be like Jane's Addiction or Smashing Pumpkins, for example, that won't necessarily get mentioned when some new rock fan is researching these dramatic, pivotal moments. So for that reason I feel like whatever we had to put up with over the years: the Seattle questions and the Seattle-sound questions and the Seattle-scene questions, it's worth it. Every time I do a Spanish interview, we still get, *'Tell me about grunge'.*"

CHAPTER 14
BADMOTORFINGER II

As previously discussed, Soundgarden toured heavily in support of *Louder Than Love* (spending a solid year on the road). So it would be understandable if they'd want to lessen the load a bit for their next world tour. But when the great grunge uprising occurred shortly after the release of *Badmotorfinger,* Soundgarden couldn't resist hitting the road for another solid year yet again. But this time, admittedly, the touring conditions must have improved greatly—as they would open for two of rock's biggest names in arenas and stadiums, as well as part of a multi-band bill featuring some of the leading alt-rock bands in amphitheaters.

Before the September 24, 1991 release of *Badmotorfinger,* Soundgarden played a handful of local shows to test-drive the new material in front of friendly faces—including a performance on September 14th at the Capitol Theatre in Olympia, which was filmed (albeit via a single camera), and featured overzealous bouncers throwing stage divers back into the crowd, as well as a pair of rarely-performed tunes, "New Damage" and "Birth Ritual." By October however, the band was ready to start playing shows outside their home state of Washington, when they performed a trio of shows in California. First up was the Foundations Forum on October 3rd (which included a Temple of the Dog reunion), followed three days later with a performance at the Hollywood Palladium as part of *Rip's* 5th anniversary party.

One of the leading rock mags of the day (it was the closest a US publication ever came to matching the quality of UK's *Kerrang!* as far as the breaking of news, exclusive interviews, and quality photographs), *Rip* was able to assemble quite a line-up at the Palladium, that just a year later, could have rocked arenas (possibly stadiums)—Soundgarden, Pearl Jam, Alice in Chains, and headliners Spinal Tap (with hair metal holdovers Thunder and Screaming Jets rounding out the bill). And once again, the audience was treated to a performance by...Temple of the Dog. There is also a good chance that guitar shredder Joe Satriani performed that evening (quite possibly as a guest of Spinal Tap), as there was a photograph that made the rounds at the time of

Soundgarden, Spinal Tap, and Satriani backstage, hamming it up for the camera.

Then on October 12th, Soundgarden was part of the Day on the Green Festival at the Oakland Coliseum. Headlined by Metallica, the bill also featured Queensrÿche and old pals Faith No More, with SG going on first, with the sun a-blazin'. Clips of the band performing have surfaced—mostly from MTV, including a news bit for *MTV News,* in which Kurt Loder was positioned in such a way that you could see a rather sweaty Soundgarden come off stage and walk by behind him.

Kim once discussed his memories of the Green performance with little old me—and that he experienced a non-performing career highlight that day. "We got to meet [legendary rock show promoter] Bill Graham. He came and posed for photos with us. And the people that worked there were like, 'Holy shit dude. Bill Graham just posed for photos with you! When he comes out and poses for photos with a band it's because he likes the band, and the bands he likes end up being huge.' And then it was maybe a month after that he died in the helicopter crash." Actually, it turns out it was *less than two weeks later* that Graham perished [October 25th].

Then on October 17th, Soundgarden played an invitation-only/secret show in New York City at an obscure venue called Warehouse 429—since it was located at 429 Greenwich Street. Unfortunately, since I was not yet a member of the press (I was still a college student, with no clue at the time I would one day be an author/journalist), I could not/did not attend. However, my photographer pal Steven J. Messina *did*—you can see the eye-poppin' proof in the middle of this book. Concerning playing industry-type shows of impartial music biz types rather than a show in front of true enthusiastic fans, Chris warned about the difference between the two. "It's more of a zoo exhibit than a performance. You just have to perform for each other and it's almost like an attended rehearsal. We play more to ourselves and have fun that way. Like it or not, you simply don't get a lot of energy and a lot of reaction from an industry audience. The biggest risk of being involved in the music industry is that it may change your perception, or make you jaded or dislike things that you would otherwise like."

Despite a few club dates in November, Chris found the time to drop by London Bridge Studios that month, to provide guest vocals for a tune by Alice in Chains, "Right Turn" (which would be released on February 4, 1992, as part of the acoustic *Sap* EP). The song was credited to "Alice Mudgarden"—due to the fact that the lead vocals are split between AiC's Jerry Cantrell, Christopher John Cornell, and also, Mudhoney's Mark Arm. And while the EP was a pleasant surprise and quite a consistent listen from beginning to end (Heart's Ann Wilson also guested on a few tunes), I would have to select "Right Turn" as the release's top tune—with all three vocalists bringing their own unique "flavor" to the composition (with the phrase "Ain't right" repeated throughout). Although honestly, Chris steals the show at the end.

And it was also in November that Soundgarden launched another handful of headlining dates, with a then largely-unknown Blind Melon providing support. "The management company that managed Guns N' Roses was overseeing them," recalled Susan. "So we were friendly with them, and I think the guys had met at the Concrete Convention—Soundgarden played and Temple of the Dog played a couple of songs, and Blind Melon played on that one. They were just all so incredibly likeable. It was so refreshing—to hear acoustic [music] and have that little bit of southern rock in there. And the eerie thing was that Shannon bore at least an energetic resemblance to Andy. And a little bit physically—in that cherubic, wide eyed, lovin' life kind of way that Andy had. Shannon had a similarity to him—the long wavy hair and open heart. So there was a healing in that—Shannon could come into our lives after we'd lost Andy. A great storyteller and such a great energy to be around."

"The first show was at Mississippi Nights in St. Louis," recalled BM drummer Glen Graham, about the show that occurred on November 7th. "Matt Cameron had this drum riser, and Mississippi Nights is like a big barn, with a high stage. His drum riser was four-and-a-half feet tall—his drums were situated so that they hung out over the edge of it. He was very close to the ceiling.

We just felt, 'What is this?' You couldn't hear—it was deafeningly loud. The next show was at a theater, then they had the whole production—the eight-foot drum riser, the '70s walls of Marshalls. They might have even had stairs like Kiss had. It was hysterical. Once you saw the whole thing, you're like, 'These guys are funny—they're great.' And nobody, I mean *nobody* in their fanbase—except maybe the people in Seattle—got it. These guys are the Beastie Boys' first record. [The audience] took it at face value. 'These guys are a bad ass metal band.' Yes, well, *they're kind of making fun of you'*."

Also on that tour, Blind Melon roadie Lyle Eaves remembered Hoon making a gift for a newfound friend. "Shannon and Chris hit it off really well. They hung out a lot—so did the crews. Chris would eat with the band and hang out. In Atlanta, Shannon made a fork necklace for Chris, which I helped him make on the sidewalk outside of I think the Roxy [on November 13th]. There was a guy who lived where we lived in LA, and this guy had this necklace—a fork that all the tongs were turned out. It was professionally done and perfect looking. Shannon liked the necklace, and he wanted me to help him make one—he was going to give it to Chris Cornell. We got a propane torch and a regular fork—it was kind of gnarly looking, the thing we came up with. But Shannon liked it and gave it to him. Chris has worn it—I've seen him on TV with it on. On that tour, Shannon gave me his wallet to keep—that was when he really started his whole stagediving thing. And the wallet got lost. It had Chris Cornell's phone number in it—that's the reason he was pissed. And it had a couple of Valium in it too, I think."

Cornell would continue to wear Shannon's fork necklace for the next few years (including in the "Black Hole Sun" video), before stowing it away after Hoon would tragically die from a drug overdose in 1995—as he once explained. "I really liked it, but I stopped wearing it after he died. Because the other thing I wore was this ring that belonged to Andy Wood, who died. It's like, 'I don't wanna wear these fucking things from people who died.' A girl outside the hotel tonight had a similar fork, and I've had people throw them onstage. I've seen hundreds of those forks, but it always reminds me of Shannon. They're making them 'cause they're thinking of me, but really it's him."

And then...one of Soundgarden's biggest career breaks happened. By 1991, Guns N' Roses was arguably at the peak of their popularity—able to headline arenas and stadiums for multiple nights globally, while their latest album, *Use Your Illusion,* was a blockbuster (chockful of hit singles and videos continuously aired on MTV). And it just so happened that G n' R were big-time Soundgarden fans—and invited them to open a string of US arena shows, from December 5, 1991 through February 1, 1992. "[The Guns N' Roses tour] was a call I got, that I was so excited to tell them about," explained Silver. "I had a bunch of t-shirt designs in a box that I needed to show them. So I went to this studio that they were at—Avast!—doing some b-sides. I get there and I can barely contain myself. 'Guys, guess what? You got offered the Guns N' Roses tour today!' Dead silence. Finally, Kim pipes in. *'What's in the box?'* Once they got on the tour, they were treated so well—the Guns N' Roses crew was incredible, and everyone was really accommodating. The hospitality was just great. It didn't take long before the Guns N' Roses crew dubbed them 'Frowngarden'." [Laughs]

"I think that might have been a name we deserved on that tour," Cornell reflected, a year later. "It wasn't a whole lot of fun going out in front of 40,000 people for 35 minutes every day. Most of them hadn't heard our songs and didn't care about them. It was a bizarre thing." Cameron however, recalled that Soundgarden was also offered a support slot by another band around the same time—that also happened to be at their career apex, popularity-wise. "We were going to go out with Queensrÿche. So we had to say, 'Later,' to those guys, and go on the Guns N' Roses ship. We really believe in our record, and we want it to be heard." And the drummer opted to "celebrate" this special occasion. "The first Guns N' Roses show I was a little bit baked. It wasn't that great of an idea, actually, thinking back on it."

Undoubtedly one of the highlights of the SG/G n' R tour was a three-night stand at one of the world's most famous arenas, NYC's Madison Square Garden (December 9th, 10th, and 13th).

While I was already obsessed with *BMF* and eager to see Soundgarden live again, the proposition of paying top dollar to see them perform a mini-set from a mile away from the stage was not all that enticing, not to mention having to endure a G n' R performance and their rowdy audience. Besides, as an unemployed college student at the time, I had far overstepped my "concert ticket fund quota" by attending two arena shows that month (Rush and Metallica).

And keep in mind, this was *not* the "kinder/gentler Axl" that we see on stage at the time of this book's release, but rather, a seemingly unpredictable/schizophrenic fellow, who regularly delayed the start of G n' R set times and sometimes abruptly ended concerts after a hissy fit. Case in point, that time at the Riverport Amphitheatre in Maryland Heights, Missouri (near St. Louis), where he dove into the audience to assault a photographer—while wearing an ill-advised ensemble consisting of white spandex shorts, a black furry jacket with no shirt, a crucifix necklace, and a biker cap—because he did not appreciate his picture being taken...which is laughable now, considering the rampant use of iPhones at concerts. Either way, it led to Axl storming off the stage, the show ending prematurely, and a riot ensuing—leading to various audience members being injured.

But looking back just a few years later at the MSG performances (the only time Soundgarden would play the venue in their career, as it would turn out), Chris wasn't blown away. "I think people growing up in different cities have different attitudes. In New York being famous is a really important thing, culturally. I mean, when we played Madison Square Garden opening for Guns N' Roses, fans would be saying, 'You're playing Madison Square Garden!' Like it was a huge deal. It wasn't the pinnacle of our career. We were opening for this other band, playing short sets in a half empty arena." However, Chris also found similarities to the early days. "It's the same feeling playing in front of a Guns audience that we used to get in some bar in Seattle when we first started out. There are a few fans of G n' R, Metallica, and Soundgarden out there, but it's mainly people who like G n' R, Bon Jovi, and Poison. Those people usually don't react too well.

This tour's cool, but it's also cool to go out and depress people and knock the air out of their stupid fuckin' party. That's fun."

Not to mention, G n' R did not yet get the memo that misogynistic hair metal shtick was becoming largely old hat (especially with the emergence of the pro-feminist Nirvana), as exemplified by a tasteless stunt they would regularly employ. "They had this thing where they'd send a guy roaming into the audience with a camera, trying to get girls to show their tits," remembered Chris. "And they'd put it all up on screens. That was a big thing in the US, two hours of intimidating girls. The way they did it was really imposing. They would walk up to a girl, try to get her to show her tits, and if she wouldn't do it, they'd get 30,000 to 50,000 people to scream at her until she did. It was pretty crazy."

Despite their sour facial expressions and not sharing the same liberal views, it turns out that at least one Soundgarden member had nothing but positive things to say about the experience of opening for G n' R—and funny enough, it's the one you'd least expect it from. "We had a blast, man," admitted Ben. "Because the whole crew of theirs and their whole band are really fucking nice. Me, I'm like a punk rocker fuckup, and I'm all cantankerous—my nickname was 'Manimal' back then. We weren't rock stars; we're not like that. Totally like the kids you'd think we'd be. And I'm all grumpy—'Goddamn it, these guys are nice, I can't even hate 'em! I hate their music, but they're nice.' Same thing with Skid Row—fucking hated their music, they knew it, but they're all so cool. Pissed me off, now I don't even have a reason to be pissed off. What the hell is this? My life is going to shit and it's beautiful at the same time! I didn't have a home life anymore—that's what happens when you tour all the time. But you've got to go for it when you have a chance."

Looking back years later, Kim recalled experiencing some backlash from longtime fans. "When we toured with Guns N' Roses, we alienated some of our Sub Pop/punk rock/indie fans. They thought, 'Soundgarden was on the fence—kind of punk rock, kind of metal. But now they're touring with Guns N' Roses, they fall into that side of the fence.' It's like, 'No, we didn't.' At that time, who were we supposed to tour with? When we signed up to tour with Guns N' Roses, Nirvana wasn't bigger than us yet. Who was there in that genre for us to tour with, that we could open up for, and play cities that we couldn't command ourselves? A lot of the cities we hit with Guns N' Roses and Skid Row were places that we probably couldn't have gotten gigs ourselves. We weren't big enough to get a gig in Omaha. We could play a small club perhaps, but promoters wouldn't have taken a chance with us, necessarily. It was an opportunity for us to play in front of a larger audience. Those tours were certainly a lot of fun. I think in retrospect, everyone understands it now. But back then, some people thought it was weird that we were taking that tour."

I recall discussing this topic once with Kim, and I explained my point of view at the time, as a SG fan. I have been guilty—and I'm sure other rock fans, too—of several instances when I discovered a band early on, and got turned off when they suddenly went massive (actually, while we're on the subject of G n' R...that was one such instance for Greg Prato!). But the '91 G n' R tour was one of the few cases where I was actually *happy* that Soundgarden was going to be introduced to a ginormous audience that probably was not all that familiar with them. So although I can't say I was/am the biggest Guns N' Roses fan, I have to give Axl and co. credit for taking SG out on tour. In fact, I have to give Axl *double* credit—for also introducing the world to another one of my all-time favorite singers and bands...the recently mentioned Shannon Hoon and Blind Melon (as Hoon sang on the G n' R hit "Don't Cry," and G n' R also had BM open shows, as well).

And it just so happened that the release of Soundgarden's "Outshined" single and video coincided perfectly with the two months' worth of G n' R dates—ultimately resulting in the group's commercial breakthrough. Released as a single in the UK in December (peaking at #50 in the UK, which interestingly, was considerably lower than the less-easier-to-digest "Jesus Christ Pose," and #45 on *Billboard's US Mainstream Rock Chart*), it featured a photo of the band on the cover that would soon find its way onto the front of a t-shirt (included in the photo section here), various non-LP b-sides would be included on different configurations issued throughout the world on promo and regular versions.

The version that packed the most tracks for your buck was the German CD single, which featured "Outshined" twice (once as an edit and again as the full-length version), plus a pair of covers—Devo's "Girl U Want" (which I will boldly declare is not only SG's greatest cover version of all-time...but one of my favorite cover versions *ever*, as SG dials down the pace of the original, and replaces Devo's stiffness with a laidback groove, which works wonders), a reappearance of Sab's "Into the Void (Sealth)," and Ben's Stones-y original, "Show Me."

On other configurations, you will find a gaggle of other b-sides (most of which had recently been recorded for *Tommy Vance's BBC Friday Rock Show*), including the Ramones' "I Can't Give You Anything," Fear's "I Don't Care About You," Jimi Hendrix's "Can You See Me," and Budgie's "Homicidal Suicidal." Once upon a time, Ben even mentioned to me that he suggested a cover of the Minutemen's "Jesus and Tequila" for SG to cover (which possibly could have been around this time), which if it got the same relaxed n' groovy type of treatment that "Girl U Want" received, could have been a dandy. Sadly, we'll never know—to the best of my knowledge, SG never took a crack at it.

And the "Outshined" video would be the first Soundgarden clip that MTV truly put some muscle behind. Directed by Matt Mahurin, the story goes that that Mahurin was working on Metallica's "The Unforgiven" video around the same time as the "Outshined" clip (including the overblown/overindulgent/boring "theatrical version" of "The Unforgiven" video, that ran eleven-and-a-half minutes...I *dare you* to try and sit through the whole thing). As a result, his attention was drawn more to the Metallicas, and the version of the "Outshined" clip that was widely seen on MTV as a "buzz bin video" (just after "Smells Like Teen Spirit" exploded and "Alive" started to gain momentum) was not the fully realized version.

It turns out that a couple of months later, Mahurin offered a truly finished version which was a major improvement...but it was too late—MTV was already done spinning the video, and had moved on. Truth be told, it was not until bloody November of 2016 (almost exactly 25 years later!) that the "new and improved" second version was widely seen by fans, when it was uploaded to YouTube. Later on, Chris summed up the two versions perfectly—"The unseen version was dangerous; the released version was a standard hard rock video."

In the "released version" of the "Outshined" clip, the viewer is treated to scenes of the band miming the song inside what appears to be a dirt-floored steel mill (how *heavy metal* is that?!), with lotsa steel barrels scattered around, and fire appearing to be the main source of lighting for the band. And for the ladies, there are plenty of gratuitous shirtless shots of Chris—including several of him climbed upon a chained fence, with wide holes in it to clearly see his face. On the other band, the "alternate version" has more of a dreamy quality to it, with slo-mo scenes interspersed with real-time ones, of the band again miming the tune in an undisclosed yet quite foggy location. Once again, Chris goes shirtless, and in several scenes, is wrapped in what looks like sheer scarf-like material—a similar effect to the front cover and inside photos of the Rolling Stones' band members for their *Goats Head Soup* album. Although the second version doesn't sound all that exciting nor enticing—seeing is believing, and I'll go with the latter over the former.

"We kind of knew prior to the album's release that ['Outshined'] was going to be slated as a single," explained Kim years later. "I actually thought they'd work more on 'Somewhere' or 'Mind Riot.' I don't know how big it was as a single—I wasn't a big radio listener or MTV watcher. I didn't get Cable TV until '94 or '95. So when I saw our videos, it was on tour in a hotel." It turns out that the song's composer was surprised by the song's commercial success. "Our biggest single was 'Outshined'," said Chris a few months after it hit, "which I feel was a stretch for MTV and for FM radio, the two places that had never played us before. That was definitely the poppiest side of our band, aside from 'Big Dumb Sex,' which apart from the language, was probably the poppiest song we've written."

"That was the symbol of things changing in the industry, and the dedication of A&M to really help break Soundgarden," recalled Susan. "['Outshined'] at a label with less support—maybe it wouldn't have gotten the sort of radio play, because the promotion staff wouldn't have been so focused on it, or the relationship with MTV wouldn't have been into play on that track. Amazing song and all the right circumstances surrounding it to have it promoted properly."

Due to MTV's and rock radio's support of "Outshined" and the G n' R tour exposure, *Badmotorfinger* would eventually climb to #39 on the *Billboard 200* (and replicating that same exact chart placement on the UK album charts). And additional publicity occurred when the album was nominated for a Grammy Award in the "Best Metal Performance with a Vocal" category—which SG would unfortunately not win on the evening on February 25th, when Metallica's *The Black Album* took the prize.

But as a result of all of this, on March 6th, the album was certified gold—for 500,000 units sold in the US alone (less than a year later, it would hit platinum, with its last certification in 1996 being double platinum). And it just so happens that about a month earlier, Soundgarden launched their own headlining tour of theaters—showing that they were seemingly fast-approaching "arena headliner status." Additionally, on March 5th and 6th, a pair of shows were professionally filmed at the Paramount Theater in Seattle, which would eventually be edited down for their *Motorvision* home video (more on that later), and with even more unseen footage seeing the light of day when a *Badmotorfinger Deluxe Edition* would be issued in 2016.

Also in the month of March (the 3rd, to be exact), the third and final single from *BMF* would be issued, "Rusty Cage." Issued in various configurations and recycling several previously released b-sides ("Girl U Want," "Show Me," "Stray Cat Blues," and even the "Big Bottom"/"Earache My Eye" medley from *Louder Than Live*), the UK did get one previously unheard track, a cover of an obscure tune from UK pop rockers, Fancy, entitled "Touch Me." Quite a sexually-charged number, "Touch Me" features the one and only male-female duet in the entire

Soundgarden discography, as vocals are provided by Stephanie Barber—the wife of former Green River/Mother Love Bone guitarist, Bruce Fairweather. And to top it all off, the cover is a shot of the band in green, with Chris striking quite the rock gawd pose (fully sunglassed, mile-long hair, shirtless, hands folded, and showcasing a six pack on his tum-tum).

Much of March and the beginning of April saw SG launch a headlining tour of Europe, before returning to the States for further theater shows. And as Ben and Kim alluded to earlier, it was also around this time that Soundgarden played a handful of shows on a bill that also included headliners Skid Row (who were promoting their #1 album, *Slave to the Grind*), as well as a fast-ascending Pantera. Matt saw it as a necessary evil—"We were in 'the metal trenches' at that point, just fully paying our dues. We were like 'the opening act' for '91-'92."

"Playing with Skid Row and Guns N' Roses, our fans would have an opportunity to see us," said Chris. "They came out and bought the merchandise. There were days on tour with Skid Row where we out-sold them in merchandise. That was a surprising thing. We knew we had an audience. If we had to do it all over again, I still can't see any other decision that would have been better. We realized we had a lot more fans in Middle America than we thought and we established new ones."

But again, Cornell sensed some distance between Soundgarden and the hard partying Skid Row. "We were up in Vancouver playing a show with the Melvins, and when we finished our set, Sebastian Bach was waiting for us in our dressing room all by himself, with his fist wrapped around a bottle of Jack Daniel's. He looked at us, and he could kind of see that we were putting on our coats or something, and he was laughing hysterically; we couldn't figure out why. We all filed out. He said mid-laugh, 'I can't believe this. You guys are leaving me alone at your own show.' We all went our separate ways and he was sitting there getting fucked up in our dressing room. A lot of those heavy metal guys seem to think that it's part of their job to keep the party going."

Another troublesome occurrence was while opening for G n' R or SR, the audience would only come alive for one song and one song only—"Outshined." "It made me hate the song," admitted Shepherd. "'Cause it means they've been watching too much TV." "That's what happens in a society when music is exposed and hyped one song at a time," said Cornell. "Whatever song they grab the ball and run with is the song they're gonna remember you for. There are a few songs that sound like Soundgarden in a nutshell. I don't think 'Outshined' is one of them, but that's the one all the kids cheer for. You might play a song that you feel is the best thing you've done in a while, and it kind of falls on deaf ears; then you play that song half-heartedly, and they love it. It can be depressing if you let it."

Undoubtedly, three memorable shows from SG's headlining leg occurred in Texas, when Soundgarden was paired with Pearl Jam (the latter of which was already on their way to superstardom, with their "Even Flow" clip now being heavily rotated on MTV)—on April 28th at the City Coliseum in Austin, April 29th at the Bronco Bowl in Texas, and April 30th at the Unicorn Club in Houston. At the last show, SG and PJ joined forces to offer the audience a cover of Neil Young's "Rockin' in the Free World" (with Chris playing one of Jeff Ament's basses!) which MTV filmed bits of, and included as part of an *MTV News* segment. And according to Kim, he was impressed with the reception Soundgarden was receiving when headlining around this time. "Sometimes, I can hear the audience more than I can hear Chris who's standing right next to me. We also get to see how each different city chants Soundgarden—the fateful three-syllable band. In Florida, they just go, 'Garden, Garden.' In Germany, they stress each syllable with equal ferocity. In Britain, they just go 'Mud-hon-ey'."

By the time it was announced that Soundgarden was going to perform a headlining show at the spacious Roseland Ballroom in NYC on May 9th, my friends and I were most definitely in. So on that Saturday evening during the spring, I found myself inside this cavernous venue, of which a large ticket paying audience had gathered (which I recall being quite chuffed at seeing, as I could see with my own eyes that the band's popularity was on the upswing)—to inspect a bill that also included openers Swervedriver and Monster Magnet. Soundgarden's eventual arrival was met by the pre-recorded beginning of "Searching with My Good Eye Closed," a song which up to that point, fell flat for yours truly. However, by seeing it/experiencing it on stage, I finally "saw the light," and it has gone on to become one of my all-time top tunes. And compared to the previous time I had seen SG live (almost two years earlier), the band looked fairly the same—except for Ben, whose hair had grown considerably, which hung down in front of his face.

I tried wiggling my way up to the front, but as many who saw rock shows at Roseland back in the day will probably also attest, the crowd surfing and moshing proved too much to take, so I retreated to a much safer/comfortable locale. And it didn't take me long to discover that the band was *on fire* the whole night—resulting in one of the best Soundgarden performances I've ever witnessed. Standout memories include Chris attempting to throw what looked like a mannequin head into the crowd (but tossing it too high, so that it got caught in the lighting truss above!), him crowd-surfing at one point all the way to the soundboard, standing up by it, and speaking into his wireless mic, before traveling back, and also at one point, thanking the crowd for attending their show instead of Kiss (who were also performing locally that evening, at the Ritz), with Matt replicating the beginning drum fill from "Strutter," immediately thereafter. Also, I recall Chris singing the Beatles classic, "Hey Jude," via a megaphone into his mic at one point between songs.

And the memories don't just stop there! Other standouts included Kim taking an unaccompanied guitar solo that mocked the shredders of the day (complete with Spinal Tap-posing and purposely poorly-executed two-handed tapping), and at the very end of the show, lighting matches and handing them one by one to the audience, to pass around. And as far as the setlist, there were plenty of highlights, including great performances of such *Ultramega OK* classics as "Flower" and "All Your Lies," a bare-bones version of "Mind Riot," and "Somewhere" starting with just

Chris singing and playing guitar, before Matt ran back to his drum kit just in the nick of time, to kick into the "Somewhere in my dreams" section, with the rest of the band joining in. It turns out that at least portions of the set were professionally filmed, as MTV aired a performance of "Rusty Cage" shortly thereafter (and included years later as part of the *Badmotorfinger Deluxe Box Set*). As a treat to your eyeballs, two vintage photos from this show are included in the photo section (courtesy of Steven J. Messina). And one final factoid—upon returning home later that evening, I was greeted by the latest issue of *Guitar World Magazine*...which had Kim on the cover! What the heck were the chances?

Once the US headlining tour had wrapped up a few days after the Roseland show, SG took a brief breather, before heading out on the road—once again opening for Guns N' Roses throughout Europe. But this time, the G n' R dates would be an all-stadium jaunt running from May 20th through July 2nd, with...Faith No More rounding out the bill (the latter of whom was about to unveil what many consider to be their masterpiece, *Angel Dust*). As Kim Thayil explained, "This was weird—our first gigs with Faith No More, we opened for them, our next gigs with Faith No More they opened for us, and then our next gigs with Faith No More, we're opening for them again. That was before *Superunknown* blew up [in 1994], so it might have turned all around again! We've toured with Faith No More probably more than anybody." Matt remembered being particularly awestruck by FNM during the tour. "That's when Faith No More was at their full, mighty power, and they were just incredible. *Oh my God.* They were just one of the most stunning live bands I've ever seen in my life."

And although footage from this tour shows that Soundgarden could certainly hold their own in front of a stadium-sized crowd (pro-shot songs from a performance at the Hippodrome in the Bois de Vincennes, France, on June 6th confirm this—which was broadcast as part of a pay-per-view event at the time), Chris preferred more intimate gigs. "I'd rather not do the sports stadium kind of thing. It would be nice to go play in front of 5,000 for the rest of my career, 'cause I don't really care about performing in front of 20,000 or 60,000. First of all, the kind of music that you have to play isn't something we're either interested in, or capable of doing."

Cameron also mirrored Cornell's thoughts on the matter. "It was very impersonal, and there's no room for our brand of music to be absorbed as it should be. You can't hear a lot of the nuances underneath this big loud bomb. And it's not a great setting because you're playing in places designed for soccer or hockey, so the sound really isn't that great. Stadiums and large arenas can be a rush, but we definitely give better performances in small theatres and clubs."

In the midst of the GNR/FNM/SG Euro tour, Soundgarden broke off momentarily to perform at the Pink Pop Festival in the Netherlands on June 8 (also performing that day— Pearl Jam, Lou Reed, David Byrne, the Cult, and PJ Harvey, among others), which was pro-filmed. And as the footage will attest, not even rainy weather nor half the audience shielded by umbrellas could hamper the band at this point—including a hypnotic thirteen-minute workout of "Slaves and Bulldozers" at the end. In the performance of that song alone, you will discover such memorable bits as getting an up-close-and-personal view of Kim blowing into the pickups of his guitar, Chris putting down his guitar for a bit to focus on scat-singing (and he doesn't disappoint—incorporating in what sounds like parts of the Doors' "Roadhouse Blues," plus "Rain, Rain Go Away," and even a phrase utilized to demonstrate rounded vowel sounds, "How Now Brown Cow"), as well as trying to communicate with the audience via speaking into a megaphone held up tightly to the pickups of his Les Paul. And it doesn't just end there—Ben models several stances to display just how low he can let his bass hang down to the ground...and still be able to play it.

Depending on when he was broached on the subject of playing shows with G n' R circa '91/'92, Chris offered varying viewpoints. For instance, in '92, he seemed complimentary— "Spending time with Axl on the Guns tour, I realized how much stuff written about them is really bullshit. They treated us better than any band ever has." But come 2012, his view had changed somewhat. "Without saying anything negative about Axl, what I remember the most was Duff and Slash and everyone else being regular, sweet, warm guys in a rock band that just wanted to play rock music. And then, like, there was this *Wizard of Oz* character behind the curtain that seemed to complicate what was the most ideal situation they could ever have been in: They were the most successful and famous rock band on the planet. Every single show, hundreds of thousands of fans just wanted to hear songs. For some reason there seemed to be this obstacle in just going out and participating in that. That is what I remember the most. It's sad."

After the final stadium show with G n' R on July 2nd in Lisbon, Portugal, Soundgarden geared up for what would be the final set of dates in support of *Badmotorfinger*—Lollapalooza. Overall featuring a line-up that was more in line with SG's alt-rock background (headlined by the Red Hot Chili Peppers, and also including Ministry, Ice Cube, Jesus and Mary Chain, Pearl Jam, and Lush), this would be the second time that Lollapalooza—which according to Merriam-Webster, means "one that is extraordinarily impressive"—toured the US. The traveling festival was originally conceived by Perry Farrell as a send-off for his band, Jane's Addiction, the year before, and was such a success that it became an annual event—and this second installment was another rousing success (particularly due to "Pearl Jam mania" peaking during the tour, with the emergence of the incredibly popular "Jeremy" video on MTV). "That was our payback for opening for all these weird heavy metal bands that we had nothing in common with," remembered Matt. "Once we got to the Lollapalooza tour, we were back with our friends."

With grunge's popularity peaking, the record companies sensed an opportunity to cash in. As a result, several Soundgarden-related items arrived on the marketplace just around "Lolla time." First up would be a limited edition of *Badmotorfinger* that included a bonus disc, entitled *Satanoscillatemymetallicsonatas* (is that the most bad ass palindrome—a phrase spelt the same way forwards or backwards—*or what*?!), or *SOMMS*, for short. Included were three of the best cover tunes that appeared on Euro singles—"Into the Void (Sealth)," "Girl U Want," and "Stray Cat Blues," as well as the largely-unheard Cornell original, "She's a Politician" (which is quite punky in nature...but admittedly, not a top SG tune), as well as a live take of "Slaves and Bulldozers."

Concerning the story behind "SaP," the tune was originally included as a free flexi-disc in the December 1991 issue of the short-lived *Reflex Magazine.* And on the mag's contents page, the song's background was described as such—"Penned by Cornell, 'She's a Politician' is based on an incident involving 'Garden guitar maniac Kim Thayil. While the band was on tour with Danzig, Thayil met a woman in a bar. As Cornell recalled, 'It went from a discussion to a violent, bottle-throwing political argument'."

Credited as simply "Recorded somewhere live in America," the live version of "S&B" is a disappointment—both sonically and performance-wise. It seems like little effort was put into locating an up-to-par rendition of the song, which features surprisingly off-key vocals from Chris at the beginning (heck, the aforementioned version from Pink Pop blows this flaccid version out of the water, and even the version filmed at the Paramount, which was to be included on *Motorvision,* would have been an improvement). And for the most part, the packaging of both the original and the *SOMMS* version of *BMF* were identical—the only thing separating the two (besides the tracklisting) are two different band photos inside.

The second SG-related release of the summer of '92 would appear on June 30th (via Epic Records)—the soundtrack to the forthcoming Cameron Crowe-written/directed film, *Singles,* which featured an all-new Soundgarden track, "Birth Ritual," as well as Chris' first-ever solo offering, "Seasons." The former track is certainly one of Soundgarden's heaviest, with a punishing guitar riff penned by none other than Matt (who would compose quite a few killer riffs for SG over the years, including "Room a Thousand Years Wide," and further down the road, "Mailman" and "By Crooked Steps"). Meanwhile, concerning Cornell's "Seasons," I will be so bold as to declare it as his greatest solo song *ever.* Featuring just voice and guitar, it showcases the immense talents of Soundgarden's frontman, albeit in quite a mellow manner—great lyrics, vocals, and even some side two of *Led Zeppelin III*-like acoustic guitar picking/strumming equate a true winner. "If you ever want a laugh, listen to it with headphones on, and you'll hear all sorts of wonderful things because I record in a closet," Chris once suggested. "The microphone is in the same room with the machine, so you can hear the machine running and turning on and off."

And the *Singles* film—which would eventually hit theaters on September 18th (and starring Matt Dillon, as well as PJ's Jeff, Stone, and Eddie, as the fictitious/mediocre band, Citizen Dick)—included a cameo by Chris (during a comical scene where Dillon's character, Cliff Poncier, tests out a new speaker system in his car) and even Soundgarden, themselves (performing "Birth Ritual," but be sure to watch the full performance of the song on the 2015 Blu-ray version, as it perfectly captures the power and unpredictability of a SG show from this era).

However, Chris voiced some concerns about the timing of the film's release. "Because it was released a year later than it was supposed to be and the scene had already exploded by then, it came off as being more exploitative than it was meant to be. It was originally very much about Cameron and how he felt, and it was going to be his independent movie." And one last tidbit concerning *Singles*—did Chris ever toy with the idea of continuing acting after his walk-on? "No, I think that's the worst fucking thing. I mean, can you imagine having to get up at 4am and sit in a trailer while someone puts makeup on you? Then stand in front of a camera and say the same lines 60 times. I feel sorry for actors and I never want to do it. I stood in front of a camera in *Singles* and that's about it."

Also around this time, A&M made the wise decision to reissue *Temple of the Dog,* which resulted in MTV putting the striking "Hunger Strike" clip in heavy rotation, and the album reaching a whole new audience—which resulted in the song reaching #4 on *Billboard's Mainstream Rock Chart,* and the album peaking at #5 on the *Billboard 200,* and being certified gold on July 24th, and platinum by September 21st. "We weren't planning on re-releasing the record, it was like, 'Fuck, this thing sold 750,000 records'," remembered Chris. "But there was obviously an audience out there for it, so we put it out again. It was re-released in more or less the same manner it was released in the first place, which was like, not a lot of hype or anything, not a poster of both bands or something like that."

Kicking off on July 18th at the Shoreline Amphitheater in Mountain View, California, and wrapping up on September 13th at the Irvine Meadows Amphitheaters in Irvine, California, Lollapalooza II hit most of the major markets of the US (quite a few of the bigger towns included multiple day stays)—36 dates in all. One show that was pro-filmed and has circulated took place on July 22nd in Bremerton, Washington, which documents an outstanding SG performance. Since they are playing what Chris refers to as a "hometown show," the band obviously put a bit more zing into their performance—including such rarely performed tunes on Lolla as a set-opening "Gun," "Big Dumb Sex," and "Ugly Truth" (I'd venture to say the latter is one of the best live renditions of the tune out there).

Other highlights include Chris sporting an interesting orange raincoat at the beginning (with the hood up, no less!), Ben spearing a beachball with his guitar that invaded his space on stage, steam rising from the heavily crowd-surfing audience, Eddie Vedder joining in on singing the chorus to "Outshined" (albeit from behind Matt), Chris criticizing the quality of fireworks someone shot off mid-set and then plugging the Jim Rose Circus Sideshow (specifically mentioning "a guy who lifts up cinderblocks with his penis...and he's going to bungee jump from his penis!"), stomping on another beachball during "Searching with My Good Eye Closed" and then wearing it as a hat...before ripping down part of the chain-link fence backdrop, and falling on his back.

And you can bet your bottom dollar that when the traveling roadshow visited the Jones Beach Amphitheater in Wantagh, New York on August 9th, I was indeed present. Despite having not been lucky to see a show on the first Lolla (a proposed date on Long Island was ultimately scraped, and with none of my pals willing to chauffeur me to New Jersey at that point—although they *would* be willing in '93—I had to take one for the team), I was aware of what to expect from all the media coverage. I recall it being an overcast day, but the skies never fully opened—thankfully (those attending the next day at the same venue wouldn't be so lucky, as a thunder storm led to a cancellation after Lush's opening performance).

Since Jones Beach is a seated venue, one did not have to endure standing the whole day...but the downside was my seat was situated quite a ways back in the bleachers. By the time Soundgarden came on—opening up with "Face Pollution," as I recall—the audience had already seen what was the day's top performer...Pearl Jam. In addition to being the artist with the highest-selling album at the time, PJ was in peak form live. And it's impossible to top a band whose singer was defying death on a daily basis, by climbing up scaffolding and lighting—and Mr. Vedder outdid himself this day by doing one of his highest concert climbs ever, up a towering cement tower (search "Pearl Jam—Porch—Jones Beach 1992" on YouTube and forward to the 2:15 mark to see the stunt...you won't be disappointed).

Perhaps as a result of this, Soundgarden's performance surprisingly fell flat—although I do recall them opening with "Face Pollution," and they did provide a surprise by offering up a cover of the then highly-controversial tune "Cop Killer" by Ice-T's heavy metal band, Body Count (which would ultimately be deleted from pressings of the group's self-titled debut album, due to pressure by such political higher ups as then-US vice president Dan Quayle). And while we're on the topic of the tune...why did they decide to perform it in the first place?

"Here's a song that people are afraid of, and it's just a song," Chris explained at the time. "And I'm gonna play it. I don't care who's afraid of it or not. It seems like people are really afraid of the wrong things." But back to the Jones Beach show, stacking it up against, for instance, the aforementioned Bremerton set, there was simply no comparison. Perhaps the gloomy weather had something to do with it, too...but then again, it didn't seem to affect Pearl Jam's performance that day, now did it?

But there were other standout moments of the remainder of the Lolla dates. Temple of the Dog reunions (on August 14th in Reston, Virginia and September 13th in Irvine, California), Chris and Eddie performing a two-man rendition of "Hunger Strike" on the side stage (on September 8th in Phoenix, Arizona), Ben flailing around wildly on stage while Pearl Jam performed "Alive" (also in Reston), Body Count's Ernie C joining SG for a rendition of "Cop Killer" (August 22nd in Miami, Florida), and at various dates, Chris indulging in some delicious/nutritious "bile beer," served up fresh from the stomach of the Jim Rose Circus Sideshow's "Matt the Tube."

And on a Lolla stop in Houston, Texas (September 5th), King's X singer/bassist Doug Pinnick had a memorable interaction with Chris. "I loved Chris Cornell. I remember I went to see Soundgarden at Lollapalooza in Houston, and I was standing on the side of the stage, and I really didn't know him that well at the time, but he looked over and saw me over there, and walked off to the side of the stage and kissed me on the lips, and then went back out onstage and started singing! I got a friend that took pictures of the whole thing. Chris was a beautiful human being—he kissed me smack on the lips every time we would see each other. We had always talked about [possibly doing an album together]."

Kim also recalled Chris discussing King's X, and how he was impressed with Doug's vocal abilities. "Chris spoke highly of King's X. I think I had seen a few King's X videos at that time on MTV, on *Headbangers Ball*, and Chris was like, 'I just met this guy from King's X. What a nice guy! He's a good singer.' I remember Chris was emphasizing the singing, and the fact that Doug was really friendly. And he took me and introduced me to him. At that time, I didn't know much about King's X—other than catching a video or two—but Chris had one of the records...or a cassette. Back then, a lot of us had cassettes—that's what worked when we were in the van, and then, later on, a tour bus. But that's my primary memory—that Chris was hyping the band to me, both as talented musicians and really friendly, amiable people."

Another musician, Meat Puppets bassist Cris Kirkwood, had a memorable Chris memory—at one of the Irvine/Lolla shows. "One time, we played with [Soundgarden] at Berkeley Square. They were good—they were metal, but not quite as 'metalled out,' with bitching songs. [Chris] is a natural—like Robert Plant, in a way. Just one of those dudes that can get up there and rock out. So afterwards, I was fucked up, and I come off stage, and kick over a table in the dressing room. I was just goofing around. And [Cornell] actually said something! And I'm a bad person—I was raised by horrible people, and I have a really shitty attitude about everything. So I'm sitting there, going, *'Motherfucker'.*"

"Years later, we were recording out in Hollywood, and Flea came out to the studio. He's an old buddy of mine. And he says, 'We're playing Lollapalooza tonight, at Irvine Meadows. You want to go with me?' So it was me, him, and [Mike] Watt. And that night, Flea wanted to have a big jam session, and he wanted everybody to come out. Gibby [Haynes] was there, Curt [Kirkwood] was there, Blackbyrd McKnight was there from P-Funk. He wanted to do 'Cosmic Slop'."

"So everybody goes out there to jam, and I'm like, 'Eh, I'm not going to go out there.' Then I decided I would. I took duct tape, and started duct-taping Gibby up, and it got all physical and goofy. And then some goon decides that I'm a troublemaker and attempts to scold me. We're talking about *punk rock* here, and it's the last show of Lollapalooza with the Red Hot Chili Peppers headlining! I was like 'Fuck you, man.' So I'm standing on the side of the stage, and I decide, 'Oh perfect...*fire extinguisher*!' I went out there with that, lit it off, and that just shut down the show. That was the end of the show. All of a sudden, I'm standing out there with all the smoke and fire extinguisher shit. Alone. Then I hear all this noise. It turns out all the noise I heard was Chris, destroying the dressing room—those guys were on the tour, too. And it was him dismantling this dressing room. It was like, 'See, see? Now *you're* wrecking things'!"

Despite Lollapalooza being portrayed in the media as an alternative to the mainstream, Kim was disappointed in its audiences' make-up. "Guns N' Roses had greater diversity class-wise. It wasn't just white, leisure-class, suburban, 18-to-24-year-old kids who don't vote. What you saw at Jones Beach, that's the way it is at every single show. With Guns N' Roses, you'd have more of a mix between working-class kids and suburban. Lollapalooza seems to foster the sort of elitism that alienates people who work for a living. It's really getting on my nerves. Guns N' Roses was really cool because a guy getting off his factory job to see a band he believed in would feel welcome. That isn't true around here." Chris also voiced similar disappointment—"I think it was the alternative culture coming together for a non-alternative audience to check out. I don't think the audience we're getting is an alternative audience."

Looking back, Ben does not have the fondest memories of Lolla '92, either. "That first [Lollapalooza tour] that we did, it was a really bizarre time of life for me. You could see the Pearl Jam thing happening—that Beatles-type phenomenon. It started on that tour—seeing the crowds and the gates, and everyone running in like motherfuckers. I would hang out with Jesus and Mary Chain—I was the only guy that would talk to them. They knew I was all dark cloud and scowling—just storm in the room, share my whiskey with them, or whatever. See—that's the problem. I started drinking too much on that first Guns N' Roses tour. I would get really depressed, and that was the only way out— or so it seemed. A lot of touring is 'hurry up and wait.' You get there and then you wait. You'd see guys that had been out for a couple of years in a row—you hit this wall where it's like, 'Why go home? There is no home, there's nothing! Let's just keep going, we'll play another show'!"

And since MTV seemed like they just couldn't get enough grunge on their airwaves at that moment, Chris would be spotted at a *Singles Premiere Party* special (which in the 2011 documentary, *Pearl Jam 20,* we find out that all of PJ were quite drunk and belligerent at), in which he re-enacted his acting cameo in the film, and is spotted at the end on stage, while PJ romps

through a cover of Neil Young's "Rockin' in the Free World."
Also, Chris was seen around the same time on MTV in a *Rock the
Vote* ad, in which he implores the youth to vote in the '92 US
presidential election (filmed at what appears to be a junk yard),
while he was also spotted on the cover of the September 1992
issue of *Spin* in a screaming/shirtless pose (alongside the headline
*THE YEAR OF GRUNGE—Seattle Spawned It, Madonna Wants
It, and Soundgarden's Chris Cornell Has It. A Special Report).*

What would turn out to be the final Soundgarden-related
release—in a year that saw a seemingly never-ending slew of
them—was the VHS home video, *Motorvision*, which was issued
on November 17th. Directed by Kevin Kerslake, the 57-minute
video features eight quality live performances (albeit as heavily-
edited versions), plus an introduction by the host of a once-popular
children's Seattle TV show, *The JP Patches Show*—"Searching
with My Good Eye Closed," "Rusty Cage," "Outshined," "Little
Joe" (YES!), "Mind Riot," "Room a Thousand Years Wide,"
"Jesus Christ Pose," and "Slaves & Bulldozers"—all filmed over
the two nights that SG headlined the Paramount Theatre back in
March.

Also added in are clips of the band riding in a vehicle
driven by Matt (who does a good job of operating it, despite
working with a very shaky steering wheel)—shot by Ben's
brother, Henry—as well as interviews with Sub Pop's Bruce
Pavitt and Jonathan Poneman, and former roadie Eric Johnson.
Although it was certainly fun viewing at the time, when
Badmotorfinger would be issued as the "super deluxe edition" in
2016, an entire performance of one of the Paramount shows
(although it fails to mention which night's performance it is—
which leads one to believe that it's an amalgamation of *both*
nights) was included without all the added bits...which is absolute
essential viewing.

Phew! So there you have it, the entire story behind
Badmotorfinger—undoubtedly one of the most action-packed
years as far as a rock band goes (if you are to take into account all
the different high-profile tours, chart success, media coverage,
etc.). Looking back on this era years later, Ben summed it up

perfectly, while giving an idea of what it was like to experience all the hoopla, first-hand. "That whole year of *Badmotorfinger* seemed like 'Whooom! Where did it go?' It was like stepping into a fucking dragster and going for it."

CHAPTER 15
93

For all intents and purposes, Soundgarden was supposed to take 1993 off...well not really *off,* as they would write and record the all-important follow-up to *Badmotorfinger*—which they did indeed accomplish. However, they just couldn't resist issuing a solo project or two, saying yes to opening a string of dates for a rock n' roll legend, and earning another Grammy nomination—this time for "Into the Void (Sealth)" in the "Best Metal Performance" category. Unfortunately, once again, SG failed to hit the jackpot on the evening of February 23rd, when they lost to Nine Inch Nails' "Wish." And also around this time, one of Soundgarden's chief members opted to alter his trademark look.

Starting around '92, it suddenly became hip to chop off all of your once shoulder-length rock n' roll hair. And not just *cut* off—chaps such as Stone Gossard from Pearl Jam opted to *buzz* it off. And shockingly, Chris' long hair—which was probably one of his most identifiable non-musical characteristics (I say "one of" because it's hard to determine if his long hair or going shirtless takes the cake)—went bye-bye via buzzcut, as well. "Susan was really busy with one of her bands," Chris recalled a few years after getting closely-cropped. "And there was about a month when I never left the house. I didn't go out in public; I didn't talk to anyone on the phone—I went a little psycho. If I hadn't been alone so long, I would not have gone as far as I actually went. But one day I went from wondering what I would look like with a shaved head to, 'That's pretty cool.' Then I put my hair in a big envelope and mailed it off to my wife."

And despite this being the pre-internet/pre-iPhone era (in which news was not nearly as immediate), it did manage to make the rounds in the news outlets. "The funny thing was, I did this really silly, personal thing for no reason, and then all of a sudden it was on *MTV News* and in *Newsweek*, and I still hadn't left the house. I thought it was strange, because I don't know how anyone found out about my hair, and I don't know why they cared." And although he just claimed in the last quote that he lessened the load on his cranium "for no reason," on at least one occasion he did give a specific reason for doing the daring deed. "Every single person in Seattle started looking like me, all the young white boys with long curly brown hair and facial hair." Another time, he simply stated, "I never liked having haircuts, which is why I had long hair in the first place, but it's not much of a challenge to shave your head."

1993 also marked the year that the MTV comedy cartoon, *Beavis and Butt-Head,* became a sensation. Based upon the daily activities of two dimwitted, trouble-making, heavy metal-loving teens, the show also proved to be a surprisingly influential taste-making tool when it came to rock n' roll—as each episode saw the dynamic duo analyzing and rating music videos. Luckily, it turned out that they enjoyed Soundgarden's clips for "Outshined" and "Rusty Cage." "I don't have cable, but they sent us tapes of that," Thayil said at the time. "At first I thought, 'Here are some goony, idiot guys who are cast as goony, idiot guys,' and I thought it was dumb. But it turns out they hate shitty music, too. That's fine. I love AC/DC and Metallica, so their judgements aren't far off."

So, now that we have these hairy topics out of the way, we can now focus on the most important occurrence of '93 for SG—recording full-length #4. Instead of hooking up once again with producer Terry Date (who had co-produced their previous two albums), a decision was made to enlist Michael Beinhorn. "We were happy with the way the last two records turned out," Cornell said. "Terry Date produced those, and he's an amazing guy. He can do anything. But we had grown a little too comfortable working with him. We wanted to try something new where we felt we really had to push ourselves to the limit."

Although Beinhorn nowadays is—rightfully—considered one of rock's great producers (having worked with the likes of Aerosmith, Ozzy Osbourne, and Marilyn Manson), by the time he was linked to Soundgarden, his resume was not all that enticing. True, he had produced what I will boldly declare are the Red Hot Chili Peppers' best two studio albums (1987's *The Uplift Mofo Party Plan* and 1989's *Mother's Milk*) and played keyboards on the album by Herbie Hancock that gave us the synth-dance classic "Rockit" (1983's *Future Shock*). But other than that, he was not particularly known as a producer who could not only steer artists to the multi-platinum promised land, but also, rock your socks off sonically.

Regardless, the band and Beinhorn set up shop at Bad Animals Studio in Seattle, and laid down tracks over a somewhat brisk three-month span (no Boston/Def Leppard-like extended studio stay here, folks). "It was good having someone new to bounce ideas off," said Cornell about the new producer. "He had a pretty strong opinion on stuff. He came from the same school as us as far as going with the approach to each song as opposed to an overall view of who we should be. It took longer because we had to form a relationship with this new guy whereas before, with Terry, we all knew where we were." And another motivation that Ben surmised for a producer switch was a simple one—"One reason why we chose Beinhorn is because he felt that we've never been recorded like we sound."

But would you believe that smack-dab in the middle of recording—from August 11th through the 23rd, to be exact—Soundgarden opted to take a break from recording, to hit the road with a chap who had recently been anointed "the godfather of grunge" (due to his amp-crackling work with Crazy Horse), Mr. Neil Percival Young. As Chris explained at the time, "This was the fourth time he'd asked us to tour with him, and every time previously we were either making a record, or it was just bad timing. We were recording this time as well but we just figured that we'd better say yes at some point. So, we've taken a hiatus from the studio for eight shows. On the day this tour's over, we're back in there."

And having not played in front of a live audience in almost a full year (the *Badmotorfinger* tour wrapped up on September 13, 1992), Chris was happy to discover that the "you never forget how to ride a bicycle" theory also pertained to the concert stage. "It seemed like it would be more unusual than it was to get back on the road. I guess if you've played for that long, even if you stay away from it for a while, it doesn't seem to make that big a difference. I mean, we were kind of rusty, and the shows haven't been our best, but it wasn't like we were on another planet when we came out and started to play. It felt pretty normal. A lot more natural and a lot more immediate than I thought I'd feel."

There were also several other "enticements" that made the mini-tour attractive. First off, their old pals Blind Melon were part of the bill—who had just scored their breakthrough hit with "No Rain." Secondly, they were able to premiere/test drive several new tunes that they were in the midst of recording (in the pre-iPhone days, there was no danger of works-in-progress massively leaking to the public)—including such tunes we would later know and love as "Kickstand," "My Wave," "Fell on Black Days," "Spoonman," "Mailman," and "Let Me Drown." And lastly, another plus was the tour kicked off in an untraveled US state for SG. "To be honest, there were a lot of Soundgarden fans there, 'cause we'd never played South Dakota before," said Chris. "There were people who knew the songs and had banners and stuff like that. It was more alienating to open for Guns N' Roses than to open for Neil Young in South Dakota! It made me want to come back and play there again by ourselves."

Automatically, Chris reaped the benefits of his near-bald noggin. "It's so much easier to play without it. I used to take a big gulp of air onstage and suck huge strands of hair right down my throat! Then I'd have to stand there and pull it back out!" And for the guitar geeks out there, it became apparent during this short run of dates that Chris had begun playing primarily Gretsch guitars—particularly the Duo Jet model—which he would continue playing through '95 (with a Gibson Firebird and a Fender Jaguar thrown in, for good measure). "I have a very strong emotional connection to that guitar [the Duo Jet, which was a 1989 reissue]. Gary Lee Conner from Screaming Trees bought it for me, and I would never let it out of my sight. It may only be a reissue, but it's a very important guitar to me because I used it in the Temple of the Dog 'Hunger Strike' video and on every Soundgarden record. It's the main guitar on 'Fell on Black Days'."

Looking back on the dates, other memorable tidbits included Chris coming down with the flu midway through the tour in Toronto on August 18th (Kim: "He ordered it six to eight weeks ago, but had to wait for delivery!") and enduring a heavy rainstorm in the midst of their performance at Jones Beach two days later (yes, the same venue that a year ago, saw the second of a two-day stay on Lollapalooza get cancelled due to a thunderstorm).

"They called it a, not a hurricane, but a gale-force storm, or some crazy thing," Susan recalled. "Blind Melon played and it was raining *incredibly hard*. By the time Soundgarden got on the stage, there was an inch of water—the wind was blowing the rain horizontal and stuff was starting to rip off the facades of the stage. I just remember after that, the huddle in the Jones Beach dressing room—both bands had just been through something that was otherworldly. It was really fun to experience that with them." Kim also remembered an on-stage comment that night—"I remember Chris saying, 'We'd like to thank God for the light show'." So after the mini-tour with ol' Neil wrapped up after a show in Mansfield, Massachusetts on August 23rd, Soundgarden returned home to complete work in the studio.

Speaking at the time of the tour, Chris discussed the status of the album. "It's sort of typically to an extreme. We've already got 26 songs, and I don't think any of us agree on which ones should be on the album. So we're probably gonna record most of them, 'cause you don't know how they'll turn out. There are a lot of titles, but I don't wanna give 'em to you 'cause I haven't really got an idea what's gonna be on the record."

Despite keeping a tight lip on the songs' titles, Chris was at least willing to disclose what to expect stylistically. "I guess the material is sort of in the *Badmotorfinger* vein, but a lot more diverse than anything we've ever done before. There are a lot of varying guitar sounds and different vocal approaches the way things are going. Hopefully, there'll be more experimentation in every direction you can think of. From one thing being more of a pop song, to something else being more of a completely atonal, noisy song. It's been pretty surprising so far."

And Kim's assessment was similar to Chris'—concerning stylistic diversity. "There's gonna be a lot of variety. The way I see it, it's just new ways of being heavy. I think there's still a depth to the songs—there always has been. There's an incredible variety amongst them, but they're all heavy. They all have a visceral element and they have an emotional and psychological element that give depth and a lasting appeal. None of them seem to be incomplete or shallow songs. They all seem to be thoroughly worked out. So we're happy and enthusiastic with most of the material. There was some stuff where the collective enthusiasm was less than on some of the other songs. But after having recorded them, the enthusiasm grew and it was great to see how the performances translated."

"We did things like layering sounds that we'd never really done before," added Chris. "I think we were trying to make each individual song sound like we thought it should do, as opposed to throwing it in there and just taking what we could get. We actually used less guitars on this record than we ever have before as far as doubling and tripling parts goes. It's just that we used a lot of different sounds that we've never tried to use before. It's mostly just the rhythm guitar sounds in general."

Matt was also willing to compare *Badmotorfinger* to its follow-up, and also, what would set the two apart. "The way the last one sounded kind of beat you up. This one's more natural sounding. It sounds real. We went into this record with the idea that we wanted to hit more of a Syd Barrett vibe on some songs." And it turns out one reason for this sound change was the use of new guitar amps by Kim and Chris. "We changed our sound around in a day and a half. We were using new amps, [Mesa Boogie] Dual Rectifiers, but neither of us knew about its full capabilities because they can do all these things. They have modern settings, vintage settings, silicon diodes or tubes, two different kinds of tubes—and this is all in one amp. They also have two different channels, and how you set that up changes the way each channel responds. We'd been screwing around with them for about a week and Kim finally figured them out. We knew we could make those things sound like us, but didn't know how."

Additionally, Chris admitted that they may had gone a bit overboard with the amount of different guitar tunings on the album. "We have eight tunings out of 15 songs. We had seven tunings on the last record. There are three tunings on this record that weren't on the last record and two tunings on the last record that weren't on this record. So, all together there are ten tunings between the two. Sonic Youth probably beat us. They carry like thirteen guitars."

This time around, the band members opted to write more on their own, and no longer jammed it out in a room together from an idea's inception. "We're tending to write a little more on our own these days," Chris admits. "But it often only starts out that way—someone will bring in an idea and then someone else will take it home and work on it. After years of touring we're less interested these days in all sitting together in a room and hashing it out. The idea of shutting yourself in with the people you've just spent 18 months with doesn't seem quite as appealing as going home and spending some time alone. But once a finished song reaches the band we'll jam on it, try new parts and so on—everybody's still involved. Kim came up with some melody parts on this record in the studio, things we never heard before, just trying stuff out. This record definitely wasn't something pre-planned, we really didn't know what it was going to be like until the last day!"

And whereas some would assume the band would be feeling some pressure to deliver—Ben remained as cool as a cucumber. "I personally don't [feel the pressure]. Maybe I'm way off track with everybody else, but I don't see any difference between this time and the last time. I've seen the pressure around us, with the people that deal with us. You know, record label people try to not put pressure on you, but they did. It's all internal—if you want pressure then it's going to be there. But we were pretty focused, we just wanted to record."

They also approached the actual recording of the material a bit differently, as well. "We recorded four songs at a time," explained Ben. "Do the basics for the four songs, then we'd stick with one song out of those four songs until that song was done, and then we would finish it off and then go to the next block of songs. So it was a lot more if we were doing one song at a time. But it wasn't really—it was four songs at a time." Chris approved of this method. "It was cool though, because you'd get the glimpse of the record in these sections, and each little period of recording was like this whole new door." And according to Ben, as a result, "Everybody was involved in the whole record."

On a personal note, Chris also tried to quit a bad habit during the recording of *SU*...which resulted in what sounded like a very messy situation. "When we were in the studio for *Superunknown* I was trying to quit smoking, so I was chewing tobacco instead. The producer guy brought in this bottle of Scotch, and I hadn't eaten that day and I took a big pull on the Scotch, and I had the tobacco in my mouth. It went down good, so I took another big swig. And then all of a sudden I was rushing to the bathroom and my whole head felt like it was going to explode, and I was throwing up pure Scotch and tobacco. It was pretty awful, but me and Scotch are friends again now."

Thankfully, according to Kim, Chris was more successful with another activity during the album's recording. "We had a PlayStation set up in the back. I do remember Chris playing some racing games and occasionally playing *Doom*. I remember sitting there for, gosh, maybe a couple hours, watching Chris play *Doom*; I was so engrossed with the graphics and the nature of the game— and it got me pretty dizzy because if you're just watching a video game and not playing it, it's like being a passenger in a speeding car. Yeah, I remember eating sandwiches and watching Chris play *Doom*."

It turned out that boredom also led to destruction, and nearly the firing of one of the album's engineers, who would soon figure prominently into the Soundgarden story. "We almost got Adam Kasper fired," recalled Chris. "He was the sole employee of the studio that was around us, the guy that we allowed to be around us. At some point, I think we just got really destructive and he didn't stop us—pretty much destroying the control room—and he almost got fired. The one thing that stopped us and got us to put our behavior in check was the fact that we didn't want poor Adam to lose his job."

Also, sometime after the tracks were recorded, there was difficulty in the mixing stage concerning getting the sound just right. "We knew we had a good record in there, but I think we were all just sick of it—we didn't care anymore," remembered Matt. "And then lo and behold, Brendan O'Brien came in and mixed it—he did it in like a week and a half or two weeks. He worked the complete opposite of the way we were working—just knocked it out. When I took the mixes home and listened to it, I realized we had a really good record."

But the same month that Soundgarden completed recording the still-not-yet-publicly-titled album, a pair of SG-related items arrived, which we should really itemize at this point. First up was the inclusion of "Outshined" in the film *True Romance* (which was released in the theaters on September 10th)—which was heard in the scene where Brad Pitt's stoner character, Floyd, is firing up a bong. Also, September would see the arrival of a side project featuring half of the band (Ben and Matt), entitled Hater—which appeared seemingly out of nowhere.

Released to very little fanfare on September 21st via A&M, Hater (which saw Ben manning the 6-string rather than his usual 4-string) was rounded out by former Monster Magnet guitarist John McBain, bassist John Waterman, and one of Andy Wood's brothers, Brian, on vocals. And with Ben and Matt also pitching in vocally, it's difficult to discern who is singing which song—as all vocalists sound remarkably similar. "Hater came about in the 'Post-Tour Syndrome' after Lollapalooza," Cameron recalled. "And we wrote most of it at Ben's house. It was so much fun and it didn't take much time either—about five days. It was my first experience writing and singing the lyrics to a whole song, and it was just nice to play with new musicians who took me in directions that I don't normally go."

While grunge artists certainly liked filling up their spare time with side bands (the most obvious examples being Temple of the Dog, Stone Gossard's Brad, Layne Staley's/Mike McCready's Mad Season, etc.), stylistically, Hater bore little resemblance to Soundgarden's punk-Sabbath style. Instead, Hater's debut (which was also self-produced by the band) focused on lo-fi/garage sounds—not sounding far removed from the Stooges' first album or early singles from the Kinks or the Who. And to get that magical sound of yesteryear, Shepherd played a pair of vintage instruments specifically for the majority of the recording—a '63 Gretsch Corvette and '67 Gretsch Roc-Jet.

However, the ten-track album blasts off with a cover of a decidedly *non*-garage rock artist—"Mona Bone Jakon" by singer-songwriter Cat Stevens. But the album really gets rockin' on the next tune, which just happens to be one of the album's best, the cheerily-titled "Who Do I Kill?". And it turned out that a video was filmed for the track—which included cameos by Mark Arm as a priest and a chap who looks very much like Layne Staley applying lipstick. Yet, the clip remained *so* unseen that I did not even know of its existence until it was rescued from the video void via YouTube—many years after the fact.

And judging from the video, it appears to be Ben who sings lead on the tune (but the lighting, camera angle, and the simple fact that the YouTube upload is not crystal clear makes it a bit difficult to know for sure), while Matt obscures his identity by letting his hair hang down in front of his face and holding the drumsticks via the "traditional grip." Another strongly-titled tune, "Tot Finder," features a guitar riff that sounds basically like a re-write of the Stooges classic, "No Fun," before leading to a surprise left-turn, with the sad-sounding, acoustic instrumental "Lion and Lamb" (which always reminded me of such glum Sabbath instrumentals as "Laguna Sunrise" and "Fluff," for some reason).

"Roadside" is another rugged yet mid-paced rocker (featuring an elastic-y guitar riff), before leading to another one of the album's top standouts, "Down Undershoe." Concerning the latter, Ben once said, "The song 'Down Undershoe' was one I was originally going to try to get Soundgarden to do. But at that time I hadn't finished recording it." And after hearing it, you could definitely picture SG doing a dandy job with it. *Our loss.* "Circles" is a rowdy rocker (which serves as a bit of a predecessor to the song "Ty Cobb," a few years down the road), which contains sloppy-yet-endearing drum and guitar breaks in the middle.

And while we're talking about drumming, Matt should be commended for showing off his chameleon-like drumming abilities, by keeping his playing so basic on this recording (which is what the songs called for) that it sounds absolutely nothing like he does on your average S. Garden release. In fact, none other than Chris Cornell had high praise for Cameron's minimalist drum approach on Hater. "The drums on the Hater record are fantastic; it's a totally raw recording. I've never heard Matt play like that before. The sound is sort of garage-y and not very slick. And then all of a sudden he does a really incredible fill, and, in the context of such a raw sound, it just blows you away. It makes him sound that much of a better drummer. When I hear that, I know why [John] Bonham is so revered."

Back to the track-by-track aspect, "Putrid" is both sinister-yet-sweet (containing the repeated phrase "star lover"), while the album's other cover, Billy Edd Wheeler's "Blistered," is a surprise country twanger that shows once again that Hater was no one-trick pony, before closing with the album's most cacophonic tune, "Sad McBain" (which I later discovered featured lead vocals by Matthew).

How does the album measure up to all of the other all-star grunge spin-offs? I'd be bold to declare that alongside Temple of the Dog's lone offering, Brad's first two albums (1993's *Shame* and 1997's *Interiors*), and Mad Season's sole studio set (1995's *Above*), Hater's debut is one of the very best. And like most of my ultimately preferred recordings, it did not immediately register. Truth be told, upon first hearing it, I wasn't all that impressed— perhaps because I was still a year or two away from discovering the mighty Stooges (and going back and thoroughly studying the Who's early work), and didn't really have much of a reference point. But I can honestly state that over the past few years, Hater's debut is probably my most listened to of the crop of non-Soundgarden recordings that its members have made over the years (and yes, dear readers, that includes Temple of the Dog and Audioslave).

While a tour was not launched in support of Hater's debut, they did manage to play at least one show that year—opening for Pearl Jam at the Seattle Center Arena (on a bill that also included Urge Overkill), on December 9th. "I thought that the Pearl Jam crowd should have heckled us more," was Ben's simple assessment backstage/post-performance. Hater proved not to be much of an ongoing proposition—apart from donating a tune ("Convicted") to the 1995 compilation, *Hempilation: Freedom Is NORML*, not much else was heard from the band for the remainder of the decade.

But Hater was not the last Soundgarden-related piece of music to arrive in '93. On October 26th, SG donated tracks to two different compilations. First up was the *BMF* b-side, "Show Me," appearing on the compilation album *No Alternative* (also featuring contributions by the likes of Nirvana, Smashing Pumpkins, and the Beastie Boys)—benefitting the Red Hot Organization, which focuses on HIV/AIDS relief and awareness globally. And secondly, offering "HIV Baby" to *Born to Choose,* which also featured tracks by REM (with Natalie Merchant), Tom Waits, and Pavement, which benefitted two groups—NARAL (National Abortion Rights Action League) and WHAM! (Women's Health Action and Mobilization).

Then, on November 9th, 4/6th's of Temple of the Dog went by another name, MACC, and offered up a cover of the Jimi Hendrix obscurity, "Hey Baby (New Rising Sun)," which was included on the star-studded *Stone Free: A Tribute to Jimi Hendrix* comp—also featuring contributions by the likes of Eric Clapton, Jeff Beck, and...Body Count! Let's backtrack and fill in the "MACC" facts, you ask? To start, the initials stand for all of the last names of the song's contributors (Mike **M**cCready, Jeff **A**ment, Matt **C**ameron, and Chris **C**ornell).

Although I personally usually automatically tune out when it comes to artists covering either Jimi, the Fab Four, or Zep (the original versions are definitive and simply can't be topped...*why bother*?), this is one of the few times when the cover matches—or quite possibly, even surpasses—the original. And the reason is because Jimi's version sounded like it was never truly completed—as it was one of the last songs he ever recorded in his lifetime (at a session dated July 1, 1970, a short while before his tragic death on September 18th), and issued on the posthumous comp, *Rainbow Bridge,* a year after his passing. As expected, McCready has no trouble replicating Hendrix-isms on his phased-out Strat, but what really makes the song a must-hear is Chris' outstanding vocals. Because as much as I love Jimi—heck, he's my favorite all-time guitarist—I would have to say that there was no comparison between the two in the vocal department. As a result, the MACC track is quite an attack.

And that's not all! On November 23rd came Guns N' Roses' latest release, *"The Spaghetti Incident?"*. And just why the heck would I be mentioning this here? I agree, an explanation is in order. An all-covers affair, *TSI?* featured Axl and co. covering the likes of the Stooges, the New York Dolls, and Charles Manson (!), plus T. Rex's "Buick Mackane." Being a long-time T. Rex fanatic myself, I admit it was a curious selection to cover, as "B. Mackane" is certainly *not* one of the best tunes Marc Bolan ever composed. But towards the end of the cover, you will find inserted—for no apparent reason—the chorus of "Big Dumb Sex"!

Interestingly, a song that Soundgarden originally offered up as a piss-take on hair metal comes off as an all-too serious statement in the manly-man hands of G n' R. Oh well, *so much for parody*. "I think they ran out of people involved with mass murders who wrote songs, so the next step was us," Cornell once kidded. Lastly, December 20th saw the self-titled debut album by the alt-electro-dance-rock duo (comprised of *Fopp* producer Steve Fisk and Brad/Satchel singer/pianist Shawn Smith), Pigeonhed. Again, why am I bring up this seemingly random factoid? Because Kim supplied some guitar work, that's why, buster!

It also must be mentioned that during '93, a Kiss tribute album was being assembled...*which Kiss was constructing themselves* (in true Kiss style, eh?). Supposedly, an invitation was extended to Soundgarden to join in on the fun—I remember the song that Gene Simmons wanted them to tackle was "War Machine," off Kiss' underrated *Creatures of the Night* album (which admittedly, could have been a potentially killer Kiss kover).

But...it was not meant to be—and for a specific reason, according to Ben. "Because [Kiss'] fans used to beat me up on the way home from school. I was into Led Zeppelin and things, which they all called 'older brother music,' so they beat me up." As a result, when the collection, *Kiss My Ass: Classic Kiss Regrooved*, saw the light of day the following year, it was entirely Soundgarden-less. But there were no hard feelings, as a photo made the rounds a few years later of Soundgarden together with Kiss (in full make-up/costumes), after attending a show on their highly successful reunion tour.

And although this following bit of music would not be released until February 4, 1994, Soundgarden re-recorded "New Damage" at some point during '93 (with Beinhorn producing). Why re-record the tune? Because it was included on a compilation entitled *Alternative NRG,* which saw some of alt-rock's biggest names (REM, U2, Sonic Youth, etc.) record via an all-solar powered mobile truck. And on their remake, SG enlisted the aid of Queen guitarist Brian May—to add some extra zest.

It just so happens that Kim once discussed his memories of re-recording "New Damage" with moi. "We got to meet Brian May—we were rehearsing at Pearl Jam's studio then. They were probably on tour. The studio was in a basement underneath Galleria Potato Head. We were there rehearsing, and all of a sudden, a limousine pulls up in this alley. We'd enter the studio through a narrow alleyway, in Belltown, Seattle. Belltown is a neighborhood in downtown Seattle. And Brian May and his assistant came walking down the stairs, came in, and introduced himself."

"I remember he had a long coat—it might have been knee-length. We shook hands, said hi, we played him the track, and he really liked it. And then the tapes went to...I don't think they went to England. They may have gone to New York, and Brian recorded his stuff at a studio in New York. [Brian recorded his parts at Pie Recording Studios in Glen Cove, New York] And then I think Beinhorn—with Chris assisting—mixed the thing. Because this was all really quick and on the fly. A lot of times, we would have a band member—Matt or Chris, or sometimes myself—sit in, to just oversee the process, and make sure things aren't being left out, or that the band's song is being misrepresented."

"It turned out really great and we were really proud of that. The way I play my solos is a little bit more...I tend to be more improv and loosely oriented, and play with some feedback and noise. I definitely like the sound of things falling apart. [Laughs] Elements of chaos and noise, and it's always improv. Only a few times—a dozen or so times—did I ever actually write a solo out in advance. And what Brian did was very Queen-like—he wrote out a very nice, simple lead melody, that he then doubled, tripled, or quadrupled the number of guitars playing the harmony part. It sounded very 'Queen,' very 'Brian May.' And it worked with that song."

So, all that was fine and dandy, but unquestionably, the most important bit of Soundgarden news in 1993 came in November, when a press release was issued via A&M Records, which finally announced the title of the forthcoming album as well as its release date. The title would be...*Superunknown,* with a release date set for March 8, 1994. And it turned out that it was Chris who coined the mysterious phrase for the album title...with a little bit of unexpected inspiration. "*Superunknown* is dyslexia, that's all. I looked at a video that said *Superclown* and I read it as saying *Superunknown* and I thought it was a cool title. I'd never heard it before, never saw it before, and it inspired me."

I recall somehow coming across the press release (or perhaps it was an article on the band that recycled quotes from it), and one quote really stuck out, courtesy of Matt—which got my hopes up as high as a kite for what lay in store. "We made an album instead of a record that has a couple of good songs and filler. We made an album in the classic sense of the term which goes back to records we bought growing up in the '70s. Bands like Aerosmith and Led Zeppelin made these records where every song counted and I think that's what we did." I am sure I was not the only SG fanatic who began counting down the days until the album's release upon reading that commanding quote.

As this chapter is winding down, how about a comical story that Eddie Vedder once shared with me about how he and Chris celebrated the completion of *Superunknown*...and almost didn't live through it. "They'd just finished *Superunknown,* and Chris had given me a copy. We went up for a hike up into the Olympic Peninsula—this eight-hour walkabout thing. And I got to talk to him about it the whole trip. [Laughs] I felt like an apprentice—he was so kind and giving with talking about whatever that process was. 'I don't use a lot of background vocals—you use a lot of background vocals, and a lot of effects.' He started laughing, like, 'I don't know, I don't really think so.' And I'd ask him about publishing—all this shit—the poor guy just wanted to take a hike and get away from this stuff! And here we are—looking at the dirt, trudging along these switch-backs going vertically, listening to this shit from me."

"Then I remember being on the side of some cliff. We had climbed up real easy, and then on the way back down, we got stuck on the middle of this cliff. He was above me and I was below. I was like, 'I don't see a way out of this'—we just sat there thinking about it for like five minutes. And then we both started laughing— it was just such a bizarre situation. Both our records were done, and we just started laughing like, 'Well, I guess the records are going to sell pretty well!' Kind of like the mystery of whatever had happened. Two nights later they played this club, I think it was RKCNDY, they were playing the *Superunknown* record. I remember that being beyond the beyond—all cylinders were firing."

"[1993] was a really good year," Ben reminisced, years later. "I tried to make a home life. My life was so fun, because we did the Hater record, did *Superunknown*. We were all really connected."

CHAPTER 16
SUPERUNKNOWN I

A long time ago in a galaxy far, far away, record companies would issue advance cassettes to members of the media many months beforehand, since the time-lag between submitting a review or article and it actually running could take many moons (again, in sharp contrast to nowadays, where with a click of a button, any old thing can be blasted throughout the known universe mere seconds after being created). And somehow/someway, an acquaintance/fellow Soundgarden fan got a hold of such a cassette of *Superunknown* a good while before its expected birth ritual of March 9th. A similar situation occurred a couple of years earlier with Faith No More's *Angel Dust,* which I promptly dubbed a copy of and went on my merry way, studying the album thoroughly before investing in an actual CD copy. But strangely, when offered to inspect the advance copy of *Superunknown,* I declined—as I felt like this would be a momentous rock album, and that I should experience it with the rest of the world, to get the full impact.

But what I *was* willing to allow myself to listen to before the arrival of *Superunknown* was the album's leadoff single, which arrived on February 15th (almost a full month before the album's entrance), "Spoonman." As it turned out, the inspiration for the song (which was in 7/8 time!) came from a prop on the set of the *Singles* movie. "I'd always thought it'd be really cool just to write down ten or twelve titles in order, as though it was a record already, and then write the songs later, based on those titles, just for fun," Chris once said. "I was supposed to come out of the Matt Dillon character's apartment, and the cassette package was in there, and I just picked it up. Cameron [Crowe] was laughing, saying how he thought it was the typical titles for the introspective solo tape from a local musician guy, and it just clicked at that point. I thought I'd just do it for him as a surprise."

"That's kind of what I do really, for fun. That's pretty much all I do, just sit around and write songs, record some stuff." And from those song titles that Chris penned music for— "Spoonman" was one of them. As it turned out, if you watch/listen to the film closely, you will hear a brief embryonic version of the song—played on acoustic guitar—at one point (during a scene in which a flier is being hung up). Perhaps most impressive is when you hear Chris' full original/solo demo of the song, almost the entire structure of the finished song is already in place—even the percussion breakdown in the middle.

Title-wise (and it should be noted that the titles on that cassette tape that Chris pilfered from the *Singles* set were thunk up by none other than Jeff Ament), the song was inspired by a Seattle street musician by the name of Artis the Spoonman, who also guests on the track by offering up a "spoon solo." When asked if the song's lyrics were specifically about Artis, Chris responded, "More or less. Him or street performers and how they're perceived by the average person, and how it's sort of a misconception that somebody who does that for a living is a street person/heathen/drug addict/low-life. It's a job—like anything else, and they'd probably rather be doing that than washing dishes for somebody."

Riff-wise, simply de-tuning the low E-string to D served as inspiration for Chris concerning "S. Man," to come up with one of his all-time most badass riffs (and certainly one of the most fun to play along to in your bedroom, which I can attest to!). Guitar solo-wise, Kim was willing to explain his approach. "Because that song is in seven and it's got a pretty straight, tight arrangement, and there's percussive orientation there, the intro to the solo was a couple of triplets that Chris had actually written as part of the song. And then you go into percussion solos. So that definitely set parameters. I would kind of play that solo a little bit more regulated—I fuck it up and vary it live all the time. I think of that as being a song and a solo that required a little bit more focus and organization, because it starts with that little solo intro riff that Chris came up with, and then it goes into the 'spoon solo.' Because of that, I am trying to have an idea of what the time considerations are of the solo—maybe in terms of length and where my location on the neck will be in terms of key."

And the UK CD single and 12" vinyl (which featured a cover image of two hands tied together with what appears to be string, tape, and...spoons) came with three additional tracks—one other *Superunknown* tune, "Fresh Tendrils," as well as a pair of non-LP ditties, "Cold Bitch" and "Exit Stonehenge." The former track (a CCC) is a strong/mid-paced rocker that features a colossal riff and higher registered vocals. And once more, the track does not include the song's title in its lyrics, but does include the repeated phrase, "In your heart, I'd freeze." However, the track was not from the *Superunknown* recording sessions—according to Ben, who quite fancied the tune.

"There was a song that was supposed to be on *Badmotorfinger*, and it wasn't, 'Cold Bitch'—it's one of my favorite tunes that we've recorded. It's been released on a few other things, yet it feels like the alienated child from the family, or the one that was left behind. It's a feeling of 'that's the one that would have proven the point a little bit more,' or 'it would have pushed it a little bit further'." And after reading Ben's quote and listening to the tune, it is absolutely much more in line with *BMF* than what was to follow on *SU*. The other ditty, "Exit Stonehenge" (credited to all four members as authors) is a silly throwaway—it's title obviously a play on "Enter Sandman" by Metallica and "Stonehenge" by Spinal Tap—which sounds like it was made up on the spot.

As expected, a video accompanied the single—directed by Jeffery Plansker (under the alias John Smithey). And unlike the majority of music videos that include some form of the artist either playing or lip-synching the song, the band only appears in black and white still photographs, while all the color/motion footage is of Artis, showing off his snazzy techniques as the world's most talented and entertaining spoonman. Also included are shots of rusted steel, Chris' bent fork necklace, rolled photographs dipped in tar, rusty spoons, and photographs being held by metal "pinchers." And while most of the times non-performance music videos prove to be a crashing bore, the "Spoonman" clip proves to be quite original and holds your interest—which shows that Mr. Plansker/Smithey knew what he was doing.

"I think we were fairly smart with 'Spoonman' in that you really don't see us that much in the video," said Chris. "You see various pictures of us, but it's not quite the same as having us in your living room all the time. We're trying to maintain some degree of mystique about Soundgarden, I guess. I remember back when I was a kid, long before MTV, the only way to see my favorite bands was to go to their concerts. It was an incredible experience. MTV has helped a lot of bands, but they've also helped rob a lot of groups of that special mystique. It's tough when you can see a great rock band on TV one second, then hit the clicker and be watching a soap opera or a sitcom the next. That's what rock and roll has become for some people." The video proved to be quite popular with MTV, and as a result, the single performed well chart-wise—hitting the top-ten in Finland (#8) and New Zealand (#10), just missing in Canada (#12), off a ways in the UK (#20), while nearly topping *Billboard's* Mainstream Rock chart (#3).

I remember the day a friend and I went to purchase *Superunknown* at a local mom and pop record shoppe (actually, make that a *CD shop,* as there probably wasn't a bloody sliver of vinyl in there at that point in time), the clerk was indeed playing it over the store's sound system, and we were taken aback by the swirling psychedelia of the song we were listening to. In fact, the portion we were listening to, the only thing that was detectable as "Soundgarden" was Chris' unmistakable vocals. Anyway, when I finally took it home (well, actually, make that *my college dorm room*) to inspect the audio findings of my latest musical investment, it was one of those few times that my high expectations were fully met. In fact, if memory serves me correctly, it did not take as many spins as *Badmotorfinger* to register in my gourd as a masterpiece.

While not as stellar an opener as "Rusty Cage" was, *Superunknown's* kick-off track, "Let Me Drown," still managed to do the trick. Built around a sturdy-yet-groovy guitar riff, the track also featured an outstanding Cornell scream right before the guitar solo, as well as a breakdown section after the solo that featured a surprisingly Bo Diddley-esque beat. Entirely penned by Chris, he once explained, "'Let Me Drown' is about—I didn't want to say this, because Nirvana put out that *In Utero* album, with the fetuses all over it—but it was originally about crawling back to the womb to die." When asked what triggered that particular line of thought, he replied, "Well, salmon always do that. They go back to where they were born, then they die. I think it would be cool if humans could do that too."

Up next was probably the album's first true classic, "My Wave." With Chris handling the lyrics and he and Kim collaborating on the music, another meaty riff is contained (that's one special thing about *Superunknown*—it was absolutely *overflowing* with memorable guitar riffs, bits, and hits), and features the album's first true standout Cornell-ism, "Don't come over here, Piss on my gate, Save it just keep it off my wave." And by the end, the song slowly unravels. "Take the end of 'My Wave'," Beinhorn once explained. "The free-form aspect offered about a million ways to play itself out. But we struck a balance on it. Kim's doing a backwards tape thing, and, in reality, he had no way of knowing where the downbeat was. He just sort of navigated by a sixth sense—or in his case, *sick sense*—and it turns out when we flipped the tape back over, there was this gorgeous melody created. He completely hit it."

Thayil later pointed out that the song would sometimes flabbergast audiences. "Whenever we start that song, the whole audience bounces up and down—it's as if they're at a Rage Against the Machine concert. But unlike a Rage Against the Machine concert, we're not going to whip you with a 4/4 dance groove. Instead, that song very quickly is established as the 5/4 song it is. That loses everybody." Lyrically, Chris once described the song's meaning as being about "Tolerance, provided that nobody tells me what to do...nobody tells us what to do. Anyone can do whatever they want, I don't care what it is. Including you can fuckin' burn crosses on your lawn, I don't give a shit...you can burn your house down, who cares? I don't. As long as it doesn't catch someone else's house on fire."

With two rockers back-to-back, the tempo and fury was alleviated momentarily, with "Fell On Black Days." While the song would eventually be considered a SG classic by many fans—heck, it would eventually become an MTV/radio hit—I have to admit, it never was a personal favorite. In fact, well, I found it to be...a bit of a bore (especially when I'd experience it performed live). Another CCC (in an odd time signature, of 6/4), "FoBD" is at least curious from a lyrical standpoint, as its author once expounded, "'Fell on Black Days' was like this ongoing fear I've had for years. It took me a long time to write that song. We've tried to do three different versions with that title, and none of them have ever worked. Someday we might do an EP. It's a feeling that everyone gets. You're happy with your life, everything's going well, things are exciting—when all of a sudden you realize you're unhappy in the extreme, to the point of being really, really scared. There's no particular event you can pin the feeling down to, it's just that you realize one day that everything in your life is FUCKED!"

The song also proved to be a personal accomplishment for Chris concerning lyric writing—"That's where I kind of nailed a whole song in terms of a specific idea; poetically, without using a lot of words." And you have to give Chris credit for utilizing the word "whomsoever" (the only time it's ever been used in a rock lyric?). "I think that 'Fell on Black Days' will surprise people," Cornell said prior to the album's release. "There again, it's hard to imagine taking people by surprise, really, because between Soundgarden and Temple of the Dog and Hater, we have all been associated with different stuff."

However, it turned out that Matt didn't go gaga from the get-go over "FoBD." "We weren't really blown away when we first heard the demos for 'Black Days,' because we hadn't made it into a Soundgarden song yet. But Ben added a great bass part that fit with the vocal melody, and Kim put in some harmony parts on the end that took the song into another gear. Chris has written a lot of songs over the years that we've never been able to sink our teeth into until now, songs like 'Fell on Black Days' that have more of a pop arrangement. And the result proved to be songs that aren't necessarily more accessible, but have more depth and are more musical than anything we've done before. Still, they didn't sound like Soundgarden songs for me until all the tracks were down."

The fast-food chain Wendy's once had a famous advertising slogan in the '80s, "Where's the beef?" Well, four songs into *Superunknown,* some fans may have been wondering, "Where's the grunge?" By the fourth song, their prayers were answered, in the form of "Mailman." With its music entirely composed by Cameron (while Cornell does the honors lyrically), its grinding riff resembles a brawny Brontosaurus, which sounds like it's being processed through a wah pedal. Surprisingly, the guitar that Kim used to record this meaty riff is not what you would have expected.

"On *Superunknown* I used a Tele on 'Mailman' and 'Limo Wreck,' probably the songs that you'd most expect I'd go for a humbucker on. The Tele just had this round sound and brightness, and it was less mushy than the S-1, especially in those dropped tunings. Because of the brightness, it also left more room for the bass, so the bass and guitar become like one big instrument." Also included on the track was one of the most "un-grunge" instruments you could think of—a Mellotron—which was mostly played by Cameron (and a smidge by Beinhorn).

And the main Mellotron man was willing to spill the beans concerning the song's composition. "I've written a lot of songs in the past, but only in the past year and a half have I actually sat down to try and write a Soundgarden song. 'Mailman' is one that I thought would be good for us. Luckily everyone liked what I'd written, so I guess I'm getting to the point where I can write Soundgarden songs. And believe me, I went through a lot of songs to get to this point—most of it crap! I just try to approach it now from Kim's shoes. He's been a big influence on how I play guitar. I just really like his style, and I was always interested in how he got his sounds. I also based some of my tunings on what he'd done."

Lyrically, the song's title is not detected anywhere in the actual song—although the phrases "I know I'm headed for the bottom" and "I'm riding you all the way" are both highly emphasized. And if I were to take an educated guess, "Mailman" is a reference to the phrase "going postal," which was coined after many violent—and often, deadly—occurrences over the years between postal workers at the workplace (although nowadays, the phrase seems to be used to describe any instance of deadly rage).

Up next, the album's title track (its title is detected within an oft-repeated phrase within the song, "Alive in the superunknown")—a musical collaboration once more by Chris and Kim, with the former also handling the lyrics, which kicks the tempo back up, after the sluggish pace of the previous two numbers. Also included is a wailing guitar solo by Kim—again, played through a wah pedal. "'Superunknown' relates to birth in a way," explained the song's lyricist about its meaning. "Being born or even dying—getting flushed into something that you know nothing about." And concerning the song's music, it wasn't so much a true collaboration as it was Cornell solving a musical jigsaw puzzle. "[Kim] had a whole bunch of guitar parts that weren't arranged; he hadn't made a song out of them. So I took the parts, because they were all really good, plenty to make a song, and ended up adding a couple more."

The album's sixth track turns out to be the sleeper on the album (and my second favorite track on the entire bloody offering...my top pick still a ways away)—the entirely Shepherd-penned "Head Down." There were a few tracks on *Superunknown* that were obviously influenced by a certain four mop-topped Liverpudlians, and this was the first. And it turns out that I was not the only lad impressed with the tune's high quality. "There's a song that Ben wrote called 'Head Down' which still kinda surprises me when I hear it," admitted Chris. "It's a big, wide, open song that sounds like the '60s English bands that were good, maybe later-period Beatles. It doesn't sound like a band, it sounds like a place that they might sound like."

"I think a lot of it has to do with the drum sound, which, for some reason, reminds me of *Revolver*," adds Kim. "'Let's rip off the Beatles so we can make some money.' [Laughs] The Beatles element, as with those of Aerosmith and Nirvana, is just something that turns up and has been an influence, either directly or indirectly. In terms of rock and pop writing lineage, sometimes the Beatles or Hendrix slips in there."

Speaking of drums, "Head Down" featured a few extra pairs of drum sticks, according to Matt. "Gregg [Keplinger, Matt's drum tech] and Ben also played drums on that. I was just thinking of this swirling whirlpool of sound, especially in the drum break at the end. Ben played this spastic, rhythmic part that swells in and out of the mix throughout the song, and Gregg brought in his own kit and just went for it."

But how about a word from the song's actual composer? Concerning its music, he recalled, "I had people over at my old house and I just said, 'I'm going down to the basement to record.' I went down, grabbed my guitar, the mic was set up by my four-track, hit record, then I started playin' and that's exactly what came out—all the words, everything. After I did the vocals and guitar, I forgot I had that tape. I watched this movie on the Beach Boys and then I just put the rest of the song down—another guitar part, drums and bass. Then I brought that down to show those guys."

And what about its lyrical inspiration, Hunter Benedict? "'Head Down' is about how a little kid is taught to smile, and then the smile is taken away. I don't know if that's heavy or not...or deep...or disturbing. I try to write happy songs, and it just doesn't work." And while we are focusing on the bassist, it seems like here is as good a spot as any for a description on how Ben approached the bass on *SU.* "I went for a lot more straight sound, more of a Motown sound. Flat wound strings and low end stuff. On *Badmotorfinger,* I tried for a fretless sound. On this record it was actually more experimental."

Then...two CCC classics, back-to-back, right smack dab in the middle of the album (which is a testament to just how exceptional the material on *SU* was, that they could pull off saving the two best tracks so late in the album, and you wouldn't already be wondering, *"Where are the potential 'hits'?"*). First up was "Black Hole Sun," which has gone on to become Soundgarden's best known song and biggest hit (and was the mysterious tune I mentioned hearing in the record store on release day). And while I will say that the song is indeed another Beatle-influenced track, I would like to clarify this statement. Whenever I would hear music that was described as such, it usually meant that it was an artist who was merely mimicking the Fab Four. In other words, writing a piece of music that was from the standpoint of it sounding like it could have been composed by them...rather than an artist letting their own personality shine through, with an *element* of the Beatles detected. And I am happy to report that the latter was the case with these two aforementioned tunes.

Interestingly, it turned out that Chris needed some prodding to commit to penning a tune like "Black Hole Sun"—courtesy of the album's producer. "I was noticing that we were starting to get off the rails a little bit," remembered Michael, concerning when material was being submitted for consideration for the eventual album. "And that kind of culminated in receiving a demo tape that had about eleven or twelve songs on them—all from Chris, because he was sending me stuff periodically. And I realized that out of all of them, there wasn't one thing there that would actually be right for a record. And I started to get really nervous. I was like, 'Oh shit. We're still kind of a ways away from having what we need.' So, I realized that I had to speak with Chris about it. We had to come to an understanding about what we were going to do with this record."

"So, I got on the phone with him, and I started to realize where he was coming from with the writing he was doing. He was really trying to write for like...'a Soundgarden thing.' And I was like, 'Now, why would you do that? You don't know who these people are. You have no idea what they're looking for. Why would you try and please people whose lives you don't have any connection with? Do you know why they're listening to you? They're listening to you because of what they're getting out of your music—not because you're giving them what they expect. It's completely the opposite thing—they're along for the ride with you. It's not like you have to create the ride for them. No, no, no. *They're* following. Do something that's amazing, and they'll follow. Music that really means something to you.' And it was something that was completely off his radar. Which was interesting to me. I was like, *'Really'*?"

"I was really suggesting to him, 'Please yourself. Please yourself first. Do something that makes you feel right, and people will want to hear it. That's all that's going to matter.' So, I was like, 'What music do you like?' And he said, 'The Beatles and Cream.' I was like, 'Well, write a song that sounds like the Beatles and Cream then.' He was like, 'Well, what if it doesn't sound like Soundgarden?' I was like, 'Chris. *You are Soundgarden. You and your band are Soundgarden.* When you play this song, it will sound like Soundgarden, because you are playing it. It's very simple."

"So, three weeks later I get this cassette tape in the mail. The first song on the cassette is 'Fell on Black Days,' there are two in the middle that are fantastic, and the last song is this. The very first thing that I heard [sings guitar part that kicks in when the vocals start]. From the very first notes from those arpeggios, I'm like, '*What am I listening to*?!' I never heard anything like it." But Chris also once pointed out a non-musical inspiration behind "BHS." "I write songs best when I'm depressed. No one seems to get this, but 'Black Hole Sun' is sad. But because the melody is really pretty, everyone thinks it's almost chipper, which is ridiculous."

Chris was also willing to explain if he thought that one of the song's standout Cornell-isms, "Times are gone for honest men," was indeed a true statement. "Yeah, I do. It's really difficult for a person to create their own life and their own freedom. It's going to become more and more difficult, and it's going to create more and more disillusioned people who become dishonest and angry and are willing to fuck the next guy to get what they want. There's so much stepping on the backs of other people in our profession. We've been so lucky that we've never had to do that. Part of it was because of our own tenacity, and part of it was because we were lucky."

And concerning how the "glistening arpeggio" sound on the guitar was created, Kim was willing to let the cat out of the bag. "It's a Leslie cabinet. [Note: A guitar amp with a spinning speaker inside] That was Chris' idea. We used a Leslie on an unreleased song called 'Blind Dogs,' but we've never recorded an interesting version of it. When we brought the Leslie cabinet into the studio during *Badmotorfinger*, it generated a lot of interest from the band as far as working out arpeggiated guitar parts through it. Chris borrowed a Leslie and was working on some *Superunknown* demos when he came up with 'Black Hole Sun.' The Leslie is perfect for that song; it's very Beatle-esque and has a distinctive sound. It ended up changing the song completely."

However, according to Chris, one element got lost in the transition from the demo to the finalized recording. "There's a Leslie cabinet I was using—a specific one—and I used it on the demo and album version, and it had a two-speed control. On the verses, it's this very fast spinning speaker and it gives it that sound for the melody, and as the chorus hit, I would click it and the speaker would slowly slow down, so the arpeggio part of the chorus would have this sweep that's changing speeds and slowing down throughout it, giving it this really drunken, cough-syrupy feeling that I really like. I forgot to do it. Thinking about it later, I thought, 'Wow, that really made it more psychedelic.' But then of course I thought that could have been the one element that might have changed the appeal in terms of radio programmers wanting to play it, and they all did."

The song also features some of the best vocals on the album by Chris—and a conversation he had with Doug Pinnick of King's X may have led to his singing approach on "Black Hole Sun." "One time, we had a conversation while they were making *Superunknown* and we were making *Dogman*," recalled Doug, "and we were laughing about how high we sang all the time, and that we didn't have anywhere to go—we couldn't go any higher. We both agreed that we're both baritones, and we didn't need to be singing that high anymore. So we both made a little pact, and we agreed to sing lower on our records. And, as a result of it, you got 'Black Hole Sun' and 'Flies and Blue Skies,' and both albums had a definite change in vocal attitude. He said, 'Let's just croon on our records,' and I said, 'Yeah! Let's do that!' I think we accomplished that."

Also, when it came to the song's guitar solo, Thayil offered up one of his best-ever. "'Black Hole Sun' was a great opportunity to play a little bit modally and a little bit chaotically, because that's definitely the type of song that boils up in the point, and the title of the song and the lyrics, it lends itself to a certain psychedelia. You almost want the contrast there of the wildness and chaos, but at the same time, you play modally, because that just sounds trippy—veering in and out of keys, and that gives it that psychedelic, [Pink Floyd's] 'Astronomy Domine' weirdness."

And concerning the use of "the p word" to describe "BHS" (no, not *that* word, you dirty devil!), Matt was adamant to point out that SG had always had a psychedelic side lurking in there, somewhere. "If you ask me, the psychedelic vibe has always been there to a degree. Before I was in the band, when these guys were a three-piece, they struck me as being a full-on psychedelic trip-out head fuck band. We're investigating that a bit on the new album." And while we're on the topic of psychedelia, Chris once pointed out—"*Superunknown* is a very stoner-friendly record, which is funny, because none of us really do drugs. If you listen to it straight, it's great, but if you get really stoned, it can seem that the whole thing was conceived for that state of mind. I can't explain why."

Then, as soon as all the purple haze had cleared, we are greeted head-on with one of SG's all-time great riff-rockers—the leadoff single, "Spoonman," which we've already discussed at length. Up next is certainly one of the darkest songs on the album (but not *the* darkest...we'll get there in a few), the outstandingly-titled "Limo Wreck." A musical collaboration between Kim and Matt (and Chris providing the prose), it took a while to get just right. "That was a tough one but it worked well, eventually," remembered Chris. "It's a 'shame-on-decadence' song. It's very strange, it's in a weird time signature and it has a real flow to it. It has a lot of different melodies and moods, and it's really dynamic, too. The bassline and the guitar lines are also really swirling, almost kaleidoscopic, but then it just clears out, and there's this vocal that's left. It's hard to describe, but it worked."

"It's a riff Matt wrote and I like it because it's so creepy, I don't even know how to describe it," offers Kim. "The song has amazing depth and emotion. It's very dark, but at the same time, very powerful and angry." Lyric-wise, Chris was inspired one day by his surroundings while in Los Angeles—"We were on a highway where you could see more limos than cars, and I had this image of how cool it would be to see a couple that had just smashed into each other, burning. You get this idea from limos you see on the highway that it's the president and normal rules of life don't apply to them because they're not in a normal car. But they're just as susceptible to car crashes and drive-by shootings."

Another album standout, "The Day I Tried to Live," follows, which is once more a CCC (boy oh boy, Mr. Cornell certainly was inspired to write for this album!). Structurally, the tune includes quite a few peaks and valleys/twists and turns (including the use of *two* different time signatures, 7/8 to 4/4), as it reflects—for the most part—softer parts for the verses and explosive/heavier parts for the chorus. Lyrically, the song was semi-autobiographical for its composer. "It's about trying to step out of being patterned and closed off and reclusive, which I've always had a problem with. It's about attempting to be normal and just go out and be around other people and hang out. I have a tendency to sometimes be pretty closed off and not see people for long periods of time and not call anyone."

"It's actually, in a way, a hopeful song. Especially the lines 'One more time around/Might get it,' which is basically saying, 'I tried today to understand and belong and get along with other people, and I failed, but I'll probably try again tomorrow.' A lot of people misinterpreted that song as a suicide-note song. Taking the word live too literally. 'The Day I Tried to Live' means more like the day I actually tried to open up myself and experience everything that's going on around me as opposed to blowing it all off and hiding in a cave."

Up to this point on *SU*, Soundgarden's punk rock side had not been exposed. But that all changed in a jiffy—upon the arrival of the blink-and-it's-over "Kickstand." With Cornell covering the lyrics and Thayil handling the musical side of things, the song lasts a mere one minute and 34 seconds, and as it turns out, served as an important track during the album's recording. "The very first song that we recorded was 'Kickstand'," recalled Beinhorn. "That was after spending about five days to a week getting the kind of drum sound that I was looking for. I'm going to say that Matt ran it down between 15 and 20-plus times, which is a lot to track a song."

And although the tune comes closest to what would be considered "a throwaway" on *SU,* it actually turned out that it was a favorite of their old friend, Jeff Ament. "A song I really, really love is 'Kickstand.' I think that's because that's a song he wrote about his bike, and my relationship with Chris is forever tied to riding our bikes. That song really does something personal for me." And these feelings were reciprocated by Chris. "It does remind me of that period, too. I think after Andy passed away, Jeff and I spent a lot of time riding mountain bikes through the hills of Seattle and talking. That's one of my best memories from that period, really."

If you're interested in actual footage of "Kickstand" being recorded, be sure to check out a segment which originally appeared on the children's television program, *Bill Nye the Science Guy.* "We always had a warm spot for kids' educational television," admitted Kim. "We always said if we were asked to do something on *Sesame Street*, we would do it, and that's no joke." Unfortunately, Soundgarden never received an invitation to appear alongside Mr. Snuffleupagus and Abby Cadabby.

Up next is quite possibly the most underrated tune on the album, "Fresh Tendrils" (in case you were wondering what a tendril is, Merriam-Webster lists it as "a leaf, stipule, or stem modified into a slender spirally coiling sensitive organ serving to attach a climbing plant to its support"). But if you're looking to find the song's title mentioned anywhere in the lyrics, you'll be wasting your time (although the opening line, "Long time coming," is repeated quite a bit).

Penned mostly by Cameron (he's the sole author of the music, and is co-credited for the lyrics with Cornell), the drummer was quite chuffed with his accomplishment. "I'm proud to say this is the first album where I've received lyric-writing credit. I wrote the music for 'Fresh Tendrils,' and when I was doing the demo for it, I had this melody idea and sang these goofy lyrics. They're just the first two lines of the song, but Chris ended up using them. But, hey, if it'll get me half the songwriting credit, I'll take it every time."

And then...a song that if you were to ask me what my personal favorite Soundgarden song of them all is, I would feel confident selecting. And that tune is a musical lumbering leviathan, otherwise known as "4th of July." Not only the heaviest song on the album, "4oJ" is the heaviest and darkest-sounding song Soundgarden *ever recorded*—as it was detuned to a dangerously string-flapping C, and contains a simple yet awe-inspiring main guitar bit, and one of the most epic "string scrapes" ever (signaling the song's end). Another CCC (he certainly deserved a "most valuable player" award for *SU,* didn't he?), it also is a testament to the variety of songs Cornell could not only pull off...but do so *masterfully* (especially if you were to stack up something like "Black Hole Sun" alongside "4th of July").

But it's the entire *sound* of the song that creates yet another masterpiece. And Cameron tried a unique approach on his drum set for the track. "I replaced all my crash cymbals with rides, and I can explain the reason I did this in one word: Bonham! I just wanted that long, elegant cymbal sound he was so known for. The riff in that song is so slow, thick and meaty that I just felt it needed that syrup on top. I also used a tambourine drum that Gregg [Keplinger] invented." Despite it being one of the biggest/best/baddest sounding tunes on the album, it had to be mixed on at least two different occasions—once in New York (at Electric Lady Studios in November) and one more time around in Hollywood (A&M Records Studio in December), before it was finally considered to be up to snuff sonically.

And as far as the song's lyrical meaning, there is quite a backstory, according to its author. "One time I was on acid, and there were voices ten feet behind my head. The whole time I'd be walking, they'd be talking behind me. It actually made me feel good, because I felt like I was with some people. At one point I was looking back, and I saw that one person was wearing a black shirt and jeans, and the other person was wearing a red shirt. They were always there. It was kinda like a dream, though, where I'd wake up and look and focus once in a while and realize there was no one there. I'd go, 'Oh, fuck, I'm hearing voices'."

When asked if Chris wrote a lot of songs while under the influence of this psychedelic drug, he replied, "No, but '4th of July' is pretty much about that day. You wouldn't get that if you read it. It doesn't read like, 'Woke up, dropped some acid, got into the car and went to the Indian reservation'." Also contained in the lyrics was another standout Cornell-ism, "Down in the hole, Jesus tries to crack a smile, Beneath another shovel load."

A few years later, Cornell was asked which SG song he was most proud of. "'4th of July' is probably the one I'm particularly proud of, because it always felt like it was entirely my own. If a song means something to you and a whole bunch of people respond to it, then it sort of changes your idea about it. And if I think a song's really great and other people think it's shit, then I almost start liking it more because I feel like I knew something they didn't."

How does one "cleanse the pallet" after offering such a hefty dose of heaviness? How about a Middle Eastern flavored number, entitled "Half"...sung in falsetto by Ben! And Chris once recalled how the song taught him an important lesson concerning expanding Soundgarden's stylistic scope. "I remember having a brief conversation with Ben about me really thinking he should sing it, because his singing on the demo was so amazing to me. The whole mood of the song was never going to be as good if he didn't do it, and his response was, 'If I sing it, and you don't, then this is a Soundgarden song on our album that you're not even on'."

"My response was, 'That's what I'm talking about. This is about the album. This is about the songs. This is about the song's best foot forward, and that should always be the most important thing.' I thought it would help us expand and push the boundaries of what Soundgarden was at the time and do it in a way we'd never done before." Admittedly a peculiar tune, "Half" has gone on to become one of my favorites off the album—undoubtedly due to its oddness. That said, not all listeners heard the song's redeeming qualities, such as a *SU* album review in

Rolling Stone, stating, "As for bassist Ben Shepherd's swirling, discordant 'Half,' suffice it to say that this song is the virtual definition of a b-side."

Perhaps adding to the song's uniqueness was the way it was recorded. For those not familiar with the recording process, if a band is not recording all in the same room at the same time, they will lay down one instrument at a time. And concerning the latter approach, I would venture to guess that almost ten times out of ten, the drums will be recorded first. But "Half" was one of the few times this was not the case.

"The drums were the last thing to go on that song, which was kind of neat," said Matt. "But there's a whole second half to that song that didn't make it on the record. It was this completely different rock section that we just couldn't get right on tape. There were tempo fluctuations going from part A to part B that we tried to overcome with studio wizardry, but it would have been a little too obvious." And if you're ever curious to hear the other half of "Half" that did not make the cut (I would venture to guess that the song's title came from the fact that only half of the full composition made the cut), all you have to do is hunt down any live performance of the song—as SG always performed the full tune as originally intended on stage.

And now, the grand finale of *Superunknown*. It turns out that the lads were saving the most depressing song for the very end (and the album's undisputed seventh CCC overall)—"Like Suicide." And when I say depressing, I mean both musically *and* lyrically. Concerning the latter, let's let Chris explain. "It's a big moment that happened while I was recording the song. I had all the music and was recording a demo arrangement in my basement. And when I came upstairs, I heard a thud against the window, and it was a female robin that had fallen into the window and broke her neck, and was just laying there. I didn't know what to do. So I ended up smashing her with a brick, putting her out of her misery. I didn't want to sit there and watch her suffer. Then when I went back down to finish recording, I decided that would be the lyrics to the song. As much as it sounds like I'm singing about a person and the metaphor is sort of the bird in flight and then [it] dies...it was literal."

Years later, Chris admitted that the song may have been influenced by how the passing of Andy Wood was still affecting him...yet he wasn't entirely sure. "Yeah, the lyrics were actually this simple moment that happened to me. I don't know that I ever directly related it to Andy, though there are a lot of songs that people probably don't know where there were references to him or how I was feeling about what happened with him. I just think that that was something that happened to me that was a traumatic thing and that I had a difficult time resolving it. I still never really have. I still live with it, and that's one of the moments where maybe in some ways it could have shown up, but I'm not really sure specifically where."

So, that takes care of the musical side of *Superunknown*. But then there was the visual side—concerning the album cover and the images included inside the CD's song lyric booklet. The album cover features a distorted image of three-quarters of the band's faces—Ben on the left, Chris in the middle, and Kim on the right. Photographer Kevin Westerberg took the pic, but no reason has ever been given as to why Matt was not included (couldn't they have somehow fit him in on the bloody cover?!)— although another distorted photo on the back cover *does* accomplish including all four members. And because Chris' mouth is wide open, the image has subsequently often been referred to by the band and fans as "The Screaming Elf." Rounding out the cover is a new Soundgarden logo on top (the font is probably "Helvetica Ultra Condensed," in case you were wondering), and an upside down forest on the bottom.

"The cover kind of suggests the dark side of the unknown, like when you look at a forest—you don't know what's in there, but it's somehow appealing to go in," rationalized Ben. "And there you go—*Superunknown*." Along with Matt being MIA from the cover, there is also another crucial piece of the puzzle nowhere to be found—*the album title* (which was included on the cover as a sticker)! And concerning the visuals inside the CD booklet, Kim once provided info—"The CD booklet has 16 pages, and there's a separate photograph or art image for each song and lyrics. Our buddy, Reyza Sagheb [credited simply as 'Reyzart' in the booklet], back in Seattle, did a lot of the photography and artwork for that. Although he gets a little name on the package—for some reason."

So there you have it—probably Soundgarden's greatest studio album ever (it's always hard for me to choose between *SU* and *BMF*, but due to its exceptional sonics, I'd probably give the edge to *SU*). In fact, make that *one of the greatest rock albums of them all*, especially since material-wise, it was an incredibly consistent listen from beginning to end (I admit, on second thought, maybe I was a bit too harsh on "Fell on Black Days"). And another reason for *SU* being so sonically rich was because Soundgarden enlisted the aid of several special guest musicians, including Matt's future wife, April Acevez (viola on "Half"), Artis the Spoonman (spoons on "Spoonman"), Justine Foy (cello on "Half"), Eleven's Natasha Shneider (clavinet on "Fresh Tendrils"), and even Beinhorn (piano on "Let Me Drown" and some of the Mellotron on "Mailman").

But Mr. Beinhorn should really be commended for what he helped the band accomplish sonically and helping guide them material-wise (especially by instigating Chris to pen a tune like "Black Hole Sun"). "All the managers that I've ever spoken to who have worked with [Beinhorn] loved working with him," remembered Susan. "As did I. He was just great to deal with in terms of the business end of things. And every musician who ever worked with him, didn't like the experience at all...and came through it usually with the best records of their careers. The process was not particularly enjoyable for those guys, but goddamn, they made a good record!" [Laughs]

And this time, the critics seemed to all be on SG's side. For instance, Matt Ashare from *The Boston Phoenix* said, "Soundgarden have always had the muscle to pull off a hundred variations on the riff from 'Dazed and Confused,' but until now they haven't been limber enough to match the rich psychedelic textures and gentle melodies that made Led Zeppelin great. As punk descendants, they've avoided some of arena rock's more loathsome tendencies, like drum solos and Stonehenge lore. Yet memorable songs, one thing the dinosaurs of the '70s had going for them, have eluded Soundgarden. In that sense, *Superunknown* isn't just an improvement; it's a songwriting breakthrough that leads the band in promising new directions."

David Browne from *Entertainment Weekly* gave it an "A" rating, and added, "On a purely technical level, *Superunknown* presents a new and improved Soundgarden. In the past, the band has come off as one-dimensional and cartoonish. This time, co-producer Michael Beinhorn, formerly of the experimental multi-genre band Material, has given them a full-bodied, thick-steak sound that finally does Soundgarden justice." Also, JD Considine of *Rolling Stone* gave *SU* a rating of 4 out of 5, and stated, "On the whole, though, *Superunknown* not only hits more often than it misses, but it demonstrates far greater range than many bands manage in an entire career. And while that probably won't be enough to place Soundgarden at the forefront of the alternative-rock scene, it ought to at least lift the band out of the metal ghetto to which it had been so unfairly consigned."

But perhaps the most glowing remarks were in a write-up by Drew Masters in *M.E.A.T. Magazine*, when he gushed "*SUPERUNKNOWN*—the title of the new album from SOUNDGARDEN, easily the most brilliant album of this young year, if not for the '90s." And that wasn't all, as he would go on to rave, "Once *Superunknown* is unleashed to the public, Soundgarden will rightfully earn the title of 'supergroup'." And lastly, "I boldly predict, due to the mega-crossover potential of this record, that sales in Canada and the US will topple triple platinum, if not more—and it will gain them a third Grammy nomination (maybe a win this time)."

And lastly, old pal Jonathan Poneman from Sub Pop offered some heavy worship in *Spin*. "There's a perspective, a natural integration of ideas in *Superunknown* that I don't think the band has really captured since *Screaming Life*. For some reason, Soundgarden has always been seen as the Seattle also-ran, though they are in many ways the defining band of the regional sound. I have been listening to this record with an intensity bordering on obsession; it redefines an entire genre of rock for the better. If anybody is going around saying that Soundgarden is any less important than any other band in this town, tell him that Jonathan Poneman is going to kick his ass."

Even Kim once told me that *Superunknown* was one of his favorite Soundgarden records...along with two others. "I think I have three albums that stand out for different reasons. *Screaming Life* is distinctly different with Jack Endino's production and our original songs from that period that Hiro played on. I just like those songs, and the sound of the production—the ambience and the feel. Just the way the room sounds. We recorded that at Reciprocal Studios, which a lot of early Sub Pop records were recorded at, including Nirvana, Mudhoney and Tad. And *Superunknown*. Once again, it's the ambience—the implied and created room. And I like the material and the performances very much. There's a dark feel to it that is powerful, and is great with headphones on. *Badmotorfinger* I love because it sounds great in a car. It's got a lot of weird quirks in it—as is typical with Soundgarden. We always added that element of crazy and weird. We had an ability to not take ourselves too seriously, while committing to the heaviness. Sort of like laughing while kicking your ass."

As it turned out, this was a case where the critical praise equated sales, as *Superunknown* would debut at #1 in the US on the *Billboard 200* for the week of March 26th—rounding out a top-ten that also included (in order) Nine Inch Nails' *The Downward Spiral,* Ace of Base's *The Sign*, R. Kelly's *12 Play*, Toni Braxton's *Toni Braxton*, Mariah Carey's *Music Box,* Counting Crows' *August and Everything After,* Celine Dion's *The Colour of My Love,* Snoop Doggy Dogg's *Doggy Style,* and Enigma's *The Cross of Changes.*

"I think [*Superunknown*] did enter at #1, but its sales were never the meteoric rise of Nirvana or Pearl Jam," explained Kim. "It sold a lot of records—but over a steady period of time. That year that *Superunknown* came out, all four of the big Seattle bands had number one records. I did an interview with some guy—he said, 'Now Seattle is the greatest rock region in history. You surpassed Liverpool. You had four bands that have had number one records from your city in one year. That's never been done before'." And Kim isn't pulling our leg concerning this claim—within the span of just *six months*, all of Seattle's Big 4 reached #1 (Nirvana with *In Utero,* Pearl Jam with *Vs.,* Alice in Chains with *Jar of Flies,* and finally, *Superunknown*).

"I think the closest to that [the pinnacle of Soundgarden's career] is when our record debuted at #1 in the US," said Chris. "We did it without having to be pop stars. That's probably the moment when all of what we've tried to do and everything we felt about music brought us to a point where we were successful." Kim remembered where SG was when they found out the news. "We were in England when that record came out and we got the news that it entered at #1, which was kind of exciting. Well, it was exciting for about an hour and then it was business as usual—interviews and touring!"

And it wasn't just in the US that *Superunknown* topped the charts—as the feat was duplicated in Australia, Canada, and New Zealand, while reaching the top 10 in Norway (#5), Sweden (#3), Switzerland (#9), and the UK (#4). *SU* also proved to have staying power—selling three million copies in 1994 alone (hitting gold and platinum on the same day, June 3rd), with its last certification taking place in 1996—5x platinum. Certainly, if/when another certification takes place, the number should increase exponentially (and who knows...maybe even result in Soundgarden's first-ever "Diamond Award"—when an album sells ten-million copies). Without question, *SU* succeeded in finally helping Soundgarden infiltrate the mainstream and established them as an arena headliner (although they—like Pearl Jam at the time—would seek unusual venues to play, rather than the expected hallowed halls), and catapulted them into the highly coveted "rock elite" group.

Amusingly, Kim once recounted about how a manager of one of rock's biggest bands had successfully predicted big success for *Superunknown*—years earlier. "I was at a Metallica gig after *Badmotorfinger* had come out, and [Cliff] Bernstein had shown me some numbers of bands that had grown in a similar way—

including Metallica. He said, 'You guys are following a similar pattern. The next record, you make 'the record of your life,' and it's through the roof'."

Rightfully anticipating that *SU* would be a blockbuster, several different configurations of collectable vinyl were rolled out by A&M (orange, blue, and a lime-ish clear), which nowadays fetch pretty pennies. And on all versions of the album—except for us unlucky bastards in the United States of America—a 16th track was included, "She Likes Surprises." A well-mannered yet not exactly remarkable melodic rocker (and yet another CCC), its creator once recounted the song's overall importance to the *SU* sessions.

"I think Michael Beinhorn's greatest thumbprint actually occurred on the song 'She Likes Surprises,' which was not on the album. That was the first song I think we approached him with during pre-production, and he attempted to get us to try a couple of arrangement ideas, and we hated them, so that was pretty much the last time we listened to him. So that was the end of pre-production, and then going in for the actual production of the album, it sort of forced us to kind of circle back and be us. We kind of shut him down right away. That was his biggest moment."

In an article about *Superunknown* for *USA Today* (dated March 11, 1994), then-editor of *The Rocket,* Charles Cross, was quoted as saying, "People have talked about the Seattle music scene being over, but that clearly does not seem to be the case. The scene is amazingly healthy."

Unfortunately, a shocking and tragic event would prove otherwise—less than a month after the arrival of *Superunknown.*

CHAPTER 17
SUPERUNKNOWN II

As with most of Soundgarden's tours, before the launch of the planned worldwide trek in support of *Superunknown,* the band played a local/invite-only/warm-up show, at the Moore Theatre in Seattle, on January 7th. It also would have been around this time that footage was shot (but not aired until March) for an episode of MTV's *Headbangers Ball,* in which host Riki Rachtman traveled to Seattle to interview the band taking a break from tour rehearsal, and to go...bowling. In addition to various chats with the band, one standout scene included Chris running down a lane to kick down pins that stubbornly had remained standing erect (and at another point, Riki pointing out a similarity between the Guess Who's "American Woman" and "Spoonman").

Then, just over a week later, SG found themselves in Australia, for their first-ever trek in "the land down under" (to borrow a phrase from Men at Work) and in "the land of the rising sun" (to *almost* borrow a phrase from the Animals). However, the shows were an example of poor scheduling, as someone/somewhere obviously was figuring that *SU* would be ready to roar earlier than its eventual release in March.

"We wanted to have it out in time, and we thought of cancelling the dates until after the release, but the promoters and the label said to come anyway," Chris explained. "We haven't really discussed yet what we're going to play, the old stuff or the new. I guess it's going to be important to play some of the older music. I think we'll lean in that direction—we're going to be touring when we would have been rehearsing, so we'll have to work our way into the new album gradually. We haven't played much of it live yet."

Playing both smaller venues as well as headlining immense outdoor shows—as part of the Lolla-like Big Day Out Festival (on a bill that also included the likes of the Ramones, Björk, Smashing Pumpkins, Primus, and the Breeders, among others), from the middle of the month until the 5th of February (with a few New Zealand dates thrown in, as well). And Chris was pleasantly surprised by the audience's reaction—"We've had the other end, where we went to Europe with Guns N' Roses, playing in front of 60,000 people who didn't give a shit about us. This is kinda the opposite feeling."

Matt also added an interesting comparison, to a show several years before. "The first time we went to New York, it was just amazing, because we played CBGB's and we just had this blue vinyl single thing out, and people actually knew the words to our songs! That was a completely freaky experience; that was a pretty magical moment for me personally, but it's cool coming to Australia, somewhere we've never been, and seeing people know the lyrics and stuff."

Just a few months after the Australian shows, *Spin* journalist Jonathan Gold offered a humorous report of when two SG's crossed paths with one SP circa the Big Day Out. "In the lobby bar of one of the tallest hotels, Cornell and Thayil are settling back with a couple of beers when Billy Corgan from Smashing Pumpkins wanders through, and decides to join them for a strawberry margarita. Corgan chatters about the pain of his life, the supposed incompetence of his band (everybody rolls their eyes), the lifesaving virtues of Jungian therapy, bands that suck. Cornell gets up to leave. Corgan tells Thayil how important Soundgarden used to be to him, and he baits him by saying that the Pumpkins sometimes do a cover of Soundgarden's 'Outshined' that segues into a Depeche Mode song or something."

Chris also once recalled an instance when Soundgarden was dared by another band to show off their dance moves during the Big Day Out dates. "We went to a bar and the highly effeminate Urge Overkill were being very critical of the fact that we were too macho to dance. But then as soon as we got up and started dancing, they started making fun of us. I think they had that in mind all along."

Up next were a handful of Japanese shows in mid-Feb, which resulted in *Melody Maker* journalist Everett True giving a first-hand account of one of the shows...plus extracurricular activities. "The lecture hall-cum-venue for tonight's concert looks very sterile. No one is allowed to leave their seats, and there's apparently a strict ban on dancing. The band's performance is equally restrained: Ben spitting and knocking mic stands over in his disgust, Chris resorting to sarcasm and false cheerleading of the frankly bewildered audience. For the finale, they can't even be bothered to play a song—instead they fool around with distortion and feedback for an eternity."

"'Standing onstage tonight was like listening to a record that's had a thumb placed on the turntable,' Kim remarks later, annoyed with himself. 'Or listening to a tape recorder whose batteries are running down.' Afterwards the whole entourage go clubbing in American bars with—as Ben puts it—'a load of has-been models with more attitude than looks.' Kim gets into a brawl with a male model, girls dance on bars. Some of Smashing Pumpkins road crew and the Ramones show up—Soundgarden have just finished touring Australia and New Zealand with both bands. We could be back in Seattle."

Afterwards, the band regrouped and set their sights on launching a European tour in mid-March, which would at least be productive in so much that *Superunknown* would be released in conjunction with the dates. And Ben quickly saw the difference. "In Australia it came out the last day we were there, but by the time we were in Europe, the record was out for a while. The fans were singing the songs; they totally knew the record." So, with a recent #1 album and their largest-ever headlining tour just getting started, 1994 looked blindingly bright for Soundgarden. Unfortunately, the same could not be said about one of rock's leading figures.

From the outside looking in, it seemed like everything couldn't have been better for Kurt Cobain in early 1994. Especially if you believed the interviews he was giving to the press and to MTV at the time—including a quite positive-sounding cover story/interview for *Rolling Stone,* entitled *Success Doesn't Suck* (dated January 27th). According to Nirvana's leader, his personal life was rosy—he was happily married (to Hole singer/guitarist Courtney Love), had an infant daughter (a then one-and-a-half year-old Frances Bean Cobain), a mysterious stomach ailment had apparently cleared up, and his drug problems were behind him. And professionally, it all was swell—his band had released an album that they were incredibly proud of (their second chart-topper, *In Utero*), its band members were getting along (especially with the addition of Pat Smear on second guitar), and Nirvana was set to headline Lollapalooza that summer.

But due to facts that would surface later, this was not the case at all—Cobain was still struggling with heroin addiction and depression, Nirvana appeared to be on the brink of splitting up, and his marriage was seemingly on shaky ground. What was later confirmed as a suicide attempt occurred on March 3, 1994 at the Excelsior Hotel in Rome, when Cobain overdosed on the drug Rohypnol (a tranquilizer that can be used to assist with heroin withdrawal), but was saved after his wife, Courtney Love, called the front desk, which resulted in Cobain being rushed to Umberto I Polyclinic Hospital and having his stomach pumped. Instead of making it known to the public that Cobain had ingested 60 pills of the drug and left a suicide note, it was decided to make it seem like it was an accidental overdose.

"We heard rumors from people that had crossed paths with him, or people that were closer to him," remembered Kim. "And of course, there was stuff that would pop up in the tabloid and the gossip mill. I don't think Kurt himself was tabloid fodder, but there were elements in his life that openly solicit that kind of attention. So every once in a while, you'd hear shit on the news, the radio, or in a magazine. I remember when there was the incident in Rome, they were calling it 'a botched suicide attempt.' I probably knew what you knew—plus some extra-added scenester gossip. That's hard to give credence to all that we hear. In retrospect, a lot of what we heard was very credible."

After leaving the hospital on March 8th, Cobain flew back to Seattle on the 12th, and on the 18th, Love called the police to report that he had locked himself in the bedroom of their house with several guns and was threatening to kill himself. Although Cobain was taken downtown by the police, he was not formally booked, but had several of the guns seized. Then on March 25th, an intervention concerning Cobain's drug use took place, which resulted in him agreeing to check into rehab. And it turns out that Susan had lent a hand, as she once explained—"Layne had been in and out of rehab, and Layne and Kurt spent a lot of time together. We were all in fear of what could happen. Alice was working with a really wonderful guy from New York, Lou Cox, a doctor who was instrumental in helping Aerosmith through their recovery."

"I got an emergency, out of the blue call from Courtney, who had no love lost for me. Previously, I had been a target of hers. She was in a very desperate, understandably frightened state. She said, 'You have to help me—Kurt's going to kill himself. What should I do?' I said, 'First thing, you have to make sure you're safe and your daughter's safe. I will connect you to the people to do an intervention—you have to make sure the people that Kurt trusts are there.' I hooked the manager up with Lou Cox. They decided to do an intervention, but they decided to use a different interventionist. And not everybody came to the intervention. I wasn't part of it—I was not 'inner circle' with them whatsoever. They did the intervention, and it went very poorly."

Kurt did agree to seek outside help, and on March 30th, he checked into Exodus Recovery Center in Los Angeles, but a day later abruptly left (by supposedly climbing over a six-foot high wall), and returned back to Seattle. On April 8th, Cobain's body was discovered by an electrician at the couple's Lake Washington Boulevard home—dead at the age of 27, from a gunshot wound to the head (it was later estimated that he had actually died three days earlier).

I remember finding out about the sad news by a friend barging into the house a few others and I were at, imploring us to put on MTV right away—where we saw the channel's then-news correspondent, Kurt Loder, live on the air, sharing the unhappy update, and discussing Cobain's short-yet-brilliant career. As I was still quite young at the time, it was all hard to process, and seemed so unfathomable that someone with that much going for themselves (and the fact that he had a young child) would want to commit suicide. But years later, Jeff Ament told me something about Cobain's passing that I completely agree with—"Unless you've been manic-depressive, I don't think you can fully comprehend those sorts of actions."

It so happened that when the news broke of Cobain's death, Soundgarden were in Paris, France, as they had a show that evening at the Elysée Montmartre, on a bill that also featured one-time Nirvana tourmates, Tad. As France is on GMT (Greenwich Mean Time), it is six hours ahead of EST (Eastern Standard Time), so probably, Soundgarden was on stage already by the time the news was first announced. Tad's bassist, Kurt Danielson, was the one that broke the news to the members of SG. "I heard this rumor that Kurt had killed himself. So I called up Van [Conner, Screaming Trees bassist]—who's my brother-in-law, married to my sister. I knew Mark Lanegan was close to Kurt, and I thought Van might know what's going on. Van said, 'There is something going on—call me back in two hours.' And I did, by that time he had the facts. So it was contingent upon me to get the Soundgarden and Tad guys all in one room, and get all the reporters out of the room, so I can have some private time with my friends, and share some bad news. There was no good way to say it. I don't remember what I said—I just went ahead and announced it after the room was sealed." Kim's memory of what immediately transpired was simple—"I never saw so many big, hairy, temperamental guys sitting around crying."

"It put a pallor over everything," recalled Susan. "It was so shocking. It's one thing to lose someone to an accident, and it's another thing to lose someone to suicide. It scared everybody— and it certainly scared me. At that time, Eddie's first wife [Beth Liebling] and I were very close—it was terrifying to think of those guys out there. They were both on tour. When the tour manager called to say that they had gotten the news, the Soundgarden guys had just gone wild. They started destroying the dressing room— out of not being able to deal with the profoundness of hearing something like that. I just told him, 'Let them go—let them do what they need to do'."

In an article for *Rolling Stone,* journalist Kim Neely was also on tour with the band at the time, and later reported, "The following day, a day off in Manchester, England, passes in an alcohol-fueled blur. The hotel is a gloomy, sprawling old building with a lot of mahogany, dark wall paper and gaudy gold fixtures;

Thayil, Cornell and Cameron, holed up in their rooms, don't turn up all day. Shepherd, a few members of Tad and a few of the crew members spend the day in a neighborhood pub. After nightfall, Thayil turns up, and he and Shepherd take up residence in the hotel bar, drinking and talking until well into the morning. Neither of them talks much about Cobain, but when they do, it's clear they're still struggling to make sense of the tragedy. 'I just wish I knew whether he won or lost,' Thayil says at one point."

Back in Seattle, Susan was helping any way she could— which in retrospect, was extremely kind of her, as she was previously purportedly a target of Kurt/Courtney (they had incorrectly assumed that Susan was a source used for an earlier controversial article about Courtney in *Vanity Fair* by Lynn Hirschberg, and the line "My favorite inside source" from the Nirvana song "Rape Me" was supposedly a veiled reference to her). "And then I went into service work at that point—literally, service work, [and helped] get the services together at a private church, and also at the Seattle Center. I went to the service with Eddie's wife. At the end of it, I had the same sort of overwhelming compassion for Courtney that I felt to a complete stranger—Yoko Ono—when John Lennon was shot. My heart just broke for her. I wanted to do something—I wanted to say something. After the service in the church, I walked up to her to offer support. About ten feet away, she noticed I was coming towards her, and she turned her back on me and walked away."

"I wasn't one of his close friends," Chris once admitted. "Kim knew him better and Ben was very close with them and with him. He had toured with them early on; there was a time when he was going to be a fourth member of Nirvana, but he didn't do it because he wasn't really necessarily invited to write songs. It was something in a way similar to losing Andy, or losing friends that died after that. It's not so much the person and the relationship with them, but the creative inspiration that person has and I would get from that person. My perception of the world of music at large artistically shrank, because suddenly this brilliant guy was gone. I'm not even talking about what he meant culturally; I'm talking about his creativity. It was super inspiring from the very first demo

I ever heard. It broadened my mental picture of what the world was creatively, and suddenly a big chunk of it fell off."

When asked if that was also how he felt about Andy, Chris added, "Yeah. The tragedy was much more than the fact that I would never see him again—it was that I would never hear him again. There's this projection I had with Andy, Kurt, Jeff Buckley [who would die in 1997] and other friends of mine that died of looking into the future at all these amazing things they're going to do. I'll never be able to predict what that is. All this music that will come out that will challenge me and inspire me—that sort of romantic, dramatic version of the perspective. When that goes away, for me in particular, it was a really hard thing. And it continues to be a hard thing."

"There's a large part of Soundgarden history, to me, that's wrapped up in that conflict of losing these incredible creative lenses of what I imagine is this incredible, infinite world of the power of creativity. These were people, and people you could share experiences with while you're learning what your power of that creativity is. So part of my memory of every record, and certainly *Superunknown*, there's an eeriness in there, a kind of unresolvable sadness or indescribable longing that I've never really tried to isolate and define and fully understand. But it's always there. It's like a haunted thing. Then there were these miraculous moments existing around a similar time, one of which is Eddie showing up and starting a new band with your friends that just lost this amazing person and having that creative output and outpouring be so phenomenal. The degree to which it changed the face of rock music in the world is this pretty incredible thing. There were these huge, amazing ups, but also these difficult conflicts I've never been able to resolve."

Ben once not only confirmed Chris' earlier claim about he being friends with Kurt, but also, recounted how they first met. "They like to say that he had charisma. *Bullshit.* He didn't have any—he was just 'Kurt,' and that was that endearing quality. *He was just Kurt.* I met him in Olympia; I don't even think he'd started Nirvana yet. I met him at a party—we were both sitting on the end of a couch and I go, 'You're like me, huh? You always wind up at this spot at the party?' And he says, 'Yep.' Everyone else is partying, and we're sitting there, being loners on the end of a couch. There was thankfully a guitar, and we'd swap it back and forth. Smoking cigarettes, talking, and kicking back."

Chris also voiced his thoughts about Kurt's supposed struggle to come to grips with fame, and what drives someone to commit suicide. "It might not have been something that he wanted, but at the same time, he made videos, y'know? Same as me. If he didn't wanna be in that situation, he didn't have to make another video after 'Teen Spirit.' It all points to something else. It wasn't just: this guy's a heroin addict and it made him crazy and he killed himself. Or: this guy gets bothered by teenagers and he hates it so he killed himself. That's probably the most romantic view, but it's not the most real view. You don't know what drives somebody to do that, but if I ever committed suicide, I would do it in a way that meant no one ever knew that it was suicide— because to me, the biggest fear of killing myself would be what it would do to my friends and family. If things are fucked enough that I want to kill myself, the last thing I want to do is go out and really fucking hurt a bunch of other people."

Instead of packing it in and canceling the remaining dates of the European tour (they had a week or so left of shows), SG soldiered on—wrapping it up on April 16th, at the Brixton Academy. And with a capacity of nearly 5,000, it was their largest UK headlining show up to that point. With over a month off before the start of the North American leg of the *SU* tour, SG found themselves serving as cover boys for the April 1994 issue of *Spin* (alongside the headline *SOUNDGARDEN KILLS GRUNGE DEAD*), while the album's second single was issued on April 25th, "The Day I Tried to Live."

With its cover image (a sunrise between two houses) recycled from the inside booklet of *Superunknown,* the UK CD single and 12" vinyl included an exceptional voice/acoustic guitar version (sounding like a 12-string guitar) of "Like Suicide," as well as a live recording of "Kickstand" (from the soggy Jones Beach show the previous summer). However, the single did not exactly scorch the charts, as it peaked at a skimpy #42 in the UK, but did manage to reach #13 on the US Mainstream Rock Chart. A so-so video was also shot (directed by Matt Mahurin)—which featured such highlights as a gentleman who continually defies gravity, Chris singing into an old school/Elvis-era mic, and the band performing amongst small fires.

Strangely, less than a month later, *another* single/video was issued, for "Black Hole Sun," on May 13th (and featuring a cover image of a chap seemingly suffering from a headache, with neon icicle-shapes surrounding his noggin). And the reason I used the word "strangely" is because it's unusual for an artist to issue singles/videos so close to each other—especially back in the good old days of the music biz—as they usually wanted to space them out to get maximum prolonged impact on radio and MTV. But Chris once gave a reason why it was rushed out in time for the most sizzling of the four seasons—"That's one reason I'm glad 'Black Hole Sun' will be out as a single this summer. 'Cause that's the time when people start thinking back about all of their other summers. Maybe I could rename it 'Endless Black Hole Summer'."

It had become clear from the get-go that "BHS" was going to be the album's go-to single. As Kim recalled, "When Hiro heard the ['Black Hole Sun'] demo, he said, 'There's your hit'—just like Ben said when he heard 'Smells Like Teen Spirit'." And Susan had similar feelings. "['Black Hole Sun']—you couldn't help but find the toe tapping and find it stuck in your head in the middle of the night. But I felt that way about 'Fell on Black Days.' You have to remember; I heard so many Chris songs along the way that were equally as beautiful, and as absorbing and memorable. A lot of beautiful, quirky songs, that no one's ever heard to this day. It wasn't a stretch to hear him write a song like that."

Hooking up with director Howard Greenhalgh, the "BHS" clip was certainly SG's most seen and most popular (*of their entire career*). And despite the song's sullen lyrics, a decision was made to make the look of the video the complete opposite. "When the director was talking to us about that idea, we thought it was a brilliant sort of juxtaposition," recalled Chris. "Get the little sunny things and the creepy things. Because both of those elements are in the song, really—it's bright and it's chipper...but it's kind of grim."

As it turns out, "the little sunny things and the creepy things" is a spot-on summary of the clip—the band miming the song with a blue screen behind them (including a fast-moving blue sky with clouds early on, then a storm blowing debris later), as well as a wide variety of characters whose faces ultimately become distorted. The end result was one of MTV's most played rock videos of 1994, and Soundgarden's first bonafide, global smash hit—hitting #5 in Canada, #6 in Australia, #7 in Ireland, and #12 in the UK, while topping the US Mainstream Rock chart (but shockingly, never registering a single placement on *Billboard's Hot 100 Singles Chart*).

Oft-times, the mark of a great song is that other artists cover it. And this was certainly the case concerning "Black Hole Sun," as everyone from Peter Frampton to the Moog Cookbook to even schmaltzy singer Paul Anka (!) have subsequently taken it out for a test drive. But one of the first artists to do so was alt-popsters Cibo Matto, who included their cover on a self-titled EP in 1995. "We thought it would be funny to cover a band like Soundgarden," explained the group's multi-instrumentalist, Yuka Honda. "In the way that they're a big guitar band and they would scream 'Black Hole Sun!' We did it in a way that would reflect French movies, but it's such a great song I can also hear doing it in a Bob Marley way, or a New Orleans way."

"I was glad," Chris admits about "BHS" becoming a radio/MTV hit. "Considering all the different songs we had, I really liked the fact that this song, stylistically, sat outside of any genre, and it wasn't really comparable to anything anyone else was doing at the time or before or since. It seems to stand on its own. And it very much did seem to lend itself to Soundgarden. But I don't think for one second I have the ability to sit down and write a hit song."

On May 27th at the PNE Forum, the *SU* tour resumed, and was followed up two days later by a show at the Kitsap County Fairgrounds. Why mention the latter date? Simple...to put in perspective how colossal Soundgarden's popularity had become—this was the same outdoor venue that they had played two years earlier as part of Lollapalooza, and now, *they* were the headliner. And when it was announced that SG would soon be setting up shop for a two-night engagement in NYC, my friends and I were most certainly eager. But instead of booking the show into one of the expected local larger concert halls (Madison Square Garden, Nassau Coliseum, Roseland, etc.), they opted to perform in a venue that I have never heard of a rock show occurring in before or since—the New York State Armory (also known as the 69th Regiment Armory, and located at 68 Lexington Avenue). Two dates were announced—June 16th and 17th—and for whatever reason, we opted for the second night.

It just so happens that this was also at the exact same time that the Long Island Railroad was on strike, so instead of taking a convenient train ride in, we had to carpool it. The summer of '94 also proved to be a scorchingly hot one in New York, and I recall it still being quite sizzling upon our walk from where we parked our vehicle over to this mysterious venue. But in the day and age of superior air conditioning, these harsh conditions would soon be alleviated, right? *Wrong.* It turned out that either the AC was not functioning properly, was not up to snuff to accurately keep several thousand human bodies cooled off, or there was simply no AC installed at all—'cause to quote the great poet Paul Stanley, it was *hotter than hell* inside the Armory. As a result, later that evening, I recall Chris either dedicating a song to or merely pointing out "men with breasts" in the audience, as I guess the oven-like heat resulted in more than a few gentlemen who hadn't visited the inside of a gymnasium in a while taking off their shirts.

Similar to Roseland '92, I felt courageous enough to wiggle my way towards the front before SG started (I unfortunately missed the other two bands on the bill, Tad and Eleven, due to traffic during our commute). And instead of SG coming right out or slowly appearing to pre-recorded music (a la the beginning of "Searching with My Good Eye Closed"), the already-sweaty crowd was treated to an odd/artsy-fartsy short-film (latter I found out it was set to a Ben-penned instrumental, entitled "Night Surf"), which followed a young boy traveling around on his bicycle, and featured one scene reminiscent of Metallica's "Enter Sandman" clip (the youngster being chased by a vehicle while on his bike). Finally, the film ended, the screen pulled up to the rafters, and...voila! Soundgarden were playing possum and were hiding behind the screen, patiently waiting for it to end, before immediately launching into a potent one-two punch of "Jesus Christ Pose" and "Spoonman."

It also became quickly apparent that although they were now headlining larger venues, Soundgarden was forgoing a Mötley Crüe-esque light show in favor of slide projections behind them which included photos or just solid colors—and with minimal use of a lighting truss above. In other words, it was more to help set the mood—and to let their performance and the music do most of the talking. Other standout memories of the Armory show include Chris giving the crowd an update concerning the score of the NBA Finals, since the New York Knicks were one of the teams competing (they would go on to win the game that night, 91-84, but ultimately, lose the series to the Houston Rockets), as well as commenting on an event that will seemingly live on forever in pop culture.

It was on this evening that OJ Simpson—with the aid of his old football playing buddy, Al Cowlings—decided to try and outrun the law, via a white Ford Bronco (as Simpson was instructed to turn himself in to the LAPD on suspicion of brutally murdering his ex-wife, Nicole Brown, and a friend of hers, Ron Goldman). Most television stations immediately broke to footage of the low-speed chase of the Bronco being followed by police cars on the I-5 freeway and Interstate 405. As a result, someone must have alerted Chris about the goings-on (he had already introduced the song "Mailman" as "The OJ story" that evening), because between songs at some point, he made another announcement to the crowd concerning OJ (to which I must admit, I thought he was joking about at first)—to which Ben stepped up to the mic and declared, "Innocent until proven guilty!"

And speaking of Ben, the three times I had seen him perform up to this point, he seemed to be pleased on stage. However, on this night, he appeared to be agitated—arguing with someone in the crowd, and even disgustingly hocking a loogie randomly into the audience. This type of annoyance/irritation from Ben towards Soundgarden's audience would only seem to exacerbate from this point on. But overlooking this one concern, the band was able to soldier on in the heat, and hand in an outstanding—and seemingly, never-ending—performance, which also included a surprise rendition of the early classic "Hand of God," and ended with readings of "Fresh Tendrils" (which saw Eleven's Natasha Shneider adding keyboards) and "Head Down" (during which, at the end, Ben and Chris joined in on percussion). Certainly, one of the most memorable SG performances I have ever witnessed/endured.

And another career milestone occurred at this point. On *Rolling Stone's* June 16th cover, all four Soundgardeners were spotted (and inside, were the focus of the aforementioned feature by Kim Neely, entitled *Into the Superunknown: Soundgarden Explore Rock & Roll's Heart of Darkness*). And yet another sign that the band's popularity had reached a higher plane—they were the focus of a news piece on CNN. During the two-minute clip, Chris and Ben are interviewed by CNN entertainment news correspondent Mark Scheerer, in which they discuss such topics as how Chris felt about a writer comparing *Superunknown* to "the best work of Led Zeppelin and Van Halen." Chris' reply? "I wish it made me feel good. I don't put that much importance into other people's opinions, really. I would think if I read that about my band or that record, I would think that that was probably laid on a little bit thick."

Other topics discussed included that some of SG's songs ("Rusty Cage," "Outshined," "Superunknown," and "Kickstand") were used in a popular video game, *Road Rash,* while snippets of both the "Spoonman" and "Black Hole Sun" videos are shown, as well as a clip of SG performing "The Day I Tried to Live" in concert. Additionally, a promo-only compilation was issued on June 28th, entitled *Foreshocks,* which featured a non-descript cover, and twelve previously-released tracks—mostly their most popular tunes ("Black Hole Sun," "Spoonman," "Outshined," etc.), but also, three non-LP tunes ("Heretic," "Come Together," and "HIV Baby").

The *SU* tour continued throughout July and into August (with Reverend Horton Heat and You Am I taking over as openers)—including a Canadian show on August 6th at Molson Park, in Barrie, Ontario, which saw both the Soundgarden and Nine Inch Nails summer tours combine together for one day, including all the tours' openers (and featuring a pre-fame Marilyn Manson on the bill). Rumors also swirled that Soundgarden would be included as part of the Woodstock '94 line-up (set to take place from August 12-14 in Saugerties, New York)—which proved to be a fabrication. "I think we'd much rather play for the twenty-somethings than have to do a little nostalgia bit for the forty-nothings," Kim explained at the time. But by the time the North American leg ended with a homecoming show in Seattle on August 13th, things seemed to had taken a surprising turn—according to Matt. "Then towards the end of that tour, Kurt died, [and] I think the whole fabric of our group was starting to unravel a little bit."

Kim remembered it a little bit differently. "It started off strong—I don't know if the fabric of the band was coming undone. I don't think there was any interpersonal tensions—I think there were stresses from being on the road. I don't think anybody was having problems with anybody else. That might have come to play more after the next album. Our last show was at Memorial Stadium in Seattle—a really bad show. Chris' voice was having a really fucked-up time. When the show was over, he just walked off stage, got in a car, and took off." As a result, a planned European tour was scrapped—including a performance at the Reading Festival on August 29th (billed right below the day's headliners, the Red Hot Chili Peppers), and no further shows were performed by the band that year.

"I think we kinda overdid it," explained Chris. "We were playing five or six nights a week and my voice pretty much took a beating. Towards the end of the American tour I felt like I could still kinda sing, but I wasn't really giving the band a fair shake. You don't buy a ticket to see some guy croak for two hours! That seemed like kind of a rip off. We've never been the kind of band that cancels a tour when somebody breaks a finger. It would have to be something fairly extreme—and to me, that was. Plus, as a singer, you've gotta be careful. If your voice is fatigued you could probably still go on, but then if you do a bunch more shows, all of a sudden you might never get to do a show again or make another record! It's pretty weird, dangerous, and ambiguous territory, 'cause nobody really knows, y'know? The doctor will say, 'Well, your voice is fatigued.' Thanks, here's 200 bucks—I already knew that!"

But despite SG being prematurely pulled off the road, two more singles/videos did appear—"My Wave" and "Fell on Black Days." The precise release dates have been lost over the sands of time, but I recall that both bubbled to the surface late in '94. The "MW" CD single sported part of an unidentified large aquatic creature jumping out of water on its cover, and featured such extra add-ons as a "Steve Fisk remix" of "Spoonman," plus a great demo of "Birth Ritual," and a live recording of the a-side (once again from Jones Beach '93). A not-all-that-memorable "MW" video was also cobbled together by co-directors Henry Shepherd and Doug Pray—which combined scenes from the "Night Surf" tour video plus live footage of the group miming the song (filmed at a show on August 11th, at the Max Bell Arena in Calgary, Alberta).

Although a great album track, "My Wave" doesn't exactly scream "potential hit single," and probably wasn't the wisest selection to follow up "BHS" (could you have really pictured it played on pop radio at the time, alongside Ace of Base's "The Sign," Lisa Loeb's "Stay," or Salt-N-Pepa's "Whatta Man"?). As a result, the single did not cash in on the buzz caused by "BHS," nor did it provide a significant chart presence globally (although it did manage to climb to #11 on *Billboard's Mainstream Rock Chart*).

The fourth/final single from *Superunknown*, "Fell on Black Days," featured a cover image of what appears to be a foggy forest at nighttime, and *did* deliver chart-wise, hitting #10 in Finland, #14 in Ireland, #24 in the UK, and #4 on *Billboard's*

Mainstream Rock Chart)—serving as further proof that "FoBD" should have immediately followed "BHS" as a single. Issued as various single configurations in the UK, several extra tracks were utilized, including a killer *SU* outtake, "Kyle Petty, Son of Richard" (co-penned by Chris and Kim), a "video version" of the a-side, a Kim soundscape entitled "Motorcycle Loop," and a live recording of the a-side (from a performance on August 16, 1993, at Pine Knob Music Theatre in Clarkston, Michigan).

Concerning "KP, SoR," as its title states, stock car racing driver Kyle Petty is the son of former NASCAR driver Richard Petty, and lyrically, appeared to get into the mindset of a determined racer. Musically based around two sturdy riffs (a main motif, and also another during the part that Mr. Cornell warns, "I'm gonna get to you"), I'd be bold to declare "KP, SoR" as one of SG's best-ever b-sides—and easily could have made the cut for *SU.* Yep, it's *that good.*

And the reason for a "video version" of "FoBD" is because for the video shot by director Jake Scott, the audio is newly recorded (however, since it wasn't a major improvement over the *SU* version, it makes one wonder...was it entirely necessary?). But the video was a winner—a simple clip shot in black and white at Bad Animals Studio, you get to see Ben scowl, Chris sporting a "90" long-sleeve shirt and a bulky Gretsch guitar he's never been spotted playing again, and close-ups of Kim soloing and Matt swatting. And it bears mentioning that two Soundgarden tracks, "Jesus Christ Pose" and the acoustic version of "Like Suicide" were included on the soundtrack to the film *SFW,* which would hit the racks on September 27th.

Although they may have been off the road for the remainder of '94, both Chris and Kim did make at least one more public appearance—at the MTV Video Music Awards on September 8th, at Radio City Music Hall in NYC. Hosted by Roseanne Barr, the show saw SG take home the award for "Best Metal/Hard Rock Video," beating out the likes of Aerosmith's "Cryin'," Anthrax's "Black Lodge," and the Rollins Band's "Liar." Both dressed quite casually/similarly (the same black long-sleeved shirt—with insect images on the sleeves—and with plain t-shirts over it), the pair were interviewed pre-show by Kurt Loder, and then post-show by Tabitha Soren, and accepted their award by presenters Denis Leary and Naomi Campbell. Chris does all the talking during the acceptance (while Kim sips a can of beer)—apologizing to Aerosmith for taking the prize, thanking Susan Silver and Howard Greenhalgh (plus others linked to the video) and stating, "I don't know if 'Black Hole Sun' is a metal song, but I'll take this."

As it turns out, one gent in attendance took exception to Chris questioning metal—Anthrax's Charlie Benante. "I'll never forget, we were at the *MTV Video Music Awards*, and we were up for 'Metal Video of the Year' for a song called 'Black Lodge,' and Soundgarden was in the same category, and they won. And I remember Chris Cornell accepting, saying, 'I don't know if we're a heavy metal band.' And we all looked at each other like, 'Motherfucker...you are the voice of heavy metal! Are you crazy? You sound just like fucking Sammy Hagar! And now you're trying to change your stripes'?"

However, Kim had a more unruffled standout memory of attending the *VMA's* that year. "The first time we met the guys in Green Day, I think we were at the *MTV Video Music Awards*, and they were performing. Outside, Kurt Loder asked Soundgarden if we were there to see Aerosmith, and I said, 'No.' Are you there to see the Beastie Boys or Green Day? 'No.' Although Aerosmith, *Toys in the Attic* and *Rocks* are two of my all-time favorite albums, and *Dookie* is definitely a classic album, and the Beastie Boys, I'm not going to turn down *Paul's Boutique* or *Licensed to Ill*. But I remember being asked if we were there to see those bands, and answering, 'No.' We came there just to see the experience, and check out what the *MTV Awards* were like, because we'd never been to one. And also, because we were nominated. We went there and we won. That's why we were there. I guess MTV wanted us to promote it, they wanted us to give this pre-promotion, like, 'Yeah! Aerosmith is going to rock! And Green Day is going to rock'!"

"And then I remember not being able to drink there. There was no beer anywhere. Someone who worked with the production staff of the *MTV Awards*, we were kind of whining, like, 'Fuck...we're here for the next couple of hours and there's no goddamn beer?!' Someone ran out and found a six-pack of some crappy beer—I think it was Miller Lite or Bud Lite. It wasn't that bad—a carrot's as close as a rabbit gets to a diamond. You can't drink it backstage, because 'We're not serving any alcohol here.' So Chris and I went down into the stairwell, and we each grabbed a beer. When we go to accept our award, I refuse to leave my beer at my seat, because I knew my friends were going to drink it, so I took it with me to accept the award. Not to show off and endorse the beer, not to show people that I was drinking—just because I knew the beer would be empty by the time I got back to my seat."

"So we were standing there, in a stairwell, drinking a beer, and all of a sudden, these two little guys come running by. They're running up this stairwell, and I'm like, 'What the fuck?' For some reason, we thought it was limited access, and we could hide and drink our beer without getting in trouble or having our manager find us. And these two kids come running up and they stop. It was Billie Joe and Mike Dirnt. They go, 'I remember the first time we saw you! You guys were opening for the Meat Puppets at Berkeley Square! *That was a cool gig*'!"

Back in the days of spending a pretty penny on bootleg CD's (and actual *mass-produced* bootleg CD's, not mere CD-R's), there was a local music vendor by me that specialized in official and unofficial releases. You would never know what new goodies lay in store (no pun intended)—you would just have to look under the listing in the racks of your favorite artists, and see if they had stocked any intriguing/uncommon titles. So imagine my surprise at some point in late '94 when I was flipping through the SG section, and happened to come across a titillating title by the name of *Stolen Prayers*. And its contents proved to be extremely enticing for me to plunk down an investment of $19.99...although crediting it as a "Soundgarden" release was a bit misleading—it was comprised mostly of previously unheard solo Chris demos (the fact that only Chris is seen on the CD case's front cover perhaps should have provided a clue).

The first four songs turned out to be plucked from the "Poncier demos" that Chris had recorded a few years earlier (as part of his exercise in songwriting, from song titles Jeff Ament had thought up for a cassette case on the set of *Singles*). All of these songs do not feature a full band accompaniment, so it's Chris and only Chris. The first tune, "Nowhere But You," turns out to be not one of the better ones, as it just meanders along for over five minutes—ultimately resulting in the realization that *there was a reason* that Soundgarden passed on recording it. Up next was a little ditty by the name of..."Spoonman," which as mentioned earlier, is quite a remarkable listen, as you hear that the entire structure of the bloody song is pretty much there, already all mapped out/for all to see.

But it would be the third track, "Fluttergirl," that proved to be the gem of the entire collection. The song would later be re-worked/re-recorded as a full band version a few years later for Chris' first-ever solo album, *Euphoria Morning,* but I always felt that this bare bones version is without question the superior version. A gorgeous ballad that due to its bare bones accompaniment (just voice, acoustic guitar, and some electric guitar overdubbed on top—as well as a surprisingly great guitar solo), I'm quite certain that I am not alone in thinking that this is probably one of the best tunes Cornell has ever penned. Perhaps ultimately sensing that the original contained a certain "something" to it, this version (as well as the aforementioned "Nowhere But You") would later be released officially as b-sides on Chris' first-ever solo single, "Can't Change Me," in 1999. The fourth and final track from the Poncier demos was a rocker entitled "Missing" (which of the Poncier tracks, was the only one that sounds as if a full band is providing back up)—and seems like it could have potentially been a worthy song for Soundgarden to take on. But for reasons unknown, was never welcomed with open arms.

Up next are three tracks listed as "Songs for Ozzy"— "Stolen Prayer," "Heartfist," and "Unholy War"—which would lead one to believe that they were submitted (or *meant* to be submitted) to the one and only John Michael Osbourne to record for his next solo offering, which would have been 1995's Michael Beinhorn-produced *Ozzmosis*. However, more astute metalheads will recognize that while although Ozzy never took on any of these tracks, another legendary shock rocker *did*—Vincent Damon Furnier, better known as Alice Cooper. On his 1994 offering, *The Last Temptation,* two of these tracks, "Stolen Prayer" and "Unholy War," were not only recorded by Alice, but Chris even provides guest vocals for both, while "Heartfist" got the old heave-ho.

And if that wasn't enough CC demos for ya...there were more! Three tracks, "Black Cat," "Angel on Fire," and "Reach Down," were listed as "Temple of the Dog demos," and one track was already familiar, "RD," as it was re-recorded/included on TotD's self-titled debut. And while the other two tracks aren't bad, again, there was a reason why they did not get re-recorded for the album—they were simply not as stellar as the tracks that made the cut. And then rounding out the disc were two live recordings— "Black Hole Sun" and "Head Down." Listed as being recorded in Kitsap, Washington (which would have been on May 29, 1994), these lo-fi audience recordings turn out to supposedly be from another show, Oslo, Norway (on March 23, 1994).

Also in 1994, three of Chris' siblings, Peter, Katy, and Suzy, were playing locally as the band Inflatable Soule, and issued a self-produced CD, entitled *So Sad.* If you are expecting grunge sounds, you will be far off the mark. The band specialized in an acoustic rock-based sound more in line with the likes of Rusted Root and the Dave Matthews Band (but admittedly, with more of a hard rock element than the other two aforementioned hippy-dippy bands)—as evidenced by a tune that a low-budget video was filmed for, "Little Bit of Heaven." Yet, the band proved to be short-lived—but did enjoy some media coverage at the time (surprising though that an indie or major label didn't take a chance on them, due to the esteemed Cornell name and all).

Looking back on 1994 as it drew to a close, it was hard for Soundgarden to make heads or tails of it from a professional and personal standpoint, according to Kim. "Around the time Kurt killed himself, the Sonics, the team with the best record in the

NBA, lose in the playoffs. Tad calls me up and says his label dropped him. At one point, you had four bands from Seattle entering the charts at #1 within half a year, and then, all of a sudden, one of these bands is gone forever. Then baseball season is canceled, aborted right in the middle of it for the first time in years. But then, amongst that period of time, our record enters at #1, goes gold, and we're on the cover of *Rolling Stone*. There were these incredible high points in our career and incredible low points in our personal lives and in the careers of other bands. It was hard to make sense out of it. Were we supposed to feel good or bad?"

Let me help by trying to put it into perspective for you, Kim—according to the Chinese zodiac sign, 1994 was the year of the dog. However, I beg to differ. *1994 was the year of Soundgarden.*

Flower single (L-R: Kim, Hiro, Chris, and Matt)

Loud Love single (L-R: Matt, Chris, Kim and Jason)

Chris and Kim live at Sundance in Bay Shore, NY:
January 20, 1990

Soundgarden shot in Seattle
(Ben quenching his thirst)

Jesus Christ pose...or impersonating his shirt's pose?

Live at Warehouse 429 in NYC: October 17, 1991

Live at Roseland in NYC: May 9, 1992

Pulse! cover (March 1994): *Superunknown* era

PATTI SMITH / BECK / IMPERIAL TEEN / OASIS / HAYDEN

SPIN

EXCLUSIVE

SIN CITY: SEX IN THE VATICAN

Soundgarden
Superwellknown by Mike Rubin

PLUS SPIN'S SUMMER ENTERTAINMENT GUIDE

JULY 1996 $2.95 CAN $3.95/UK £2.25

Spin cover (July 1996): *Down on the Upside* era

Artifacts: sticker, t-shirt design, backstage pass

Live at Jones Beach, NY: July 9, 2011

Chris

Kim

Ben

Matt

Backscreen images and Chris in the crowd

Chris Cornell: 1964-2017

CHAPTER 18
9 5

Similar to two years earlier, 1995 was supposed to be a year off for Soundgarden—to write and prepare for the follow-up to *Superunknown*. However, shortly after the dawn of the new year (January 8th), the lads accepted an invite to appear on *Pearl Jam's Self-Pollution Radio Show*, via a broadcast that originated from Eddie Vedder's house, that included additional performances by the likes of Pearl Jam, Mudhoney, and Mad Season.

For the SG portion, the hits were forgone in place of four uncommon tunes or renditions—"Blind Dogs" (which would soon be issued on a soundtrack, more on that soon), a complete overhauling of "Fell on Black Days" (which did not resemble the *SU* version at all), the *SU* b-side "Kyle Petty, Son of Richard," and a preview of a song that would appear on the next SG album, "No Attention." Video footage also exists of their appearance, but it is single-camera shot and focuses almost entirely on Ben and Matt (both seated), so it's not exactly the most exciting SG footage to choose from. But it *does* include Chris at one point apologizing to Eddie for spilling coffee in his kitchen. And the following evening, Chris, Kim, and Ben appeared on the nationally syndicated radio show, *Rockline* (emanated from Bad Animals Studio), where they took phone calls from listeners.

Then, on the night of March 1st, all four members of SG were spotted at the Shrine Auditorium in Los Angeles. The occasion? The 37th Annual Grammy Awards—hosted by Paul Reiser. While they did not perform, SG did collect two awards that evening—"Best Hard Rock Performance" for "Black Hole Sun" (beating out Alice in Chains' "I Stay Away," Beastie Boys' "Sabotage," Green Day's "Longview," and Pearl Jam's "Go") and "Best Metal Performance" for "Spoonman" (beating out Anthrax/Public Enemy's live version of "Bring the Noise," Megadeth's "99 Ways to Die," Pantera's "I'm Broken," and the Rollins Band's "Liar"). They were also up for two additional awards that year—"Best Rock Song" for "Black Hole Sun" and "Best Rock Album" for *Superunknown,* but lost out to Bruce Springsteen's "Streets of Philadelphia" and the Rolling Stones'

Voodoo Lounge, respectively. They did televise the win and acceptance speech for "Best Metal Performance" (with the award being presented by BB King and Al Green), which saw Matt get a round of applause when he said, "I just want to thank my mom, for letting me practice drums in her house for over ten years. This is for you!"

Chris later discussed his thoughts on finally winning Grammy Awards. "Being given credit for your work is fun. I may not have felt particularly comfortable standing on stage thanking people for our award, but it was the right thing to do. [Susan] is always good at advising us about the right thing to do in those situations. You've got to go out there and let the people know you appreciate the fact that they like your music. It might seem cool to just stay at home and ignore them, but it's not smart, and as we get older we're trying to be cool and smart."

A month later (on April 1st), the soundtrack to the film *Basketball Diaries* was released, which finally gave a loving home to "Blind Dogs." Another strong non-LP track that featured a thick-as-molasses guitar riff (with music penned by Kim and lyrics by Chris), by this point, it was established long ago that Soundgarden's outtakes were better than the vast majority of rock bands' supposed "grade A" material. Again, when you have four strong songwriters in one band...an overabundance of quality material is bound to be left on the cutting room floor. Luckily, SG has served up these tasty scraps on soundtracks, comps, and b-sides.

It was also around this time that a new crop of bands who were clearly mimicking Seattle's Big 4 (some of them so bold as to assemble a "musical Frankenstein"—borrowing elements from *all four* bands) began getting some major airplay on MTV. In case you forgot, I'm talkin' 'bout the likes of Bush, Silverchair, Sugartooth, Seven Mary Three, and Sponge, among many others (heck, you could even detect quite a few Vedder-isms vocally via Hootie & the Blowfish's Darius Rucker). And Chris was not impressed with this new crop of grunge copycats—"These bands have no history or substance. Looking at them, you know exactly what they're about, it's all marketing, all package."

Having had to cancel their second go-round of Euro dates in '94, SG opted for a maneuver in the summer of '95 that was a carbon copy of what occurred in the summer of '93—they put recording their next album on hold (Chris and Matt started working in the studio in July), so they could perform two weeks' worth of rocking festivals and larger halls. Instead of starting small and building up to the larger shows (since they had not performed on stage in over a year), SG opted for the bold option of starting big, with four festival dates from the get-go— Sunstroke on August 23rd (Dublin, Ireland), Lowlands on August 25th (Dronten, Netherlands), Pukkelpop on August 26th (Hasselt, Belgium), and finally, Reading on August 27th (Reading, England).

The main reason for agreeing to do the dates was undoubtedly to finally make good on their aborted Reading slot from the previous year, and this time, the bill saw SG placed only below headliner Neil Young (backed by Pearl Jam), and above White Zombie, Pavement, Mudhoney, Blind Melon, Babes in Toyland, and other acts. Pro-shot clips of the band performing aired at the time on MTV in Europe and America, and confirmed that whatever vocal troubles Chris was experiencing the previous year were clearly in the rearview mirror. So much so, that Chris had no problem scolding an overzealous interviewer ("Shut up! We're talking now!") during a chat with MTV Europe post-Reading performance.

After the festivals, SG opted to play further Euro shows as a headliner—which in most cases were mostly "indoor festivals," as the bills included a semi-rotating cast of bands, including the likes of White Zombie, Blind Melon, Mudhoney, Kyuss, and Sponge, among others. And as they had done back in the summer of '93, the summer shows of '95 saw a few newly-penned tunes receive airings, including compositions that would eventually go by the official titles of "Ty Cobb" and "Kristi." The shows also included a cover of the Doors' "Waiting for the Sun," and would conclude with a long, meandering, all-instrumental rendition of the Beatles' "I Want You (She's So Heavy)"—which would end with the audience only seeing the band members' silhouettes, as they would ultimately only be illuminated by lights against a curtain behind them.

To get a taste of this mini-tour, there is great footage of a complete performance from the September 6th show at Turbinenhalle in Oberhausen, Germany (albeit single-cam shot, but thankfully filmed totally steady and not motion sickness-inducing-jumpy). The tour would wrap up three nights later at Festa Dell Unita, Reggio nell'Emilia, Italy, which concluded with an occurrence that was becoming all too familiar by this point—Ben getting into some kind of bruhaha with an audience member.

And according to Mudhoney's Steve Turner, he witnessed first-hand proof of Matt's earlier "fabric starting to unravel" comment concerning SG. "We did some big festivals with Soundgarden in '95. It was just the worst. The Soundgarden guys—none of them [were] really talking to each other, everyone angry. It was no fun. It was one of those things that we immediately knew we shouldn't have done. I judge a lot on what our drummer, Dan [Peters], thinks about things. And that, to this day, is his least favorite trip he's ever been on. So that says a lot to me. They were acting miserable, like they were having the worst time of their lives. Well, then fucking don't do it! The same thing with Nirvana—if you hate it so much, don't fucking do it. Either deal with the situation that you created, or don't. Don't continue doing it and acting like a little spoiled child—with really nasty parents." [Laughs]

With there already being multiple Nirvana and Pearl Jam books on bookstore shelves, it only made sense that Soundgarden would be the next grunge act in line to receive "the book treatment"—especially due to their recent breakthrough commercial success. And on September 15th, the first-ever S. Garden book was published via St. Martin's Griffin, entitled *New Metal Crown*. The 224-pager was penned by Chris Nickson (who has also penned books on such musical subjects as Melissa Etheridge, Mariah Carey, and John Martyn), and while not including anything too groundbreaking info-wise (and only going up to the *Superunknown* era), it was pleasing to finally have a book—whose cover featured a black and white pic of the band circa '94—that dotted the i's and crossed the t's, and attempted to make sense of the band's story up to that point.

Sadly, on October 21ˢᵗ—barely a month and a half after Blind Melon wrapped up their Euro dates with Soundgarden—singer Shannon Hoon tragically died from a cocaine overdose on his band's tour bus, at the age of 28. "That was the 'shock call'," recalled Susan. "To get that call, and know the horror that the guys had to have gone through. We had a similar situation with Layne. I didn't even know [Shannon] had a drug problem, so it just shocked me. Chris was never one to have phone chat relationships with people—he and Jeff Buckley were as close as it got. They didn't talk often, but when they did, it was definitely a deep connection. But Chris adored Shannon. When I got the call, Chris was over at our cabin at the time, writing. I was trying to get him to come home, so I could tell him in person, but he could tell that something was wrong and wanted to know what it was. It was another incident where to me it felt like he buried the grief—Chris buried the grief. He didn't react, he didn't respond—he went dead silent. I think it had to do with his continuing depression—unresolved grief. And Shannon's death was another significant blow."

Reminiscent of Kurt Cobain painting a picture of everything being fine and dandy in the press circa late '93/early '94, Cornell seemed to be doing the same thing a year or so later, as he was quoted as saying, "Most of the winter I did snowboarding and a little bit of songwriting and I didn't really take anything too seriously. That's the first time I've ever done that since I can remember, ever, taking a certain amount of time off."

But according to Susan, Chris' depression only worsened around this time. "I think Chris was really starting to suffer from untreated depression—the way he wasn't focused on what he needed to be focused on, in terms of making the record. And stopped participating in a way that was productive for everybody. Chris would come home and literally be on the floor in a ball, crying, in the middle of the night. He was inconsolable. They weren't communicating—try as I may to get them to sit down and have meetings, and go talk to some kind of a group counselor."

"I had a book I had given them at one point, that Aerosmith's manager had told me about—something that Aerosmith had read collectively, and helped them a lot—called *The Paradox of Success*. They laughed at me when I gave it to them. [Laughs] They were not group therapy candidates. So eventually, everybody retreated into their own corners and stopped communicating. The key to everything, and any relationship that's going to survive is communicating. We watched Pearl Jam go through it and come out the other side, because as difficult as it is at times for anybody to sit down and talk when they're not feeling good about each other or themselves, it's the only way to get to the other side. And Soundgarden wasn't willing to do that."

Despite growing tensions and troubles behind the scenes, to their credit, the band continued work on full-length #5—which would eventually go by the title of *Down on the Upside*, and recorded at Studio Litho and Bad Animals. But according to Kim, everyone was not on the same page. "Came back, Chris was in the studio doing some demos, and then I went into a studio trying to do some demos. At some point, what I thought was preproduction ended up being production. What were demos and preproduction ended up kind of 'the thing'—everything was in gear. It was like, 'Wait a minute.' There was a huge miscommunication in the recording process of *Down on the Upside*—just in terms of pacing and tempo. Stuff was at this one tempo, and then all of sudden, the pace really sped up. The next thing I know it's like, 'We need your guitars...*now*'!"

But at the time, it sounded like the other members of the band welcomed the change in how they approached the recording process—including Chris. "We've always done demos and then we'd make a record and spend the whole time trying to capture the essence of the demo. It seems really stupid! Why not just make the demos your record? This album's been way faster and way easier." And Chris described what made the sound of *DotU* different. "Something about this record seems more sonically direct, possibly less larger than life than what we've done on previous records. The kick drum sounds less like a gun shot off in a gymnasium and more like a drum. To my ears what you hear in these songs is the closest we've ever gotten to capturing the 'true' sound of Soundgarden."

Sound-wise, Matt seemed as pleased as Chris. "Litho is a converted woodworking/lithography factory that [Pearl Jam's] Stone Gossard put a studio in. It's been up and running now for about two years. It's fully analog. He's got a really nice API board with a Studer. It's a medium-size room, so the drum sound I was getting wasn't as enormous as the last record, but they just had a nice, ambient sound. They sounded as big as that room, so I was very happy with the way everything came out, as far as the room sound goes."

And despite a more back-to-basics approach, Kim loaded up on the gear he utilized. "I used a lot of different amps, a lot of different guitars. On *Louder Than Love* and *Badmotorfinger*, I used a lot of humbucking [pickups]. On this album I used the Guild S-100 quite a bit, but I used a lot of Telecaster and Jazzmaster as well. And there is more acoustic guitar on this record, plus dobro, mandolas, and the occasional keyboard—but it's never overdone, it's just there for color."

Another difference of the *DotU* session was Chris altering his vocal recording approach in the studio. "When I was younger doing this, I used to, as far as singing went, beat myself up way too much, singing way too much, and the songs would end up sounding sterile because of it. My voice would get tired and I wouldn't give in to that. I'm gonna keep going, and going. I guess it kind of comes down to realizing that on previous records, a lot of performances I did vocally on demos I usually ended up liking more. I didn't give a shit. I wasn't worried about it being something that was forever, because to me, at the time, it was just the demo."

It was also reported at the time that the band considered recruiting Brendan O'Brien as producer, but due to prior commitments, the idea was scratched. Instead, the former "assistant engineer" on *Superunknown,* Adam Kasper, was promoted (listed as co-producer of the album—along with the band). Kasper would reflect on the sessions a decade later. "It was a long six months. Basically the same approach to *Superunknown*. We had so many songs since all the guys were writers. This is before Pro Tools—you were limited and it was a whole different way of recording. Nowadays, you can keep everything and never make a decision until the last day. It was the last sort of analog era—and we did it all analog. If you listen to that record, it's got tons of stuff on it. The band seemed pretty good—they were all fairly independent at that time, as far as writing their songs. Particularly Cornell."

"It was my idea to record it at Studio Litho with Adam Kasper, because I felt our last situation was intense—all these big named producer guys involved," remembered Matt about the sessions, that would wrap up in early '96. "It just wasn't our scene at all. We just went back to the homemade method of making records with our buddy, Adam."

However, beneath all the positive vibes radiating in the press, Kim was disappointed in his lack of input concerning songwriting for *DotU*. "I ended up just writing and completing 'Never the Machine Forever.' I did it on my own, there wasn't an iota of collaboration with that. There was a lot more collaboration with the band on all the previous records. Collaborations were getting fewer and further between. My participation was diminishing."

For Ben, it was not the best time for him personally—but he did recall a curious collaboration, which remains unreleased. "For me, it was more painful. Because my honey was leaving me the whole time that was going on. But the music, it was way more us. We actually recorded with Randy Johnson [then-pitcher for the Seattle Mariners], after he'd won his first Cy Young. He came to the studio—he played drums, and me and Kim played guitar. We actually made a song and recorded it. Chris was going to sing on it, but never did." When asked about the tune, Adam replied, "I don't remember much about the song. Let me just say he's a better pitcher than a drummer."

As it turned out, towards the end of the album's creation, an inebriated Chris almost made a drunken decision that would have proven detrimental to the sound of at least one track. "The last night we mixed *Down on the Upside*, we were up 'til six in the morning mixing the last song, and I was too drunk to hear it. I was just about to start changing everything and everyone else was saying it sounded good. I was thinking, 'OK, let's have another beer then'!" That said, a stone cold sober decision was made after the album was completed—a BMW motorcycle was purchased for Kasper, as a gift for his hard work (a 1995 R100 PD Classic, with a price tag of $10,400...in case you were wondering).

While we're on the subject of motorcycles...it sounded like Chris was quite the bike buff around this time, as *Kerrang!* writer Morat reported, "Cornell is much bigger than you'd expect from his photos, solidly built like he works out, and it soon becomes apparent that he is far from being the poser you might imagine. He has a couple of Harley Davidsons, not because they are rock star accessories, but because he enjoys riding them. One of his first biking experiences, the one that made him get his own bike, was when he got spat off the back of a friend's Z1000 Kawasaki and landed on his head, filling his helmet with dust."

With the band smack dab in the middle of working on *DotU* in late '95, a couple of Soundgarden-related releases were rolled out in time for the holiday season (both on November 21st)—a CD+ entitled *Alive in the Superunknown* and a CD EP entitled *Songs from the Superunknown*. Just what the heck is a "CD+" you ask? An understandable question. It was a format that never caught on, that combined audio tracks and data tracks (images, video, animation, etc.) on the same disc—sounds sorta like a CD-ROM, if you ask me.

And on the *Alive in the Superunknown* release, you would find four audio treats—the title track from *Superunknown,* the "video version" of "Fell on Black Days," the non-US *Superunknown* extra track "She Likes Surprises," and Chris' solo acoustic version of "Like Suicide." But that's not all! Also included were photos of the band, videos of Artis the Spoonman, a videogame, an animated *Badmotorfinger* logo, the videos for

"My Wave," "Fell On Black Days," "Black Hole Sun," and "The Day I Tried to Live," plus a live video of "Kickstand."

Perhaps sensing that the average SG fan was not interested in a CD+ (heck, back then, most people I knew didn't even have home computers yet), the *Songs from the Superunknown* CD collected all four aforementioned audio tracks, as well as tacking on an ambient/experimental/instrumental throwaway, entitled "Jerry Garcia's Finger" (concerning its title, it was in reference to the fact that the late Grateful Dead singer/guitarist accidentally had part of his right middle finger chopped off by an axe—as a mere lad). "We wrote that as a space jam on the day the Grateful Dead played their last show in Seattle," remembered Chris. "I originally called it 'Jerry Garcia's Dead,' but 'Finger' was better." Wise decision, as Garcia actually *would* die on August 9, 1995.

Moreover, another SG-related piece of recording occurred sometime during '95—Kim joining the likes of Nirvana's Krist Novoselic, Alice in Chains' Sean Kinney, and the one-and-only Johnny Cash (!), for a cover of Willie Nelson's "Time of the Preacher." The tune was included as part of a tribute album to the pony-tailed singer/songwriter—by various grunge and alt-rock artists—entitled *Twisted Willie* (released on January 30, 1996, via Justice Records). The little-heard tune is certainly worth a listen, as the rendition alternates between the style of musical accompaniment you would expect from a Cash-sung tune and a grungy tune from the '90s (in other words, the strum of an acoustic guitar, followed by fuzz guitars). Surprisingly, the tune also features one of Kim's noisiest guitar solos ever recorded.

A month later (on February 20th), Soundgarden appeared on the multi-artist comp, *Home Alive,* when they donated "Kyle Petty, Son of Richard" for use—which benefitted the Seattle-based women's self-defense collective called Home Alive (which was formed after the tragic rape and murder of Gits singer Mia Zapata, in 1993), while Ben and Matt served as the rhythm section on another track on the comp, "Joyride" by Kristen Barry. '95 would also see several SG members guest on other artists' albums, including Matt appearing on Eleven's *Thunk* ("Why," "Seasick of

You," "Big Sleep," and "No Ground") and Seaweed's *Spanaway* ("Magic Mountainman"), while Kim would supply a guitar solo to the track "Naked and Famous," off the self-titled debut by the Presidents of the United States of America.

And while there would be no *Rolling Stone* cover story again like there was back in '94, the band did get a story in the magazine reserved for only top-tier musical artists—a "studio report" about how the album was coming along (in their February 8, 1996 issue). Titled *The Joys of Noise: Soundgarden Throw a High-Frequency Sludgefest* by Charles R. Cross, the article is best remembered for detailing a recurring practice that Chris would indulge in during the recording of SG albums—constructing handmade wallets out of duct tape. Also around this time (February 1st), a Soundgarden entry in the "CD Books" series was released, penned by Jon Ewing—who had also written other entries in the series, including the Beatles and Alanis Morissette. For many years, this and *New Metal Crown* remained the only books on the marketplace that chronicled the band's history...that is, until *Dark Black and Blue* boldly changed all that!

But things were clearly no longer so cheery in the world of Soundgarden. And it was becoming obvious within their inner-circle—including *DotU's* co-producer. "I think [Kim] felt that during *Superunknown* things were getting commercial-oriented and radio friendly. So that struggle started back then. And the more Chris had hit songs, Soundgarden turned into 'a hit radio band.' They never were before that—they were heavy, disturbed. That was Kim's leaning. *Down on the Upside*, it was even more evident. Kim was more on one end and Chris the other."

Unsurprisingly, Kim agreed with Adam's assessment. "Overall, I don't see it as a pleasant experience. It fucked up the momentum of band personnel dynamics and creative dynamics. To the point that I was not satisfied, and I don't think Chris was satisfied either. And that's something that we carried on the tour. Maybe if I was more frank, sat down, and bitched with the band, things would have worked out."

Despite Matt's positive outlook earlier, looking back on the sessions years later, even *he* had mixed feelings. "It was good, but we weren't all on the same page. I was certainly trying to keep everyone motivated and just try to get it off the ground, but if people don't want to do things, it's hard to get them going. We weren't enjoying the process as much as we had been."

CHAPTER 19
DOWN ON THE UPSIDE

Judging from the end of the previous chapter, not all was well in Soundgarden-land when the highly-anticipated *Down on the Upside* was released on May 21, 1996 (appearing a week earlier on limited edition double vinyl, with 1,500 being issued on *clear* vinyl). But I would assume that the common thought behind the scenes was by taking the album out on the road, maybe it would lift morale and get the band back on track. And if this was the case, then the plan got off to a rollicking start—as it was announced that Soundgarden was invited back to tour as part of Lollapalooza (the first major band to be asked back).

The first piece of music that the public was treated to from *DotU* was the tune "Pretty Noose," which was issued as a single two months before the album's arrival. I remember upon first hearing "PN," I was not entirely impressed—thinking that it sounded a bit like what you would expect from SG. But after repeated listens, it did indeed grow on me—as it was probably merely a case of SG having set the bar so bloody high with their previous offerings, you'd expect every time for them to offer up a "Rusty Cage," a "Jesus Christ Pose," or a "Black Hole Sun."

It turns out that the tune was a CCC, which starts with a slow riff once more squeezed through a wah pedal, before the rest of the band joins in and provides added metallic muscle. And while the phrase "pretty noose" is uttered quite a bit in the tune, it is the phrase "I don't like what you've got me hanging from" that stands out most. When asked what the tune was about lyrically, Chris' explanation was concise—"An attractively packaged bad idea. Something that seems great at first, but comes back to bite you."

A video was also shot for the tune—directed by Frank Kozik (who is best known for his attention-grabbing art for concert posters). And quite frankly...it was a snoozefest. At first, it seems like the basis of the video is that we are following SG around in their normal, everyday lives, so you see Kim shooting pool and Matt riding his motorcycle. Then suddenly...a gentleman (who looks like Chris, but his identity is not entirely clear) gets violently arrested by police on the hood of his automobile! Elsewhere, we see a shot of Ben sitting atop a VW Beetle and smoking a cigarette, plus scenes that seem to be randomly thrown in—a sinister looking go-go dancer, a woman getting a tattoo, the inside of a diner, etc.

And the last shot is of Chris sitting at the edge of a bed, with what looks like either a sleeping or dead lady laying underneath part of the sheets, before the final image is of a close-up eyeball, that flashes both the *Badmotorfinger* logo/image and the "S" logo circa *Ultramega OK*. Supposedly due to the implication that the woman may have been murdered in the bed, it had to be edited somewhat for MTV, to which the director took exception—"They got a dead girl in that lame Stabbing Westward video so I don't understand their problem." Seems like the same old baffling situation SG found themselves in circa the "Jesus Christ Pose" clip—it was acceptable for artists such as Madonna to stir up controversy with her videos, but for a rock band like SG, it was a great big no-no.

The "PN" CD single issued in Europe (which featured a photograph of the band made to look like a black and white drawing on the cover, below a huge red "SOUNDGARDEN" plopped on top) would include two tracks plucked from the forthcoming *DotU*—"Applebite" and "An Unkind," as well as a near-ten-minute long interview, conducted by SG's old tour mates, Alain Johannes and Natasha Shneider from Eleven. Chart-wise, "PN" performed fab—peaking at #10 in Finland, #14 in the UK, and #18 in New Zealand, while also topping *RPM's Canada Rock/Alternative Chart* and peaking at #2 on *Billboard's Alternative Songs Chart* in the US.

A day before the May 14th arrival of the vinyl version of *DotU*, all four S. Garden members were interviewed by MTV VJ/radio DJ Matt Pinfield for a radio broadcast produced by *Album Network*, in which tracks from the album were also played/premiered. I remember staying up to tune in, and being pleased with what I heard. And one standout piece of conversation I recall between Matt and SG was that the band enjoyed how the album's title sounded when Pinfield pronounced it.

Another undoubted career highlight occurred on the evening of May 18th—Soundgarden's one-and-only appearance on *Saturday Night Live.* I remember staying up late that evening to watch the Jim Carrey-hosted episode, and being quite concerned that the VHS tape I was recording the two songs (musical artists are usually confined to performing only a pair of tunes per episode) on was nearing the end, and that both may not fit properly. Luckily, the second song ended just in the nick of time.

I was already familiar with the first song performed, "Pretty Noose," of which the band sounded good (although Chris' vocals were a bit ragged, but that's the thing with *SNL*—the few times I have seen musical performances, as I'm not a regular viewer, the mix was rarely up-to-snuff). But I recall besides the musical portion of the performance, noticing that Cornell's hair looked different (my girlfriend at the time explained that his Sid Vicious-esque spiky hairdo was the result of hairspray—not gel, pomade, nor mousse) and that he looked much skinnier/less muscular than in the past. Additionally, I spotted Chris and Ben playing instruments I was not accustomed to seeing them play—a Telecaster and a Mosrite (similar looking to the bass that Dave Alexander of the Stooges played circa *Funhouse*), respectively.

But the second song was the real story—a tune that I later discovered was entitled "Burden in My Hand." It turned out to be a much better sounding performance than its predecessor (especially Chris' vocals), and the tune overall reminded me a bit of a Rolling Stones/classic rock tune. In fact, I will go as far as saying that I prefer this version of the song over the studio version that would be included on *DotU* (more on that in a bit). And at the end of the episode, the members of SG could be spotted standing alongside the host and the rest of the cast, bidding viewers sweet adieu. As it turns out, SG was not all that excited about appearing on *SNL,* but as Chris explained, eventually did so for a sole reason. "We had two things we said we'd never do. One was play when the sun was out, which we've now done, and the other was live TV. But Jim Carrey said he wouldn't do the program unless we were on, so we relented."

So, when the day finally came for the CD version of *DotU* to be obtained, I was fully prepared. It was the first cardboard/digipak CD version that Soundgarden ever offered of a full-length album (rather than the usual hard plastic case), while its cover showed that the band continued to get a kick out of obscuring their identities on album covers. Case in point, all you see are their silhouettes in what looks like an airplane hangar or some spacious storage room (once more supplied from the same photographer responsible for the *Superunknown* cover image, Kevin Westenberg). Title-wise, I would soon learn that the phrase was a lyric tucked away within a song entitled "Dusty," and later on, I would discover that Kim originally had another album title in mind. "I wanted to call it *Devil-King of Children*, but some people had a problem with it."

Kicking things off with the song I was already familiar with, "Pretty Noose," I was eagerly awaiting to hear what else the lads had in store...but didn't dare forward it (I would later discover that the song featured an interesting guitar tuning—C, G, C, G, G, E—which would also be utilized on several other selections on the album). Soon enough, the amusingly titled "Rhinosaur" was up to bat. Featuring Chris handling the lyrics and Matt the music, if anything, it showed that Matt had proven an old joke wrong (that Dave Grohl once retold on *The Howard Stern Show*)—"What's the last thing the drummer said before he got kicked out of the band? 'Hey, *I wrote a song*'." Built around a swaggering riff that struts around at the same mid-pace tempo until just before the two-minute mark, before it's almost as if someone detonated a "hyper speed button" (while Kim provides a wailing solo over it).

Then, one of the album's underrated tunes (and a song I enjoy the title of), "Zero Chance." A collaboration between Chris (lyrics) and Ben (music), the song is not musically what we've come to expect from Mr. Shepherd—as it's a gorgeous-yet-sad ballad, which also showcases the exceptional singing and vocal melody talents of Cornell (especially two parts—the chorus, and the bit in which he sings "Why doesn't anyone believe, In loneliness, Stand up and everyone will see, Your holiness").

And Ben continued his winning streak—providing the music to "Dusty" (with Chris again serving as wordsmith). As previously stated, the tune is probably best known for providing us with the album's title, but it also turns out to be one of the album's standouts. Featuring a Stones-y acoustic guitar groove, it turns out that the song was intended for Hater's proposed sophomore album (an album that wouldn't surface until several years later), but perhaps sensing that a whole lotta people would hear it on a SG record rather than a Hater one...the hand-off was understandable. Interestingly, the "Hater version" of the tune has never surfaced.

Then comes the album's most furious tune, "Ty Cobb." Although a punk rocker to the core (as evidenced by the repeated use of an ill-mannered word) the song features several acoustic/folk instruments plopped on top—including mandolin (plucked by Chris) and mandola (picked by Ben). While the song would be titled after a tough-as-nails Hall of Fame baseball player (who served as center fielder for the Detroit Tigers from 1905-1926, before finishing his career with the Philadelphia Athletics from 1927-1928), it turns out that the song was originally titled "Hot Rod Death Toll," from a line in the song.

To be honest, I would have preferred the tremendous original title, but Ben had his reasons for the switcheroo. "It was basically coming from the frame of mind of some sort of hardcore pissed-off idiot, and that's why we titled it that. We weren't writing the song about Ty Cobb at all—I didn't even know anything about him. I was just thinking of a character who was a combination of a lot of people I've met and didn't like."

After all the venom of the previous number had been thoroughly drained, we were met with one of the album's undisputed classics, the melodic and more composed "Blow Up the Outside World." A CCC, the verses are a bit Beatle-y sounding (especially Chris' vocals), before the pre-chorus and chorus dial up the heaviness. And Kim seemed to agree with the Beatles comparison...*somewhat*.

"People said there was a Beatles-ish element. I suppose there is a bit of Paul McCartney and a little bit of Lennon in the flavor of the song. Everyone in the band grew up with the Beatles and we had a certain degree of respect and admiration for them that's not uncommon. I think many people were Beatles fans, especially for that period in time. There's a number of acoustic guitars on the track as well and then, towards the end of the song, it gets louder and aggressive and goes to these power chords, and is maybe a little reminiscent of AC/DC."

Chris, on the other hand, was willing to list the similarities and dissimilarities between "BUtOW" and an earlier, similarly-titled tune, "Fell on Black Days." "It's not the same [as 'Fell On Black Days'], but it's a much longer song. But it isn't very wordy, either. The lyrics are similar in vibe to 'Fell on Black Days,' as is the feel—a heavy guitar and drum presence, but with more focus on the melody." And Kim wound up approaching the song guitar-wise from a standpoint he rarely had previously.

"Even though there's an aspect of blues guitar playing—which I definitely picked up either by osmosis or just assimilating rock guitar—I'm not generally a huge fan of blues in general. But I am with specific artists. And with 'Blow Up the Outside World,' which is sort of a pop arrangement, I remember approaching that with a blues sensibility. It was very strange, because it is a pop arrangement, but it had a feel to it like a blues song, so that's why I came up with the blues solos for that."

And then a tune that we've discussed only but a pinch previously, "Burden in My Hand." As mentioned earlier, I always preferred live renditions of this song over the studio version—especially with clean electric guitar strumming the beginning (which Chris would play live) rather than acoustic guitar (the studio version), and also, Chris' vocals (feel free to compare the *SNL* rendition to the *DotU* rendition—go ahead and do that now if you'd like, I'll wait for you to come back). Kim also saw similarities between "BiMH" and an earlier classic rock standard. "I thought of 'Burden in My Hand' as the contemporary 'Hey Joe.' I thought there was something to the melody, the lyric, and the feel—the overall emotive sort of discomfort and beauty that that song elicited was very similar to that sort of squirming beauty that 'Hey Joe' elicited."

Up next is a throwaway that I always found myself skipping, "Never Named" (with lyrics by Cornell, music by Shepherd). But according to Chris, the lyrics had special meaning, as he described them as "Out of my childhood, which is something I've never done. The line, 'I'm just a baby who looks like a boy,' I always looked really young for my age, but I never wanted to. I could always get away with acting younger, because I could pull it off. With such a boyish look, I could get away with ridiculous shit like going to school fucking high out of my brain and no one would ever figure it out, because I didn't look like somebody who would do that."

A song that I consider an instrumental—but isn't really—follows, entitled "Applebite." With music provided by Matt and lyrics by Chris, the reason why I look at the tune as an instrumental is because there aren't very many lyrics in the song at all, and also, you can barely make out what is being sung (without the aid of a lyric sheet). And to the best of my knowledge, the song features the first-ever appearance of a Moog synthesizer on a Soundgarden album (supplied by Matt), plus piano (plunked by Adam).

And the composer of the song's music once explained, "'Applebite,' for example, is pretty much a study in dynamics. It starts out in one dynamic and attains this other dynamic through theme and variation, basically. There's one constant motif going through the whole thing, and we were able to give it different colors with the dynamics. It's pretty difficult to write good, solid pop-structure tunes. I've definitely done that in the past, but it's easier for me to write riff-based tunes." And it turned out that Chris quite fancied the tune, as well. "Yeah, I loved 'Applebite.' Matt played the demo for that. That's the one I really pushed for— I definitely wanted that song on the record." Chris' wish would be hereby granted.

Up to this point stylistically, "melody" seemed to outweigh "metal" on *DotU*. But the latter made a triumphant comeback seemingly out of nowhere, with the 100% Kim composition, "Never the Machine Forever." Certainly one of the most cacophonic and heaviest tunes on *DotU,* it was the only track that the guitarist would have any compositional input in (which was quite astonishing, as he previously had pitched in on several tunes per album). And he once discussed the inspiration behind the song's gnarly guitar riff and peculiar time signature.

"The inspiration was, Greg [Gilmore, ex-Mother Love Bone drummer] and I were doing some jamming. I was doing some preproduction for *Down on the Upside*. Chris had done some demoing on his own—4-track or 8-track stuff, and Matt had done some demoing on 4-track stuff. I wasn't recording on 4-track, since I didn't feel comfortable with songwriting that way. I would write riffs and then just turn on a regular tape player and record the riff. I could record a melody over that and record that simply. I didn't worry about demoing 4-tracks, and still don't."

"But I decided to go into a friend's studio and jam with Greg and work out some ideas in preproduction before going into the studio, and 'Never the Machine' came from that. Greg was jamming out of the drum riff and I started noticing, 'Hey, this is kind of a weird sort of groove or feel.' And Greg said, 'Yeah, I think it's in 9/4.' So I thought, 'OK, well, I'm going to write music in 9/4, then.' So I came up with the guitar riff and all the guitar riffs, and of course then eventually the vocal melody and the lyrics for 'Never the Machine Forever.' So, basically I wrote a song in the time signature 9/4, that tempo. And so for that reason, I gave sonic inspiration to Greg Gilmore for identifying this jam as being 9/4, for being that time signature."

Kim also once gave a teeny glimpse into what the song's cryptic lyrics were about. "It's about a life-and-death match between an individual and a less specifically defined entity. And, yes, it's based on personal experience." Alrighty then. And as it turns out, "NtMF" is a tune that Ben quite fancies. "While we were mixing it, I was like, 'That's so fucking SST'—meaning [the way] that time period, that record label sounds, like [then-SST producer] Spot drum sounds. Sounds like old Soundgarden. He wrote it the last goddamn day too. Finished tracking and then put it into the mixing."

Next...another throwaway, I'm afraid—a CCC entitled "Tighter & Tighter." In fact, so much of a throwaway that other than describing its tempo as "sluggish," I think it's best that we just go right to next tune, which was one of the album's standouts. After several attempts to get the next song on a SG album (going back to *Badmotorfinger*), "No Attention" finally found a warm and loving home on *DotU*. Another CCC, the tune is a punk thrasher which I will be bold enough to declare as the album's biggest ass-kicker (and one of my personal faves). And the tune contains something that I've always relished concerning Soundgarden's song constructions—they were adept at inserting in a killer part, seemingly out of nowhere. And here, such a section occurs at the 2:36 mark, when the song's main guitar part is played, but sounds different due to a change in tempo and feel. Job well done, lads!

A Chris/Ben collab follows (I will let you take a wild guess at who was responsible for the lyrics and who was responsible for the music), "Switch Opens," which seems to be a forgotten tune on the album, but a worthwhile listen. And while the song's title is mentioned here and there, it's actually the phrase "Switch is on" that gets repeated the most. Chris would also later reveal how this mid-tempo'd tune was written mostly in the studio. You want another CCC? You got another CCC— "Overfloater"! Although you could probably consider it a throwaway (pretty sure it was never performed live), it does include some fine vocals from Chris, who also tickles the ivories of a Rhodes piano—an instrument most recognizable on such rock classics as the Doors' "Riders on the Storm" and the Beatles' "Get Back."

And then...we are thrust back into the manic world of Ben, who is the sole author of another furious punk rocker, "An Unkind," which turns out to be another one of my album faves (although admittedly not the most highly recognizable of SG tunes)—and another composition that was supposed to be for Hater's planned second effort, but instead, was transplanted here. The tune races by at a NASCAR-like pace (clocking in at a mere 2:08, it's the album's shortest tune), and while the song's title is not truly uttered in the song (although "*and* unkind" is). The phrase "On the storm, It's time to go" is repeated throughout, while the rarely used in rock n' roll word "penultimate" is also featured, and the phrase "We couldn't look a saint in the eyes" always stood out for yours truly (in a strange personal quirk, years later, I would adopt a little doggy whose previous owners had named him...Saint!).

Closing the album is what sounds like a not-so-distant-relative of "Overfloater"—a tune entitled "Boot Camp." And the reason why they both sound like they were cut from the same stylistic cloth is 'cause they certainly are more ambient-sounding than yer average SG tune. While not as gripping an album-closer as say, "Like Suicide" was, it does help provide some much needed "musical resolution."

My thoughts on the album? It was not as jaw-droppingly brilliant as the previous two SG albums and not as consistent (you could certainly make a valid argument that *DotU* was the first SG album since *Louder Than Love* to be padded with filler). In fact, when thinking back on the band's discography, I often find myself writing off *DotU* as being not in the same league as *BMF* or *SU*...but whenever I actually put the album on and dig deep, I am reminded that the album is indeed a keeper.

· Again, it just had the misfortune of following up two stellar recordings that have gone down as being amongst my all-time favorites (and I'm sure many other SG fans, as well). But knowing what I know now about tension within the band's ranks at this point, it makes it understandable why the album wasn't quite as inspired nor unified-sounding as the prior two triumphs (but again, remains impressive that they could pull off a strong offering amidst the turmoil).

Unexpectedly, it appeared as though the critics had cooled somewhat concerning their admiration of Soundgarden. Reviewing *DotU* for *Rolling Stone,* Rob O'Connor gave it a very lukewarm three out of five star review, before saying, "Chalk up a few points since Soundgarden don't rip off their sound from the many interchangeable bands in *MTV's Buzz Bin*. But even with all four members writing, the best the band comes up with is the same ol' metal machine music. Soundgarden represent a changing of the guard: The band comes from an underground stoked by its hatred for the limited perspective of the hair-metal bands of the

'80s. Now clearly in the mainstream, the group has the opportunity to expand its music beyond the usual rhythms and attitudes that have already been established. It's a shame that Soundgarden don't live up to the challenge."

Elsewhere, *US Magazine's* David Browne also voiced his concerns (although giving it a more adequate B+ review)— "*Upside* has its downside. The album was produced by the band, and like many self-produced efforts, it shows. With arrangements that crest and fall to the point where a road map would have helped, the overlong (16-song) album is often unwieldy and could have benefited from judicious trimming. Also, in avoiding outright anthems, it stints on metal catharsis—which is, after all, the very purpose of this most purging of genres."

When *DotU* was finally released, it would peak at #2 on the *Billboard 200* (kept out of the top spot by the Fugees' sophomore effort, *The Score*), but actually did take the cherished next step on both the Australian and New Zealand charts—while peaking at #2 in Canada, #3 in Sweden, #4 in Finland, #6 in Norway, and #7 in the UK. And at last count (August 14, 1996), *DotU* was certified platinum.

By 1996, it was becoming quite apparent that although grunge and alt-rock certainly helped shake things up a few years earlier, it was unable to sustain itself. Case in point, the influx of not just grunge copycats, but bands that were using elements of alt-rock, yet softening and shaping them in a way that was not nearly as confrontational, risky, or passionate as say, Kurt Cobain or Trent Reznor. "Nirvana were a great band, but their success sure ushered in a whole bunch of wimpy clones that kind of gibber away on MTV," explained Kim about this troubling phenomenon. "It does seem like it's just a matter of time before bad things come back into music. It's what children and housewives like!"

Chris also sounded unimpressed with the new competition. "Now there's this endless stream of shitty alternative college music. It's all politically correct and you're not allowed to be too aggressive or too soft. It's wimpy little guitars played by guys wearing spazzy glasses. [Laughs] That's just as annoying as hair farmer rock. But there's always going to be a large amount of shit in any genre and a small amount of stuff you're actually gonna like."

Although SG's latest studio experience didn't sound like it was the most enjoyable one, they did have a whopper of a tour lined up—Lollapalooza—which could have potentially put everything back on track. But according to Matt, this proved not to be the case. "The sessions were certainly strained. And once we started touring, the shows were increasingly bad. Just horrible. A lot of drinking, bad vibes, rock star bullshit. I was actually thinking about bailing at that point. Ben couldn't really get through an entire show without having some kind of temper tantrum. It was so not about music."

As previously mentioned, beginning at some point during the tour in support of *Superunknown,* Ben began acting increasingly erratic and hostile towards the audience (and his poor defense-less equipment)—which continued throughout the tour in support of *DotU.* "As far as Ben smashing stuff up, it was not an unusual occurrence by then," remembered Susan. "He had a lot of unseated anger that he didn't deal with in his own life. It became almost like a stage antic, to exhibit all this tension and discontent onstage. And it became an issue. I'd say the same thing over and over: 'Ben, you're giving up your power. There were 3,000 people there tonight—2,999 of them got ripped off, because you focused on one guy.' It became like a circus act, where everybody's focused on 'Why is the bass player so mad, and who is it that he's threatening to beat up?' So we talked about it, and I'd send him magazine articles about different things—how to not give away your power, basically. And other public figures that had gone through that frustration of that catch-22—of wanting to be in front of an audience, and resenting it at the same time."

A friend of the band, Jeff Gilbert, had an interesting theory behind Ben's troubled state. "[Ben] was horribly lonely, depressed, and heartbroken. I felt so bad for him, because nobody wanted to be on the road at that point. You know where it started? When they were on the road and got the news of Kurt. They were so far away from home, and they weren't around their support system—their friends, their family. Kim told me, 'It wasn't fair.

We didn't get to grieve, and be around our family during that period. We were supposed to be on the road. And that's when it began to suck.' People dying out of the Seattle music scene simply was not supposed to happen."

Before embarking on Lolla, SG was enlisted by Molson Beer to perform as part of their "Blind Date" concert series, in which if you were to be the first, or ninth, or hundredth caller on your local FM station, and then were to win a draw, Molson would fly you to a destination to watch a renowned band in a small venue. The only thing is...the attendee would not know which band it was until they got there. So, on June 15th at the Town Pump in Vancouver, BC, 500 lucky buggers witnessed Soundgarden in a local watering hole.

But about two weeks later (and after a warm-up gig at the Showbox in Seattle), SG was ready to ride aboard the Lolla choo-choo train once more. Up until this point, Perry Farrell and his pals were dead set against welcoming heavy metal into the stable of artists for their touring festival (in fact, it would later become known that when Ozzy Osbourne was denied a spot on Lolla one year, his wife/manager, Sharon Osbourne, wound up launching the highly successful/metal-based Ozzfest). And the reason why I bring this up is because 1996 was the first year that a tried-and-true metal band, Metallica, was finally "welcomed into the club."

However, many years later, Perry stated his true feelings concerning letting Metallica in on the fun. "I was very angry the first time they played Lollapalooza. I helped create the genre alternative, and alternative was against hair metal, teased-out hair, spandex, bullshit rock music. Metallica, in my estimation at that time, wasn't my thing. I was into alternative and punk and underground. My friends were Henry Rollins and Gibby Haynes and Ice-T."

At the time though, Chris had some not-so-nice words for Lolla's mastermind. "Have you noticed how Lollapalooza isn't this multi-cultural, multi-sexual, multi-racial event at all? What Perry Farrell never admits is that it's just a slick rock concert with a good name and his ambition is to make a lot of money. Perry has a very good manager. He even has a percentage on the parking.

It's a huge draw, and what people don't realize is it's far from being just the 'alternative college' crowd who go. It's very mainstream and very middle class. Even when we did it in 1992 with Ice Cube, the whole audience was entirely white."

Kim also voiced his concerns about appearing once again on the festival (which Ben jokingly referred to as "Larsapalooza," at the time—in tribute to Metallica drummer Lars Ulrich). "I had my criticisms about Lollapalooza the first time we did it, all the pretenses, the notion of alterna-culture. But this isn't that trip. This is more like Metallica and Soundgarden on the road, and you throw in the Ramones and Rancid. I don't see it as being part of some collectivized neo-hippie experience: 'It's our Woodstock.' If I was 17 back in 1969, I wouldn't have gone to Woodstock. I would have gone to Detroit." Sensing that they may get some backlash for appearing on such a testosterone-heavy bill, Chris beat the critics to the punch, calling it "Metal-sexist-apalooza. I'll dress like a woman if it will make people feel better."

But really, the organizers had no choice in the matter, as Metallica was one of the highest-drawing and most popular rock bands on the planet (and remain so, at the time of this book's birth), and were launching a tour in support of their first album in five years. Admittedly, that album, *Load,* stunk to high heaven— both musically and visually. Concerning the former, they had dialed down the "metal" part of the equation on such ditties as "Until It Sleeps"—as they were obviously trying to attract the alt-rock crowd. And concerning the latter, all you have to do is take a gander at the embarrassing and pretentious Anton Corbijn-shot photos of the band inside the CD booklet, trying oh-so-hard to look "alternative" (but coming off as bad U2 impersonators).

And although Metallica was billed as the festival's headliner, Soundgarden was seemingly looked upon as a co-headliner that year—due to their popularity and the fact that they had already toured Lolla once previously (and actually had some honest-to-goodness alt-rock roots and cred—unlike the headliner). And rounding out the line-up on the main stage was the Ramones (on their last go-round, before riding off into the sunset), Rancid, Shaolin monks (!), Screaming Trees, and

Psychotica. Additionally, there was a slot that year on the main stage which saw the appearance of rotating "surprise guests," which included the likes of Rage Against the Machine, Devo, Cheap Trick, Cocteau Twins, Waylon Jennings, and Wu-Tang Clan, among others.

Running from June 27th (Longview Lake in Kansas City, Missouri) to August 4th (Irvine Meadows in Irvine, California), I am ashamed to admit that this was the first SG tour since *Louder Than Love* that I did not attend a single show of. Why? I can't recall, exactly. But judging from the footage of the Lolla tour— there is quality (yet not pro-shot) footage of the tour's stop at Downing Stadium in New York on July 10th, among other dates— SG was still a solid live band, although not as animated on stage as say, their spring '92 shows were.

"There were too many days off," Chris complained after the tour had been completed. "It was kind of a dumb tour in the way it was routed. The whole idea stemmed from the Metallica camp not wanting to play in any major markets because they wanted to come back and do their own tour. There were so many days off that it didn't kick in. We were out for two weeks and it didn't seem like we were on tour, because we would play a show and have two days off. It seemed like we were doing a bunch of one-offs, but about two weeks in it started to kick in and started to be really fun."

Chris also offered honesty when asked if there were any politics between his band and Metallica. "There was a little bit going on. It was more or less between the Soundgarden and Metallica crew, really. I think their crew are used to Metallica headlining shows where they can do what they want and are used to calling the shots. I didn't have any ego problems about that. I would assume that there would be more Metallica fans than anyone else there because they sell way more records than anyone else on the bill, so I didn't care."

"But it wasn't a Metallica tour. They started eliminating our volume and little things headlining bands always do. It wasn't Metallica's fault at all, it was just the way the crews were used to working. They just hadn't done anything like that ever since they've been a big band. For years and years it's been Metallica headlining, and it took their crew a while to figure it out."

Looking back at Lolla '96 today, it did not seem to attract as much coverage nor hoopla as the '92 version did—except for one bit of unwanted coverage, when Kim was arrested and then freed on an assault charge in the early morning hours of July 21st after SG rocked Rockingham, North Carolina. "It's all just bullshit," Chris said at the time over the incident. "I don't think it will stop him from doing anything. The problem is that he is so recognizable. Nobody looks like him. You would stare at him even if he wasn't a famous person, and he gets hassled a lot. He can't really go anywhere without getting recognized."

On a more positive note, Soundgarden was granted their third cover story for *Spin* circa Lolla—a black-and-white shot of the band on the cover and a feature story (entitled *Superwellknown*) by Mike Rubin were the main selling points of the July 1996 issue, as well as discovering by the photos that Ben now appreciated sporting black leather trousers. But when asked about Lolla '96 a decade later, Matt's memories were *not* positive. "We'd done the Lollapalooza tour with Metallica around that time, and that was a total nightmare. We weren't playing good—sounded bad, really bad shows. Kind of embarrassing."

Two days after Lolla wrapped, the Ramones played what would be their last-ever show at the Hollywood Palladium, at which Chris and Ben were present. Highlights included Chris addressing the crowd at one point, and Ben strapping on one of Johnny Ramone's trademark Mosrite guitars, and strumming along for a rendition of the tune "Chinese Rocks" (both incidents being documented on the CD/VHS, *We're Outta Here!,* issued on November 18, 1997).

Also, it was during the summer of '96 (July 2nd) that the *Superunknown* standout, "My Wave," appeared as part of the comp *MOM (Music for Our Mother Ocean)* which benefitted the Surfrider Foundation (described as "a non-profit environmental organization dedicated to the protection and enhancement of the world's waves and beaches through conservation, activism, research and education"). "It's an issue with everyone, whether they know it or not," Chris once said about the sad state of the Earth's environment. "All the people who sit around and don't seem to care if there are trees or fresh water, all those people who are just as vulnerable to what it does to our bodies and how we live and whether our environment can survive or not."

A month after Lolla was palooza'd, SG would launch a Euro tour, which coincided with the release of the second single off *DotU,* "Burden in My Hand," on September 18th. Issued in several different formats throughout the world, the most enticing was the CD single issued in Australia, which included two stellar outtakes from the *DotU* sessions, "Karaoke" and "Bleed Together," as well as a reappearance of the demo version of "Birth Ritual."

Concerning the mid-paced n' moody "Karaoke," Chris once explained that lyrically, it was about "Following a formula is what seems to be successful right now. It's about how loads of bands are imitating bands that already exist." "Bleed Together," on the other hand, was much more uptempo, and sounded like it would be an absolute ass-kicker if performed live. However, to the best of my knowledge, it never was aired on a concert stage. Either way, the single managed to crack the top-ten in Canada (#9), while also topping *Billboard's Mainstream Rock Chart* in the US, and coming in at #33 in the UK. I was a bit disappointed that "BiMH" was not a bigger hit, though—as I thought it would have attracted the same pop fans who fancied "Black Hole Sun."

As expected, a video was filmed for "BiMH." And as it turns out, is one of their all-time best...yet not oft-seen. Directed by the same bloke who directed the "Fell on Black Days" clip (Jake Scott), the "BiMH" vid contains stunning landscape shots of the Mojave Desert, and of Chris strumming an acoustic guitar while situated atop a wooden structure, a sweat-dripping Matt taking a breather by a collection of animal skulls, crawling critters, a flaming tree, a hand buried in sand, and all four members strolling through the vast dunes during a wind storm (as well as a rain storm), among other visual delights. And the single's cover reflected the vibe of the video (a desert scene consisting of a bare tree, sand, and a mountain in the distance).

The Euro leg of the tour ran from September 16th (Barrowlands in Scotland) through October 18th (Johanneshovs Isstadion in Stockholm), which also included at some point an in-studio performance for a MTV Europe show entitled *Live and Loud.* The five-song set has been oft-bootlegged and circulated, and due to its lighting and camera work (heavy on the close-ups), gives off a late night/hallucinatory/dream-like quality throughout the top-notch—albeit not exactly high energy—mini-performance, which included "Burden in My Hand," "Spoonman," "Blow Up the Outside World," "Mailman," and "Black Hole Sun."

Photographer Ross Halfin once recounted an encounter with Chris during this leg of the tour—which supposedly would have taken place after Soundgarden's performance on October 9th at Le Zénith in Gay Paree. "I was in Paris, and I saw them do a great show—this was the beginning of *Down on the Upside.* Afterwards, I remember being in a room with [Chris] drinking, having a good time. And Chris ended the night by throwing a lamp through a window. What's the point of drinking if you can't enjoy yourself with it? Maybe it's the Irish in him—just wants to start fighting and being stupid. There's no point in being like that if you can't fight."

Shortly after the Euro dates ended, a compilation entitled *Guitars That Rule the World, Vol. 2: Smell the Fuzz: The Superstar Guitar Album* was released (on October 22nd), which featured some of biggest names of rock guitar showing off their skills—Rush's Alex Lifeson, Kiss' Ace Frehley, Smashing Pumpkins' Billy Corgan...and Dark Load. *Dark who?* Let me explain. Turns out that Kim must have had some free time on his hands at some point, and was part of a side project that went by the mysterious name of Dark Load—of which only a single track has ever surfaced from the band, on this comp. Entitled "Brewicide," it's an entirely instrumental affair—featuring a repetitive chord progression, with plenty of space for Kim to solo about one-third of the way through. And who else were members of this brief band? Then-Ministry drummer Bill Rieflin, Kim's friend Jeff Gilbert on second guitar, and a bassist by the name of

241 DOWN ON THE UPSIDE

Paul Larkin. But after this track, it all went Dark for the Load—nothing was ever heard from them again.

Around the same time that the US headlining leg of the *DotU* tour was launched in early November, the Doug Pray-directed documentary, *Hype!*, was issued, which included interview clips with such SG-related persons as Kim, Matt, Susan, and Jack Endino, among others, with a great live rendition of "Searching with My Good Eye Closed" featured (filmed on August 11, 1994, at Calgary's Max Bell Arena, which was the same show that also gave us the footage utilized in the "My Wave" video).

Also the same month, one of popular music's all-time greats opted to cover a Soundgarden tune. The gentleman in question was none other than the man in black, Johnny Cash, and the tune was "Rusty Cage." Released on November 5th and included on Cash's Rick Rubin-produced *Unchained,* the song was reworked from more of a roots rock standpoint, particularly with its unmistakable rockabilly gallop (with Johnny's backing band being none other than...Tom Petty and the Heartbreakers!). "I was simply knocked over that Johnny Cash would record a song that I wrote," Chris once said. "I remember when my brother brought home *At San Quentin* when I was nine. We listened to it over and over for about a year. Short of the Beatles covering a song that I wrote, it was the biggest fan experience I've ever had."

And another SG single was rolled out before year's end, "Blow Up the Outside World," on November 18th—with a front cover image of a beefsteak tomato with a single worm burrowing its way out of it...and a back cover image of the worm and a bunch of his cronies atop the poor fruit (yes, *tomato is a fruit*). By this point, the well was running dry regarding exclusive material for b-sides (Australia received near-decade old live tracks from *Louder Than Live*), but the Brits did receive one of the better remixes SG ever offered—of the tune "Dusty," reworked by Moby.

As I believe I have stated earlier, I find remixes to be a waste of time (does anyone actually really listen to these things/take them seriously?), as they rarely improve upon the original or have anything worthwhile to even add to it. But this is one of the few exceptions. While certainly not *better* than the original version, this remix at least offers a different sonic viewpoint, as it largely strips away the music and focuses primarily on Chris' vocals (decades before vocal-only versions of songs began flooding YouTube), and even features moans and groans throughout—similar to Moby's eventual breakthrough hit, "Natural Blues."

And wouldn't ya know it, *another* video was filmed! The "BUtOW" clip was directed by none other than Devo bassist Gerald Casale (who over the years not only directed classic Devo videos—including the iconic "Whip It"—but also, clips for the Cars, Rush, Foo Fighters, and even grunge wannabees Silverchair), and while it had good intentions, it surprisingly falls flat.

Featuring the band miming and playing along to the song in front of a blue screen, the main focus is Chris strapped to a chair and being forced to watch footage (presumably of his life), with his hands outstretched...a la a *Jesus Christ pose!* The whole "confined to a chair, being forced to watch unpleasant scenes on a screen" idea had been done to death by this point (Alex DeLarge in the film *A Clockwork Orange*, Dr. Hans Zarkov in the film *Flash Gordon*, W. Axl Rose in the music video for "Welcome to the Jungle," etc.), which results in an overblown clip that appears to have cost oodles of money to make.

Beginning on November 7th at Salt Air Arena in Salt Lake City, Utah and wrapping up on December 18th at Mercer Arena in Seattle, the *DotU* US headlining leg would feature various supporting acts (Rocket from the Crypt, Tenderloin, Pond, and the Presidents of the United States of America). And set-list-wise, a few treats were included—Chris performing "Black Hole Sun" all by his lonesome, as well as such covers as Iggy & the Stooges' "Search and Destroy," the Beatles' "Helter Skelter," and the Doors' "Waiting for the Sun."

The tour also had its share of sneaky sneaks sneaking in hand-held video cameras and documenting the events the best they could—one such bootlegged show I was able to acquire back in the day on VHS was the November 29th performance at the Mesa Amphitheater, in Mesa, Arizona. Highlights include an explosive version of "Ty Cobb," Chris dedicating "All the turkey souls floating around in turkey heaven today" before "Black Hole Sun" (due to it being the day after Thanksgiving), as well as Ben smashing his bass to smithereens at the conclusion of a set-closing "Jesus Christ Pose."

With Soundgarden's popularity in New Zealand and Australia seemingly soaring to an all-time high, the lads were invited to headline the Big Day Out Festival once again—on a bill that also featured the Offspring, the Prodigy, Fear Factory, Supergrass, and Shonen Knife, among others. And by golly, they accepted—touring as part of the fest (as well as headlining their own shows) from January 16th-February 4th. And on a side note— since it pertains to this month/year—Pigeonhed released their sophomore effort, *The Full Sentence,* on January 28th, which once again, featured the guitar work of Kim.

The *DotU* tour cycle would grind to a halt once and for all with a pair of shows in Hawaii—at the Maui Cultural Arts Center in Maui on February 8th, and Blaisdell Arena in Honolulu a day later. And it sounds as if the last performance may have been the straw the broke the camel's back. In a review that ran in the *Honolulu Advertiser* a mere two days after the concert, writer Gary CW Chun reported the following. "What made the last show of Soundgarden's world tour at the Blaisdell Arena memorable was not the great-sounding music, unfortunately, but the surly behavior of Ben Shepherd. Shepherd, who plays his low-slung bass with an assertive, rumbling pulse, made his bad mood known both to his bandmates and the audience more than halfway through the concert last night."

"What triggered his tantrum could have been problems with his instrument, but in any event he spent the remainder of the concert kicking at a side stage light, making obscene gestures to the audience and occasionally spitting in the general direction of bandmates Matt Cameron and Kim Thayil. Lead singer and guitarist Chris Cornell had some words with Shepherd, but that apparently didn't appease him. At the end of 'Blow Up the

Outside World,' he brought everything to an abrupt halt as he took off his bass, threw it up in the air, gave the audience the finger and stalked off stage. Hopefully Shepherd's onstage behavior was the result of exhaustive touring, and not the manifestation of ill feelings that may threaten the band's existence. There's still a lot of music from this Soundgarden."

Years later, Ben explained his side of the story, as to why he wasn't in the jolliest of moods that evening. "That last show we played in Hawaii was the night that I found out it was our last show. Because our bass tech, I'd gotten him out of rehab—which is another harsh thing about our family that was going on. I got him over to Hawaii, because they were the last shows we were going to do [on the tour]. I thought we'd do 'the Beatles thing'— take it easy for a while. Not fucking break up. So we played our last show, and he called a band meeting. He's the only guy besides one of us that can call a band meeting, because he had seniority— he was on tours before I was in the band."

"He goes, 'What's this shit I hear—this is your last show and you're breaking up?' Everyone didn't rebut that, they just sat there. I was like, 'What the fuck?' And of course, my equipment died that night. The opening band had already left, so there was no other equipment in the building. I got pissed and smashed my bass. I was totally out of my head—angry and pissed off. Drunk. And I was lividly sad, because that was the end of the tour after my honey had left me. And that was it, the last show of the tour that she should have been with me on. The last tour was the most creative and destructive music that I'd ever heard or been part of. The final magic."

Upon returning home, Chris kept up the facade that everything was fine and dandy with SG. Appearing at the 39th Annual Grammy Awards on February 26, 1997—"Pretty Noose" was nominated for "Best Hard Rock Performance"—he was interviewed briefly before the show by MTV's John Norris. And when asked if he was "jonesing" to get back to writing and recording, he replied, "Yeah. For the amount of time we spend not recording, it kind of seems silly, because that's what bands do— they make records. People write songs and make records. It seems like we don't spend enough time doing that. So, hopefully we'll be doing that real soon." And in case you were wondering, Soundgarden did *not* get to take home the prize that night—Smashing Pumpkins did, with "Bullet with Butterfly Wings" (a song from '95 winning in '97...oh well, whatever, never mind).

However, by this point, Kim could see the writing on the wall. "On tour, Chris did the best job of anyone in trying to communicate. He was grossly inadequate in that department in previous situations—but I think he really took a leadership role on our last tour. In terms of communicating, and trying to get the band on the same page. And I applaud him for that. It might have been too little, too late. I didn't see the band as breaking up—I just saw myself and Ben as being unhappy. Matt was also unhappy. Probably why Chris took a leadership role in trying to direct communication and bring the band together—I think he saw that there was a lot of dissatisfaction. He was definitely ballsy and courageous in trying. But like I said—*too little, too late*."

Judging from all the turbulence Soundgarden was experiencing as discussed in the previous chapter, it shouldn't come as much of a surprise that by springtime, the band was finished. And it turns out that the member that supposedly made the most effort to try and keep it rolling along during the past year or so, was the one that made the decision to split up.

"At the time, I was trying to get some songs going for the next one," remembered Matt. "One morning, I took my dog out for a walk, came back, and Chris's truck was in my driveway. I was like, 'Cool, Chris never comes to visit—we'll play songs together, work on some stuff. What a great opportunity!' So I go into the house, and my girlfriend at the time, April—who's now my wife—goes, 'Chris is in the basement.' I go down there, and he just reeked of alcohol. I think he'd been up all night drinking, and he looked a little odd. We started talking. We never really hung out that much, so I was like, 'OK, why is he here?' [Laughs] And then he was like, 'Well...I'm here because I'm leaving the band'."

As it turned out, Ben also received a similar visit from Chris. "Chris Cornell shows up—he's got a bottle of, I think, Canadian Club. We're all standing in my living room, and my friend goes, 'Today's the day the Beatles broke up.' And Chris goes, 'Here man,' and hands me the bottle. I take a swig, we go down to my car, and he says, 'I'm quitting. I'm breaking up the band. How do you feel about that?' I looked down at the ground, spit on the ground, and went, 'Alright.' That's how I joined the band—when they asked me 'Do you want to join the band?' I looked down at the ground, spit, looked up, and said, 'Fuck yeah!' It was kind of fitting for me."

"One of the first things I told [Chris] was I felt relieved," recalled Kim about a similar discussion he had. "And he was really surprised—he said that was the same thing Matt said. I think Ben took it the hardest. It bummed me out, but I did not shed a tear. Ultimately, we were a band for thirteen years—that survives most relationships or most people's employment periods."

"We started out doing everything ourselves, and we were always talking to each other," Chris explained years after the split. "But as things slowly transitioned into bigger business and required more people to help, the band just stopped communicating. We were always really happy in the studio. We were always really motivated, never pulling out our hair. But dealing with what the music business version of what Soundgarden had become..." And speaking of business, Chris also personally phoned the chairman and CEO of A&M Records, Al Cafaro, to tell him that a split was imminent. "I was shocked but not surprised," Cafaro once said. "It was getting harder and harder [for them] to keep a shared vision."

Despite still being married at the time, Chris opted to keep his plan secret from Susan. "Chris kept it away from me—for reasons of protection, and what he thought would be legality. He consulted with someone else—got another lawyer, and was very thorough about making sure everybody would be safe and protected. Once he got all that in line, [he] let me know what he was intending to do, and then did it a couple of days later. Came home absolutely distraught."

So, on April 8th, a statement was issued by A&M Records to the public, which simply stated, "After 12 years, the members of Soundgarden have amicably and mutually decided to disband to pursue other interests. There is no word at this time on any of the members' future plans." Later in the week after the announcement of Soundgarden's split, Silver was contacted by *The Rocket's* S. Duda, who reported she "Would only characterize the split as 'heroic,' while praising the band for having the courage to come to the decision and 'look into the unknown'." However, a decade later, SG's manager was more willing to open up.

"There wasn't any overt hatred between them—it was that dysfunctional relationship, where they're figuratively living together and not talking to each other. Which literally is the way Chris became as a husband. Here we are living together—not in this period, but later years—but he's not talking. That became the seat of dysfunctionality. There are these guys that have a career that could continue to grow, they can make it on their own terms.

They're unhappy with things about each other, but nobody's saying what they are, or talking to each other about what they are. So it decayed from within. And Chris just kept getting more depressed."

A mere two days after the split was announced, it was reported by MTV that Shepherd had joined the obscure Seattle band Devilhead (as a guitarist)—which was led by one of his co-Haters, Brian Wood. It was also stated that the new line-up of the band had already been rehearsing for a month, had written a handful of new songs, and had performed their first show together on April 4th, at Moe's in Seattle (debuting some of these new tunes, as well as a cover of AC/DC's "Dirty Deeds Done Dirt Cheap"). Unfortunately, the public never got to hear the fruits of Devilhead's "Shepherd era," as the group splintered before issuing any recordings.

Interestingly, the same month that SG announced their split, the fourth and final single from *DotU* would be issued (albeit only in Australia, featuring a cover photo of the band colored in red and black), which was a surprise selection for its a-side—"Ty Cobb." After all, picking a track that has "the f-bomb" dropped throughout will not exactly appease your average tight-ass radio programmer. And the b-sides were simply underwhelming— "Rhinosaur," the golden oldie "Big Dumb Sex" (I guess if you're going to say "fuck" on the a-side, why not indulge again for the b-side?), and a remix of "Rhinosaur" by Ministry's then-drummer, Bill Rieflin. Dubbed "The Straw That Broke the Rhino's Back Remix," it unsurprisingly sounds rather...industrial (a style trailblazed by Ministry)—particularly due to the clang of percussion and Chris' vocals being dipped in distortion. And since the band was kaput by now, no video was ever filmed for "TC."

And as if Soundgarden's split wasn't bad enough, it seemed like by and large, rock music continued to take a major swirl down the toilet around this time (OK, OK—*besides* Radiohead and Queens of the Stone Age). Case in point, the unwelcomed arrival of Creed, Nickelback, Puddle of Mudd, Staind, and Godsmack—all of which were mining similar sonic terrain as the grunge greats...but failing to inject any originality nor putting a unique spin on things.

As Ozzy Osbourne/Black Label Society guitarist Zakk Wylde once told me, "I remember my one buddy, when Creed was huge, I was like, 'Who's buying these fucking records? These guys are fucking gigantic.' And I went over to my buddy Eric's house, and in his CD player was the Creed record. And I'm like, 'So *you're* one of the fuckers that buys this Creed stuff!' And he goes, 'Well yeah, of course you asshole. Look at it, there's no more Alice in Chains, there's no more Soundgarden—besides listening to your dumb ass, how much more can I listen to my Zeppelin and Sabbath records? I'm not going to listen to fuckin' DMX and Dr. Dre and all that shit. Creed, at least they're playing guitar!' And I was like, 'Never mind...there's your answer, right there.' Hey listen, if we can't get any Coca Cola, give me a Mr. Pibb—I'll drink that shit. It's supply and demand."

In the wake of the split, it was reported that Chris—as widely expected—would embark on a solo career, while Ben and Matt would not return to Hater, but rather, had formed a new combo, Wellwater Conspiracy. With John McBain welcomed back into the fold, the trio's debut full-length, *Declaration of Conformity,* was issued on June 17, 1997, via Third Gear Records. And similar to their previous side-band, the release of the album was so hush-hush, that I only discovered it while briefly employed by a music publication, and spotted the album in a buncha bins of CD's that were up for grabs, and I had a foggy memory of hearing somewhere that the band had some kind of link to Soundgarden.

By inspecting the credits inside the mysterious CD, I was able to put 2 and 2 together—Matt was listed under the alias "Ted Dameron," while Ben was listed simply as "Zeb." But unlike Hater, WC saw Ben strictly handling lead vocals and no instruments, while Matt was credited with "drums, vocals, Minimoog, simulated rain, acoustic guitar, guitar solo on 'Lucy Leave'," while John was credited with "guitars, bass guitar, drums on 'Far Side of Your Moon' and 'Palomar Observatory'."

"We recorded it at my old house and here in my new one," Matt once explained. "It's basically some 8-track stuff that we did in the basement. We did two singles, and those came out, but there were only a thousand or so printed of each. It was a blast. I got to sing on a couple of tunes and play guitar. John pretty much wrote all the music. He's a retro king. He knows how to get the early, garage, punk style sounds. So it was a lot of fun." When I finally plopped the CD in my boombox (whose front cover was a mysterious illustration of what looked like a crab and a winged moon, with three Hindu-looking gents beneath), I was pleasantly surprised to discover that while it retained elements of Hater's lo-fi garage rock, it also welcomed in more psychedelic and experimental sonic components.

The majority of the fourteen-track CD was written by all three or at least some combination of two members, while three covers were included—"Lucy Leave" by Syd Barrett, and a pair of obscurities off a compilation entitled *Teen Trash From Psychedelic Tokyo '66-'69* ("Sandy" by the Carnabeats and "Nati Bati Yi" by the Spiders). Other highlights included such instrumental psych-surf ditties as "Shel Talmy" (titled after a record producer who produced such '60s classics as the Kinks' "You Really Got Me" and the Who's "My Generation"), "Far Side of Your Moon," "Space Travel in the Blink of an Eye," and "Enebrio" (the latter of which sounds like an outtake from the cult classic *Oar* by Skip Spence), plus such vocal-featured compositions as "The Ending," "Green Undertow," and "You Do You." However, by the time a second Wellwater Conspiracy album would be issued, Ben would no longer be involved. But still, to this day, *Declaration of Conformity* remains one of the more interesting/experimental SG-related side projects.

Since Soundgarden had never issued a best-of collection, what better way to wrap up their career (in time for the holiday season, no less) than with the 17-track strong *A-Sides,* released on November 4th. Sporting a semi-blurry, green-tinted photo of the band on the cover (that looks like it was from either the *Superunknown* or *Down on the Upside* eras), the CD booklet featured band photos plus a solo photo each of Chris, Kim, Ben, and Matt, with Ben's photo taking the cake (him doing a wild jump through the air mid-performance).

And while the tracklisting for the most part follows what its title advertises (collecting all the a-sides of Soundgarden's singles from 1987-1997), there were a few flubs. For example, the album opens with "Nothing to Say" (which was *the b-side* of the "Hunted Down" single), "Get on the Snake" is included (which was never a single), and a pair of a-sides were skipped over entirely ("Room a Thousand Years Wide" and "My Wave")—in order to include another b-side, "Bleed Together." Chart-wise, *A-Sides* only managed to peak at #63 on the *Billboard 200* and at #90 in the UK, but did reach #6 in New Zealand.

Post-split, Kim kept the lowest profile, as it appeared as though he had retreated from the public spotlight altogether. Though he was willing to discuss the break-up with his old pal, Jeff Gilbert, in the February 1998 issue of *Guitar World*. During the Q&A, Kim explained, "The break-up isn't filled with as much drama as you'd like to believe. We simply got to the point where we didn't want to be Soundgarden anymore."

When asked if he had any desire to play with anyone else at that point, he responded, "No. I was with the best singer, bass player, and drummer that I could want to play with. I don't want to go and get into another situation and ultimately feel disappointed. Anything else, by comparison, is going to seem second-rate. What I'm saying is that this is what I did for twelve years of my life. I don't know if I want to ever do this again. I do not see it as being an important thing to my life, outside of that time in a person's life when he's maximizing his prime abilities. Your prime ability might be to be a pitcher or a writer or a musician/entertainer. That may not be where your desire is."

But the last exchange in the interview proved to be the most interesting—concerning if Soundgarden would ever consider reuniting at some point in the future. "If we ever did it again, it would be for the creative element and the camaraderie. I think everyone likes and enjoys each other's company. We would do it for that reason. If someone were to dangle a million-dollar carrot in front of our faces, they wouldn't get a nibble because we're not interested."

"There are plenty of other things we can do. Music is just one of many employment opportunities available to us. We're talking about four individuals who are capable of retiring if they so wish. Employment opportunities are not the issue here, sabbatical is. As long as we're all alive and kicking and enjoying ourselves, nothing's over. Sure, there's a certain finality to what we did. It would be foolish and pretty stupid to say, yeah, it's over. But we ran our course. We had fun."

Needless to say, I was not only disappointed and upset by the split, but was downright shocked. Because judging solely from interviews in the press and on TV, it seemed like the band was getting along, remained a strong concert draw, and while *DotU* wasn't exactly a blockbuster sales-wise, it was still highly successful. And in a strange quirk, almost exactly a year later—April 20, 1998—my other favorite then-modern-day rock band (and oft-tourmates of SG), Faith No More, announced *their* split. Was there any correlation between such high quality bands as Nirvana, Soundgarden, and Faith No More going the way of the dodo, and the influx of such stinky styles as nu metal and rap metal taking its place on the radio/MTV? I'll let you be the judge.

However, the biggest SG-related news of '98 would be concerning Matt, when on April 17th, it was announced that he had joined...Pearl Jam! Up until this point, PJ experienced Spinal Tap-like troubles concerning retaining drummers—Dave Krusen, Matt Chamberlain, Dave Abbruzzese, and Jack Irons had all occupied the drum throne up to this point. So when Irons announced he no longer was interested in touring—in support of their just-released fifth studio effort, *Yield*—Cameron was summoned and accepted. Initially announced as not a permanent member but just a *touring* member, as of this book's release in 2019, Matt most certainly is a permanent member—having subsequently played on the albums *Binaural* (2000), *Riot Act* (2002), self-titled (2006), *Backspacer* (2009), and *Lightning Bolt* (2013), kept the beat on countless tours, and would be inducted into the Rock and Roll Hall of Fame with PJ in 2017.

Both Ben and Matt would appear on Black Sabbath guitarist Tony Iommi's debut solo album, *Iommi,* in 2000—which saw a renowned guest vocalist appear on each of the album's ten tracks (Ozzy Osbourne, Dave Grohl, Phil Anselmo, etc.). SG's former rhythm section would appear on tracks both separately, and in one case, together (the album-closing "Into the Night," featuring Billy Idol on vocals). Ben would also appear as part of Josh Homme's the Desert Sessions (1998's *Vol. I/Vol. II,* which was recorded at Rancho de la Luna in Joshua Tree, over a week in August '97), and would play on two solo albums by ex-Screaming Trees singer Mark Lanegan (1999's *I'll Take Care of You* and 2001's *Field Songs*), and tour, as well.

And in addition to his PJ duties, Matt seemed to be one of the most in-demand drummers in all of rock during the late '90s/early 21st century. For a taste of the artists he worked with during this time, here ya go—Queens of the Stone Age ("Born to Hula"), Smashing Pumpkins ("For Martha" and "Because You Are"), Geddy Lee (most of his solo album, *My Favourite Headache*), Chad Kroeger ("Hero"), and Peter Frampton ("Blowin' Smoke" and a cover of..."Black Hole Sun"). And let's not forget further work with Wellwater Conspiracy, which after their debut album, became a two-man band—Cameron and McBain—with guests (1999's *Brotherhood of Electric: Operational Directives*, 2001's *The Scroll and Its Combinations*, and 2003's self-titled), before splitting up.

While Kim kept the lowest of profiles of the four, he couldn't help but appear either on the odd recording session or part of a live performance, including teaming with ex-Dead Kennedys singer Jello Biafra and ex-Nirvana bassist Krist Novoselic (plus drummer Gina Mainwal), as part of the No WTO Combo—which billed itself as an "anti-globalization punk band," and played a single show on December 1, 1999, of which five tracks were released on May 16, 2000, as the album *Live from the Battle in Seattle.* Additionally, Kim provided guitar on the Wellwater Conspiracy album *The Scroll and Its Combinations* (the songs "C, Myself and Eye" and "The Scroll"), a pair of tracks on the 2004 self-titled debut by Dave Grohl's star-studded metal project, Probot ("Ice Cold Man" and "Sweet Dreams"), plus the

2006 Boris and Sunn O))) collaboration, *Altar* (the track "Blood Swamp").

　　Concerning Chris' post-SG exploits, seemingly ever since he offered up one of the best songs on the *Singles Soundtrack* way back in '92, there had been anticipation concerning if/when he would be launching a solo career. The first bit of solo Chris material that was offered was a song by the name of "Sunshower," as part of the *Great Expectations Soundtrack*—issued on January 6, 1998. The consensus? Another classic. Like "Seasons," "Sunshower" puts the focus on acoustic guitar and Chris' vocals, but manages to introduce percussion and also wah guitar lines into the mix, as well. As a result, this probably led quite a few fans to assume that his debut solo full-length would follow the same path of these two tunes.

　　With the arrival of *Euphoria Morning* on September 21, 1999, this turned out not to be the case. Instead of going at it alone, Chris enlisted two-thirds of the band (and once upon a time touring partners) Eleven—guitarist Alain Johannes and keyboardist Natasha Shneider. And besides playing on the album, all three would be listed as co-producers of the album, with the trio being credited as co-writers of the music for five of the album's twelve tracks (with Chris contributing all the lyrics on the album, and penning the rest of the songs solely by himself).

　　In addition to the aforementioned trio, a host of drummers were also utilized, with popular drummer-for-hire Josh Freese appearing on the most tracks (seven total)...and none other than Matt Cameron appearing on one. And concerning the business side of things, Chris' solo career would surprisingly not be managed by Susan, but instead, by Jim Guerinot...while the album was not issued via A&M, but rather, Interscope.

　　As far as the content of the album (whose cover featured a close-up of Chris' face—who may or may not have been sporting a bit of eyeliner—and a beam of light), it would suffer from the same criticism that I would have with most of Chris' solo material—it was certainly good, but lacked that certain special something that he was only able to achieve whenever he joined forces with his Soundgarden chums. And speaking of his former band, if you were expecting at least a few tracks that reflected their trademark grunge sound on *EM*, you'd be barking up the wrong tree—it was comprised entirely of material that caught Chris in a singer-songwriter mode, with bits of soul and R&B mixed in, for good measure.

But of all of his solo albums, *EM* would be the one I enjoyed and listened to the most—especially such tunes as the single/album opener, "Can't Change Me" (which featured a great spaghetti western soundtrack-esque guitar line), "Wave Goodbye" (a tune inspired by the tragic death of Chris' friend, Jeff Buckley), "Moonchild" (written about Susan), "Disappearing One" (the tune featuring Matt), and "Pillow of Your Bones" (quite a S. Garden-esque title, eh?).

One misfire was re-recording "Fluttergirl" and adding in electronic bits (the original demo is far superior, which would be included as a b-side of the "Can't Change Me" single). However, the album performed respectfully on the charts—peaking at #18 on the *Billboard 200* and #14 on *Billboard's Canadian Albums* chart—but came nowhere near what a new Soundgarden album would have achieved on the charts nor the airwaves.

Chris' touring band in support of the album included both Alain and Natasha, as well as bassist Rick Markman and drummer Greg Upchurch, and featured a setlist that leaned heavily on *EM,* as well as including "Sunshower" (the set opener), "Seasons," Temple of the Dog's "All Night Thing," and only a few S. Garden tunes—"Fell on Black Days" (which was one of the few instances during the performance that Chris would strap on a guitar, as he was primarily only holding a mic throughout the night), "Boot Camp," and "Like Suicide."

I was lucky to catch two performances of the tour in support of *EM*—on September 14, 1999 at Town Hall in NYC, and again on February 24, 2000 at the Vanderbilt on Long Island. And to be honest, there were not many standout memories (again, unlike the many Soundgarden shows I have seen over the years), although I do recall at one point at the Vanderbilt show, Chris told the audience we should all go to sleep, and he stood at the mic for an extended period of time with his eyes closed...until he ended the joke, by admitting that it felt odd to be in front of an audience with his eyes closed for so long. And while the solo performances that I witnessed were enjoyable, they would suffer the same fate as any time I would see a member of SG in an outside project—*I wished I was seeing the real deal.*

To get a taste of what the *EM* tour was like, there is an exceptional sounding pro-shot/full-length performance of the last night of the tour—March 7, 2000 at the House of Blues in Las Vegas, which I wholeheartedly recommend you check out (Chris is in exceptional voice throughout—and there is a simply *sublime* version of "Seasons" that needs to be seen/heard to be believed). And one last tidbit concerning the album—when it was reissued on CD and vinyl years later (on August 14, 2015), its title was reverted back to the spelling that Chris wanted in the first place— *Euphoria Mourning.*

And then, after the tour for *EM* had wrapped up...Chris' life seemed to become completely unhinged. But not entirely, as he and Susan welcomed the birth of their daughter, Lillian Jean, in June 2000. And from the view of the public, things looked like they were going swell for Chris, as rumors began surfacing that he had formed a new "supergroup" with three-quarters of Rage Against the Machine—guitarist Tom Morello, bassist Tim Commerford, and drummer Brad Wilk. Supposedly assembled (or at least, instigated) by Rick Rubin, it was initially rumored that the band was to be called Civilian, but later confirmed as Audioslave (ah, there's that "slave" word again!) and I recall Sharon Osbourne announcing on *The Howard Stern Show* that the new group was going to tour as part of an upcoming Ozzfest. But behind the scenes, not all was well with Chris.

First off, the Ozzfest appearance never materialized, because it appeared as though this promising band might be over as soon as it began—due to conflicts concerning business. With Chris being represented by Jim Guerinot (of Rebel Waltz) and the former Rage members being represented by Peter Mensch (of Q Prime), an agreement could not be reached to please both sides. In fact, Guerinot went as far as confirming to *Yahoo! Music* that Chris was no longer the singer of the band on March 26, 2002.

Then, to add insult to injury, thirteen early and unfinished versions of original songs were leaked to online file sharing services. Also, on April 19th, Alice in Chains singer Layne Staley's body was found in his Seattle apartment (in a sad twist, it was approximated that he died on April 5th...eight years to the day that Kurt Cobain died)—from the results of a "speedball," i.e., a combination of cocaine and heroin. Chris was spotted on April 20th at the Seattle Center as part of a memorial for Layne, sporting bleach blonde hair (a photo made the rounds of he and Jerry Cantrell at the gathering, sharing a laugh).

But as Susan alluded to earlier, Chris was suffering from depression, and around this time, his alcoholism and drug addiction worsened. "Unfortunately, being a child of two alcoholics, I started drinking a lot, and that's what eventually got me back into drugs," Chris once admitted. "You often hear that pot leads to harder drugs. But I think alcohol is what leads you to everything, because it takes away the fear. The worst drug experimentation I ever did was because I was drunk and didn't care."

When asked what specific drugs that alcohol led him to, he responded, "At first to prescription medication and then to pretty much everything. I'd had several years of being in control of my alcoholism. I was pretty reliable; I took care of business. And then when my personal life got out of hand, I just got loaded. So I went through a couple of years of depression again. I didn't eat, I drank a lot, I started taking pills, and at some point you just get sick of it. I was pretty sure that nothing like that would ever happen to me. Then I ended up having as bad a problem as anyone's going to have and still be alive. So I realized I'm not special. I'm just like everybody else."

As it turns out, one of his new bandmates came to his aid in a big way—and it sounded like he may have even saved his life. "We got together and wrote songs quickly," Tim Commerford once recalled. "Then we had some turmoil regarding management. We had a different management company than Chris and that caused a few problems. The next thing you know, it felt like things were falling apart before it even began. We had written a record, but for a second it didn't feel good."

"Chris kind of went MIA. Chris is such a different person now. He's on top of his game and on an all-time high, but at that time he was Seattle Chris Cornell. He went Seattle on us. I personally went to Seattle. I searched for him and I found him. By finding him, I found myself in jail. Not because he was there, but because I ended up in there. That trip to jail cost me a ton of money. I look back on that and think that was money well spent because that was a big part of why Audioslave actually became a band. It was worth every penny. I found Chris and I dragged him out of Seattle and we became a band that made a lot of records in a short period of time."

Thankfully, Chris had the wherewithal to agree to a stint in rehab (after an intervention took place, which included Susan and the other Audioslave band members). "Realizing how I was affecting people I cared about made a big difference," explained Chris in his decision. "The other three members of Audioslave didn't know me that well, and when we started making the first record, I was pretty much at my worst. I think they just looked at it as 'Oh, this is the kind of guy we have in our band now.' [Laughs] And we were writing great songs, but then it got scary from them. Their urging didn't come from a place like 'We're concerned about our careers.' It came from a place like 'We're concerned about you.' I felt a sense of sadness and fear in them that made me wake up. It was being around people who weren't part of the bad part of my life that I then saw how bad it was."

And it turns out that Filter singer/guitarist Richard Patrick was at the same rehab as Chris, at the same time. "On September 28, 2002, I was ready to stop drinking so I went to a facility in Malibu to get sober," he once recalled. "I was extremely skeptical and as an atheist I did not want to really try. Newcomers like me always want to shit-can everything. I woke up to some old guy saying 'I hear you're a singer.' I said 'Yes' and he said, 'There's some other guy here from a band called gardens of sound or some shit. You guys might get along.' He was talking about Chris

Cornell. I took my first baby steps into a program of recovery that lasted all this time with Chris' help. Chris said 'I know this shit feels goofy but it's the only deal in town that seems to work.' I wouldn't have gotten it if Chris didn't legitimize the whole thing for me. For 28 days, Chris helped lead the way. You saved my life buddy. I'll never forget you."

Eventually, both sides in Audioslave came to an agreement—the band would be managed by only one company, the Firm, and Audioslave's self-titled debut was finally officially released November 15, 2002 (co-produced by the band and Rick Rubin, and issued via Epic/Interscope, and with a cover image designed by Pink Floyd's go-to-guy, Storm Thorgerson). Again, a decent effort—especially the singles "Cochise" and "Show Me How to Live"—but A. Slave never came close to scaling the same heights as S. Garden. Although commercially, one cannot argue that the debut was a success—certified 3x platinum in both the United States and in Australia, while peaking at #4 in New Zealand, #5 in Norway, #6 in Canada, #7 on the *Billboard 200*, and #8 in Australia. I was able to catch a pair of performances by the band during their first tour—both when they were part of multi-band line-ups.

First up was NY radio station K-Rock's "Claus Fest" at Nassau Coliseum on December 12, 2002 (on a bill that also included Coldplay, Queens of the Stone Age, Zwan, etc.), and then again at Lollapalooza at Jones Beach on July 30, 2003 (featuring Jane's Addiction, Queens of the Stone Age, Incubus, etc.). Again, unlike Soundgarden performances, not a lot stands out for yours truly as far as memories of the Nassau show, apart from discovering that Tom Morello could leap rather high in time to the music.

The Jones Beach show stands out for the fact that at one point, a fit-looking Chris held up a recording device to the audience (who were whooping and hollering), and he said something along the lines that one day when he was an old man he would listen back to it. But the top highlight was at one point when Chris jumped into the crowd (which there was seating), and ran around an entire section of seats with his wireless mic, before returning to the stage.

And then, in 2004, Chris and Susan's marriage ended in divorce. As it so often seems to turn out with divorces, it did not go smoothly—as there were lawsuits and some public discrepancies. Audioslave would continue chugging along for two more albums—*Out of Exile* in 2005 (which topped the charts in the US, Canada, Norway, and New Zealand) and *Revelations* in 2006 (reaching numero uno in Canada, Australia, and New Zealand, while peaking at #2 in the US)—before running out of gas in 2007. After his exit, Chris returned back to his solo career, issuing *Carry On* in 2007, and the quite criticized *Scream* in 2009 (the latter of which saw Chris team with Timbaland as the album's executive producer—resulting in a very dance/pop/R&B-flavored recording), with each peaking at #17 and #10 on the *Billboard 200,* respectively.

In case you're wondering why the brevity concerning Chris' post-SG projects in this chapter, hey, this is a book about *Soundgarden,* so let's keep it as such, OK? And it was also during the early 21st century that Chris met Paris-based American publicist Vicky Karayiannis—resulting in the pair getting married in 2004, and the same year, the birth of a daughter, Toni (in September), and a year later, the birth of a son, Christopher Nicholas (in December).

It turned out that Chris was not the only ex-SG member to fall on hard times during this period. "My whole life seemed over," Ben once admitted. "Soundgarden broke up; my other band, Hater, broke up; my fiancée broke up with me; and then I broke three ribs. I got addicted to pain pills, drank a ton, and wound up OD'ing on morphine. I was laid out in my house for five days, and no one knew it. It was a fucking horrible time—this total rock n' roll cliché."

But it was right around this time that I first personally crossed paths with most of the members of Soundgarden. At the time—2005—I was a regular writer for the UK publication, *Classic Rock,* and when I received a press release that Hater was issuing their long-awaited sophomore effort, simply entitled *The*

2ⁿᵈ, I was able to convince my editor to let me interview Ben about Hater as part of the magazine's *Welcome Back* section (in the front of each issue). *But also,* I could interview him about Soundgarden, in hopes that I would be able to speak to others associated with the band—for a feature article about their history. Luckily, I got the go-ahead, resulting in the Hater article running in the May 2005 issue, and the larger Soundgarden feature running in the Summer 2005 issue.

For the Hater article, Ben and I chatted about why the material on *The 2ⁿᵈ* was recorded back in 1995, but not issued until ten years later. "It was just more or less a demo session that Matt and I were doing, getting ready to record *Down on the Upside.* We had the recordings going, just kind of messing around. Some of the songs were taken off the recording sessions and put on the Soundgarden record—that's how 'demo friendly' it was. And it wound up being called a Hater session, because the guy that we were recording with wrote on the cassette *Hater Sessions Two.*" After A&M folded, Ben eventually hooked up with friends who started an indie label, Burn Burn Burn, who offered to issue the recording.

A few SG-related topics were discussed in the Q&A, including a rumor at the time that he was working with Kim on music again (not true), and that a pair of tunes that wound up on *DotU* were originally recorded for these Hater sessions—"Dusty" and "An Unkind." When asked how the Hater versions differed from the SG versions, Ben replied, 'Well, Chris' voice fucking rules and Kim's guitar playing rules. Right there, it makes it ten times better. There's a fine line between being a demo and being a finished thing. 'Dusty' was just an instrumental on the Hater stuff, so Chris saved that song right there."

And as much as I'd like to go track by track concerning *The 2ⁿᵈ,* I am a firm believer in fairness, so since I did not do so for Chris' solo work and Audioslave (since all were released during "Soundgarden's wilderness period"), I just wouldn't feel comfortable doing it here. But...I will list my two top tracks—"Downpour at Mt. Angel" (which contains one of the boldest statements ever uttered at the end of a song) and "Curtis Bligh" (which could have easily fit on Hater's self-titled debut). Speaking of which...to be honest, *The 2nd* proved to be not as fun nor as strong as its predecessor—perhaps due to the fact that Ben and Matt didn't know the material would be the basis of a second Hater album.

In the same *Classic Rock* interview, Ben also discussed that he had formed a new band, Unkmongoni (a phrase that Tarzan used to yell to the animals to run and be free), which also included ex-Void guitarist Bubba Dupree and bassist Drew Church. However, by 2008, Unkmongoni was kaput (with no material ever being released—despite having recorded at least 20 songs), and it was later reported that Ben was completely seemingly through with music afterwards, as a thief robbed all of his equipment (including his cherished "Tree" bass), and as a result, "I slipped into a comatose state and went to work as a carpenter's grunt."

For the Soundgarden feature in *Classic Rock* (which, as I mentioned in the book's intro, was entitled *Black Hole Sons*), in addition to interviewing Ben, I was also able to speak with Matt, as well as producers Jack Endino and Steve Fisk, plus photographer Ross Halfin. As a long-time SG fan, this was obviously one of my top journalistic highlights up to this point. And I learned quite a few bits of trivia from Soundgarden's history that I did not know beforehand—such as Ben recounting how a band member would spend his evenings during the recording of *Badmotorfinger.* "Kim would be outside at night, smoking cigarettes in his van, listening to the Mariners games."

Elsewhere, Halfin discussed the band members' personalities circa the *BMF* era. "The thing about them—they were all actually quite quiet. They were very nice, but they were one of those bands that as soon as they started drinking...when people drink, everybody becomes a wanker. Matt Cameron, I never saw him like that. Kim Thayil would always get very morose and started wanting to be your best friend—crying and stuff. Chris would be alright to a point, and then he'd start doing things like kicking doors or tables."

"And Ben Shepherd would just go crazy. It would be like 'Fuck you and fuck you!' to whoever he could. It got to a point where they ended up getting security in England. Ben was walking across Camden Town, there was a bunch of English guys outside a pub, and he's like, 'Fuck you assholes,' and they came over and whacked him. So security was [needed] because they would just go off when they drank."

I can't recall how long after the article ran, that—to borrow a quote from Colonel Walter E. Kurtz in *Apocalypse Now,* "I realized...like I was shot...like I was shot with a diamond...a diamond bullet right through my forehead"—I had the basis (and contacts) to put together a book. But not just about Soundgarden, but the *entire* grunge movement—as I felt that the books up until this point written about the subject were either hard to follow or simply not thorough. Shortly thereafter, work began on what would eventually become *Grunge Is Dead: The Oral History of Seattle Rock Music,* released on April 1, 2009, via ECW Press. For the book, I was able to interview many of the main characters of the Soundgarden story at length.

Unfortunately, Chris' publicist at the time declined my request for an interview with him for the book, as it appeared as though his relationships with even former bandmates had become non-existent, as evidenced by this surprising quote from Jeff Ament in the book—"I don't think anyone in Seattle has heard from Chris in a long time." But to counter the disappointment of not landing an interview with Chris, I was lucky to conduct several lengthy interviews with Kim, plus a two-and-a-half hour whopper of an interview with Eddie Vedder, which was not only quite an accomplishment (he had declined to discuss Pearl Jam's early days for a *Rolling Stone* cover story in 2006), but to this day, remains my favorite interview that I've ever conducted.

Kim, Ben, and Matt didn't seem all that enthused about the prospect of a Soundgarden reunion when broached about the topic in *GiD*. But all that seemed to change in a flash, when Kim, Ben, and Matt reunited on March 24, 2009 at Seattle's Crocodile Cafe, to perform at a stop of Tom Morello's Justice Tour (a tour initially formed in celebration of the 60th Anniversary of the Human Rights Declaration)—with Tad's Tad Doyle stepping in for Chris behind the mic. The one-time performance (referred to as "Tadgarden" in the press) consisted of three songs—"Hunted Down," "Spoonman," and "Nothing to Say."

"Tom Morello was coming through with the Justice Tour, and he had asked Susan Silver—Tom wanted to get some notorious rock locals," recalled Kim. "Ben Shepherd and I were asked separately—we were going to be on the bill separately. As things worked out, it was getting close to the gig date, and Ben had not put together any project, and the guys that I was jamming with, our ideas were not gelling. We were going to do some old punk rock covers, and have Mark Arm sing. That fell through. And Tom called, and said, 'Would Ben and Kim like to join me on stage to do 'Spoonman'?' And we said, 'Sure. But we heard Matt is coming down to the show, and I'm not going to play it *in front* of Matt—I would play it *with* Matt'."

"So I called Matt, and he said sure. Ben said, 'Let's do the first single, 'Hunted Down'/'Nothing to Say,' and then we'll do 'Spoonman.' And then this left a problem with who we would get to sing with us. A lot of people that I asked were real hesitant—they didn't want to replicate Chris' performance. So it had to be Tad, right? It had to be the guy with *God's Balls* to say, 'Fuck yeah, I'll do it!' We went down to the Pearl Jam rehearsal space and had one practice on a Monday and rehearsed for an hour and a half. The next day, we went over them at soundcheck, and then we busted out those three songs [at the Crocodile Cafe]."

Almost exactly a month after the Tadgarden performance, I was invited by Easy Street Records in Seattle to do a signing/reading for *Grunge Is Dead* (on April 25th), which resulted in me meeting a lot of the folks I had interviewed for the book face-to-face, including Nirvana's Chad Channing (as well as Krist Novoselic, although I did not interview him for the book), Truly's Robert Roth, Mudhoney's Mark Arm, and three major names connected to Soundgarden—Kim, Ben, and Susan.

Due to our phone chats for *GiD* and our meeting in Seattle, Kim and I struck up a friendship, and as a result, I convinced him to do his first interview for a publication in quite some time—*Rolling Stone*—in an article published on July 21, 2009, entitled *The Soundgarden Songs You Haven't Heard: Kim*

Thayil Breaks His Silence. In the article, we discussed the recent Tadgarden performance, the possibility of a b-sides box, and his recent inclusion as one of *Rolling Stone's 100 Greatest Guitarists* (coming in at #100). But the last two questions I asked and Kim's answers proved the most interesting:

> **Ben told me he thinks that if Soundgarden were to get back together, you guys could pick up exactly where you left off.**
> I think he's right. We all play enough and are acquainted with the material enough that I think it would take a few rehearsals. When Ben, Matt, and I got together with Tad, it was like falling off our bike and getting back on.
>
> **That said, could Soundgarden ever reunite?**
> People would have to want to. I think more importantly, tending to the merchandising catalog is something that would be satisfying for the band members and for the fans. I never say never...but I'm not losing too much sleep over it, either.

For the remainder of '09, not a peep was heard from the Soundgarden camp. But...on October 6th, all four members were in the same place at the same time—the third night of Pearl Jam's four-night stand at the Gibson Amphitheatre in Universal City, California (which also included Chris joining the PJ lads during the encore for a rendition of "Hunger Strike").

And then, on January 1, 2010, Chris tweeted out a mysterious tweet—"The 12 year break is over & school is back in session. Sign up now. Knights of the Soundtable ride again! www.soundgardenworld.com".

CHAPTER 21
10 11

As expected, with such a bold statement (actually, make that a bold *tweet*), rumors started automatically swirling about Soundgarden's future, and especially, if they were back in business again. The band was not quick to confirm nor deny, but later in the year, Kim explained the true meaning behind it. "We're not the Knights of the Soundtable, that was our fan club. We were just re-upping it with the new website. But the rumors generated offers. The demand was overwhelming. I wouldn't say we acquiesced, but we kind of warmed to the idea." Matt said that it may have been an earlier business meeting that got the wheels in motion. "We got together, and decided we wanted to relaunch our catalog, get a website, be on Myspace. Just basic shit. We weren't online at all. We've also got a bunch of unreleased stuff we wanted to try to put out."

But getting back to the mysterious "Knights of the Soundtable ride again" message, it was linked to a site that showed a photo of the band playing live, and when you entered your email address for future updates, it unlocked a previously unseen video for "Get On the Snake" (which I never even knew existed!). Although low-budget, the video was arguably better (or at least approaching "just as good" territory) than the more costly clips from *Louder Than Love*. The half-color/half-b&w vid captures the band circa '89 miming the song, with both Kim and Matt sporting their best rock t-shirts (the Butthole Surfers and Nirvana, respectively), Chris showing off his topless torso and a pair of hole-ridden dungarees, and...none other than *Hiro* on the bass. And as an added bonus, shots of cows in a pasture and of a forest.

The next official announcement from SG (to their email subscribers) occurred on March 1, which simply stated that they would be reissuing their first-ever single, "Hunted Down"/"Nothing to Say" in time for Record Store Day (on April 17th), while also offering a free download to fans of a kickass live recording of "Spoonman" from the Del Mar Fairgrounds in San Diego, California in 1996—on what was their final US tour of the '90s. And then, *finally* what everyone was waiting for—the band confirmed they would be playing their first shows in well over a decade that year.

Now, I must warn you that the following bit may sound like I'm patting myself on the back...maybe I am. Or, maybe I'm just stating the facts. I recall having a conversation with Kim after it was announced that Soundgarden had reunited, and he brought to my attention that it was his answer to my last question in our 2009 *Rolling Stone* interview that helped put the wheels in motion for Soundgarden's reunion, as it showed the other members that he was open to the idea of getting back together. Of course, I'm not saying that they wouldn't have eventually gotten back together at some point anyway, but still, for a mega-SG nerd like myself, it was sweet music to my ears. Undoubtedly, that compliment will forever remain one of the top highlights of my entire journalistic career.

The first performance was a hush-hush affair, and not announced until the day of the show—SG was billed as "Nudedragons" (probably the finest anagram of the word "Soundgarden," although "Nursedgonad," "Raddungeons," and "Dadsneonrug" ain't too shabby, either) and were set to play the tiny Showbox in Seattle, on April 16th. And because the band posted the following request beforehand, "Please leave your camera and video recorders in the dungeon," precious few video or audio clips have surfaced over the years.

But one clip that did manage to magically appear was an official/pro-shot rendition of "Beyond the Wheel," which leads one to believe that the entire show was documented, and could one day see the light of day. And judging from just this one nugget, the band sounded swell—particularly Cornell's voice, as he had no trouble reaching the song's Mount Everest-esque high notes with the greatest of ease. But the 18-song set sounds like it was a jolly good one overall—kicking off with "Spoonman," and then touching upon all eras of the band—"Gun," "Rusty Cage," "Flower," "Pretty Noose," etc., and wrapping things up with a cover of the Doors' "Waiting for the Sun."

And this was confirmed from reviews of the show, including Travis Hay from *Seattle PI* exclaiming, "I was lucky enough to see the band twice when the group was in its prime—once in 1994 at the Kitsap Bowl and again in 1996 at the Gorge as part of Lollapalooza where they performed after the Ramones and before Metallica—and Friday's show was on par with how I remember Soundgarden." However, Ben thought otherwise—"It was boring; the crowd was dead still, and everyone was like, 'Yay! The antiques are moving?'!"

But the main show of the year would take place on August 8th, when it was announced that Soundgarden would headline Lollapalooza. But before taking the mammoth stage, they played a warm-up show at the Vic Theatre in Chicago on August 5th, of which fan-filmed footage was much more readily available than the Showbox gig. And once more, most eras were touched upon material-wise (except for no tunage from *Screaming Life* nor *Fopp*).

By this point, Lolla was no longer the traveling festival it was back in the '90s, but rather, a multi-day event held annually at Grant Park in Chicago, Illinois. For the first time ever for SG/Lolla, the band would be hitting the stage at nighttime/in the dark, on a day that also featured performances by the likes of Nneka, the Cribs, X Japan, and Wolfmother. As expected, the show was pro-shot, and a near 50-minute set of highlights would eventually make the rounds on select music TV stations.

While SG still sounded mighty and Chris could still hit all the notes, looks-wise, Kim was decked out in all-black and was now sporting a fedora (while keeping his long mane of hair in an easier-to-manage ponytail), Ben had "filled out" since the last time we saw him, Matt looked the same, while Chris had grown his hair long again and was now favoring Gibson ES-335 guitars (a model that Chuck Berry made famous).

And you couldn't complain about the edited TV version—especially such standouts as the set-opening "Searching with My Good Eye Closed," "Rusty Cage," "Outshined," "Get On the Snake," or the final tune, "Face Pollution" (although I would have been more interested in some of the tunes that did not make it to the TV version—"4th of July," "Like Suicide," and the *real* set-closer, "Slaves and Bulldozers"). Once more, I'm quite certain there is a complete version of the performance hibernating somewhere, which if combined with the Showbox gig, could make a fab "SG Live 2010" DVD/album combo.

The next substantial bit of SG news was when they were granted the cover of the September issue of *Spin*—a black and white photo of the lads outdoors, alongside the headline "SOUNDGARDEN: Exclusive! After 13 years, the grunge gods return. Now what?" Penned by David Peisner, the article didn't really answer the tough questions—was SG back for good? When would a world tour be launched? What about a new studio album?

But perhaps it is most memorable for painting the picture that Ben was homeless—due to his response after the interviewer asked where he currently lived. "Nowhere. Literally. I've been sleeping on studio couches and at friends' houses. I'm totally broke." Peisner would go on to elaborate, "Shepherd is part owner of a bar 15 minutes from here called Hazlewood, but he says he sinks any money from it into the solo album he's been working on since last fall. Six months ago, he split with his girlfriend and moved out of their house. 'This is my home now,' he says, holding up the sides of his slightly gamey overcoat."

With no new studio album ready to go in 2010, the decision was made to assemble a career-spanning retrospective, instead—entitled *Telephantasm*. And this time, they had another shot at correcting the tracklisting faux pas that plagued *A-Sides*. Released on September 28, 2010, the album was issued in several formats—digital, a single twelve-track CD (which was also bundled with initial shipments of the video game, *Guitar Hero: Warriors of Rock*), a deluxe CD version comprised of two discs/25-tracks (and a DVD of all their promo videos), and a three-LP vinyl edition.

Concerning its mysterious title, according to Kim—who coined the name—it means "Either a ghost from afar or an illusion from afar or an illusion at a distance," while the album's cover image features a wolf-dog in front of what looks like a destructed/abandoned city (and was designed by Josh Graham, who also handles the visual art side of things for Neurosis), with the *Badmotorfinger*-era Soundgarden logo making a surprise comeback.

Regarding the single disc version of *Telephantasm,* we finally get "Hunted Down," "Birth Ritual," and "My Wave" (all of which were sorely missed on *A-Sides*). However, we don't get a single bloody selection from *Ultramega OK*, while arguably the best-known tune off *Down on the Upside,* "Pretty Noose," has gone bye-bye, too. But we do receive a stellar, previously unreleased ditty, "Black Rain"—a track (lyrics by Chris, music by Kim and Ben) that began life circa *BMF,* but was never completed...until now.

Built around a massive riff (that sounds like a not-so-distant relative of "Cold Bitch"), "Black Rain" also features Chris singing in a high register—something he seemed to do less and less of after the *BMF* era. Also, it contains another stellar Cornell-ism—"Can't stutter when you're talking with your eyes." Released as a single prior to the album's release (August 17th), it went on to become SG's sole song to ever chart on the *Billboard Hot 100* (#96), which is un-freaking-believable—again, how the heck did "Black Hole Sun" not make at least *an appearance* on the chart? Can I get an amen?! Also, a best-forgotten video was offered for "BR," which features comic book animation, and a bunch of eye candy-ish effects...without a whole lotta substance.

The deluxe edition of *Tele* proved to be superior to the single disc—which is expected, since it more than doubled its tracklisting. But instead of including the best-known studio versions of songs, either alternate or live recordings are featured instead...which serves as a good news/bad news scenario. In other words, instead of including the splendid version of "All Your Lies" off *Ultramega OK,* we get an "'86 version" of the track, which pales in comparison (but does mark the first—and only—time that early drummer Scott Sundquist appeared on a SG album), the BBC version of "Flower," a live version of "Jesus Christ Pose" (from the "Black Hole Sun" single) in which Chris botches some of the lyrics, etc.

But probably the biggest fumble is the inclusion of the *Saturday Night Live* version of "Pretty Noose" (in which Chris' vocals aren't on par with the studio version), rather than "Burden in My Hand" (whose *SNL* version *was* better than the studio version). And tacked on as an iTunes full album download bonus track was a near title track, "The Telephantasm"—a mostly-instrumental tune penned by Kim, which was recorded but never released from the *Screaming Life* sessions (which would later be issued as a single on November 26th, with a version of "Gun" recorded at the Nudedragons/Showbox show as its b-side).

And as far as the contents of the DVD, it included either original and/or uncensored versions of the promo videos for "Jesus Christ Pose," "The Day I Tried to Live," "Pretty Noose," and "Blow Up the Outside World," as well as all the original clips (plus the little-seen vid for "Flower," among other visual goodies). Chart-wise, the single-disc version performed respectfully, peaking at #24 on the *Billboard 200*, #20 in Australia, #15 in Canada, #12 in New Zealand, and #11 in Greece. And when it came to certifications, *Telephantasm* was quickly certified platinum upon its release. Wanna know why? Because in somewhat of a cheap trick, sales were based on the first day of retail availability of *Guitar Hero: Warriors of Rock*, which as explained earlier, was bundled with copies of *Telephantasm*.

To promote the release of *Guitar Hero,* SG performed a "secret show" at the game's launch event on September 27th, at Paramount Studios in Los Angeles. The mini-set only lasted a grand total of nine tunes, but did prove significant in that it included the first-ever live performance of "Black Rain." And as spotted from fan-filmed footage, the band played in front of a black *Guitar Hero* banner, while Kim was spotted sans-hat and hair not confined to a ponytail—something he rarely did during the "reunion era." And then on November 9th came SG's final performance of 2010, when they played a pair of tunes, "Black Rain" and "Hunted Down," on the late night comedy talk show, *Conan.*

So, with *some* activity in 2010 (I can't go as far as saying *a lot*, as there was no significant tour or new album), I was curious to see how much of a workload SG was going to take on for 2011.

On February 15th, I was simply overjoyed when I read the following news item posted on the band's official page:

> *Over the past few months, we've been busy jamming, writing and hanging out together—exploring the creative aspect of being Soundgarden. It feels great. We have some cool new songs that we are going to record very soon. Thank you for all of the support!*
>
> *Loudest of Love,*
>
> *Ben, Chris, Kim and Matt*

And that wasn't all that SG fans could look forward to in the near future. While interviewing Adam Kasper for *Grunge Is Dead,* he offered a quote that certainly perked my ears up. "I'd gone on their last tour to record a lot of their live stuff—there's a whole great album's worth of live Soundgarden stuff that's just been sitting. Cool covers like 'Helter Skelter'." Strangely, although the grunge bands of the '90s were all great live acts, none managed to issue a truly classic live album that captured them in all their fully electrified glory—a la Kiss' *Alive*, Ramones' *It's Alive*, Cheap Trick's *At Budokan*, etc.

For example—Nirvana of course came closest with 1994's *Unplugged in New York*, but that was *electrified acoustic*. Alice in Chains offered 2000's *Live*, but was assembled from various tours from throughout several tours with Layne, and came off as sounding cobbled together (as did Nirvana's *From the Muddy Banks of the Wishkah,* from 1996). And Pearl Jam would eventually issue a seemingly never-ending smorgasbord of concert recordings, but such earlier offerings as *Live on Two Legs* didn't match the fury nor focus of their early years (although their live radio broadcast from Fox Theatre in '94 would have taken the cake if the entire thing was ever officially released...with *Live in Seattle 1992* coming in second place).

Finally, on March 22, 2011, SG released their first-ever live album (consisting of the concert recordings that Adam mentioned), entitled *Live on I-5*. For those who don't live on the west coast of the United States, the album's title is in reference to Interstate 5, which runs along the Pacific coast of the United States—which you could cruise on to reach the venues of the shows recorded for this live collection. Rather than feature a complete show from beginning to end, *Live on I-5* collects highlights from several concerts, which were then edited together to create a set list similar to what you would have heard as an attendee on the *DotU* tour.

Taped during November and December 1996, the recordings were from six shows—Del Mar Fairgrounds in Del Mar, California; Mercer Arena in Seattle, Washington (two nights); Pacific National Exhibition Forum in Vancouver, British Columbia; Salem Armory in Salem, Oregon; and Henry J. Kaiser Convention Center in Oakland, California. And kudos to Mr. Kasper, who did a marvelous job editing together and creating a vibe that sounds remarkably like it could have been a single show. And for a band that was on their last legs (mere months before splitting), they still sound highly inspired and ferocious—which shows once again what a special live act SG was.

Sporting a cover image of smeared neon lights on a freeway, the album was issued in a few different configurations— a download, a 17-track CD, a couple of pre-order goodies (an 18th track tacked on the end, "Blow Up the Outside World," or a five-track bonus EP, entitled *Before the Doors*), or a bonus DVD only available when purchased at Best Buy, of three tracks filmed at Lollapalooza 2010. And if you acted fast, maybe you were lucky enough to have obtained the limited edition double vinyl edition (which came with the *Before the Doors* CD as an added bonus). So now that we have all the technical mumbo jumbo out of the way...what was my assessment? I will borrow a quote of mine that appeared in *Rolling Stone*—"It's funny that for a genre of music that was so based on live performance, there hasn't been a definitive live grunge album, and *Live on I-5* finally sounds like it."

The opening one-two-three punch of "Spoonman," "Searching with My Good Eye Closed," and "Let Me Drown" is hard to beat, while the classics ("Outshined," "Rusty Cage," "Fell on Black Days," "Black Hole Sun," "Jesus Christ Pose") are balanced with some of my all-time fave SG album tracks ("Head Down," "Nothing to Say," "Slaves and Bulldozers," "Dusty"). And since they were still promoting *DotU,* the set tends to weigh in favor of that album ("Burden in My Hand," "Boot Camp," and "Ty Cobb"). But it's not to say that there is a flub or two. For instance, the decision to include covers (the Beatles' "Helter Skelter" and Iggy & the Stooges' "Search and Destroy") rather than a few more originals ("My Wave," "4th of July," or "The Day I Tried to Live" all coulda been a contendah). Also, not a single bloody selection off of *Ultramega OK* or *Louder Than Love* was included.

But by tacking on the five tracks from *Before the Doors* (titled as such because the material was recorded during soundchecks on that tour), all is forgiven—"No Attention," "Never the Machine Forever," a cover of the Doors' "Waiting for the Sun" (which is actually *better* than the two covers on the main album!), "Room a Thousand Years Wide," and "Somewhere." Song for song, an exceptional live album (although it didn't exactly rock the charts—peaking at only #47 on the *Billboard 200*)...and as I can attest, the perfect soundtrack to listen to at high volume, when you're trying to stay awake while driving home at 4:00am, after witnessing your baby daughter being born.

I was also granted another interview with Kim for *Rolling Stone* around this time (published on February 18, 2011, under the title *Soundgarden Prepare Live Album, Plot Return to Studio*), in which we discussed *Live on I-5.* "Ben and I were just talking about this last weekend—we're both still in awe of this album, the performances and the songs. It's kind of ridiculous how fast we're playing 'Jesus Christ Pose' or 'Ty Cobb'—it's much faster than the studio version. And there are some crazy fills in there from Ben, Matt, and me. Guitar solo things, weird bass runs and drum stuff. I think everyone was listening to the recordings and were surprised by individual performances, flourishes, and collective performances."

And Kim also weighed in on *Before the Doors*. "What's unusual about [the songs] is that they sound live, but there's no audience present. These amazing performances played to an empty arena, but you get the ambience and sound of the arena, and you get the reverb and echo that is emanating from the stage. It's a pretty trippy thing, it's like we're playing alone in a canyon or a cathedral."

When asked about the possibility of a full-on tour, Kim responded, "I think Matt's got some Pearl Jam commitments coming up, but we're always talking about stuff. There's always ideas. I don't mean to be vague, but we're always talking to each other and jamming with each other, and I think it's probably likely that we'll be playing live. And I think we would be happier to do that in tour form than just to do it as one-offs. If nothing's on paper or in stone, I wouldn't want to disappoint people—other than we want to do that and we're definitely talking about that."

In May, it was *finally* announced that Soundgarden would launch their first considerable US tour since 1996—spending almost the entire month of July crisscrossing the States, with a variety of strong openers dropping by (Coheed and Cambria from July 2-13, the Mars Volta from the 14th-23rd, the Meat Puppets and Queens of the Stone Age on the 29th, and then the Puppets, QOTSA, and Mastodon on the 30th). So of course, when it was announced that SG and C&C would be performing at Jones Beach Theater in Wantagh, New York on July 9th, I was ready. The last time I had seen Soundgarden, it was at the broiling show at the Armory in '94, which despite the less-than-ideal circumstances, remained one of the best SG shows I ever witnessed. So...my expectations were high.

I am happy to report that the lads certainly delivered that evening (the first time they ever performed at this open air venue without the threat of rain hanging overhead—*literally*). And the setlist was perfectly placed—all eras/albums were represented, with standouts being simply slammin' renditions of two *LTL* standouts, "Gun" and "Ugly Truth," as well as "Hunted Down," during which Chris jumped in the audience—as he had done previously at the same venue with Audioslave a few years earlier—and traveled a few rows in before standing on a chair, where he continued to sing, while audience members slapped him five and took shots with their phones.

And unlike the previous times I had seen SG live, now, they were no longer just going with a bare bones lightshow, but rather, now had a giant screen behind them, that showed moving images at various points—which appeared to be courtesy of Mr. Graham, a la the imagery that adjourned the *Telephantasm* art. And two tunes that the back screen phantasmagorias (yes, that's really a word!) seemed to work best with was during "4th of July" (elements of the *Telephantasm* cover) and "Loud Love" (moving neon highway smears a la the *Live on I-5* cover). And what better song to end it all than with a nice and long rendition of "Slaves and Bulldozers" (complete with the expected feedback finale). Quite a few powerful pix taken at this show by my pal Kurt Christensen can be viewed in this book's photo section.

And from a personal standpoint, I was lucky to snag a VIP pass for the show, which resulted in briefly catching up with Kim before the show, and him introducing me to Coheed guitarist Travis Stever—which led to a spirited discussion about both our admiration of Shannon Hoon. I also spotted Ben backstage and re-introduced myself, and he told me he and his friends were about to go listen to his solo album that he was working on (which would later be issued under the title *In Deep Owl*—more on that later). And after the show, I was allowed backstage, where I was introduced for the first time to Chris and Matt, and also, Matt Pinfield!

My meeting with Chris was fleeting—just a quick intro and a swift picture snap (he was with his two young children, so I didn't want to take up too much of his time). But I was able to chat for a much more substantial time with both Matt and Kim—staying so late that by the time we made our way through to the parking lot, our car was the last one left in attendance, amongst all the emptied/discarded beverage receptacles.

A few days later (July 14th), I traveled to the Borgata Events Center in Atlantic City, New Jersey, to enjoy another SG show. While it was not as memorable as the Jones Beach show, I was impressed that SG took the time to mix up their setlist (realizing that quite a few NY-based fans would probably be attending both shows). While both concerts opened with "Searching with My Good Eye Closed" and "Spoonman," new additions included "Big Dumb Sex" (which contained an intro by Chris explaining how it was a goof on hair metal bands of the '80s), "Black Rain" (the first time I ever experienced it live), and "Mailman."

One memory of the show—which is actually a non-musical one and quite sad—was a gent who was standing in front of me, who kept passing out and falling backwards (at least two times, from what I recall). After a brief post-show congratulatory meet-up with Kim and Matt, I was on my way to the casinos—to watch my friends lose some dough (I'm not much of a gambler, I'm afraid) and to breath in some secondhand smoke. From there, the tour continued on for another two weeks—wrapping up with the largest show of the tour (27,500 capacity), at the Gorge Amphitheatre in George, Washington.

But Soundgarden was not finished performing for the year, as they squeezed in two more dates at the end of October— the 26th at the Verizon Theatre at Grand Prairie, Texas, and a headlining spot at the Voodoo Music Festival at City Park in New Orleans, Louisiana, on the 28th (on a mucho varied bill that also included My Chemical Romance, Band of Horses, Ani DiFranco with Ivan Neville and Herlin Riley, and countless others). And just before the year expired, Chris issued an acoustic live solo album, *Songbook,* which featured covers (Led Zeppelin's "Thank You," John Lennon's "Imagine"), as well as two S. Garden tunes ("Fell on Black Days" and "Black Hole Sun"), plus various originals from his past ("Can't Change Me," Temple of the Dog's "Call Me a Dog," Audioslave's "I Am the Highway," etc.), as well as new compositions (including the album's lone studio track, "The Keeper"). While the album was not a major seller Stateside (#69 on the *Billboard 200),* it did fare better in Australia and New Zealand (#21 and #20, respectively).

So, for Soundgarden, all in all, 2011 wasn't just another brick in the wall—they had confirmed that they were indeed once again a legitimate touring band. So naturally, the next question would be...was new music on the horizon for 2012?

CHAPTER 22
KING ANIMAL

Probably the biggest bit of news to come out of my chat with Kim for *Rolling Stone* in 2011 was when I asked him if Soundgarden was working on new material. "We are jamming. Just getting to re-learn and re-love each other in a creative fashion. And it's wonderful, it's been going great. Everyone's happy, and there are a lot of ideas being thrown around."

"We do apologize that we haven't been able to share the past few months with our fans, because it really has been a couple of months of a lot of creative insight and sharing amongst the band members. Although there are many of our fans that would love us to be entertainers, we love that too, but the one element that we hadn't fully re-explored and re-established is the creative element. The creative partnership is certainly the one we wanted to set aside time to enjoy, and that's what we've been doing over the past few months. And I really would like the fans to know that."

But when I asked pointblank, "Is the band's goal to get into the studio at some point and work on a new album?", I was met with a rather vague reply. "Now, we are not currently recording, but we plan to—and will. The time we've been spending as a creative partnership playing music together and writing, with the definite objective to record and release new material. We're not yet recording, we're not yet releasing new material, we are writing—for that purpose."

By the dawn of 2012, no new album had appeared...but a new *song* would be offered for public consumption—a tune donated to the film *The Avengers* (am I the only person on planet earth who did not see, nor have any desire to see, this $1.519 billion grossing superhero flick?), entitled "Live to Rise." Released as a single on April 17, 2012, "LtR" was composed entirely by Chris and co-produced between the band and Adam Kasper, and starts off promising (with a worthy guitar riff)...before it transforms into a tune that sounds more like a solo Chris composition (especially the verses), rather than a true blue SG-sounding song. Certainly not the most memorable tune SG ever recorded (in fact, I firmly believe that "Black Rain" was far superior).

And equally forgettable was the song's music video, based mostly on clips from the film, as well as scenes of the band miming the tune in what seems like a humongous empty hangar, and by the end, they are performing in a windstorm (reminiscent of a previous sticky situation they found themselves in—towards the end of the earlier "Black Hole Sun" clip). Still, "Live to Rise" made its presence felt on *Billboard's* myriad of rock-related charts they have nowadays (topping both the Mainstream Rock and Canada Rock charts), while peaking at #69 on the good old fashioned Canadian Hot 100. Also, the tune would be included on *Avengers Assemble (Music from and Inspired by the Motion Picture)*—released May 1st—which, truth be told, besides Soundgarden, was comprised mostly of foul songs by foul artists, but did manage to peak at #11 on the *Billboard 200*.

I also somehow learned around this time that SG was indeed working on a sixth studio effort—recording at a pair of studios in Seattle (Avast! and Bad Animals) and one in Los Angeles (TNC). When I found out this tidbit, I tried convincing my then-editor at *Rolling Stone* to give me the OK to do an on-site "album update" report on how Soundgarden's album was coming along. Ultimately, the stubborn schlemiel passed on the idea (guess preventing more article space for such oh-so exceptional talents as Kid Rock and the cast of MTV's *Jersey Shore* proved too terrifying for him). Hence, a disappointingly missed opportunity.

But during the summer, the band did take a break from recording to perform at two mammoth outdoor festivals in England—Download on June 10th in Donington Park (on a bill below headliners Black Sabbath, but above Megadeth, Lamb of God, Black Label Society, Anthrax, Kyuss Lives!, and DevilDriver), and headlining the first night of Hard Rock Calling on July 13th at Hyde Park (over Iggy & the Stooges, Cold Chisel, Black Stone Cherry, and Kids in Glass Houses). The show was professionally filmed, with a particularly fine reading of "4th of July" being quite popular on YouTube (which is prefaced by Chris complaining about being hungry while being forced to smell the aroma of a nearby pizza vendor), while Led Zeppelin's riff-master Jimmy Page is spotted enjoying the show from the side of the stage.

Then, on September 17th, the news all Soundgarden fans had been waiting so patiently for finally broke—a new studio album would be released on November 13th, entitled *King Animal* (and released via Seven Four/Universal Republic, as A&M went bye-bye in 1999). When discussing the possibility of a Soundgarden reunion back in 2009 for *Grunge Is Dead,* Ben said, "I think we could fall back right to where we were, actually." So, as the date of November 13, 2012 drew closer, I thought back to Ben's quote...and was tempted to set my expectation level on an optimal setting.

Yet, I did have in the back of my mind that I did not care all that much for the recently-released "Live to Rise," but...had thoroughly enjoyed "Black Rain." So, it could go either way. Instead of going with a big name or surprise name concerning the album's producer (Beinhorn, Rubin, etc.), Soundgarden went with their old friend, Adam Kasper—the same chap that previously worked on such offerings as *Superunknown*, *Down on the Upside*, and *Live on I-5*.

With an album cover image showing a heap of animal bones in a wintry forest (done up by their now go-to-guy, Josh Graham), *King Animal* was issued in several formats—standard vinyl, CD, and digital download, and for those who craved more, a deluxe box set was in store, featuring a CD with three bonus tracks (demos of the songs "Worse Dreams," "Black Saturday," and "By Crooked Steps"), double vinyl, a DVD of SG's Hyde Park 2012 performance, and five lithographs. Additionally, if you preferred to purchase the *KA* CD at Best Buy, you would have received *five* demos as bonus tracks (add on "Bones of Birds" and "A Thousand Days Before" to the aforementioned tunes).

And furthermore, come 2013, you had even *more* options—the six-track EP *King Animal Demos* was released on Record Store Day (April 20th) as limited edition pink vinyl ("Halfway There" being the sixth track). Additionally, *King Animal Plus* featured five tracks from *Live from the Artists Den* ("Taree," "Blind Dogs," "Rowing," "Non-State Actor," and "A Thousand Days Before") plus an acoustic tune from Chris ("Halfway There") on September 10ᵗʰ.

So, let's get down to the real nitty gritty...was *King Animal* a keeper or a stinker? The album's opener also turned out to be the first single/video, "Been Away Too Long." If you were expecting to have your socks knocked off upon ignition, this was not entirely the case, but it did come close with this merry rocker, which seemed to lyrically be about returning to the party after being absent. But when you stack this punky-ish tune up against previous SG album openers ("Flower," "Rusty Cage," "Pretty Noose," etc.), it comes in last place. With Cornell handling the lyrics and collaborating with Shepherd on the music, it also contained a guitar bit at the 2:29 mark that bears some resemblance to the ending guitar motif of "My Wave."

Video-wise, the song's clip was directed by (who else?!), Josh Graham. Not featuring the band one iota, it shows a young woman breaking free of a straightjacket, residing in what appears to be an abandoned mental institution, being chased by dogs, discovering masked men made of snow or sand, and a room that recreates the *King Animal* album art. The outcome? A clip that comes off far too artsy fartsy and indulgent—that actually recalled the era of MTV in the '80s when directors spent big bucks trying to create overblown "mini-movies."

When it came to the "BATL" single, no b-side was offered (something that has become oh-so-common in the days of streaming and digital downloads)—but the single did precede the album by a bit, when released on September 27ᵗʰ. Featured on the single's cover appeared to be black and white flowers and a skull, as well as a design that resembled the horned skull on the *KA* cover, that would go on to be used as part of the album's iconography (especially concerning merch). Despite my slight criticism, the tune did prove to be popular with rock radio, as it topped both *Billboard's US Mainstream Rock* and the *Canada Rock* charts (and peaking at #5 on *US Rock Airplay*).

Song #2, the oddly-titled "Non-State Actor" (lyrics by Chris and Kim, music by Ben) is a fine n' underrated rocker—based around one of SG's trademark tricky guitar riffs (something that Chris never seemed to get proper credit for was his knack for being able to play these off-meter and/or complicated rhythm guitar bits and sing so impeccably at the same time). Kim once recalled that early on, the song was "Jokingly referred to as 'Punk Rock World Pop' for a while. I thought the title 'Non-State Actor' would fit with this...I don't know if 'international' is the right word for it, but something about it seemed rhythmically to be evocative of other countries, other parts of the world."

But getting back to my earlier point, the reason why I call it "underrated" is because while it *is* a good tune...it held the misfortune of being placed right in front of what is probably the best tune on the entire album, which unfortunately resulted in me oft-times forwarding it to get to song #3! In fact, I did not come to fully enjoy "NSA" until hearing a live version of it years later, on the *Live from the Artists Den* release (as its great guitar riff is much more emphasized). But before becoming fully acclimated with the album's contents, I recall becoming a bit concerned—the first two compositional offerings were OK...but not earth-shattering. Did I set my expectations too high with *KA*?

Thankfully, with the arrival of "By Crooked Steps," all was forgiven. With all four members pitching in (Chris lyrically/Kim, Ben, and Matt musically), the tune features not only the best guitar bit on the entire album, but make that one of the best they've *ever* offered! I'm not pulling your leg, either—I'm as serious as a heart attack. Which looking back on the tune now and the way the tracklisting fell into place, if SG wanted to really wow you straight away, *THIS* should have been the bloody album opener. The song would go on to become the album's second single (released on February 12, 2013)—featuring a cover design that resembled an image of a biker club logo, and would once more top *Billboard's US Mainstream Rock* chart, while coming in at a respectable #4 on the *Canada Rock* chart.

And unlike the album's first video, the clip for "BCS" delivered in a big way—in fact, I'd go as far as saying it was SG's best video since all the way back to "Burden in My Hand," in '96. As it turns out, mega-SG fan Dave Grohl enjoyed the song so much that he volunteered his services to direct the video— resulting in a comical clip (for whatever reason, SG never really showed their humorous side in video until this one) that shows the band as a Segway-riding gang, and bravely serving as what appears to be "good music police," as they take over a dance venue occupied by a lame DJ, and perform the song...before getting arrested by cops at the end. In fact, Matt once commented on the group's alleged "lack of humor." "Ultimately, we took our music real seriously, but we weren't humorless fucks like most people think the whole grunge scene was. Kim and Chris are two of the funniest guys I've ever met in my life."

Discussing the background of "BCS," Kim once explained, "That main riff is Matt. That's like in 5/4 or something. Matt brought that riff to us and he had that change, the little change modulation. He came up with that, showed it to us, and we jammed on it. And while jamming over it, I came up with that C section, that dreamy part. I'm not sure what the lyrics are, I'm not going to attempt to sing them, but that dreamy C section, that was Chris'. That was my guitar part and music and Chris came up with that dreamy lyrical part."

"And then the intro was mine, which was this delayed guitar part to evoke the idea of being stranded on a highway in North Dakota. It's this kind of meandering riff that kicks into this cool, aggressive 5/4 groove. And then Ben wrote that ending riff, that really quick one that sounds like something Jimmy Page came up with on *Led Zeppelin I*—you might know what song that is." Um, that would probably be "The Wanton Song" off of *Physical Graffiti,* Mr. Thayil.

Something I've always enjoyed about Soundgarden was that they would sometimes incorporate Middle Eastern-sounding bits into their music ("Half" being the most obvious example). And here, this exotic influence comes to the surface once more, in the Cornell/lyrics and Thayil/music collaboration, "A Thousand Days Before." It turns out that the tune had a working title of "Country Eastern," because as Kim explained, "This riff that I came up with, it sort of had an Eastern or Indian feel to it. But then I had other friends who when they heard the riff or the demo, thought it had what they would call a little chicken pickin' thing to it."

Up next is another champion—"Blood on the Valley Floor." This awesomely-titled tune (would've made a grand title for a Clint Eastwood western, doncha think?) utilized the same songwriting tandem as the last tune, and turns out to be a prime cut of SG—a big ol' guitar groove that rumbles along at a leisurely pace, that is one of the album's best. Up next is the first CCC of the album, "Bones of Birds." If there is a tune on the album awarded the "sleeper" of the bunch, I'd feel confident going with this composition, as it contains some of Chris' best lyrics of the entire offering and an outstanding vocal.

And Chris once explained the meaning of "BoB." "Lyrically kind of inspired by being a father, and having children, and having that stress...y'know that stress about you don't want to see them lose their innocence in a way that when children lose their innocence, they sort of learn about the real world, it's never a good thing. It's always because of loss, something bad happened, something they weren't expecting. I guess it's the stress that I feel about it. Not wanting them to go through those things, but obviously knowing it's going to happen."

To this point, Ben hadn't made his presence felt all that much (besides collaborating with the others on "By Crooked Steps"), but that was all about to change—starting with "Taree"—in which the bassist offers up a bit of a slow, Stones-y number (I know I've used the Mick/Keef-led band as a description often for Ben's tunes...but he was obviously a fan), which as it turns out, was penned prior to SG's split in '97. This is followed by the 100% Ben-penned "Attrition," a punk rager that sounds like it would have fit well on the second half of *Down on the Upside*. But as it turns out, according to Ben, it was written circa the *Badmotorfinger* era. "It was a commentary—it was two or three weeks after we went into Iraq. So I was kind of pissed off—'Look at this crap going on'."

Up next are three CCC's in rapid succession, which surprisingly, mostly fall flat, and slow down the momentum that the album had achieved over the last handful of stout selections. The first one, "Black Saturday," is largely forgettable, although lyrically, Chris explained it as "It's like one of those conversations you have with your buddy when you're in your twenties, and you say, 'If I ever turn out like my father, hit me over the head with a brick, and then cut me in half and put in a freezer, and then when I'm frozen, either put me through a vegetable slicer or a wood chipper.").

The second, "Halfway There," suffers from the same problem as "Live to Rise"—it sounds like it would have fit better on a CC solo album. And the tune was astonishingly released as the album's third and final single (on September 3rd, whose cover merely recycled the "Been Away Too Long" cover, albeit in a lighter shade), featuring yet another Josh Graham-directed video, which proved to be spacey and psychedelic, with close-up shots of an astronaut's face and glowing lights. The band would largely be absent from this clip (except for their faces making a cameo towards the end, as well as the horned *KA* doohickey), and overall, the clip proved to be reminiscent of the "Star Gate sequence" of the classic Stanley Kubrick-directed film, *2001: A Space Odyssey.*

Rounding out this CCC trio is "Worse Dreams," which is his best offering of the three (starting off sounding similar to the beginning of the early SG tune, "Entering," or even Bauhaus' "Bela Lugosi's Dead," before leading to a resilient chorus). However, Kim likened its feel to the early Pink Floyd classic, "Lucifer Sam," while Ben equated it to 1931 German drama-thriller, *M,* starring Peter Lorre. So, to be frank, while Chris was still in fine voice and provided some inspired lyric-writing elsewhere on *KA*, he certainly didn't bring his A-game to the table concerning the quality of most of the songs he composed entirely on his own (unlike say, *Superunknown*)—the exception being "Bones of Birds."

Thankfully, *KA* ends on a high note, with two killer tracks back-to-back. First "Eyelid's Mouth" (now if that isn't a blatant Cornell song title, I don't know what is!), which was a collaboration between Chris and Matt. A mid-tempo rocker built upon a solid riff and a Superman-strong chorus (plus a great guitar solo by Kim—perhaps his best of the entire album), it is certainly one of the album's standouts. Which leads to mentioning—Matt just may deserve the MVP award on *KA*, as he played a crucial role in the composing of two of the top tunes on the album. So on that note, I congratulate you, Mr. Cameron, on receiving this award!

And then...on to the album's grand finale. For quite some time, it was clear that "By Crooked Steps" was my top tune of the album. But upon repeated listens, its closer, "Rowing," has become tied. For starters, the song (which sees Chris provide the lyrics, and Chris and Ben collaborate musically) is probably the most original-sounding of the album, as it is not comparable to *any* previous SG tune. In fact, if anything, its repetitive bassline is more reminiscent of one of Kim's faves, Tool. It also contains some of my favorite lyrics that Chris ever penned, with the line "Don't know where I'm going, I just keep on rowing, I just keep on pulling (polling?), gotta row" repeated throughout as if it was a mantra.

But really, from beginning to end, "Rowing" contains some of my favorite Cornell lyrics *ever*—if you're not familiar with the words, you should really make it a point to sit down and study them at some point. For a gentleman that never completed high school, it's amazing how gifted Chris was at writing poetic lyrics and summing up universal feelings...which is obviously not an easy thing to accomplish (which ultimately, makes him one of my favorite rock lyricists of all-time—up there with the lofty likes of John, Stevie, Freddie, Sting, and Kurt). Comparing "Rowing" to SG's earlier album-enders, I would be bold enough to proclaim it amongst their all-time best—perhaps only outdone by, or even possibly tied with, "Like Suicide."

Sonically however, *KA* contained the same problem that the majority of hard rock records of the early 21st century suffered from—it sounds as if the low levels were pushed to the max, as if you were only going to listen to it in a car with a Dr. Dre-approved subwoofer. As a result, if you were to listen to say, *Louder Than*

Love directly after *KA*, you will probably be diving for the volume control to properly adjust it—to prevent your party guests from dropping their cocktails and holding their ears in discomfort. So, a far less gonzo mix—more like, oh say, *Superunknown* or *Down on the Upside*—would have proven far more beneficial and enjoyable...and not so much "of the time" (I predict that this era—years from now—will be looked upon as one in which rock albums suffered from this common sonic slip-up).

Even with my critiques and concerns, I think *King Animal* was a very solid album, and ultimately, did indeed manage to satisfy my expectations. Is it in my top-ten rock albums of all-time, like either *Badmotorfinger* or *Superunknown* is? No. But...still impressive—especially if you consider how long a layoff there was between SG studio albums (so, it turns out that Ben wasn't pulling our legs with his earlier prediction).

Another way to gauge the high quality of *KA*—quite a few rock and metal bands whose classic line-ups had been frozen in carbonite had been recently thawed, and offered comeback albums all around the same time—Faith No More (2015's *Sol Invictus*), Stone Temple Pilots (2010's self-titled), Primus (2014's *Primus & the Chocolate Factory with the Fungi Ensemble*), Anthrax (2011's *Worship Music*)...heck, even three-quarters of Alice in Chains came back with a new singer, William DuVall (2009's *Black Gives Way to Blue*). However, if I had to pick the best of the bunch when stacked up to their classic work, I would confidently go with *King Animal*.

But as it turned out, the reviews from others were mixed. Reviewing the album for *Rolling Stone,* Jon Dolan gave it a 3.5 out of 5 star rating, saying, "Now, there isn't much of a rock mainstream left to dominate; big, heavy, high-protein bands like Soundgarden are all but extinct. Which is exactly why *King Animal* is a weirdly cool beast to encounter in 2012—like running into a mastodon in a Melvins t-shirt."

Stuart Berman from *Pitchfork* was less impressed, giving it a tepid 5.9 review, saying, "And in the decade and a half that Soundgarden were out of commission, there have been many art-metal aspirants—from the Deftones and Queens of the Stone Age to Mastodon and Boris—who've aimed for a similar balance of brains and brawn. The best hope for *King Animal* was that Soundgarden would be inspired enough by their spiritual successors to want to outdo them, and set a new benchmark for ambitious aggression. Instead, the group's first album since 1996 just sounds like the one they would've churned out in 1998."

And one of the better reviews was from Mary Ouellette from *Loudwire,* who said, "In music, it's sometimes difficult to stand the test of time but Soundgarden prove with *King Animal* that they did not reassemble simply to preserve a legacy but to build on one that's already firmly in place."

While there was no tour to coincide with the album's release, there were a handful of shows and TV performances—including a November 6th appearance on *Later with Jools Holland* in England (which included performances of "Been Away Too Long," "Rusty Cage," and "Taree"), followed by two full concerts. The first would be at the Westend Indoor Festival in Dortmund, Germany on November 7th, and the other at the O2 Shepherd's Bush Empire in London, England on November 9th. Returning back to America, the band then performed a mini-set in front of a small audience at the Ed Sullivan Theater in NYC on November 12th—as part of the *Live on Letterman* concert series ("Worse Dreams," "By Crooked Steps," "Incessant Mace," "Beyond the Wheel," "Taree," "A Thousand Days Before," "Eyelid's Mouth," "Non-State Actor," "Fell on Black Days," and "Rowing" were all performed).

On the day of the album's release, Soundgarden performed a special show at the nice and cozy Irving Plaza in NYC, which I was able to score tickets for. And it turned out to be one of my all-time fave SG gigs that I have ever attended—due to a fine performance by the band, strong setlist, hearing the new tunes performed live, and a prime standing spot—in the first row of the balcony opposite the middle of the stage (getting to the venue early always pays off, folks!). And this time, I *did* get the go-ahead from *Rolling Stone*—to review the show. In a piece entitled *Soundgarden Thunder Through Album Launch in New York* (with the subtitle *Intimate show for 'King Animal' proves grunge vets are still 'Ultramega OK')* that ran the next day (November 14th), here is what I had to say:

> Although Soundgarden has been gigging off and on since reuniting in 2010, it was not until a recent mini-tour of smaller venues in England and North America that fans were finally able to hear a healthy helping of new material. At the group's Tuesday night stop at New York City's 1,025-capacity Irving Plaza, many new songs from *King Animal*, the group's first all-new studio album in 16 years, did battle with countless grunge classics.
>
> When a black curtain parted, the *King Animal* album cover greeted the crowd as the stage's backdrop. Guitarist Kim Thayil and bassist Ben Shepherd donned hats for the performance (a fedora and a newsboy cap, respectively), and Chris Cornell rekindled his grunge-god persona, complete with long hair and black stomp boots. Keeping the beat throughout was sometime Pearl Jam drummer Matt Cameron, who is one of the few major rock drummers to forgo a Peter Criss-approved drum riser, instead opting to remain close to the stage with his modestly-sized kit.
>
> Straightaway, you knew it was a "hardcore fans only" type of show, as the band chose to go with such tracks as the *Ultramega OK* obscurity "Incessant Mace" (the set opener) in place of expected stand-bys (like "Black Hole Sun"). During the set's second tune, "Gun," the mostly older crowd behaved like young kids again, slam dancing into one another after the mid-song advice to "buckle up." The leadoff single/video from *King Animal*, "Been Away Too Long," was featured, as was a smattering of other new tunes, some of which could use a bit more onstage honing ("Taree") and some that already sounded like behemoths ("By Crooked Steps").

However, it was the classics that drew the biggest crowd response, especially "Hunted Down" (which stirred up the mosh pit once more) and "Outshined" (which featured the crowd singing the lyrics nearly as loud as Cornell).

Foo Fighters drummer Taylor Hawkins, who was spotted by the soundboard, seemed to be having a grand old time. One person who didn't appear to be having such a jolly time was Shepherd, who prowled the stage all night, as if looking for something to set him off. At one point he yelled at someone offstage before kicking a few monitors out of his way.

For an encore, Cornell threatened a "45-minute version" of "Slaves & Bulldozers," which didn't meander that long, but did conclude with five minutes of swirling feedback. After the curtains closed and the prerecorded strains of Deep Purple's "Speed King" came on, some headed for the exits. But after chants of "one more song," Soundgarden did return with a slamming rendition of the *Badmotorfinger* gem "Rusty Cage." (Unfortunately, the feedback and break time prevented a performance of "Flower," which was on the set list). As the band left the stage, a sweat-drenched Cornell thanked the crowd; Thayil was the last one to exit, but not before toasting the crowd with his Budweiser.

For those unable to score tickets to this cozy gig, some relief will soon be on its way: a far more extensive Soundgarden U.S. tour has been announced for early next year.

After the show, I was able to quickly congratulate Kim on a job well done, for which he gifted me a cold can of Bud. He also was kind enough to briefly introduce me to the gentleman who was now managing Soundgarden, Gary Gersh, who was then the CEO of The Artist Organization (TAO) management firm, and had previously worked with the likes of Nirvana, Rage Against the Machine, and the Beastie Boys. Due to the small dressing room being jam-packed, Kim apologized for not being able to chat at length, but did promise that we would be able to catch up soon—as Soundgarden would be launching a more substantial tour in support of *KA,* and returning in the new year to NYC.

But there would be three more performances to go in 2012—November 16th at the Phoenix Theatre in Toronto, Canada, the 26th at *Jimmy Kimmel Live* in Los Angeles (where the songs "By Crooked Steps," "Been Away Too Long," "Rowing," "Rusty Cage," and "Beyond the Wheel" were performed), and a final performance at the Fonda Theatre (also in LA) on the 27th. But it was in 2013 that the real touring in support of *KA* would commence. Kicking things off on January 16th with a show at Terminal 5 in NYC, SG would remain on the road for the next month touring North America, including a three-song performance at the Commander-in-Chief Ball at the Walter E. Washington Convention Center in Washington, DC on the 21st (including a photo op between all four band members and Barack and Michelle Obama), before beginning a two-night stand the following evening at the Hammerstein Ballroom in NYC. And it just so happens, I attended the first evening.

I remember it feeling like one of the coldest nights of the year (oh how much fun it is to wait on a train platform when a nice and refreshing January breeze comes whooshing along), but hey, this was *Soundgarden* we were talking about, so I was most certainly willing to brave the elements. But to be honest, the show was not entirely enjoyable, for reasons outside the band's hands— due to a ticket snafu, I had to move my seats several times due to moronic ticket ushers changing their tune repeatedly about where I was to sit. Eventually, I just gave up and retreated to the only empty seats in the venue—way in back of the balcony, and with a partially obstructed view.

But when I *could* focus on the show (which opened with "Jesus Christ Pose" and closed with "Beyond the Wheel," and surprisingly, contained no "Slaves and Bulldozers"), some standouts I enjoyed included "Outshined," when an audience member held up a sign, inquiring if he could come up onstage to play guitar with the band. Chris surprisingly accepted this odd request, and handed him one of his guitars. But just as the young lad strapped on the instrument, Chris' guitar tech quickly appeared and took the instrument away—as it turned out it was in another tuning (which would have sounded like a limo wreck). This resulted in Soundgarden's special guest standing by himself for a spell on stage while the song was being played...until he was presented with an instrument that was in the proper tuning. And it turned out that the mysterious man could indeed play well—as he kept up with the others.

However, the real treat was witnessing two tunes that had either not been performed in a long time or never at all—the *Down on the Upside* classics "Rhinosaur" (first performed since 1997) and "Zero Chance" (its live debut). It was surprising to learn that "ZC" had never been played onstage before—especially after Chris announced that it was one of his favorite SG songs. Another memorable moment was at the beginning of "Blood on the Valley Floor," there was a moving image behind the band on a screen that replicated the front cover image of *KA*, but had snow gently falling on the buncha bones—which created a hypnotic effect when merged together with the song's goliath groove. And a final memory occurred after the show—when chatting with Kim, he warned that he was either suffering from, or just getting over, the flu. So, as a precautionary measure, I kept a considerable distance and kept our post-performance chat brief.

Soundgarden continued the first leg of the *King Animal* tour throughout mid-February, when they closed it out with a three-night stand at the Wiltern Theatre in Los Angeles, from the 15th-17th. And the last night was filmed for the PBS series, *Live from the Artists Den*—which would premiere over a year later (the week of July 8th) in edited form, before the entire mammoth 28-song/2.5 hour set would be released on July 26, 2019, as several configurations—download, CD, 4-LP vinyl, Blu-ray, and of course, the obligatory behemoth box set (comprised of 4 LP's, 2 CD's, a 40-page book, band member lithos, and other assorted tchotchkes).

As I stated earlier concerning the *Live on I-5* release, my main complaint with most rock artists' live recordings (particularly the ones in the '70s) is that they are not entirely live, as they sound heavily doctored in the studio. Now, of course I could care less if one or two overdubs (to fix flubs) occur...but quite a few foolers way back when would often re-record entire songs (in some cases, *entire albums*) in the recording studio, add in an audience track, and consider it "live." The reason I bring this up again is because on *Live from the Artists Den,* it is very apparent that few—if any—overdubs were utilized. Case in point, some of the tunes catch Chris' voice sounding a bit ragged (particularly "Been Away Too Long," the beginning of "Jesus Christ Pose," etc.). But I'm sure I am not alone in stating that I would *so much* rather hear an honest document of a live rock band—including a few mishaps or bum notes—rather than someone trying to pull the wool over my eyes. Heck, that's the whole point of seeing a band live—to see if they can pull it off live. And that is what makes *LftAD* a winner.

And it also features a stellar tracklisting, as well. Similar to when I saw them the previous November, they opted to open the set with "Incessant Mace," which I wouldn't have thought would make a solid set starter (compared to say, such other more uptempo options as "Jesus Christ Pose" or "Spoonman"), but its moody Zep-groove works wonders as an opener. As expected, we receive a healthy helping of *King Animal,* since they were promoting the album, and in two cases, "By Crooked Steps" and "Blood on the Valley Floor," the riffs sound even heavier and grander when performed on stage.

Also, I may go as far as to boldly proclaim the version of "Non-State Actor" here being *better* than the studio version. You also have to admire that they took on two obscurities that evening, "Blind Dogs" and "New Damage," which just so happen to be amongst the best performances of the set. Elsewhere, you can't go wrong with "My Wave," "Flower," "Rowing," "Taree," "Hunted Down," "4th of July," nor an explosive rendition of "Ty Cobb."

After taking a two-month breather, SG resumed the tour on April 22nd at the Fifth Avenue Ballroom, in Royal Oak, Michigan, before wrapping things up on May 31st at the Palacio de los Deportes in Mexico City. And in between, they also performed at two humongo festivals—DC101 Chili Cook-Off at RFK Stadium in Washington, DC (on May 4th) and Rock on the Range at Crew Stadium in Columbus, Ohio (on May 19th). After surprisingly not taking part in any summer Euro festivals (you'd think they'd be eager to—with a new album to promote), they did launch a brief *indoor* Euro tour on September 4th at Hartwall Areena (yep, it really was spelt "Areena") in Helsinki, Finland, that wrapped up on September 19th with the second of a two-night stand at O2 Academy Brixton in London, England.

And it was right in the middle of this tour (August 27th) that Ben released his first-ever solo album, *In Deep Owl,* credited to HBS (as in...Hunter Benedict Shepherd). The focus of the album appears to be on voice and guitar, as well as barebone song structures, with Ben handling all vocal, guitar, and bass duties (as well as mandolin and a bit of drums), while several renowned drummers drop by—Matt Cameron, Matt Chamberlain, and Greg Gilmore.

Standouts include the album opening "Stone Pale" (which sounds reminiscent to Queens of the Stone Age's "This Lullaby"), "Koda" (which includes frog ribbits throughout), and "Baron Robber" (which sounds quite Hater-like). Concerning the album's mysterious title, Ben once explained, "That's an old nickname for the neighborhood where I hang out," while its cover was not the most stunning artwork ever—a green backdrop with what looks like rope in a circle, with sunlight rays emanating from it, and the artist/album title within the loop.

On November 13th, a message was posted to Soundgarden's official website from Matt, explaining that he would be taking 2014 off from working with Soundgarden, in order to promote Pearl Jam's latest album, *Lightning Bolt* (but made it a point to state that his absence was only *temporary*, as to prevent any "Matt has left Soundgarden" rumors). The note also confirmed that Soundgarden would be touring in 2014 with a substitute drummer. It eventually was announced that—in a funny twist—one-time PJ drummer Matt Chamberlain (that's him in the "Alive" video) would be the fill-in. However, Mr. Cameron *would* actually occupy the drum throne at a handful of 2014 shows—including a performance on June 2nd at Webster Hall in NYC.

Webster Hall turned out to be quite a special show, as SG performed *Superunknown* in its entirety to celebrate its 20th anniversary—and was later aired on *Howard 101* (one of Howard Stern's two channels on Sirius Radio). Probably my biggest SG concert regret was that I was offered tickets to this show, but a mere day or two beforehand. I could not find someone to accompany me on such short notice...so I wound up not going. If I were to do it all over again, I would have simply flipped my friends the bird and flown solo—to witness this once-in-a-lifetime concert event. But I admit...I fumbled the ball when it mattered most. I hope you can forgive me.

It turned out that as a result of this special performance, Chris gained a new appreciation of the album, and also, specific songs. "'Limo Wreck' is one we haven't played since getting back together in 2010. It was one of those where if it were someone else's song, I would have thought, 'God, why didn't I write that?' or 'How brilliant is that?' And it's complicated. There's a lot going on, and it's in a strange tuning and there are a lot of things musically that don't make sense; those things are fascinating to me."

"I was listening with fresh ears, so I was maybe not quite as cynical. As for doing the album in context, I'd forgotten some of the songs that were on there. I'd forgotten 'Fresh Tendrils' and 'Let Me Drown,' which I'd viewed as an older song, came from there. Then the songs we played a lot, like 'My Wave,' in the context of the album in order [were] interesting. I had a really welcome feeling that it belongs on the album; it rescues it from too much of other moods. Usually when we play it live, it's bunched into a bunch of midtempo rockers, and it isn't as important there."

And as it turned out, right around the same time as the *Stern* taping, a special reissue of *Superunknown* appeared—as two special editions. The deluxe edition featured two CD's, with the first being the remastered album, and the second consisting of demos, rehearsals, and b-sides. The super deluxe edition though expanded the tracklisting significantly, as it was a five-CD set, featuring all the aforementioned goodies, plus the album mixed in Blu-ray Audio 5.1 Surround Sound, plus a hardbound book and newly reimagined album artwork by Josh Graham. Additionally, a two-LP vinyl version was issued, while the *Superunknown* singles (also with newly interpreted artwork sleeves by Joshua G) were reissued on April 19th (Record Store Day), as a set of five limited-edition 10-inch vinyl records.

But getting back to SG's touring workload in 2014, Cameron would also appear with the band as part of SXSW on March 13th and 14th. Though it was Chamberlain on the drums in late March/early April, which included a show at Estadio Nacional in Lima, Peru on March 27th, and three outside-of-the-States Lollapalooza performances (March 30th in Chile, April 2nd in Argentina, and April 6th in Brazil)—the first time SG ever visited those exotic locales.

However, for a performance on *The Tonight Show Starring Jimmy Fallon* on June 3rd (which included performances of "Spoonman" and "My Wave"), Cameron was back in black (literally, as he sported a dark t-shirt). But by the time a European tour was launched on June 6th as part of the 100% Fest at Maçka Küçükçiftlik Park, in Istanbul, Turkey, Chamberlain was back in place. And he would remain as SG's timekeeper for most of the remainder of the summer, which included spots on several Euro fests (including the Greenfield Fest on June 14th in Switzerland, Nova Rock on the 15th in Austria, Hellfest on the 22nd in France, and Graspop Metal Meeting on the 29th in Belgium, amongst other stops). But the top Euro appearance occurred on July 4th that year, when Soundgarden came in just below Black Sabbath on a bill that also featured Faith No More, Motörhead, and Soulfly—in a return appearance to Hyde Park (which saw Cameron magically reappear behind the kit).

After a handful of Canadian dates from July 12-18, SG jumped on an intriguing co-headline bill of the States—with Nine Inch Nails, from July 19-August 30. Interestingly, if everything went according to plan, this bill would have toured back in 1994 as well, but Chris' vocal troubles prevented it from happening. But now, 20 years later, the time was finally right—with NIN experiencing a career renaissance of sorts, when Trent Reznor won the Academy Award for "Best Original Music Score" three years earlier for *The Social Network,* while the band's latest album, *Hesitation Marks,* peaked at #3 on the *Billboard 200.*

When the tour visited Jones Beach on August 1ˢᵗ, I was curious to see if "the other Matt" could cut the mustard. And he did a surprisingly solid job—passing his test with an uncommon mid-set appearance of "Jesus Christ Pose" (a song that usually resides towards the beginning or ending of the set). Songs from *King Animal* were kept to a minimum by now (only "Been Away Too Long" and "A Thousand Years Before" were included), as the expected classics and album cuts were performed—a set-opening "Searching with My Good Eye Closed" (which was prefaced by a recording of "The Telephantasm"), "Gun" (the song's debut on this tour), "The Day I Tried to Live," "Blow Up the Outside World," and a splendid set-closing of "Beyond the Wheel."

After the show, I found myself chatting once more with Kim, and asking if a follow-up to *King Animal* was in the cards. He said it was, to which I replied that I got the same vibe as the era between *Louder Than Love* and *Badmotorfinger*—insomuch that I had a feeling that the band had sufficiently built upon *KA* and all the touring since first reuniting, and were now ready to take a significant leap forward. Little did I know, this would be the last time I would ever see Soundgarden live.

Once the SG/NIN tour had wrapped, Cameron united once again with Chris, Kim, and Ben, for a mini-set outside of Centurylink Field in Seattle on September 4ᵗʰ (which included a performance of "Flower"—no doubt as a wink to their locals who had been there since the '80s), to celebrate the home opener of the then-reigning Super Bowl champs, the Seattle Seahawks (in a game against the Green Bay Packers, in which the 'hawks would win, 36-16).

And the last two performances of 2014 would occur on October 25ᵗʰ and 26ᵗʰ at the Shoreline Amphitheatre in Mountain

View, California, when S. Garden was invited by N. Young to take part in his annual Bridge School Benefit concerts. Both performances saw virtually the same setlist—"Fell on Black Days," "Blow Up the Outside World," "Black Hole Sun," "Burden in My Hand," and "Dusty" (although the second show would swap "Burden" with "Zero Chance").

With the band never afraid to incorporate acoustics into some of their songs, an obvious question may have been inquired by some—why didn't Soundgarden ever partake in MTV's *Unplugged* series way back when (especially since Pearl Jam, Nirvana, and Alice in Chains were all responsible for classic performances on the program)? Kim once explained, "We were asked to do *Unplugged* a number of times, but we didn't, because we were in the middle of doing all kinds of other stuff. We were either touring or recording. It's like, 'Hey, MTV wants you to do an *Unplugged*,' and we're like, *'Not now.'* But it's interesting, of the big four bands, we're the only one that never did *Unplugged*. I think we probably should have in retrospect, but we had a lot of things up in the air, a lot of things we were doing at the time, that we just couldn't get around to that."

However, another SG musical offering was on the schedule before the end of the year—*Echo of Miles: Scattered Tracks Across the Path*. It was during the interview process for *Grunge Is Dead* that I made another discovery that proved intriguing— there had not only been an overabundance of SG b-sides that had never been neatly compiled into one collection, but also, a multitude of tunes that had never been released in any shape or form.

So on November 24, 2014, Soundgarden finally bit the bullet and put out *Echo of Miles*—a b-sides/rarities comp. With an album cover again designed by Josh Graham (which appears to be of a valley between two mountains, with extra objects added, and the *BMF* era SG logo placed a top), it also was once more issued in various formats—a download, a 3-CD set, a streamlined single-CD, and a whopping 6-LP vinyl set. Concerning the 3-CD, each disc was categorized—"Originals" (disc one), "Covers" (disc two), and "Oddities" (disc three), while the single-CD was strictly the "Originals" disc (with a few less tracks).

The first disc is the best of the set, as it collects all of the worthwhile b-sides from SG's Euro singles. And at 18 tracks strong, it most certainly feels at times like a long-lost SG studio album. It includes all the uncommon tracks we've already covered in previous chapters—from 1988's "Sub Pop Rock City" all the way through 2012's "Live to Rise" (although the latter was not a b-side, it had never been included on a Soundgarden album, hence, why not include it here?). And of course, the quality of some of these tracks are every bit as good—and in some cases, *better*— than some of the material that made the grade, including "Heretic," "Fresh Deadly Roses," "Birth Ritual," "Kyle Petty, Son of Richard," "Blind Dogs," etc. But the last two tracks on the disc are what longtime fans were probably most curious about, as they were never released anywhere before—"Kristi" and "Storm."

Concerning "Kristi," it was a tune that was performed during SG's tour of Euro festivals in '95, and was apparently eyed for inclusion on *Down on the Upside*...but fell short of the finish line. Which is baffling, as it is a far stronger tune than say, oh, "Never Named" (with music by Kim and lyrics by Chris, it features another towering riff and Chris offering a list of things that you could not do without him, including repeatedly warning at the end, "You're gonna die without me!"). And "Storm" was an early recording by the band, but was not fully completed until *EoM.* Another Cornell/Thayil collaboration, "Storm" definitely does sound like it could have fit on *Screaming Life,* as it leans more towards the goth-y side of things rather than the headbanging side.

Similar to Metallica, it appeared that in most cases, Soundgarden would cover other artists' tunes for b-sides in order to try and turn their fans on to the artists. Case in point, Budgie's "Homicidal Suicidal," Fear's "I Don't Care About You," Fancy's "Touch Me," etc. Or what was more common—covering a lesser-known tune by a renowned artist, such as the Beatles' "Everybody's Got Something to Hide Except Me and My Monkey," the Rolling Stones' "Stray Cat Blues," Devo's "Girl U Want," etc. And that is exactly what comprises the second disc.

And the third disc I predict was probably the least-listened to of the set for many, as it is comprised mostly of either improv/noise jams ("A Splice of Space Jam," "Jerry Garcia's Finger," "Ghostmotorfinger," etc.) or remixes ("Big Dumb Sex," "Spoonman," "Dusty," etc.), while a few honest-to-goodness tunes are included as well, which really belonged on disc one, but because of time constraints, wound up washed ashore here ("Twin Tower," "Night Surf," "Black Days III," "Karaoke," etc.).

As earlier reported, a single disc version of *Echo of Miles* was issued—featuring fourteen tracks total, and comprised solely of the best original compositions...while a few deserving tunes ("Toy Box," "Karaoke," and especially "Kyle Petty, Son of Richard") get the boot. Overall, I was extremely pleased to finally have all of this material on a single release. Although myself—and I'm sure many other SG scholars—had been long familiar with the material that had been previously issued on b-sides and soundtracks (back in the wild west days of Napster and Audiogalaxy, I recall making a CD-R entirely of SG b-sides, which received plenty of spins while riding along in my automobile, and made me quite a hero in the eyes of my fellow SG-loving friends). But one thing I did notice that was absent from this comp...the multitude of still-unheard SG tracks, sitting on a shelf somewhere (or more appropriately nowadays, *stored in a hard drive* somewhere).

After all, as I mentioned earlier, when I spoke with Kim for *Rolling Stone* back in 2009 and asked him about this unreleased material, he was quite forthcoming to discuss titles ("Dirty Candy," "Ocean Fronts," "Open Up," "Summation," "Beast," and "No Shame") and descriptions. And then of course, one mustn't forget the other unreleased early tunes off the demo *Songs for Bruce* ("I Think I'm Sinking," "Bury My Head in Sand," "In Vention," and "Out of My Skin"). Or whatever lurks deep within *The First 15*. Or the overabundance of songs SG members demoed back during SG's first go-round that never surfaced, and in particular, by Chris (don't forget Susan's earlier comment when asked about "Black Hole Sun"—"You have to remember; I heard so many Chris songs along the way that were equally as beautiful, and as absorbing and memorable. A lot of beautiful, quirky songs, that no one's ever heard to this day.").

Ben even once told me how much superfluous material was written for SG albums that never made the cut, and that he had a potential solution at the time to get the music heard. "Every record we made, there were so many extra songs. We didn't even bother to rehearse them, or we'd get them to the point where they could be tracked and then decide not to. We always had an extra album's worth of shit to do. That's what I always wanted to do, like, 'Fuck this, let's record two records now, go on the road for this one record, and then while we're on the road, we can release the second record.' No one ever liked that idea." [Laughs]

"We could have recorded two records in a row every time. Just eliminate the middle process and go for it every time—have one in the vaults, so when you're touring, you can have more time off. Like working to get ahead, instead of just subsistence. I think towards the end, we started just bringing in songs almost finished to each other. There would probably be logistically more, because the time of accumulation of songs and stuff." Hopefully, one day these worthwhile contents imprisoned in the SG vaults will be set free, for all the world to see.

2015 saw Soundgarden lighten their workload substantially—which included only a handful of festival dates in Australia and New Zealand from February 21-March 3 (involving several different Soundwave appearances, most of which included the rarely-performed "Kyle Petty, Son of Richard"), before only playing one more show that year—July 11th at Canada's Big Music Fest, in McLennan Park, Kitchener, Ontario.

Later in the year, a pair of mega-SG fans, Jaye and Mike English, assembled a gorgeous photo book, entitled *Photofantasm: Nudedragons to King Animal* (released on August 6th, via the Spoondog Entertainment Group) which as its title suggests, chronicled this exciting reunion era. Utilizing images from a variety of photographers and including all-new interviews with admirers of the band (including yours truly), the coffee-table sized book—with all net proceeds going to Canary Foundation (which is solely dedicated to the funding of early cancer-detection solutions)—is a must-see for fans, which was limited to 1,000 copies total.

And on September 18th, Chris issued his fourth solo studio album overall, *Higher Truth,* which reached #19 on the *Billboard 200.* While doing the rounds of press for the album, I was lucky to finally get a phone interview with Chris—the one and only time I ever interviewed him—for the now defunct publication, *Long Island Pulse.* The article (entitled *Searching for the Truth*) ran online September 25th, and here are the contents of our short-but-sweet chat:

What are some differences between creating songs for Soundgarden and a solo album?
Soundgarden is something that you sort of write into. You imagine what this band is, and what it means, and that identity kind of changed over the years. And then up until this album, really, I think writing solo songs has always been whatever I feel like. There was no identity to worry about. In *Higher Truth* I clearly had a goal in terms of writing—all the songs needed to work in an acoustic context, stripped down entirely to just acoustic guitar and singing. And if they didn't work that way, then they weren't going to make it on the album.

Looking back on the grunge movement, do you feel it was the last significant one in rock music?
It could feel that way to me, but I'm viewing it from a different vantage point than maybe, somebody who's 15 years old and just discovering rock. To me, there's always two ways to look at it. One is, it is kind of a guitar, bass and drum thing. These instruments were accessible, anyone could pick them up and make a song. So it has to be a grassroots/blue-collar/homemade thing. And I think that's what hip-hop became. [Anyone] can sit in his bedroom with a laptop and make a record, and it's grassroots, it's homemade—it's all the things that rock music was when I was a teenager. But if you want to look

at the sort of guitar/bass/drums/longhair/white person version, then yeah, I think Seattle is sort of the last great cultural shift in traditional rock music.

Grunge was similar to psychedelic rock of the late '60s and punk of the mid '70s because it went beyond the music—it affected fashion and even political outlook. Can these broad-sweeping movements happen again?
It was the sort of purging of a lot of ingredients that started with pop culture that then spilled over into a lifestyle. I think we still have different movements or subgenres of music, it's just that now it becomes so scattered and fractured that it's smaller groups. And they don't make one big sweeping impact. There isn't enough time now for the spore to culture. The bacteria won't grow enough to actually become an illness and take over and change everything. We move on. And that next clique is the sort of antiseptic that wipes out whatever it is that was about to start.

Outside of playing live, how do you connect with your audience?
One of the great things about being able to connect with fans through social media is to remember these are real people. That part really draws you in. It can become kind of isolating when you're able to just focus on one thing and your life's passion all the time. But sometimes, we get distant from what the music can actually do. And social media can remind me of that.

With a lessened schedule in 2015, SG chose to scale back even further the following year—they did not play *a single show* in 2016. Which was surprising, as the year marked the 25-year anniversary of the release of *Badmotorfinger,* so at least a few special shows recreating the album from start to finish would have been most welcome. But what the band *did* find the time to do was to assemble several different "25th anniversary editions" of the album, celebrating this fact. Released on November 18th, you could choose from a limited edition seven-disc super deluxe edition, a 28-track two-CD deluxe edition, a single CD edition and a two-LP, 180-gram audiophile black vinyl edition. Additionally, a two-LP vinyl in metallic silver vinyl was issued in a limited pressing of 1,000.

I was lucky to snag a copy of the super deluxe, which was housed in a box whose cover replicated the original (but with the blades now looking like mirrors, and when a button was pressed, the blades spun around rapidly!). Inside, it came with all sorts of goodies—a book complete with photos from the era and countless renowned rock artists singing the album's praises (I was going to say "kissing the album's keister," but that may have come off a tad too strong), as well as various thingamajigs (a patch, a sticker, four frameable photos of each member's face, etc.).

Music-wise, the original album was included as both a remastered version *and* as a Blu-Ray Audio 5.1 Surround Sound & Remastered Stereo version, plus outtakes (nothing too earth-shaking), and b-sides. But the real reason why I paid the big bucks for this version was that it included both the audio *and* the video of the *Live at the Paramount* performance from 1992 (which way back when, was issued in edited form as *Motorvision,* which is include here, too!). The *Live at the Paramount* DVD is truly Soundgarden in their prime as a live band—the whole thing is a must-see/hear (trust me, you'll thank me later).

But it's not to say that there wasn't a significant SG-related live event in 2016—how about a string of live dates from...*Temple of the Dog*?! As the story goes, there was a lawsuit in 2015 between SG/TotD's former label, A&M Records, and one of the co-founders of the studio that TotD's self-titled debut was recorded at, London Bridge Studios (Rajan Parashar, as Rick passed away in 2014). The reason? Because A&M claimed the master tapes of the album were never returned to them from the studio. Finally, on May 24, 2016, Chris tweeted on his Twitter page a message that read "Temple of the Dog masters returned today. History made whole 25 years later!"—with a photo featuring six boxes of tapes sitting atop a white conference table.

The lads wasted little time in scouring through the tapes' contents and reissuing the album on September 30th, in a variety of formats, including a four-disc super deluxe version with 48 unreleased tracks and/or mixes (which included two CDs, one DVD and one Blu-Ray Audio disc), plus a 180gram, two-LP vinyl edition of the original (remastered with gatefold jacket), plus double CD and single CD versions. The reissues were also newly mixed in stereo by Brendan O'Brien, while the 5.1 surround sound was handled by Adam Kasper.

And what better way to promote these releases than with eight US live dates in November? Running from November 4-21, TotD (Chris, Matt, Jeff, Stone, and Mike—Eddie opted not to participate) played two night stands in a trio of theaters (the Tower in Philly, Bill Graham Civic Center in San Fran, and the Paramount in Seattle), while performing one night each in probably the two most famous arenas in the States—Madison Square Garden in NYC and the Forum in LA.

Although I was unable to purchase a ticket for MSG (I recall tix costing a pretty penny...and it sold out in a New York minute), it was hard to not be impressed by the tour's setlist, which of course featured material from the classic album, plus tunes from Mother Love Bone ("Stargazer," "Stardog Champion," "Man of Golden Words," etc.) and a variety of covers (Jimi Hendrix's "Hey Baby," Black Sabbath's "War Pigs," Harry Nilsson's "Jump into the Fire," etc.) and even songs by TotD members outside projects (Chris' solo song "Seasons," Mad Season's "River of Deceit," etc.).

It also appeared as though the band was open for a return to the studio in the future, as Chris was quoted at the time as saying, "There's always a chance [we'll record more songs]. Just from my perspective, it would have to feel great. It's a scary thing. I don't want to say it would have to live up to the [first] album, but I wouldn't want to take away from it. That's the issue with me. I don't want to detract from what happened before."

Soundgarden was apparently more willing to "hit the ground running" (to quote another great poet, David Lee Roth) tour-wise in 2017—when it was announced in February that year that they would be launching a springtime US tour—running from April 28-May 27, with the Pretty Reckless and the Dillinger Escape Plan alternating as openers. And prior to the tour's ignition, *Ultramega OK* was reissued by Sub Pop Records on March 10th (it probably would have made more sense to wait a year to do so, as 2017 marked the 29-year anniversary rather than the 30-year anniversary, but whatevs). Not as over-the-top as the *BMF* set just a few months earlier, the *UOK* offering saw the band work with Jack Endino on remixing the album (as they were never quite happy with the sound of the original Drew Canulette production), with six additional "early versions" of songs tacked on at the end. And as expected, several formats were offered— 2xLP, CD, digital, and even cassette.

Beginning with a show at the Amalie Arena in Tampa, Florida (as part of "98 Rockfest"), the 2017 Soundgarden dates appeared to be a warm-up to dust off the cobwebs, as from interviews at the time, it sounded like they were finally getting serious about recording their next studio album. With the other dates being split between festival and theater appearances, judging from video footage, the band was still offering worthwhile performances—with setlists that seemed to alternate between "Searching with My Good Eye Closed" and "Incessant Mace" as the set-opener, and mostly keeping *King Animal* material to a minimum, to focus on vintage material.

The night of the band's performance on May 17th at the Fox Theatre in Detroit, Chris posted a tweet at 8:06pm to his official Twitter page, which included a photo of the marquee outside the venue, and with the following message—"#Detroit finally back to Rock City!!!! @soundgarden #nomorebullshit".

CHAPTER 23
CHRIS

The morning of May 18, 2017 started just like any other day for yours truly—checking emails and news stories shortly after waking up. As I clicked on the Blabbermouth site (a site that specializes in metal news, in case you didn't know), I simply couldn't believe the headline of the top story— "SOUNDGARDEN Singer CHRIS CORNELL Dead At 52."

Like I'm sure many who read this headline, I first thought/hoped it must be some kind of mistake. From the outside looking in, all appeared well with Chris—he was in the midst of a tour with Soundgarden, had just performed a show with the band, and judging from his recent tweets, interviews, and news reports, was a loving father and husband (even tweeting on Mother's Day—just three days earlier—to Vicky, "To my @vickycornell you are an angel and a lioness. The perfect mother and the perfect wife. I love you! Happy #MothersDay2017"), and seemed to have overcome the troubles he had earlier disclosed—addiction and depression.

But after noticing the top mainstream news sites were also posting similar news stories, I had to accept this as a sad fact. I also remember feeling similarly to when another one of my favorite singers died years before also while on tour, Blind Melon's Shannon Hoon—I immediately not only felt bad for him and his family, but also, for his bandmates, as the shock and horror they must have felt I'm sure was indescribable.

Due to social media, renowned rock musicians immediately began posting tributes to Chris on Twitter, including Elton John, Jimmy Page, Tony Iommi, Paul Stanley, and Joe Perry. Additionally, a wide variety of artists performed Soundgarden songs in tribute at their concerts either in the coming days or over the next few months, including Megadeth ("Outshined"), Living Colour ("Blow Up the Outside World"), Coldplay ("Black Hole Sun"), Guns N' Roses ("Black Hole Sun," which would become a permanent staple in the setlist of their *Not in This Lifetime* reunion tour), while U2 played a recording of the original version of "Black Hole Sun" before going on stage on

May 20th at the Rose Bowl in Pasadena (which included the entire crowd singing along and holding up their iPhones with the flashlight option on). And perhaps most moving was when Norah Jones performed "Black Hole Sun" on May 23rd, at the same venue that Soundgarden had just played at six nights earlier (and Chris' last-ever performance)—the Fox Theatre in Detroit.

From what I could later piece together from police reports, at about 11pm on May 17th, Soundgarden finished their performance at the Fox Theatre. Looking back at footage of the show, by this point, Soundgarden had worked in a new light show—with several columns of horizontal "lines" of lights in the background (gone was the screen that showed *Telephantasm* or *King Animal* cover-related images). Also, unlike say, the *Superunknown* era, where properly illuminating the band was a great big no-no, it seemed like the band had finally relented in allowing themselves to have apt lighting shone on them. Don't get me wrong, SG's 2017 stage set-up would never be confused with a Kiss, Dio, or Metallica concert production (no props, explosions, lasers, fire columns, or confetti), but still, it was a definite progression.

In some of the close-ups of Chris' face from this performance (particularly during "Black Hole Sun"), he does appear to be glassy eyed and even a bit dazed. And on "My Wave," the vocals are a little off, which offers evidence that Chris may have been having difficulty with his in-ear monitors. But overall, it was not a bad show at all—so there's no clear evidence to support that Chris' state of mind was dramatically affecting the quality of the band's live performance. In other words, a poor performance or peculiar behavior during the show (i.e., if he had stormed of the stage mid-performance or done something that drastic) could have possibly served as a warning sign. But this was not the case. The last song performed that night was "Slaves and Bulldozers"—which included lyrical snippets of Led Zeppelin's "In My Time of Dying" (complete with an extra-long feedback exploration at the end). And here's a tiny tidbit of trivia—judging from the footage, the first song played over the soundsystem after the show was finished was one of my favorite Stevie Wonder tunes, "Too High" (a song about a girl who dies from a drug overdose).

Shortly after the end of the show, Chris went to his room at the MGM Grand Hotel in downtown Detroit (a suite on the eleventh floor), and was accompanied by bodyguard Martin Kirsten, who gave Chris two sleeping pills (for anxiety). Kirsten then left Chris and went to his room (which was only two doors away). By about 11:30, Kirsten received a phone call from Chris, complaining of TV troubles (of which it was arranged for a member of the hotel staff to bring a new remote). At 11:35, Chris spoke to Vicky on the phone, in which he slurred his words, and was repeatedly saying "I am just tired," which led to Vicky becoming concerned, and contacting Kirsten to check on Chris.

Kirsten did so at about 12:15am, and had difficulty entering the room, as Chris did not respond. Vicky instructed Kirsten to kick open the door, which he did, and had to then kick open the locked bedroom door. When he finally gained entry, he spotted Chris on the bathroom floor, with an exercise band around his neck, bleeding, and unconscious. Kirsten loosened the band and tried resuscitating Chris, before a hotel medic arrived on the scene at 12:56, who started CPR on Chris. A call to 911 was placed, with first responders arriving at 1:00. At 1:30, Chris was pronounced dead. Later that day (at 1:39pm), the Wayne County Medical Examiner's Office released a statement, stating that an autopsy was completed, and that Chris' death was ruled "suicide by hanging."

A toxicology report would eventually be released on June 2nd, in which it was learned that several drugs were in Chris' system at the time of his death—butalbital (usually used for the treatment of pain and headaches), lorazepam (also known as Ativan and as a benzodiazepine or "benzo," which is an anxiety medication), pseudoephedrine (a decongestant) and its metabolite norpseudoephedrine, caffeine (from NoDoz tablets), and naloxone (medication used to block the effects of opioids—especially in an overdose situation). However, according to Michigan's Wayne County assistant medical examiner Theodore Brown, "These drugs did not contribute to the cause of death."

Immediately following the release of the toxicology report, Vicky issued the following statement to *Rolling Stone*— "Many of us who know Chris well noticed that he wasn't himself during his final hours and that something was very off. We have learned from this report that several substances were found in his system. After so many years of sobriety, this moment of terrible judgment seems to have completely impaired and altered his state of mind. Something clearly went terribly wrong and my children and I are heartbroken and are devastated that this moment can never be taken back. We very much appreciate all of the love we have received during this extremely difficult time and are dedicated to helping others in preventing this type of tragedy."

In an interview with *ABC News* nearly a year after Chris' passing (that aired on February 21, 2018), Vicky pinpointed when her husband began using pills again. "Approximately a year before he died, he was prescribed a benzodiazepine to help him sleep. He had torn his shoulder...the pain in the shoulder was waking him up at night and it was keeping him up." This led to a relapse, and Vicky recalled as a result, "He had really delayed speech. He was forgetful." There was even a screen shot of an email displayed from Chris that he sent to an undisclosed friend in the music business (dated March 22, 2017), in which it read, "[Name blurred out] is in, maybe send him the mix you want him to hear. Would love to talk, had relapse."

According to the Recovery Village website, concerning Ativan use, "Some of the more severe symptoms on the brain and body can include mental and mood changes, such as hallucinations and depression, weakness, memory and cognition problems, and trouble walking or talking." And shortly after Chris' passing, celebrity doctor Dr. Drew Pinsky explained, "Benzos over a long term (more than two weeks) are a very dangerous class of medications and extremely dangerous if you have a history of addiction."

Pinsky would also add, "This man should have never been on this medication. He is a long-standing drug addict in recovery—he should not be on that medication. Period. End of story." Additionally, conspiracy theorists speculated about the possibility of Chris being murdered, but since the facts surrounding his death I feel are solid (Wayne County Medical Examiner's spokeswoman Lisa Croff stated "We stand by our cause of death," while Detroit police media relations director Michael Woody specified "We investigated all possible angles, and there were no signs this was anything but a suicide"), and since this is a book about Soundgarden—not solely Chris—I will leave that to others to ponder.

On May 26th, Chris was laid to rest at the Hollywood Forever Cemetery (sadly, on the same date Soundgarden would have played their second to last show of their never-completed springtime tour—at the Bomb Factory in Dallas). Eulogies were delivered by Kim and Matt, as well as by Jeff Ament, Tom Morello, actor Josh Brolin, and film producer Eric Esrailian (Chris had recently penned/recorded a song, "The Promise," for Esrailian's film of the same name, which dealt with the Armenian Genocide, with the single's proceeds going to the International Rescue Committee), while attendees included the likes of Ben, Hiro, Brad Pitt, Christian Bale, James Franco, Fred Armisen, Dave Grohl, Krist Novoselic, Courtney Love, Pharrell Williams, James Hetfield, Lars Ulrich, Nile Rodgers, and Joe Walsh (among many other renowned names from the entertainment business).

Also, Linkin Park singer Chester Bennington and guitarist Brad Delson performed Leonard Cohen's "Hallelujah"—a song made famous by one of Chris' friends, Jeff Buckley. Tragically, Bennington—who was the godfather of Chris' son, Christopher—would also commit suicide by hanging less than two months later, on July 20th...on what would have been Chris' 53rd birthday. When the ceremony (which was private) ended, mourners were led to Chris's final resting place in the "Garden of Legends" section of the cemetery, while Temple of the Dog's "All Night Thing" played during the procession. Chris' grave marker read "Voice of our generation and an artist for all time," while his grave was located in close proximity to the grave of one of his friends— Johnny Ramone of the Ramones.

Noticeably absent from the funeral was Eddie Vedder, who would not comment about the tragic death of his friend until the following month, during a concert in London—"About two days after the news, I think it was the second night we were sleeping in this little cabin near the water, a place he would've loved. And all these memories started coming in about 1:30am like woke me up. Like big memories, memories I would think about all the time. Like the memories were big muscles. And then I couldn't stop the memories. And trying to sleep it was like if the neighbors had the music playing and you couldn't stop it. But then it was fine because then it got into little memories. It just kept going and going and going. And I realized how lucky I was to have hours' worth of...you know if each of these memories was quick and I had hours of them. How fortunate was I?! And I didn't want to be sad, wanted to be grateful not sad. I'm still thinking about those memories and I will live with those memories in my heart and I will...love him forever."

Something that I've contemplated after Chris' passing was...could anything have been done differently to have saved his life? Had there been any earlier suicide attempts over the years? Were there any warning signs to those close to him? Especially after recalling that Vicky in 2016 credited Tim Commerford for saving Chris' life circa Audioslave's formation, by saying "Chris was dying in Seattle. Timmy C stepped up like a real friend and saved him. He will always be one of the most special people to Chris. If only others had half the balls or the heart of Timmy C." However, according to Dr. Michael Miller (an assistant professor of psychiatry at Harvard Medical School), "Many people who commit suicide do so without letting on they are thinking about it or planning it."

I also thought back to something Chris said a few years before when appearing on *The Howard Stern Show* (during one of the most revealing interviews he ever gave). When asked about Kurt Cobain's suicide, he responded, "I had friends die before that. And the way that he did it was kind of a twist, but other than that, I had been through it before. And it was a shame. But it's a shame for his daughter for one, it's a shame for fans. But really, it's a personal thing, and I don't know...it was a drag and I wish it didn't happen. And I also think like, if he would have just hung on for six months, who knows? Six months later, he would have been a completely different guy." And I also recalled another quote (previously mentioned in this book, from *Grunge Is Dead*), which Jeff Ament once told me about Cobain's death, which sadly, now also applies to Chris—"Unless you've been manic-depressive, I don't think you can fully comprehend those sorts of actions."

And as with any time a singer-songwriter dies, their lyrics seem to take on a whole new meaning, and this was certainly the case with Chris. Case in point, such lyrics as "Born without a friend, And bound to die alone" ("Zero Chance"), "'Cause you're better off alone than with me" ("Fluttergirl"), and "Nothing seems to kill me, No matter how hard I try" ("Blow Up the Outside World"). Additionally, almost all the lyrics to the final song on the last Soundgarden album released during Chris' lifetime, "Rowing" (especially "Moving is breathing and breathing is life, Stopping is dying, You'll be alright, Life is a hammer waiting to drop, Drifting the shallows and the rowing won't stop" and "Rowing is living and living is hard, But living beats losing all that we are"). Certain song titles also now proved eerie, including "Pretty Noose," "Like Suicide," and "Cleaning My Gun," and especially the music video for his solo song, "Nearly Forgot My Broken Heart" (in which Chris plays a prisoner about to be hanged, and a noose is placed around his neck—however, he is not hanged, but rather, rescued).

Understandably, the surviving members of Soundgarden kept a low profile after Chris' passing—although Matt did issue a solo debut, entitled *Cavedweller,* on September 22nd, of which the message "For Chris" was etched into the vinyl version. But in 2018, they slowly began being spotted—including Matt touring once more with Pearl Jam. And on August 10th, on the second of a two-night stand at Seattle's Safeco Field, none other than Kim joined PJ for a rendition of the MC5's "Kick Out the Jams," and later, Iggy & the Stooges' "Search and Destroy" (along with Mudhoney's Mark Arm and Steve Turner on the latter) and displayed a shirt that featured the likeness of Chris' face (a play on the Starbucks logo) on it.

In the fall, Kim also hit the tour trail for the first time since Chris' passing, when he joined the newly-assembled MC50. Including original MC5 guitarist Wayne Kramer, the band toured to celebrate the 50th anniversary of the release of their classic album, 1969's *Kick Out the Jams*—comprised of singer Marcus Durant (Zen Guerilla), plus an alternating rhythm section, which included either Doug Pinnick (King's X) or Bill Gould (Faith No More) on bass, and on drums, either Brendan Canty (Fugazi) or...Matt Cameron! I was lucky to catch a performance by the band on September 14th at the Paramount in Huntington, New York, and I was, quite honestly, blown away—especially by Durant's vocals (who I was not familiar with beforehand). And it was great to see Kim onstage having fun again, and also, to catch up with him after the show. I don't think he would mind me sharing one topic we discussed during our chat that lasted late into the evening—"Which Kiss album is the best?" Kim's selection? Their classic recording from 1975, *Alive!*—which I would have to agree with him on.

On November 16th, a compilation album was released, simply titled *Chris Cornell,* which was released as both a standard single disc and deluxe edition comprised of four discs—which touched upon highlights throughout Chris' career. Featuring a cover designed by Jeff Ament—of a youthful, longhaired Chris from the *Badmotorfinger* era—the expanded set also included previously unreleased material, including a song entitled "When Bad Does Good" (which would win a Grammy award in the "Best Rock Performance" category at the 61st Grammy Awards in 2019) and Prince's "Nothing Compares 2 U," plus previously unreleased live songs, including a touching rendition of Bob Marley's "Redemption Song," sung as a duet between Chris and his daughter, Toni.

And on January 16, 2019, a star-studded concert took place at the Forum in Los Angeles—*I Am the Highway: A Tribute to Chris Cornell.* Hosted by Jimmy Kimmel, members of Soundgarden, Temple of the Dog, and Audioslave all performed, as did such artists as Metallica, the Foo Fighters, Queens of the Stone Age's Josh Homme, Miley Cyrus, and Maroon 5's Adam

Levine (among many others)—playing a mixture of their own songs and their favorite SG songs. *Almost* included was Faith No More's Mike Patton (who I would have been curious to hear how he would have tackled a SG classic or two), but he had to cancel due to being under the weather. And closing the concert was a performance by the surviving members of Soundgarden, joined by special guests, including:

"Rusty Cage" (with Taylor Momsen)
"Flower" (with Marcus Durant)
"Outshined" (with Marcus Durant and Stone Gossard)
"Drawing Flies" (with Taylor Momsen, Buzz Osborne, Matt Demeritt, and Tracy Wanamae)
"Loud Love" (with Taylor Momsen, Tom Morello, and Wayne Kramer)
"I Awake" (with Taylor Hawkins and Buzz Osborne)
"The Day I Tried To Live" (with Taylor Hawkins and Buzz Osborne)
"Black Hole Sun" (with Brandi Carlile, Peter Frampton, Tim Hanseroth, and Phil Hanseroth)

While it was great that such a variety of top-notch musical talent paid tribute to Chris, I'm not the biggest fan of tribute concerts nor tribute albums—as almost always, there is no comparison between the original versions and the tribute versions. But if the show helped provide any sense of closure or peace of mind for Chris' former bandmates and/or family members, then I'm absolutely all for it. As of the time of this book's release, an official DVD or album of the tribute show has not been released, but I would be surprised if either/or do not surface one day. But what *was* released in 2019 (July 26th, to be exact) was the *Live from the Artists Den* album—which was previously discussed at length in the last chapter. As far as future Soundgarden-related releases, I'm sure further anniversary editions of their albums are forthcoming that have not yet received such a re-examination, and as previously discussed, hopefully worthwhile unreleased material will be issued one day, as well as finishing off the songs the band was working on at the time of Chris' passing, which were to be included on Soundgarden's projected seventh studio full-length.

Without question, Chris will go down as one of the all-time great vocalists/songwriters/lyricists, as I wholeheartedly believe that his work is comparable to the legendary likes of John Lennon, Jimi Hendrix, and Freddie Mercury—especially when he was joined by Kim, Matt, and Ben or Hiro, and collaborated on music together.

We were lucky to have had Chris in our lives for as long as we did.

CHAPTER 24
IF YOU LIKE THE SOUND

So...for the book's final chapter, how about we figure the right ingredients required to create a Soundgarden sonic stew? First things first though—let's wash our hands thoroughly and put on our chef's hat/apron, before we try and determine the ideal measuring cup amounts.

There have been many descriptions of Soundgarden's music over the years. Early on, "goth punk" was fitting. Then it was "punk Sabbath" (which I found much more apropos than "punk Zeppelin"). Before finally, the best known of the bunch, "grunge." But it turns out that the handful I already mentioned weren't the only ones—there were quite a few others offered up...all documented by Mr. Thayil below!

In an article from 1989 for *Raw Magazine,* Kim offered up "heavy muddle." The same year in *Kerrang!,* he mentioned that one journalist described Soundgarden as "big rock." A year later, he explained, "There were two really good descriptions of us back when we first started...somebody said we were 'Killing Joke meets Rush' and then there was 'XTC vs. Black Sabbath'." Then, in 1992, Kim offered another depiction, "An alternative underground punk rock metal band?" By 1994, he provided two more zingers in *M.E.A.T. Magazine*—"zen metal" and "acid punk."

However, there was one description that Kim did *not* appreciate. "We were typed as macho and testosterone-fueled, and for years we thought it was unfair. It's unfair that we have a metal tag, but in the past year or two I've realized we are a pretty macho band. We're macho like Clint Eastwood, as opposed to macho like Andrew Dice Clay."

When it came to influences or comparisons, either members of Soundgarden or members of the press have mentioned a variety of artists. Some of these include—Bauhaus, Joy Division, Sonic Youth, Hüsker Dü, Killing Joke, Blue Cheer, MC5, Budgie, Ramones, Jimi Hendrix, Black Sabbath, the Beatles, the Rolling Stones, Velvet Underground, Led Zeppelin,

Metallica, Jane's Addiction, the U-Men, Melvins, the Cult, Danzig, and Masters of Reality, among others.

"At the beginning, a lot of people thought we sounded like Led Zeppelin," Kim once said. "Mainly because we have a singer who can hit the high notes without sounding screechy. That's what every writer compared us to, because that's what everyone had told them." As a result, Kim and his bandmates would often clear up this misconception—"We weren't influenced by Led Zeppelin and Black Sabbath. The past few days in interviews we've been asked that. We said, 'Look, if anything, *you* drew a parallel'."

"If they say that we sounded like those bands, we'd say OK, and I might be able to accept that. But if you say that we drew from their body of work and created what we do out of that, it's like, 'No, that was never the case.' When I started playing guitar, I was listening to Johnny Ramone, the MC5. There may have been things we've done in the past that sounded similar, but that certainly wasn't because of influences. It was probably happenstance."

But one band that *did* prove influential for Soundgarden—but is rarely (if ever) mentioned—was reggae-hardcore-punk-metallists the Bad Brains. And as Kim once explained, it was not just musical, either. "I think in that they are part of the American hardcore movement, which was influential to [Soundgarden]. And in that they were a significant part of the progressive post-hardcore movement of the mid-to-late '80s, that we found ourselves in. Yes, in that way, they're very influential. I mean, we didn't end up doing any reggae, but they're definitely influential."

"I think it was important to Soundgarden as well, that the Bad Brains were a band of color, because that's what Soundgarden was. For our first half-year, we were pretty much an Asian band—a Japanese guy [Hiro], an Indian guy [Kim], and Chris. But the fact that the Bad Brains were a band of color I think was important to us, because that was how we identified with them."

And according to Jack Endino, another possible influence on Soundgarden—especially early on—was obscure psychedelic-experimental-industrial rockers, Chrome. "Chrome, which was also a band I heard about through working with Soundgarden, that I had missed. Chrome was a late '70s band that was a post-Hawkwind, but they were based in the Bay Area, and they were very psychedelic and industrial and weird. Helios Creed was the guitar player, who's still going strong today in his own little indie world."

"They made a lot of just really weird, alien-sounding, dark, noisy, psychedelic kind of records. A whole series of them that they made, that made them into a sort of underground cult band that persists—there are certain people that are into Chrome. Chris Cornell turned me on to Chrome." And if memory serves me correctly, it was Chrome's 1982 offering, *3rd from the Sun,* that was the album that Chris introduced Jack to (which would make the most sense sonically, especially after hearing the title track).

Earlier, Michael Beinhorn recounted Chris telling him that the Beatles and Cream were two of his favorites. And it turns out he also fancied another '60s era Brit band—Pink Floyd. And particularly, their "psychedelic era," when led by singer/guitarist Syd Barrett. He even went as far as selecting their 1967 debut, *The Piper at the Gates of Dawn*, as one of his all-time favorite albums for *Classic Rock Magazine*—discovering it right around the time of Soundgarden's formation, via the record collection of the owner of a house that he and Hiro were renting, and eventually, even painting a Pink Floyd image on the back of his motorcycle jacket!

"It includes some of Pink Floyd's best-known songs, including 'Astronomy Domine' and 'Interstellar Overdrive,' and every song is fantastic," Chris explained. "It connects with me in a way that I just can't describe, creating a very special environment that no other record can achieve. It's more capable of removing you from wherever you are when you hear it than any other record I know."

"I'm also a big fan of the band's follow-up album, *A Saucer Full of Secrets*, but for different reasons. Syd Barrett wrote just one song, 'Jugland Blues,' for that one. But save for Roger Waters' 'Take Up Thy Stethoscope and Walk' and the instrumental 'Interstellar Overdrive,' *The Piper At The Gates Of*

Dawn was mostly attributable to Syd. I like both of those albums more than the ones Pink Floyd made without Syd, as an arena rock band. I guess I was too afraid of crowds."

While Kurt Cobain will probably forever be considered the patron saint of *Meat Puppets II* (due to having the Kirkwood bros play three tunes on Nirvana's *Unplugged*), I actually first read of a notable musician singing the album's praises via...Kim (in *Rip,* to be precise). As he recounted to me in the book *Too High to Die: Meet the Meat Puppets*, "When Soundgarden formed, [*Meat Puppets II*] got played a lot. I remember playing it for Hiro and Chris all the time. Here's the weird thing—I still don't have *Meat Puppets II* on vinyl, because a good friend of mine in college gave me a homemade cassette. He had the album or he had borrowed it from somebody. So he gives me this cassette, and on one side is Blue Cheer—it had a bunch of stuff off *Outsideinside* and *Vincebus Eruptum*. And the other side of the cassette had *Meat Puppets II*."

"That thing, I would just play it and watch the sun rise, I would play it and watch the sun set. I'd come home from college from classes—I'd go by a local convenience store and buy a couple Buckhorn Beers, a pack of cigarettes, and some string cheese, and go and sit in my bedroom. My bedroom was a sort of walk-in closet and the window faced west. So I laid there eating string cheese and drinking my Buckhorn Beer, and I'd put on *Meat Puppets II* and watch the sun go down. I had to do that all the time. It tripped me out, and it was the coolest feeling—being mildly intoxicated."

"And *Meat Puppets II* was great if I smoked pot, which I rarely did, but on the occasion I did, I was like, 'I've got to listen to the Meat Puppets!' And on the occasion of doing MDMA or anything else that may cross the path of a 22-year-old musician who is a student. That album tripped me out—it seemed to be heavy and wild in these other ways. Psychologically and emotionally. I loved it. That Meat Puppets' second album became not only my favorite Meat Puppets album, but perhaps one of my favorite albums of all time."

An additional glimpse into the artists that helped shape the Soundgarden sound came in 1992, when Kim was asked what his top-5 albums of all-time were for *Rock Power*. His responses signaled his—and his band's—varied listening tastes. And those selections included...Frank Zappa's *Freak Out*, MC5's *Kick Out the Jams*, Voivod's *Rrröööaaarrr*, Nirvana's *Bleach*, and Corrosion of Conformity's *Blind*.

Another major component of the group's sound was Chris' lyrics. Oft-times, Chris specialized in a lyric-writing style that strung together phrases that if you were to read them apart from the song, would prove to be largely nonsensical ("Black Hole Sun" being the most obvious example of this, as well as "Searching with My Good Eye Closed"). But when combined with the music, the lyrics would create all sorts of images inside your noggin—a style that such other rock n' roll wordsmiths as David Bowie, Kurt Cobain, and Scott Weiland would also employ at times (it was also once stated in the now-defunct magazine *Pulse!* that "Cornell is heavily influenced by author Sylvia Plath").

But according to Matt, he felt that these lyrics were often based on reality. "Chris' lyrics deal with inner struggles he's gone through but a lot of people can relate to them." The man himself who was responsible for the vast majority of SG's lyrics also once explained lyric writing. "Lyrical ideas happen a lot. Sometimes I'll try a lyrical idea on a song I wrote and it just doesn't work, and someone else will bring in a song and it works for that. Or I'll have a lyrical idea lying around and I'll just be waiting for the right feel."

And with such a vast amount of songs penned throughout his career, it's not a surprise that Chris came up with the perfect solution concerning navigating around bouts of writer's block—he'd just break on through to the other side. "Sometimes I think I'm having a writer's block, and I'll write a bunch of songs anyway, and a couple cool songs come out. Writer's block for me—as opposed to being that I can't write or be creative—is that what I'm writing, I don't really feel is inspired, or it's not inspiring me, even though it might inspire someone else. I tend to write faster when I'm in a bad mood. It'll happen really fast because I'm not as self-conscious about it. I'm in a bad enough mood that I don't really care. Usually I like the song a lot when that happens. Those are some of my favorite songs. Maybe it's more immediate."

Steering now to the musical side of things, a definite S. Garden sonic trademark was...tuning their guitars down *low* (the most obvious example being "4th of July"). Once upon a time, Kim discussed just who was the first Seattle band to detune, which helped open the floodgates for other local acts. "I'd say the Melvins, probably. I remember a conversation I had with Buzz Melvin. We knew that Kiss tuned their guitars down a half step. And Buzz said, 'Yeah, and Sabbath went down to D.' The Melvins started to use that, and we eventually started to write in drop-D." As a result, Soundgarden certainly contributed to trailblazing the genre that rose to popularity in the early-mid '90s—"stoner rock" (including such bands as Kyuss, Clutch, Sleep, Fu Manchu, and Monster Magnet). However, most of the members of Soundgarden did not sound like they were major stoners, themselves.

"I smoke pot maybe four times a year, but that's about it," Kim explained in the early '90s. "I used to do acid but then I had a terrible trip one time. I've tried pretty much every drug once, but never really got into anything. Except beer. I don't know what it is about beer..." Around the same time, Matt added, "On long drives Ben and Kim and I will smoke out, but they normally are drinkers. Chris will take a hit every now and then, but it's pretty rare. He stays pretty clean on the road."

Additionally, Matt also once discussed if he ever got stoned when he played with Soundgarden. "Sometimes. I think it helps when I'm at home and I'm in the right mood to create. A little pot, coffee and time is normally a really good combination for me. Sometimes it helps open up a different side of my creative brain that might not open if I'm not relaxed enough. For the most part, it's always been helpful."

Another musical element that the band embraced was working in peculiar time signatures (the most popular tunes being "Outshined" and "Spoonman," both of which were in 7/4, with one of the more zanier being "Face Pollution," which utilizes both 9/8 *and* 6/4). But while prog bands seemingly try and pen tricky compositions *on purpose*, this proved not the case with Soundgarden. "That happened naturally—that was never premeditated," explained Kim. "It was something our drummer would end up pointing out to us. I'd write a riff and Chris would start singing over it and Matt would go, 'Hey guys, that's in 7/4.' I had no idea. Matt was a little more musically trained than the rest of us."

Kim also once explained how it was sometimes a challenge learning tunes penned by the other members. "I have the hardest time learning Chris' songs, because even though Ben's songs have a lot of freaky shit in them, they tend to be freaky in the way they're assembled, not in how they're played. Chris does this offbeat thing a lot, whereas I grew up on the Ramones downstroke. In Chris' songs the A section might transition into the B section on the last upstroke—the last 'and'—of the A section, rather than on the next downstroke like you'd expect."

While not as frequent as the other aforementioned items, exotic Middle Eastern sounds can be heard from time to time in Soundgarden's compositions, as well (especially on such tunes as "A Thousand Days Before" and "Half"). When once asked if he drew on any of his own ethnic influences, Kim responded, "Mine is East Indian. There might be a little bit of influence there, but it's funny, because Chris often writes parts that have that sort of Eastern flavor, and I'll often write parts like that and so will Ben. So I don't know if it's necessarily something I picked up from the ethnic thing—it might have been more from listening to the Beatles or to Indian music when I was a kid, perhaps."

Also according to Kim, it turns out that inspiration for their music was often drawn upon from literature and film. "Just the idea of dynamic, the way the story develops. There's a dynamic and a certain drama. I've often thought a lot of our music was very cinematic. *Superunknown* was quite that way, and we've often had that told to us by people. We don't draw that often from rock. Right from the beginning, when me, Hiro and Chris formed the band, we would discuss how the most boring rock we ever

325 IF YOU LIKE THE SOUND

heard was rock that was influenced by rock. So it's just the mood, a feeling that you might get from a movie or a book or even a painting, and you write a song that tries to describe that. Usually the band is very good at reading each other that way."

And as previously mentioned—Kim was named the #100 "greatest guitarist" by *Rolling Stone* (out of a possible 100) in 2010. But despite this accomplishment, one of rock's all-time guitar greats was not necessarily smitten with guitar solos. "One of my favorite solos with the band is on 'Slaves and Bulldozers.' When our A&R guy came in we played it to him, and he was like, 'This is finished? Huh? C'mon guys.' I just said, 'You don't get it, do you? That's it, finished!' To me it's great—it seems free, it's real kinetic, it gives the song this great jarring feel. 'Like Suicide' is another one I like, but I play that note-for-note every time, the same patterns. 'Slaves and Bulldozers' live is when I'm real free. I just approach the fretboard with a 'what do I do now?' attitude."

"Sometimes it's great, sometimes it doesn't work. That's what music is like. I think there's a lot of guitar geeks out there who get caught up in the idea of difficulty. They constantly play faster, try and invent new chords—but I kinda think that's a pretty sophomoric approach. This isn't the hurdles, y'know? Playing the guitar is there to make music, and it should be easy!" And this mindset was reflected when he was once asked, "Any advice for kids just starting out playing guitar?" "Don't take lessons. Listen to your records. And watch other people play. I think the fun thing is just discovering stuff on the guitar, not having people tell you what to do. It's more fun to have it be something you explore."

Unquestionably, an Electro-Harmonix Big Muff Pi Fuzz guitar pedal became largely synonymous with grunge (thanks to Nirvana's and Mudhoney's fondness for them). But it turns out that Kim utilized another guitar pedal—that despite being on the opposite end of the sonic spectrum of a fuzz box, still served as a building block for the Soundgarden sound. "I got an Ibanez Stereo Chorus pedal, and I always used it. Eventually I started turning it off for the more visceral, harder rhythmic parts, because it would smear their clarity, but I turned it on for the arpeggios and harmonics. Mark Arm of Mudhoney used to give me shit for that:

'Y'know, Kim, you guys would sound a lot heavier if you'd just get rid of that chorus!' I'd tell him, 'Hey, we're not just a heavy band; we have a trippy element too'."

Another contributing factor to the Soundgarden sound was their rhythm section—which on their studio albums, was comprised of either Hiro and Matt or Ben and Matt. Unlike most alt-rock bassists at the time that played with a pick, both Hiro and Ben mostly played with their fingers. Also, for both, bass was not their first instrument—for the former, it was mandolin, and for the latter, it was six-string guitar. In fact, Ben had never seriously played bass until joining Soundgarden.

"I played pretty well immediately, because of Hiro's influence and some other real bass players I knew growing up," recalled Ben. "You have to decide right away how you're going to learn. Playing with a pick can throw you into the realm of being a guitar player on bass. But that's not really what it's about; it's about tone and texture. I thought of my favorite bass players— including Hiro, Chuck Dukowski from Black Flag, and Mike Watt—and most of what I liked was fingerstyle. I decided I'd better learn to play that way. I started listening to Charles Mingus because I wanted to learn how to play some dirty, weird shit."

As a result, Ben's inexperience on the bass helped shape his playing style, particularly early on. "Sometimes I would go for a note and miss it entirely, either on the fingerboard or with my plucking hand because the string spacing was so different from playing guitar. I'd hit the gap. Rookie mistake!"

Another unique twist was when Matt would write music for SG, he did so from a not-so-common vantage point for most songwriters. "I think a lot of my music and ideas come from playing drums. I approach songwriting very rhythmically. It's really hard for me to sit down and write a folk song. I just can't do it. My music is more riff-based and it takes me a while to come up with something I like. I'm known for being a drummer, and I'm grateful for that. I was really lucky to be able to grow as a drummer in Soundgarden and other bands I've played in. But I also think it's important as a musician to expand into other areas, be it songwriting or production or whatever. I'm just trying to find another tool as an artist and expand on the tools I already have."

But in all honesty, if I were to be bold and try and predict what people will remember most when it comes to Soundgarden for years to come, it will probably be Chris' incomparable vocals. Besides Freddie Mercury and Robert Plant, few singers could handle singing as many *popular* styles (which eliminates the experimental-leaning Mike Patton from the running, while sadly, Jeff Buckley's body of work was too small for a true comparison), and pull each off masterfully.

However, during what many consider Chris' peak era vocal-wise (the '90s), he surprisingly did little to protect or preserve his voice. Case in point, if you are to inspect off-stage photos of Chris during Soundgarden's first-go round, you are bound to eventually see an image of him with a cigarette in hand. "Smoke a lot, drink a lot," Chris admitted in 1994. "I used to do daily vocal training, but for me it didn't work. I hate to say that in print and then some kid will go and wreck his voice, but I did learn a lot from my lessons. For the first couple of years though, I would learn the theory and then it would all just go straight out of the window as soon as I got on stage, I'd just start screaming again."

"Gradually though, it became automatic, knowing the right thing to do and the wrong thing to do. It took a lot of years of experience to make my voice strong, and so now I don't even need to warm up, I just do the soundcheck and then go sing. There was one time we did 18 shows in a row, so I've put my voice through a lot of shit in the past and I think it's paid off." Right around the time of Audioslave, Chris finally quit smoking and drinking.

And it turned out that he built his remarkable vocal range by pushing himself beyond his comfort zone. "I always used to waver between secure and insecure, which is the nature of a vocalist, because the voice isn't like other instruments—some days it sounds better than others. My voice has progressed over a long period of time, just through screaming. We would write songs where it sounded like the singer should do something extreme. If I was singing in a higher range, I'd push my voice so it would break up because I like the way it sounded. After a while it didn't break up, it went to the note—that's basically how I got my range."

Vocal influence-wise, Chris once admitted, "I'm influenced by a lot of singers whose music I don't really like, which is strange. I think Smokey Robinson is an amazing singer but I don't really listen to his records. I like Sly & the Family Stone and I do like their records a lot. I have influences that you can hear, like the Beatles, who were the band that got me into music."

"Chris had very strong regard and respect for Freddie Mercury," Kim once told me. "Certainly, they were both very dynamic with their vocals. If you want to add someone else to that mix—maybe not someone as 'grand' in vocal style, but certainly with a huge spectrum of technique—you might want to add Robin Zander [of Cheap Trick] to that. Once again, he's not grand—he doesn't have the grandness of a Freddie Mercury or that Chris could tap into at times—but Robin Zander certainly is an incredibly dynamic vocalist, as is Freddie Mercury and as is Chris. He can bring it down, he can scream, he can do a beautiful Beatles melody."

In addition to his vocal talents, over the years, Chris transformed into a tremendous frontman. But as he once explained, it did not come easily. "If I didn't do what I do, I think for the most part I would have very few friends and be a shut-in most of the time. It's sort of a battle between that person and then the guy that wants to just let it all out in front of 2,000 people and rant and scream and say anything he wants."

But as it turns out, Chris was inspiring other singers and performers—whether he knew it or not. "Chris Cornell was a huge influence for me," Devin Townsend once said. "The first Soundgarden album I really got into was *Louder Than Love*. I just loved that record. And then when *Badmotorfinger* came out, that was one of the ones when you're 18, you have a strict regimen of records that everybody allows each other to listen to. And *Badmotorfinger* was part of that. I remember listening to it and going, 'Holy shit. Can that guy ever sing!' That became a real 'practice record' for me, too—driving around in the car and singing to *Badmotorfinger* was really a great way for me to build some chops."

Former Dio guitarist Tracy G also once admitted how Chris had even inspired the late/great Ronnie James Dio. "When I was in Dio, Soundgarden was coming out with something new at the time, and Ronnie and I were talking about Chris, and Ronnie was giving it to him. He was like, 'Yeah, that guy can sing.' When we were writing a song on *Angry Machines*, 'This Is Your Life,' it ended up being a ballad with just him singing, I wrote it all on baritone guitar, but there is pretty piano behind him. Ronnie is singing it, and it's something that Chris or Freddie would have sung—it's real pretty, operatic. A beautiful song."

"And I told him at the time...he was wondering what he should do, how much he should put the vocals in or where he should go with the vocals. Not that he ever had to ask us for advice, but sometimes, he would ask. I said, 'Just go for it, dude. Do like a Chris Cornell thing—the way he does. Just rip!' And Ronnie's like, 'Well, I don't want to overdo it.' And I'm like, '*Fucking overdo it*!' There were only a few people who can sing like that."

And since we're on the topic of Ronnie James Dio and metal, I once had the opportunity (for an earlier book, *Survival of the Fittest: Heavy Metal in The 1990's*) to ask quite a few renowned rock names about if they heard a similarity at times between Chris and Ronnie (particularly the latter's first two albums with Black Sabbath, 1980's *Heaven and Hell* and 1981's *Mob Rules*), and also, if Chris was a metal singer...or not. Some interesting points were made:

LONN FRIEND [Editor of *Rip Magazine*]: That is what made Chris so unique, is he hit the Rob Halford/Ronnie Dio...he hit the registers that the pure, like, "Geoff Tate sort of metal singers" hit. He got those ranges. But there was this sandpaper underneath the surface. He wasn't a clean, pristine...he didn't hit those notes unscathed. It was like he was going over broken glass to get to them.

And I think that's what made Chris that sort of a fusion of a pure metal vocalist like Bruce Dickinson/Rob Halford/Ronnie James Dio/Mercyful Fate [King Diamond], with that kind of growl of metal. He is that. And yet, at the same time, Chris experimented solo and went into his lower registers and released some rather odd pop tracks, a Michael Jackson cover ["Billie Jean"] and things like that. Just like Metallica, he's always exploring.

WENDY DIO [manager/wife of Ronnie James Dio]: Soundgarden was a band [that Ronnie James Dio] really liked a lot. He's a great singer, that's the thing—Chris Cornell has a strong voice and he's a great singer. But I think if you listen to him singing something and you hear Ronnie singing something, you can tell the difference. Both great singers, but they have their own "independence."

JACK ENDINO: I kind of superficially do [see similarities between the vocals of Cornell and metal singers], because Chris has a high range. I more saw that when they did "Beyond the Wheel," which is a song on *Ultramega OK*, which I actually did the demo for it years ago. We did eight-track demos of that whole record. And I thought, "This is fucking Rob Halford here!" Because here is a song where he suddenly goes up like two octaves in the middle of the song. And I thought, "This is a classic *Sad Wings of Destiny* move that Rob Halford would do, with Priest." And he had never heard Judas Priest. He just looked at my blankly, like, "What? What the hell is that?" *He had no idea!* He didn't even grow up listening to that music from what I can tell.

So, that's what makes it so strange—yeah, Chris Cornell, people perceive him as a "metal singer," because he has that classic '80s high range to his voice, and he's not afraid to use it sometimes. But that's not the music he grew up listening to. So it's kind of accidental. It's a weird parallel of evolution in his case. I don't think he listened to any of that shit until probably years and years later, when somebody would have sat him down and said, "Wait a minute, listen to *this*."

That was what I remember at the time—him looking at me like, "What are you talking about? *Who's Rob Halford?*" [Laughs] To him, it was just like, "Well, this is the voice I've got, and this is how I'm going to use it right now." It was interesting. I never thought of him as Dio, because he didn't sing about demons and shit. He didn't quite have that kind of vibrato. To me, it was a little more Rob Halford. But whatever...and it's accidental. [Laughs]

Another observation concerning what made Soundgarden so unique and distinctive was the same thing that made such bands as Queen, Led Zeppelin, and the Police extraordinary—without those specific four band members in place (three in the latter's case), it would not have been the same. In other words, it was the push and pull of Chris, Kim, Ben/Hiro, and Matt that made it so darn special ("Kim's a flake, Matt's stable, and Chris is as weird as I am" is how Ben once described his bandmates).

And Kim was not oblivious to the fact that he was involved in a very exceptional creative situation—"Chris is a great singer who has really developed. Ben's been in the band for four and a half years and he's world class. Matt is God's drummer. Someone once said to me, 'Kim you make the band arty, Matt makes the band professional and Chris makes the band commercial.' I've seen bands with great ideas and great singers, but without a great drummer, they weren't able to pull it off." Certainly, all of Soundgarden's members contributed their part.

While thinking of how I could end this portion of the book, I kept thinking back to two standout quotes. The first was one from Chris, circa 1995. "I'm not the one who's gonna guess how history might view Soundgarden. That would be kind of silly to me. When you start thinking like that, you're destined for a big fall. All we can do is make sure we make the best records we can, and then hope people like them."

"We've always made records to please ourselves, and that attitude isn't going to change. Just because more people may know who we are and what we're about doesn't mean we're going to start changing the way we work. To me that sounds like a very dangerous way of working." To Soundgarden's credit, they were one of the few bands that remained true to their artistic vision from their inception through to the very end.

And the other quote was from photographer Ross Halfin, circa 2005. "Soundgarden were probably my favorite band of the '90s—they were the most original out of all of them. I like them better than Nirvana. They wrote doomy love songs with a heavy edge. Soundgarden albums improve as they go, where, like, Metallica albums don't. *Kill 'Em All* is probably their best album...then it goes all downhill from there."

I'll take it one step further, Ross. For most of the time they were in business, *Soundgarden was the best rock band on the planet.*

INTERVIEW

PHIL ANSELMO
Pantera and Down singer,
toured with Soundgarden in 1992

In an interview with *Loudwire* in 2013, you called Chris "The Best Modern-Day Rock Vocalist."
If the man was still alive, I would probably feel the same way. He's got all of the earmarks of a classic rock vocalist. He's got it all. Put it this way—when I first started listening to Soundgarden in 1989, he reminded me at times of a very young, *Sabbath Bloody Sabbath*-era Ozzy Osbourne. He also reminded me of Robert Plant. And then later, to my ears, he sounded like John Fogerty. That's a great mixture of rock voices that are staples. He had all of that going for him. It's a pronunciation thing, it's absolutely a range thing. I would think he was a tenor, and he utilized it greatly.

And another thing—and this is coming from a singer—he could switch from full-out voice, and slip directly into falsetto pretty seamlessly. And that is not as easy as it seems. It's actually pretty tough. It's tough for me—it was always tough, because I never had a falsetto. Back in the day when I was hitting high notes, I was doing like, Rob Halford—and that was full-out, singing full-voice. I talked to Terry Date about Chris, and how he used his voice—especially when we were recording *Cowboys from Hell*. And I was surprised that he did use the falsetto as much as he did, but still, it's evident to me—his ability to slip between the full-voice and falsetto-voice was pretty uncanny.

Pantera played some shows with Soundgarden and Skid Row in 1992.
We had a good time. In those days, there wasn't much separation between us, because Skid Row were fans of Pantera...but still there was a big wall of separation, because we were the newcomers and they were established. And with Soundgarden on the bill, it was like we had a chance to hang out. We had met before though. As a matter of fact, when Pantera was recording *Cowboys from Hell,* Voivod, Soundgarden, and Faith No More were doing that tour, and they came through Dallas. That's when

I first met Chris—in Dallas. Very nice guy. A really quiet guy. Later on, at that Skid Row show, he opened up a little bit more. A very fun guy. An absolutely pleasant person. Lovable. And the rest of the band too, for God's sake. Matt Cameron, that dude sat down and listened to the first Down demo with me. Totally cool. Kim was super-cool too. I don't remember meeting Ben or the other bass player. But the rest of the guys were just delightful people.

Favorite Soundgarden songs and albums?

Well man, this might get a little long here. I'm going to go with *Ultramega OK*—"Beyond the Wheel" is fucking insane. It's classic—I don't need to say anything more. And then off *Screaming Life*, "Hunted Down" is a great song. This is kind of a weird story, but the first record I ever had from Soundgarden was *Louder Than Love*, and that was just a by-chance thing. I was living in Texas at the time, and my phone rang. I picked it up, and it was this lady on the other end of the line, and she was desperate. She was talking about her boyfriend who I knew very well, who started his own underground station, and had a fanzine. So, he would get all these advance records. Anyway, he got tossed in jail, and she was freaking out, and was trying to sell anything she could of his to get him out of jail.

So, I was like, "Well, if you're selling discount music, I'll stop by and help out." It was weird—I was looking through all this cat's stuff. And laying in a big pile of cassette tapes was *Louder Than Love*. And it didn't have a cover to it, it didn't have anything—except it was one of those clear cassette tapes. And it just said Soundgarden: *Louder Than Love*. The name alone, "Soundgarden," I don't know what it was or why it appealed to me, but I just bought it on a whim. And funny enough, it's a great record, and also, produced by Terry Date—and just a few months later, we were working with Terry Date! It was all pretty tripped out. But *Louder Than Love* is excellent, and *Badmotorfinger...* those are my favorite records, man. For sure.

How does Chris compare to the all-time vocal greats—Freddie Mercury, Robert Plant, Ronnie James Dio, etc.?

He's just as good. Just as important. Equally as talented. He's probably one of the greatest rock vocalists of all-time. I know it's tough going up against the likes of Dio and anybody else you mentioned. But man, I believe that. It is my opinion, but hey...*it is my opinion.* [Laughs] I think the motherfucker is great.

Did you ever discuss singing techniques or favorite singers with Chris?

Sure. Actually, I brought up the stuff I talked about a little bit earlier with you—about how at first, I thought he had that "Osbourne edge." And then I heard different little things in his voice. And he more agreed with me about Osbourne than he did with Robert Plant. Another thing that caught me off guard—this was in 1989—was that he smoked. I couldn't believe it! I was like, "Damn man...I'm not the only one!" I asked him, "Does that ever bother you?" He said, "No," and I said, "Yeah, me neither."

Did Chris' death surprise you?

I was stunned, amazed, and gasping for air. And still—to this day—I don't believe it went down the way it went down. There's something funny there. I don't know enough about it, but...put it this way—I'd seen him at a festival in Europe or Australia. And he wasn't with Soundgarden, he was just doing his own thing. He was sitting outside the dressing room, kind of early evening—the sun was just going down. I stopped, and just said, "Hey man, what's going on?" He was really mellow and cool as fuck.

I don't know—I just didn't get any dire vibe from the guy. It probably is not enough to give a correct diagnosis of the situation, but I don't know man—I don't believe it. It still seems unreal. It feels very much like one of our favorite artists got taken *way* before his time. It really feels like us fans got chiseled out of hearing where this guy was going to go musically. It feels like we got dicked, man. I can't even imagine what it must be like for people who are really close to him. It feels like a raw deal.

Were there any Pantera or Down songs that were influenced by Soundgarden?

Not to my knowledge. But I know especially in the Down camp...with Pantera, we were so doing our own thing, and so busy. It's similar with Down, but at least with Down, we got a chance to reflect on where we thought we fit—with the bands that were heavily influenced by Black Sabbath. The first wave of bands— like Saint Vitus, Witchfinder General, etcetera, etcetera. I know for a fact that with Down, we had a huge respect for them. I'm sure all the guys in Down still do. We would discuss Soundgarden, for sure, because of the similarities in the music that we had together. Great respect for them.

How do you think Soundgarden's music holds up today?

It's classic. Hands down classic. It holds up 100%. It is forever, as they say.

How would you like Chris to be remembered?

As a gentle soul who was most probably the best of his era.

INTERVIEW

DAVE WYNDORF
Monster Magnet singer/guitarist,
toured with Soundgarden in 1992

When did you first discover and hear Soundgarden?
In the late '80s. I think probably the first record I heard from them was a single I think, and I remember *Ultramega OK* in my head very strongly—because it had some great songs on it. They were just amazing. And I saw them in '89—they co-billed with Mudhoney at Maxwell's in Hoboken, New Jersey, and it was *fuckin' great.* I was like, "ROCK IS BACK!"

Both of those guys, they were firing on all cylinders that night. That show, the minute it got me was Soundgarden was good on record, but it wasn't anything like they were live. They needed the volume. The whole show itself was amazing, because Mudhoney was one of my favorites, so it was just like, this is so much rock in one room, when there hadn't been *any* fuckin' rock around. In '89, there was plain old punk rock, grown up punk rock, and we didn't get much of the stuff that was coming out of England—some of the cooler stuff. So, this was just amazing. This was like, *the real deal.*

Soundgarden came on, and I think they opened. And the first thing they played was "Working Man" by Rush...and then went into "Communication Breakdown" [by Led Zeppelin]! It was like a split song—they went right into it. It just completely freaked me out. It's exactly what they wanted. I think they were playing it as a goof—trying to make fun of old rock. And those guys were pretty much from a punk rock pedigree—at least their attitude was. Long-haired punk rock, but punk rock anyway—and very "indie scene-y." So, they were doing it as, "As a 'wink,' we're going to do the dumbest song in the world, 'Working Man'." But the way they did it was *fuckin' great.* I was just like, "Yeah. This is exactly what I want. I want to see a band do 'Working Man' and 'Communication Breakdown'." And with Cornell singing it, you can just imagine how great it was.

What made them unique at the time?

They knew what to avoid in punk and indie to not be cliché, and they knew what to avoid in metal not to be cliché. But they had the best of both of those things. They had their own thing. Like, Kim played guitar like nobody else—he had those weird tunings, and he would let stuff go over. He wouldn't hit chords all the time, which is what most metal guys would do—they would hit everything so it was all banged out—sort of like old Zeppelin. It was almost like watching the Edge or somebody—one of those guys that just lets stuff go. So, that was weird. And it was unusual—it had nothing to do with the music that I saw coming out. On the indie side they didn't go corny—it wasn't like a total twee thing. It wasn't wimpy.

A lot of the indie stuff out there was just like...nerd rock, or something. Not that there's anything wrong with that, but you go to a show, and you're like, *"Come on now."* I was of the age where I was probably in my late twenties, so I had been to real rock. Real rock had come and gone, and then punk rock had come in. Most of that stuff was built on a certain amount of power. When the college rock radio stuff got big, a lot of the stuff kind of tweed out. It was nice and it was grown up—it was grown up young people and well-behaved. And it was just not that interesting. And Soundgarden and Mudhoney had this sort of *"ARGGH!"* ferocity to it, that I was like, "Oh yeah, I recognize this."

When did you first cross paths with Soundgarden?

We released a record, *Spine of God*, and Soundgarden were making their way up, and they started doing a lot of MTV—they were in "the system" at that point. And sure enough, they appeared on MTV, on *120 Minutes* or something, and Kim was wearing a Monster Magnet shirt! Which was a big deal—MTV was a big deal at that time. There was nowhere else to go, and if you wore a shirt, that was a decision—those guys made a decision, "I'm going to wear this shirt." And it just completely blew me away. It was like, "This guy is doing it...*for us*."

The next thing you know, by '92, they had released *Badmotorfinger,* and they had requested that Monster Magnet be on the tour with them and Swervedriver in the United States. That was in the spring of '92. We were on tour in Europe and had a bunch of dates left. We found out about that, and I just said to our manager at the time, "We've got to cancel these dates and go tour with those guys." *You can't not.* They were doing theaters— perfectly-sized places. And then the next thing you know...we're there. I think we started in Oregon. It was fantastic.

What sticks out about Monster Magnet touring with Soundgarden in '92?
It was a really, really great time. It was the first time I had played on stages that big. It was a huge learning experience for me. Also, it was a big learning experience for how the music business works, and once a band goes from indie to major. Which was a really big deal at the time. Everybody wanted to do it...but nobody wanted to do it. [Laughs] Everybody wanted to do it, but nobody really wanted to *own it.*

It is hard for people to remember nowadays, but it was almost like, "If you do this, you've pretty much sold a bit of your soul, and there's going to be a certain amount of people who hate you forever." And I watched that with Soundgarden. They were really aware of it. And I met those guys, and they were really fucking nice guys. They were cool. Smart, funny—like *real* guys. Like dudes. They were serious about what they were doing and the music, but they were really concerned about how people were going to take them, now that they were three albums in.

The one thing I noticed about the tour was the fantastic shows they did every night—they didn't do one bad show. They were on fire back then. Later on, we played with them again, and they weren't on fire. But they were going for it at that point. Especially Cornell was going for it, and Ben. The one thing I remember is seeing them agonize over the whole thing. Really upset. And I remember saying to myself, "What are you guys complaining about? You're two albums in on a major label."

And this album, *Badmotorfinger*, was a *phenomenal* record. That's a hard rockin' record. There is no way in the world that any serious music listener can listen to that and go, "These guys sold out." I didn't see it that way. But they were really concerned about it. And they come from a place where press really matters. In Seattle, the business would eat people alive over there. People kept talking about what was cool and what wasn't cool. And I think a lot of rock writers and indie press had a lot to do with how the bands felt about things—although the bands resented it. But there was no real way back then to have an idea about what the fans thought of you. They either bought something or didn't buy something.

And there was a lag time between when something came out until its ultimate assessment would come out. And with the grunge thing...I hate to call it grunge, but with the grunge thing and that indie scene that happened in the late '80s, there was a buffer zone between what you did, how the people accepted it, and how it was interpreted by rock journalists in between. And the rock journalists would form this thing about what this record meant. And a lot of bands thought that was the final word to the fans—forgetting that no, *the music* really is.

It was a really interesting time, and I remember being kind of scared too, because I was on an indie, and I wanted to be on a major...but I didn't want to look like I was on a major. It was the same thing. It was like, "Well, how can we continue a life in music without a major? Is it possible?" No, it didn't seem possible. Anyway, Soundgarden were very concerned about that.

You said before that Chris and Ben were really "going for it" at that point live.
What I remember was Chris was like a messianic frontman. Like, old school. Although he was doing it...not with a nod and a wink, but he was almost doing it begrudgingly. He was doing it athletically. He was like a "shirt's off guy." And that's why I couldn't believe he would come and complain about, "Oh...these people look at me like I'm some sort of Robert Plant or

something." And I remember going, "Well dude, why don't you put your fuckin' shirt on? You're sending out signals here!"

When you go out with a mic in your hand and you look at the ceiling with your shirt off, you look like you're trying to be Robert Plant. They didn't get it. But I think he was trying to play with it. All I know is I remember having a conversation with him once—he was a super-nice guy—and he was talking about that. And I was like, "Just fuckin' eat it up. Are you crazy? If I looked like you and sounded like you...I'd already have platforms built! Nobody cares as much as you think they do. They want you like that. They don't mind. And the smart people will find out you're having fun, the dumb people and the people who think they're smart will go with the current press, which was like, 'Fuck you if you make any money or if you have fun'."

But the Nirvana thing really, really fucked with everybody back then. Nirvana's success really fucked with everybody's heads, because Nirvana came out and made it bigger than anybody by being miserable. And all of a sudden, that became a gimmick—be miserable, don't like it. It was bankable, and I think it fucked with everybody's heads, like, "Am I supposed to be miserable, too?" I know it fucked with my head. And then of course what happened to Nirvana—the ultimate thing, where you make it...and then kill yourself. It was like, "*This is horrible!*"

But back to Soundgarden, they were going for it. I don't think it bothered them that much, because if it did, they wouldn't have put on the shows that they did—which were smokin'. Ben was a maniac—he was like Spiderman on stage, jumping around, and he would drag has bass on the ground. And Chris just looked like a million bucks, and he would stage-dive every night. The crowd was the most giving to a singer I've probably ever seen—they would float him around the crowd to the back of these theaters, up and down stairs. And he really looked like Jesus Christ. I was like, "*This is amazing.*" And he sounded fantastic. And Kim was just doing his thing, just flying. And Matt is one of the best drummers I think I've ever seen. So, it was all there. It was real rock. They were going for it. They were not throwing up their hands in disgust or rolling their eyes—which they did later.

John McBain was still in Monster Magnet at that point, right?
Yeah. His last tour with Monster Magnet was doing the *Badmotorfinger* tour with Swervedriver.

Did his leaving come as a surprise?
Well...we kind of asked him to leave. It was like, "This isn't working." He was just freaking out over the whole thing. I never figured out just what was going on in his mind. But I think he was kind of bugged out about the whole thing that I was just talking about—about the press and what's cool or what's not. Because he had his issues with it, too. I'm out there, rocking. Like, "Come on! Stick it up their ass!" And he's like, "Oh, that's not cool." We got back, and he had been really talking it up with those guys, and started riding on the bus with them. And the next thing you know, when John was out of the band, he moved to Seattle, and he got in that project, Hater, with Ben [and Matt]—which was pretty good. And that was it. It was a really weird time with John. Very strange.

What did you think of the Hater and Wellwater Conspiracy projects that John was involved in, with members of Soundgarden?
Oh, I loved it. I was like, "Keep going!" I was hoping that John was going to bust out and do what he wanted to do—whatever that was. He never said anything. John wasn't a guy who would say what he wanted. He'd just say what he *didn't* want. He was one of those guys, "Uh...I don't like this." "Well, what do you like?" "I don't know." It's kind of hard. Everybody goes to school with one of those guys. But I loved it. I thought that this was the best thing that could possibly happen—being that John was not a "road guy," obviously.

As far as Monster Magnet was concerned, I was a huge fan of what Monster Magnet stood for—at least in my mind. I was the guy who kept coming up with the whole thing, like, "It should be like this, it should be like that." And the fact that if John didn't want to play, if John wasn't into it, it was unworkable. In fact, that he would still go on and play and not go back to New Jersey and like, hide in a hole, that was the best thing ever. So, I was totally psyched.

Did you continue to keep in touch with Soundgarden after the tour?
No, unfortunately I didn't. I wish I could say I did. I just kind of went forward. I'm pretty much a homebody, so I would just go out to work, and come home and hang out. I wasn't the kind of guy that would call—I didn't want to bug them. Now, I wish that I did. Ben and I kept some phone calls every once in a while. He's crazy as a bed bug, sometimes! And I was not—contrary to popular belief—a drug guy. I was not all fucked up. I was completely into this, "I just want to write music and make music and keep going." So, I didn't. And I kind of wish we did, because I probably could have learned something about the business from those guys.

You mentioned that Monster Magnet played shows again with Soundgarden—in 1995.
It wasn't a lot of dates, but it was in Europe. From what I could see, they were great as ever, but...they didn't seem that into it. They toured *a lot*, man. They did the whole thing. They signed to a major label, and did everything you're supposed to do in the rock business. When you do that, you always die a little bit. There's no way on earth that your emotions and your brain can withstand that kind of punishment. *It's a lot.*

So, when we saw them, they were wearing button down shirts and stuff...and not even sweating. That kind of thing. Which is fine, I guess—but not exactly what I had in mind. They were getting haircuts and shit. [Laughs] "Boo! Where's the rock?!" But they were at that point, like, here these guys were, just by the sheer amount of work they did was so much more mature than us—even though I was a couple of years older than them. But they were more mature because they had lived more of it. So, I understood what was going on. I talked to them a little bit then, and they were just like, "Yeah, *whatever.*" Like, "When does the plane take off?" By that point, they had money—that changes a lot of things.

What are some of your favorite Soundgarden albums and songs?

From the early days, "Nothing to Say" is one of my favorite songs...ever, still. It's an *amazing* hard rock song. A heavy song. "Hands All Over" is another great one. Almost the entirety of *Badmotorfinger.* "Outshined" and "Jesus Christ Pose" were like, *"Holy shit."* Just the sound of it and their delivery...fucking potent. *Superunknown,* there was "Black Hole Sun," I really liked "My Wave." And "Burden in My Hand" is a really great song.

Probably a little earlier is when it got me, but I don't think that has to do with quality of songs—it just has to do with new excitement. But they never jumped the shark. They were always good. And I really liked the stuff at the end, when they started integrating big piano into the music. It really worked. It was like the Stones—they started doing stuff with a big, giant piano at the bottom of everything. It's cool.

Were you surprised by their split in 1997?

No, not at all. I thought it came late. Us guys on the lower rungs were all like, "They're going to break up," because they had the money. And as soon as you get the money, everything changes—you just don't care as much anymore. You don't have anything to prove, and when you work for that money like they did, there comes a point where everyone has to take a break.

And taking a break in a band is usually the kiss of death for any band. As soon as you take a break, it's like, *"Why did I marry you again?"* You look at other people. Not that you're not friends, but that's what I see. You take a while, and then you either get back together...or not. I guess it all depends on if you officially say, "We break up." Never say never, in my experience—you never say you're breaking up, even if you are. So, I wasn't surprised that that happened.

Did you see any shows during their reunion?

No, I wish I did. I saw some Cornell solo shows in Europe in the mid-aughts—2005/2006—which were OK. But nothing like

Soundgarden. Very slick—it wasn't as raw as Soundgarden. Did you see any of those?

Yes. I've seen Chris solo, with Audioslave, and with Soundgarden.
Oh, I forgot about Audioslave. Yeah, I always wondered about Audioslave—it should have been a lot better than it was. I don't understand...they should have been over-the-top.

Whenever I saw Audioslave or Chris solo, I would always be thinking, "This is good...but I'd much rather be seeing Soundgarden."
There was just a certain ferocity. Not only that, but the way the songs were done, they were one of those bands that really is *a band.* You start taking the components out, and all of a sudden, this isn't a modular unit—you can't just swap out one thing and expect it to go the same, like some bands. There are all kinds of weird quirks and stuff that happened when those guys played together. Which is probably why I loved them so much. I didn't realize at the time...or maybe I did, I was like, "This is why this is great."

But there was really nobody like them—not even around in Seattle, either. They were way classier than everybody else. And they would play it down, like, "No, we're not." And it was like, *"What are you talking about?!"* And they would say, "No, we're just punk rock." I was like, "Dude...if that's punk rock, I'm a fuckin' frog. That is not punk rock! You've got like, Indian music coming out, there's weird psychedelic shit, plus there's Sabbath and Zeppelin." *Awesome.*

I miss those guys. I was happy when they got back together, and I thought they were at that point where they would be like, "Fuck it. We'll just completely cream everyone and do whatever we want." And I guess they were on their way back to doing it...and then Cornell commits suicide. The most bizarre fucking thing...ugh, *horrible.*

Did Chris' death come as a shock?
Totally. Yeah. I don't think anybody could see that coming. I knew he was a thinking man—a deep thinker—and I knew he was disappointed by the rock business early on. But he'd gone on and survived for so long, and he had a wife and kids...I guess you never know. Like his wife says with that drug, I can totally believe that. Because I was on benzodiazepine for a while, and coming off it, that was the first time and only time in my life that I ever considered suicide. And it was a direct result of that drug. Benzodiazepine will do that. You can look at case histories of suicides due to drugs, and you'll see just a long line of people— "The guy was perfectly fine for four years...and then he jumped in front of a train." And what was he taking? Benzos. It was horrible. And what a rotten way to go. Poor bastard. I feel bad for him. He must have been very, very lonely and despondent at that point in his head. For you to go that way...it's foul. *Yech*.

The whole thing is heartbreaking.
Yeah. It just didn't have to be. I'm convinced it had something to do with all those drugs. Y'know, everybody's got it in them. It's just, what does it take to get it out? Sometimes, you take these foreign substances, and you go into a place that normally you would never go into, and the next thing you know, *boom*. Really bad. I think their legacy will overcome that—hopefully, in a couple of years, the suicide thing will fade, like it does. And the music itself will be the lasting part of it.

How do you think Soundgarden's music holds up, and do you think they will go down as one of rock's all-time great bands?
Well, they already went down as one of the all-time great bands for me, because they did something that nobody else did and nobody else had even tried to do—that's a good sign. Nobody could even try to put that combination of stuff together and pull it off—it would be too sloppy and weird and shitty. So, yeah, I think they'll go down in history as one of the greats.
It all depends on how history itself is formulated in the future. The information age thing that is going on has to shake out

first, and rock history and rock in general right now is on shaky ground—just because there's so much stuff. But if you look back, in any circles of musical innovation, as opposed to pop phenomena, if you look at musical innovation, what it means to music—they'll be one of the greats. Absolutely.

How would you like Chris to be remembered?
As one of the most kickass rock singers of all-time. I'm sure he'd be like, "Can't I be remembered for something deeper than that?" But that's how I remember him. They had very good lyrics too, but I never figured out who wrote what in that band. I think everybody wrote a lot of different stuff together. Including lyrics. But I remember him as being the "it doesn't get any better kind of guy." I could turn around and they can show anybody from any age, and if anybody asks me, "What a great rock singer should be," I would point to him. *That guy.*

INTERVIEW

JIM ROSE
Founder of Jim Rose Circus,
toured with Soundgarden on Lollapalooza '92

When did you first cross paths with Soundgarden?
It was Lollapalooza. Chris had come to my shows in Seattle—my show was popular in Seattle way before internationally. But I came from a little place, and I'm ten years older than those guys. He came to my shows, but I didn't meet him.

How would you describe the Jim Rose Circus Side Show at the time?
I was doing a regular run every Thursday, Friday, and Saturday night at the Ali Baba's Middle Eastern Restaurant on the belly dancing stage. A lot of people came to that show—it sold out every night. It was only 80 capacity though. It was just a little show, and people paid I think it was eight dollars, and I ended up making good money just doing 80 people a night for three nights. We had pierced weight lifting, human blockheads, human pincushions. I incorporated some magic with it and some silly burlesque stuff with it. It was a comedy show—we didn't take ourselves real serious. Basically, I spun humor around atrocities.

And how did the show get involved with Lollapalooza?
That's a direct connection to Soundgarden right there. Susan Silver recommended me. And I didn't know her, but she stepped in there and did that. And then Perry Farrell looked at some video stuff, and said, "Yeah, let's do this." That's how I ended up on Lollapalooza. And I didn't realize that they were fans. Then, I get to Lollapalooza, and I was clueless, man—I'm ten years older than all these people. I had just gotten off heroin—I had been on heroin for ten years, and I had just gotten off about a year earlier. I remember somebody pointing at a big crowd of people, and said, "There's Jane's Addiction." And I said, "Well, *I hope she gets treatment.*" Because I wasn't aware of any of these bands at all. But I realized pretty quick that there was this thing going on—

later called alternative-whatever. And these guys were darlings of that movement. Somehow, I ended up in it.

How soon after your stint on Lollapalooza began did you realize it was causing a stir with the crowd?
Well...then we're going to sew it back to Soundgarden again, because people think I was an immediate success on Lollapalooza. But, the fact is there was no advertising of when I may or may not even be there. They didn't promote me on that festival. And it's a second stage, which people weren't used to at the time. And it was really far from the main stage—you needed alligator repellent and a weed whacker to get to it. So, I could shoot a canon through my crowd and not hit anybody for the first week.

But the people that were showing up—every show—were the Pearl Jam guys, the Soundgarden guys, Ministry. And then whatever town we were in, whatever locals. Somehow, people were figuring out who I am. But it was just so underground that the kids coming...it just hadn't happened yet. So then, one night, I look up, and it's just *thousands* of kids. I go, "What the fuck?! How did this happen?" And somebody told me, "Soundgarden's show just ended, and they just announced on the main stage for everybody to come meet them over at the Jim Rose Freak Stage." So, that was Chris. Without him, I'm not sure we would have this conversation right now.

Afterwards, I saw Chris, and I really thanked him for it. And he said, "Hey, why don't you start introducing Soundgarden every day? And then at the end of my set, I'll say, 'Hey, let's go meet up at the Jim Rose Freak Stage'?" I said, "OK!" So, I started announcing. And I did a really big bally—bally is kind of a term used for freak shows—but I really pumped them up, "THIS IS THE OFFICIAL LOLLAPALOOZA WAKE-UP CALL! EVERYBODY, STAND UP! STAND UP! STAND UP!" I got them all following instructions. Then, I would bring them out, and they got really big applause, so, it was good. But they were getting good applause anyway. It was a nice synergy there. And we became good friends for a few years. I hung out with them a lot. I remember one time, he threw a TV out a window at a hotel, and I was the one walking on the sidewalk at the time, and it just barely missed me. But he didn't know that—he was just frustrated about something.

I would joke around with him, I told him and Eddie—because they were tired of doing interviews at a certain point, and also it was part of that whole thing, to act all down and whatever—"Listen, Eddie, why don't you do Chris' interviews, and Chris, you do Eddie's, and see what happens?" And the journalists never knew the difference! They were talking to Eddie Vedder when they thought they were talking to Chris, and they were talking to Chris when they thought they were talking to Eddie, for a couple of weeks there.

Susan and Chris were still together at that time.
I hung out with them a lot, actually—even after Lollapalooza, for a few years. Then I got lost—I went off with Nine Inch Nails and Marilyn Manson, and I never looked back. And I had moved at that point from Seattle. So, I didn't really see them after that too much. But to be honest, they just didn't show any affection towards each other. I assumed there was some there—they had a daughter. But I didn't see it—they weren't public with any affection.

There are several photos online of you and Chris together circa Lollapalooza—one of you and him eating together, and a few others.
I don't really have memories of eating with Chris—although I did it almost every day, because they served lunch at the same time, at the same place, and I was there. Soundgarden was not stealing Lollapalooza. They had a really nice following, but "Black Hole Sun" hadn't come out yet. But they were absolute gods in Seattle. And Chris' reputation was to be inclusive. And if he believed in you, it wasn't just words—he put *effort* into helping you do better.

That's the reason why he announced us from the stage, without even mentioning it to me—he wanted me to do better. I can get a little emotional when I talk about Chris, because it was just an amazing turnaround once he took me under his wing, and helped me with that. One of my huge regrets, I kept telling myself, "I'm going to get in touch with him again." And I knew he moved to France, and I live in France...but it just never happened.

But anyway, more memories from Lollapalooza—you know that one photo where he's got the biggest smile you've ever seen Chris Cornell have? I'm guessing we were on mushrooms, because I remember we did mushrooms once on Lollapalooza, and that may have been the day. But for the most part, we were from Seattle, we might meet new friends, but Seattle meant something to Chris. And Eddie was there, and Chris really helped Eddie in the beginning, as well.

So, Pearl Jam, Soundgarden, and the Circus...and Ministry would show up all the time and crash the thing, and of course Al [Jourgensen], he would suck up all the oxygen, because that's what he wanted to do. Which was fine, because none of us were really talking a lot, anyway. Eddie at the time was all worried about becoming mainstream and on MTV all the time, and he wasn't happy about that. That was the thing he was brooding about.

Remember, this whole grunge-y thing...they should have called it "broo-gey"—there was a lot of brooding going on, man, they should have been fucking jumping up and down and throwing babies in the air with the breaks they were getting. It was just a little town—Seattle at the time, the poster said, "The last one out of Seattle, please turn out the lights." It was not the Seattle of myth and legend that it is now. But it was a very brooding kind of thing going on. It was the same with Kurt Cobain—Kurt was always down and "*Life's hard.*" I was just a guy who was happy as fuck that I had gotten off a ten-year heroin habit, and I wasn't about to get sucked into all that.

I already had my brooding period, where I only read Beat writing, and the occasional Louis-Ferdinand Céline. I'm ten years older than them, and I think they all knew it. I was really tired because I wasn't used to touring like that—that was my first tour like that. I wasn't like this guy that burst into a room and sucked up oxygen. But I definitely talked more than they did. And the point is, if I was talking too much, they'd quit hanging around me.

I never went looking for them—they always came to me. So, I must have provided something that was of interest.

You mentioned taking mushrooms with Chris. How much partying was going on during Lollapalooza?
I'll tell you this—Soundgarden and Pearl Jam did not party a lot. There were some beers around, but nobody was going crazy. Now, a couple of years later, I used to drink like a fish and play ping-pong with Chris. We used to do that a lot, and I used to drink with Eddie—Eddie got to where he loved red wine. And Eddie and I used to love to play pinball and air hockey. So, we'd just go find a dive bar. And the same with Chris—there was a dive bar that had a ping-pong table, and we would play. That worked.

How was Chris as a ping-pong player?
Not very good. He was OK, but I was a pretty good ping-pong player. Mostly, I was keeping the ball in play—I could have smacked it any time I wanted to.

You mentioned earlier that it took a while for the Jim Rose Side Show to gain popularity on Lollapalooza, but by the time I caught your act at Jones Beach (on August 9th), you had quite an audience.
I don't remember that show specifically...was that the one that had the hurricane?

No. There was supposed to be a second show on the 10th, but it got cancelled right before Pearl Jam went on.
I've got a great story for you. Backstage at Jones Beach, there's this little boat dock, where Guy Lombardo used to drive his boat in, pop up, do his show, jump on his boat, and get the fuck out of there. It's been a venue for a very long time. So, I'm back there, and it's just me and the promoter, Ron Delsener. He's in just some shorts, and he's laying in the sun, and he's got one of those silver things to reflect the sun in a certain place. And he knows that I'm getting a little bit of heat, so he's being my friend—because he probably wants to promote me in the future—and he invites me.

I'm laying around, it's kind of hot, and I really don't want to be there. It's *really* humid.

Then, this big burly guy comes up, and whispers something in Delsener's ear, they put a robe on him—he's real shaky—and he walks out. Now, I didn't have a clue what the hell just happened. But I found out about a week later that I was right there when he found out that they were going to have to shut the show down...*and Delsener had no insurance.* All of that had to be paid out of his pocket. And that was an expensive...I don't know, it had to have been a million or so dollars. I actually saw him getting that bad news.

Chris was asked by MTV to do *Rock the Vote*. He asked if I could be on with him, they said we need to ask our boss. Chris said, "Tell them that I only want to do it with Jim Rose." So, we did it together about ten minutes later. I forget what city but it poured rain and kids created a giant mud slide. Chris and I went. Chris kept his hat real low—no one recognized him. We did the slide and it was a blast—we were covered in mud. We didn't even recognize each other at first—we were just part of a mud horde. I went around saying "CC" until I heard back from one of the mudded in a whispered voice, "Jim, *is that you*?" We hung out for hours doing the slide and talking with other muddy buddies. That I think was the most fun day that Chris had on Lollapalooza.

Let's discuss one of the show's main attractions, bile beer.
We would pump this guy's stomach [Matt the Tube], and the stuff that came out of his stomach, we would offer to the audience. And by the time we got to Jones Beach, where you saw it, fans rushed the stage. We just didn't have enough vomit for everyone. But it didn't used to be that way. We used to offer it to the audience, and nobody would come up, because they didn't want to drink it! And I don't blame them. We used to do the show, never thinking anybody was going to drink the damn stuff.

One day we offer it...and Chris walks out and says, "*I'll drink it!*" The fans go crazy. Because remember, a lot of them were Soundgarden people, because he had just told them to come meet there. And remember, the person that came on after

Soundgarden was Ice Cube, and Ice Cube was *not* the genre that was really hitting and sticking with that alternative movement in 1992. So, it was easy to get a lot of Ice Cube's crowd to come see me. Now, I know you put him in a different situation and he would go through the roof, but there weren't a lot of people at his shows—which was really lucky for me, as well.

So anyway, Chris drank it. And the next day I offered it, Chris came out again, but this time, *Eddie Vedder* followed up! Then the next night, it's Eddie, Chris, and Al Jourgensen. Well, by that time, it ends up on MTV. And MTV meant something back then. Now, not only are a lot of people coming to my shows, they're even waiting during Soundgarden for us to come out—because it was more intimate, and you could sit down there and not worry about getting trampled on or anything. Then, I offered it, and fans just rushed the stage. I'm talking 40 or 50 of them. Our equipment was getting destroyed.

So, I told the Lollapalooza people, "Look, I'm going to stop doing this, because I can't afford to replace my equipment every night." And they said, "No, no, no. We'll get you extra security. We like you doing this." "Oh...OK!" So then, every day, it's Eddie, Chris, Flea, and whatever rock star was in whatever city that wasn't part of the tour but was there and had access backstage—Gibby from Butthole Surfers, somebody from Aerosmith. They all came, because they knew they were going to end up on MTV. And as much as they act like they don't want press, they actually do—and they also want to act like they're wild and crazy.

That's how I ended up with all these friends. I'm a nobody, but other than Chris, Eddie, and Al, everybody just wanted that badge of craziness I guess, so they would want to hang out. But then Chris stopped doing it after a while, and other people kind of quit doing it after a while. But Eddie Vedder and Al Jourgensen—*every day*. And then it got out on MTV that they were in a race to see who could drink the most vomit. And at the end, it turned out that Eddie had drank it two times more than Jourgensen did. And when Jourgensen was asked about it, he said,

"Fuck it, I'll just make my own." But anyway, Chris got that thing going.

People may forget how shocking some of the things in your act were at the time—I remember several people fainting in the audience during the performance.
Yeah, yeah. But you know what? Presentation has a lot to do with that kind of thing. The act that they would faint on was the Human Pincushion. But that's only because I kept suggesting that people might be fainting during this. And I had a little presentation where I set them up psychologically to create things. If I had presented it differently, I don't think I would have really gotten any.

I never thought of it that way. But you're right—if you put a thought in someone's head, then you get a different reaction.
Yeah. That's something I knew a lot about. When I was a heroin addict, I had to come up with money every day. So, the psychology of how to manipulate humans to act in my best interest was just ingrained in me. I mean, I was fucking *dangerous* when I got off heroin—with everything I knew how to do.

Regarding bile beer, it wasn't just beer, but other things too, like ketchup and chocolate, right?
Oh yeah—Maalox, ginseng. Ginseng was popular back then.

Did you ever drink the bile beer yourself?
Fuck no! So much of my show, I couldn't even watch. My later years I could, with women sumo wrestling and Mexican transvestite wrestling and all that. That show that I was doing on that tour, it was put together for a purpose. I wasn't the biggest fan of it. [Laughs] I'm not my biggest fan. But it's what I thought people wanted at the time. I wrote some jokes around it, and spent a lot of time in Europe—that's where I learned all that stuff.

What didn't you like to watch in your show back then?
Oh, that whole bile beer thing—I almost threw up every day. That pincushion thing, I hated it—especially if it was a hot day and he

was bleeding. That's the reason why it wasn't in my show after. I took it out for one more go-around, because people expected it, but then it was gone and I never did it again. I tried to not do the bile beer thing, but boy, the fans really reacted negatively, so I had to bring that back. I didn't want to do it, but there it was. Mr. Lifto, that never bothered me. Sword swallowing never bothered me. Just those two.

And you kept hanging out with Chris after that tour, right?
Yeah. We could turn it on, but we don't want to turn it on if we're just being social. And we both had—and I still have, and he would too, if he were around—social anxiety. I don't know if anybody's talked to you about Chris and that, but he was not the most comfortable human around. We mostly let other people talk that were around—Susan was always there, and there was another girl, Susie Bridges. Chris wrote a lot of his hit songs at her house— before he became famous.

But as far as after Lollapalooza, for a couple of years, Chris would call pretty often, or at least somebody would call me, and say, "Chris is going to be here, and asked if you would go." So, I would go often and we would hang out and basically listen to other people talk. And then, when we played ping-pong, he started drinking. I forget what year that was, but he wasn't a good drunk. It didn't take much to get him there, and it could get sloppy pretty quick. But we would be drinking beer when we would play ping-pong—that I remember.

How would you describe Chris' personality?
I would say loving, magnanimous, shy, and because I'm kind of into psychology, I could tell immediately...that's another reason I've had so many rock star friends, because they're all insecure. So, a lot of them have social anxiety—they just do, it's amazing. And since I have that and I am able to talk about it early in a friendship, something happens there. And I knew he had social anxiety, so we talked about that. That was probably my bond with Trent Reznor. But I'll tell you somebody who wasn't—David

Bowie. Man, Bowie could walk into any goddamned room, and he was just as comfortable as hell.

How would Chris' personality change when he would drink? Would he become violent?
No—I didn't see violent. He was a little aggro, but I don't think he would punch anybody though. And that's what I call violent— if it's to another human or an animal. Maybe I've got my definition of violence wrong. He could be aggro, but I never saw him get into a fight or even come close. You've got to remember, when I'm hanging around these guys, they don't have their security guys with them, because we're not going anywhere where that's needed. They're just being who they are—as best they can. There's nobody protecting Chris in a little dive bar playing ping-pong.

Realistically, he was a little aggro, but it quickly turned into sleepy. [Laughs] Slurry, actually. But he was such a sweet guy—he doesn't deserve negativity, because of how much he's helped people. And his heart was always so good. Y'know, I've got this weird thing about religion—I can't believe in something or someone that's over a thousand years old. But I do believe that you can believe in someone's heart, and then you hope to emulate that heart. And me, I call them "living buddhas." And for me, Chris was a living buddha. His heart was something I realized was a goal. Because I'm always into self-improvement, and Chris' heart was a goal for me, and I vividly remember that. And he did change me. He didn't know he did, but he did change me in a lot of ways.

I remember why it got weird for me to go see Chris. I had a choice between Nine Inch Nails with this other band that was the opening band—I was the middle slot—which was this kid named Brian, and now, we know him as Marilyn Manson. I had a choice to go out with that tour, or to go out with the Soundgarden tour [in 1994]. And I chose Nine Inch Nails. And I chose Nine Inch Nails because I didn't tap into that audience at Lollapalooza, and I was trying to build my fanbase up. I just didn't think that more exposure to a grunge audience was going to make much difference for me. And this whole goth-y thing, they seemed to be into theater, and theatrical type stuff—more than a grunge fan. And I thought, "Maybe I'll fit there better." And I was right—that tour is really what did it for me.

You—because you were maybe hyper into reading stuff—knew my name, but most people at Lollapalooza were vaguely familiar or aware of a "Lollapalooza freak show." MTV took my brand, basically, and turned it into "Lollapalooza freak show"—they showed footage of me all day long, and underneath it was "Lollapalooza freak show." When I got off Lollapalooza, I was kind of sad about that, because I had put a lot of effort into this thing, and I didn't think I built my brand that strong. And sure enough, I did a tour right after, and it didn't sell a ton of tickets. So I figured, "OK. I'm going to have to do something to fix this." And the Nine Inch Nails tour is the one.

So after that, you lost track of Chris?
Yeah, and it wasn't Chris' fault—Chris didn't care [about Jim turning down the Soundgarden tour]. I did see him one time after, and we were good—we played ping-pong and we drank. Everything was the same. But I wasn't running in those circles, and I moved out of Seattle, and I was just never in the same city again. I was in the same city as Pearl Jam many times, but I don't think Soundgarden really toured that much. So, '95 was the last time I saw Chris, and then I never did again. But there was always a city where Pearl Jam and us were in—very often.

Were you a fan of Soundgarden's music?
I was talking to Trent Reznor the other day, and I said, "Trent, you know that song, 'I want to fuck you like an animal'?" And he said, "*You mean 'Closer'*?" I mean, Trent has been one of my best friends forever, and I still don't even know the names of *his* songs! So, for me to name Soundgarden songs...I'm not going to be able to give you a whole list of them. I loved "Outshined." And then of course, that whole "Black Hole Sun" album, there was a lot of good stuff. Because remember, I'm ten years older. Kim Thayil's style of guitar—he takes from the '60s. There are riffs he's doing

that are very '60s-type riffs. He wasn't doing '80s riffs, as much. He was kind of playing around and doing a different tuning of '60s-type stuff. Kim's guitar was a big part of all that.

And then Matt Cameron...I ended up living with him after Lollapalooza. We were roommates—my wife, and him and his wife. I came back to Seattle after that tour, and my car had been towed, and I had given up my apartment, because I was going to be gone for a while. I had toured Canada right before Lollapalooza, so I had been away for months. I didn't have a place to stay, and I was looking for a place, and Matt said, "Well, you can stay with me until you find an apartment." And I ended up with him for a few weeks.

It was Seattle man, and they were just really good to each other there. And by the way, that whole supporting each other, if you go to LA, all those bands that are competing, they'll pretend to like each other, but there's no support there. It's competitive. With Seattle, it was very supportive. If you were from Seattle, we took care of each other. That was a very interesting thing for just a geographical location. I'm ten years older, etcetera, etcetera, and I'm not in a grunge band, but yet, we're all friends, and I'll be damned if they didn't take care of me, because of a geographical location.

Soundgarden and Nine Inch Nails toured together in 2014. Did Trent ever discuss that with you?
Yeah, but they didn't really hang out. It was two ships in the night. I asked Trent about that, and he was professional. I think it's just another in a huge blur for him. Actually, I can't speak for him, ever. Especially using the word "blur," because he remembers *everything*. So, it was not a blur—I was just using that for some throwaway.

Concerning Chris' social anxiety and whatever other troubles he may have had; do you think it fueled his creativity and made him such a special talent?
Yeah, of course it impacted his art. How could it not? Of course it did. I can't put my finger on exactly something in his catalog that

directly says, "This is how this happened," but he obviously was...I just recognized it immediately, because again, that psychology stuff is kind of interesting to me, and this was back in the early '90s, when people weren't putting labels on specific things like that. But I zeroed in immediately, and said "social anxiety." Yeah, he's living with it, and he knew he was living with it. If he didn't know he was living with it, he would have never bothered to go to a doctor to get medication for it. It's all part of the fabric of where he's creating from. I know so, but I can't point to anything.

Did Chris' death come as a surprise?
Yeah, it was a surprise. I've had a lot of friends commit suicide, and a lot of them were not surprising. Chris was. I hadn't spoken to him for several years, and it was always in the back of my mind to go thank him for everything he did for me. And I always thought, "We're going to be in the same city at the same time at some point," and it just never happened. I felt really bad. I didn't feel bad about not getting in touch with him, because that's just some selfish thing on my part—as far as feelings go. Because that wouldn't have made any difference. I just felt sad for Chris to be in that place. By the way, he was on medication. He didn't used to be. Back when I used to hang out with him, he wasn't on anything.

Remember I told you he had social anxiety? I'll bet you that medication he was on, that was part of what he was being medicated for. See, I don't know anything about that, but I just made that connection now, because he wasn't on that medication back then. It's just sad to be in that place. I used to go out with a girl, and her mother committed suicide, and she got so upset that she would always talk about, "She took the easy way out." I was like, "Wait a minute..." Sometimes people say that about suicide. But the thing is, it's a sickness. There is *a thing* going on there. There's no easy way out—they're having a tough fucking life, or they wouldn't go that far. I forget who said it, but "Suicide is the sincerest form of self-criticism." [Note: Author Robert Heinlein is credited with that quote] I always remember that line.

How would you like Chris to be remembered?
To be fair, he had a Buddhist heart. He could see an ant, and if he believed in that ant, *he would turn it into a tyrannosaurus rex.*

INTERVIEW

GILLIAN GAAR

Journalist, author (Entertain Us: The Rise of Nirvana, She's a Rebel: The History of Women in Rock and Roll, World Domination: The Sub Pop Records Story)

When did you first hear Soundgarden, and see them live?
It may have been just getting stuff from Sub Pop, because I was at *The Rocket,* and they were always sending over their promo things—the early catalogs, with those great descriptions. I definitely remember Dawn Anderson's review of *Deep Six,* which would have come out in '86. I think the first time I saw them was in New York—in '88.

They were playing CBGB's, when I was there for the New Music Seminar—which was in July. I remember seeing someone recording their show, and I pointed them out to Susan Silver—so they got busted! Then later, some people I know who tape everything, said, "Why did you do that? It could have been a valuable document!" But I don't think I saw them in a club after that. I saw them in the Moore Theatre, and that was probably the smallest other show I saw. Which even that was on the small side—I think it's 1,500 people. But still, a pretty big deal for a local rock band to play.

Do you have any specific memories of the CBGB's show?
It was just so dark—not well lit. These clubs I always thought were so strange, because they were like these long "railroad cars"—just so long and they went so far back. And you were just sort of like, "*Ooo*, this is the famous CBGB's," which you'd read about so much in *Creem Magazine.* It was interesting that someone was interested enough in the band to want to tape them at that stage. Because they couldn't have been known much beyond Seattle—at that point. It wasn't like a packed house with people moshing or anything like that. Kind of more laid back and relaxed—if one can imagine seeing these bands in a circumstance like that.

What about memories of the Moore performance?
I remember I had called to get a comp ticket, and I think it was Chris I spoke to on the phone—because I was calling trying to get Susan. I never interviewed him. I did interview Kim, and that was more about Sub Pop than about Soundgarden. But funny enough, there was this local filmmaker, who made these really strange, mondo film-like things, and I was in two of them, and they were having a screening of it one night, the same night as the Soundgarden show. And it was at a little screening place not far from the Moore. So, we went to the film screening with a couple of people from *The Rocket*. We didn't stay for the whole thing because we wanted to get over to see Soundgarden.

I remember even then, Chris had the "sex god image," and "He plays without his shirt on...or in the long board shorts barely hanging on his hips" sort of thing. They didn't move around the stage as much as say, later—they just had this tight intensity. Like, Chris might lean over or walk around, but he wasn't leaping or jumping in the air—but it was still pretty intense the way he did it. Like someone really tightly wound, and they don't have to move a lot for you to know they're very intense.

You described Chris as having a "sex god image" on-stage.
The whole Sub Pop attitude was very tongue-in-cheek, and not taking yourself too seriously. You took your music and your work seriously...but you also *didn't* take it seriously. When they'd do these kind of poses, it was kind of like they were sending it up— even though they were serious about it. And maybe some of this came through with the interviews, but Chris was pretty quiet and soft-spoken. He was really like someone stepping into a role—that was his stage persona, and then off stage, he just seemed to be a more quiet and introverted person.

While they were obviously a rock band, they didn't act like what you would think a typical rock band would act like. Think about all the bands on the Sunset Strip—all the hair metal stuff—and none of the Seattle bands were like that...*at all*. Well, maybe with the possible exception of Andy Wood in Mother Love Bone. But you could tell he was totally joking with that. Even then, you knew it was tongue-in-cheek. The Sunset Strip guys, they were taking it seriously. So, even though Chris might have come across as a sex god, people knew there was a bit of a joke going on underneath, and he wasn't taking himself too seriously. He wasn't some narcissist, preening about it.

How would you compare Andy Wood as a performer to Chris?
A totally different kind. It was like the difference between Robert Plant and Freddie Mercury—and you know who the Freddie Mercury is in this one. Andy was flamboyant, and he just had such fun with it. And that's what made you love him—he was having such a good time. I remember seeing him at the Vogue—it was one of his last performances. I think it must have been that they could just do a show that night, because there weren't those many people there. And they were already signed with PolyGram, so they were on the way up. And you'd think Andy was playing an arena—the way he was out there. He was joyful...and playful. Chris...well, none of Soundgarden really came off as "playful."

Something else that I find interesting with Chris, is there were some contradictions, such as the song "Jesus Christ Pose," in which he seems to be railing against Axl Rose type rock stars, but yet...Chris was photographed quite a bit at the time making Jesus Christ-like poses, himself.
They would do things like that, and they must have known by then that people were going to read these other things into it, like, "This is a commentary about this thing, and not a celebration of it." And "Big Dumb Sex"—the same thing, which was this ludicrous, over-the-top thing. How many people take it seriously? But I guess you have to get past that as an artist, put it out, and think, "Well, people may *not* get the message"...unless you want to be explaining it in an interview every time. When your audience grows and you get a broader audience that didn't come from your community and your culture, they're going to come at it from a different angle. That seemed to throw someone like Kurt more than it did Soundgarden.

But Eddie Vedder got a lot of that, too—people calling him and wanting him to solve their problems, because "You must understand my problems, because your lyrics mean 'such and such' to me." It must be overwhelming. You've got to shut yourself off from that. There's not enough of you to give out to those kind of people. And, "No. I don't know how to solve your problems. I'm like you—I have my own problems, too." People project so much.

That must be a really disorienting thing to happen when you get famous. They must all go through that in the first year or so of really big fame...or even the first couple of months. Like Kurt was talking about in his suicide note—"All the warnings from the punk rock 101 courses over the years." It must be disorienting to go from your small community and into this worldwide community, and people projecting all kind of things on you, and feeling like they owe you, because they cried to or first had sex to your record. But they don't know you.

Strangely, some of the greatest rock artists seemed to struggle with depression—whether it be Chris or Kurt.
I think there are have been articles about a number of artists who have manic depression or bipolar—I think across the artistic spectrum, going back to Van Gogh and other people, too. But I hadn't thought of his addictions as being a way to deal with depression—but that makes total sense.

Something else that now is sadly similar between Chris and Kurt—if you are to read their lyrics, they reference suicide, and their lyrics take on a whole new meaning after they both committed suicide.
Neither of them wrote a simple song, really. Something like "Sliver" isn't a simple song. Kurt never really wrote a traditional or conventional love song. I might say "About a Girl" and "Drain You" are love songs, but of a very dark nature. People would always talk about the sweetness of "About a Girl" because of the sweet sound, but the lyrics are not that nice.

But there are even more obvious things, such as Nirvana's song, "I Hate Myself and Want to Die," and then Soundgarden had the songs "Like Suicide" and "Pretty Noose." Now, those song titles and lyrics take on a whole new meaning.

Yeah, they do. I know with Kurt, people were saying, "Oh, he's just being ironic." But still...I remember thinking about this at the time about Kurt—Michael Azerrad's book had come out in '93 [*Come As You Are: The Story of Nirvana*], and Kurt talks *a lot* about suicide in that book. Just the slightest provocation—"I was so mad about it, I was going to blow my head off" or "I was so depressed about this, I just wanted to kill myself." Again and again and again. I thought at the time, "Man, he talks about it *a lot.*"

Lastly, something that I've always found fascinating—how such a small, concentrated location gave the world such great rock vocalists all around the same time, with Chris, Eddie Vedder, Layne Staley, Kurt Cobain, and Mark Lanegan.

That was interesting. I thought about that a lot when I was working on my Sub Pop book [2018's *World Domination: The Sub Pop Records Story*]. I give a lot of credit to them—Sub Pop—for really taking things to the next level. Not that all those bands were on Sub Pop, but most of them were. I think Sub Pop showed the way, like, "You can do it from here. You don't have to go to New York or LA to do this." Bruce and Jon always talked big, "Yes, we're going to be world stars." And I guess on some level they did think that, but at the time, I sure didn't. I just thought it was their usually braggadocio. And besides, it just didn't seem possible. It just seemed like there was this huge gulf between playing the Ditto Tavern and then playing the Coliseum, and being on a major label and getting on the radio. It just seemed like some other world, that I had no idea how you got there.

I think it just freed people to do things themselves, because we were isolated, we didn't really have to pay attention to what was going on in New York and LA, because this was our own thing. I remember some people would go to New York and LA, and they would just get lost, or their band would disappear and dissolve, because it was too big and there was too much competition, and they did not have an identity. Seattle was small enough that all the bands had this regional identity. Even though Soundgarden and Alice in Chains didn't sound the same, they all came from the same culture. So, they had common roots. And everyone developed in their own way. But still, there was this unifying thing underneath.

.

INTERVIEW

THE REVEREND HORTON HEAT
Singer/guitarist, toured with Soundgarden in 1994

When did you first cross paths with Soundgarden?
It just came out of the blue that they wanted us to open for them.
So, that was it. The next thing you know, we're out there on tour—
playing 10,000-seat arenas. It was awesome.

**Soundgarden was on Sub Pop early on, as were you. What was
your experience like on the label?**
I really appreciate the chance they gave us. But I think it might
have felt like...maybe they needed to focus more on the Seattle
bands, because that's what "Sub" stands for—Seattle
Underground Bands. There were a couple of instances where I
think they may have taken us for granted. But I don't really blame
them, and I really appreciate them giving us a chance. Other than
that, it was really just kind of a business deal. It wasn't like we
were hanging out with all the bands, partying all the time.

**You toured with Soundgarden in 1994—when they were
probably at their most popular.**
One of the standout memories was just how Chris Cornell and his
wife were to us. He was a very nice, mild-mannered guy. He
would come on our bus a couple of times—hung out, maybe did a
shot. But he wasn't really a big drinker—we might have coaxed
him into doing a shot with us. I don't know what we were drinking
back then—Jägermeister or whatever it was. Whiskey...I don't
know. One of the funniest things was when he started arm-
wrestling everybody. And man, *he was strong.* He was one of
those guys that was super-lean and kind of lanky, so he wasn't all
that jacked-up. But he was strong. Our drummer was 6'5", Taz
[Bentley], and he easily beat Taz in arm-wrestling.

The only thing that I do remember is he would get mobbed
by girls. *Just mobbed.* It was insane. He had to be a little bit
careful. He'd kind of look out the window before he walked off
the bus before he walked out the door, because he never knew
what he was walking into. But a very nice, mild-mannered guy. I

think at the end of the day, he was one of the best—if not *the best* rock singers—in history. I think he's above Robert Plant, I think he's above a lot of other guys. It's hard to compare people, and I don't like doing that, but gosh, the range and his voice sounded honest and real—even up at the higher ranges. And that's a hard thing to do, because it's one thing to sing high and sound like the "Mikey Mouse voice." But it's a whole other thing to sing high and have balls and have power, and have authenticity—a *realness* to it. To this day, whenever I hear a Soundgarden song or the other bands he was in, it's like, "Man...this guy was the best ever."

From what you could see, how was he handling all the fame and success at that point?
I thought that he was handling it probably better than—or as good as—anybody else in any band, because it seemed like he wasn't very picky, and he was just a mild-mannered guy. But it was cool too that he played—and I don't know how long he did this— Gretsch guitars. I always thought that might have had something to do with how we got on the tour, because we were a Gretsch guitar-type band. They were big rock stars, and those shows were off-the-hook.

The biggest show we ever played was on that tour. The Soundgarden tour fused with the Nine Inch Nails tour, so we got to stagger. Since Soundgarden was bigger than Nine Inch Nails, their opening band got to play fourth bill. The top bill was Soundgarden, the second bill was Nine Inch Nails, the third bill was us, and the fourth bill was Marilyn Manson! So that day, *Marilyn Manson opened up for Reverend Horton Heat.* But they were still real fresh at that point. We had been around for seven years, I guess. But that was the biggest show I've ever played—I think there were 32,000 people in Toronto for that gig. So, you start considering that Soundgarden was playing these giant shows like that, they had a little bit of pressure. When you have the #1 record in the world, the #1 tour in the world, and 20,000 people every night...they really weren't just hanging out with us, drinking until they puked. None of that was going on.

Did you hang out at all with any of the other members, though?
A little bit with Ben, and I think our drummer connected with Matt a little bit. We were a little peashooter band. I saw all of them in the lobby of the hotel in LA, and they were super-nice. I hung around and chatted for a while, and Chris and his wife were still together. Very nice people. That gets me into another thing, where I'll win "controversy of the year"—I think somebody murdered him. I think he was too level-headed of a guy to do that. I don't know what all he was up into, but you might want to research that angle of it.

He was one of these people that knew what he had accomplished. He knew that he could write these songs that were incredibly cool and unusual, as well as having accessibility to people. People loved him, loved his voice. I don't know what happened, but that's very suspicious. Chester Bennington, he was his friend, and he committed suicide the same way not long after that. I don't know—that was suspicious, too. You might want to research it.

How was it playing in front of a Soundgarden audience?
Some of those shows were *scary*. Like that big one I was talking about in Toronto, when we were playing, it was the biggest mosh pit I'd ever seen. And people were throwing stuff. I had to quit looking up at the people in the crowd, because every time I looked up, somebody was getting hit in the head with a bottle, or somebody would get slammed to the ground. It was intense.

Did you get the chance to watch Soundgarden perform during that tour?
Oh, we watched them just about every night. I think the Olympic [in Los Angeles], that was killer. There was one in San Antonio at a place called Sunken Gardens—it was big and held a lot of people. But it was outdoors—it was a little bit rough because it was San Antonio heat. It's *really* hot there. But they pulled it off. He was an amazing singer.

One funny thing that I will say that they had that I had never seen—this was a big rock n' roll tour, but they didn't necessarily have a whole lot of pyro, but they had all the lights and bells and whistles, and one thing that they had was what they called a "gig butt protector." And the gig butt protector were these giant air conditioning units, that on the outdoor shows, it blew air conditioning on. But they had them labeled "gig butt protector." But they were smart, because some of those shows were...like I was saying, that San Antonio show was pretty intense—95, 98 degrees outside. Especially for guys from Seattle...it's not that hard for us, we're from Texas. But for them, it was crazy.

Do you remember anything about playing what was the last show of the *Superunknown* tour, at Memorial Stadium in Seattle?
Artis the Spoonman was there. And I'd known Artis for a long time—Artis is the guy who was in the video for "Spoonman." I knew him since before I think Soundgarden was even a band, because he used to travel around—he would come to Dallas with this Scarborough Faire thing. But that was amazing because it was outdoors in a stadium and really good weather and really good sound.

And their music crossed over—like when Johnny Cash covered "Rusty Cage" and reworked it as a rockabilly song.
I think it's a classic. Johnny Cash managed to pull off making one of his classic albums [1996's *Unchained*] towards the end of his life. "Rusty Cage," gosh, that song *rocks*. I saw them play that song at a big outdoor festival—I think it was Lollapalooza, and this is before we had a chance to go and tour with them. I might have met them—I was backstage at that show. A lot of stuff is kind of a blur. When I saw them play that song at Lollapalooza, it just brought down the house. You could tell that they were really something special. They basically just kicked every band's ass on that day. But that guitar riff is fantastic.

But that tour [in 1994], we were a little peashooter band out there with Soundgarden—the biggest band in the world. And we had done shows with Guns N' Roses, but very few of those bands are cool enough to come hang out with us and talk to us. I can't blame them, because it's a lot of pressure being the #1 band in the world. White Zombie we toured with, and they were super-cool to us. We still stay in touch with those guys. Some of them were more accessible than others.

I try to understand that this is a lot of pressure, so if we do a show with Guns N' Roses, I'm not sitting there going, "Axl Rose didn't even come say hi to me." But I did appreciate the times Chris came and hung out with us, and it was a great chance for our career. Even when I saw Kim this last summer, I said, "Hey man, thank you for that tour. It was a big deal to our career."

I remember when I interviewed you for *Vintage Guitar Magazine*, you said you were indebted to Soundgarden for taking you out on that tour.
Oh yeah, absolutely. Totally. To this day, I have shows and I talk to the fans, and so many of them say, "I saw you at the Soundgarden show." On that tour, we were in Canada, too, so I'm getting that a lot here in Canada—we're in Canada right now. I'm still getting it, 25 years later. It's crazy.

What do you think of Kim as a guitar player?
Extremely innovative. And very proficient. I mean, he always had something unusual to play, and he always was heads and tails a better guitar player than most of the other grunge or alternative bands. A lot of those bands were actually really good bands—but they weren't top notch musicians, like Kim. And Matt Cameron was amazingly talented. So, they were ultra-pro, ultra-talented players—right in the pocket, right in tune. And unusual and exciting guitar riffs. That's one of my favorite things about "Rusty Cage"—that frantic guitar riff at the beginning is just killer.

Did you keep in touch after the '94 shows?
No, I really didn't. But I did see them one time I ran into them at the Mondrian Hotel on Sunset, and chatted for a while. They were real nice, and were kind of surprised to see me. It was good to talk

to them, shake their hands, and see what they were up to. I wish I could have known Chris later in his life. I think he was a really cool guy. Maybe I'm a conspiracy theorist, I don't know—but I don't think he killed himself. You might want to research that a little bit—there's this whole thing on the internet.

What do you recall about finding out about Chris' death?
I was shocked. He was always a level-headed guy. If you consider his stature in the music business as a rock star, he was probably way more level-headed than anybody else I ever met that was up in those upper-echelons. By far the most laidback, regular guy, mild-mannered, nice person. And I can't blame these guys—I can't blame Axl Rose for being a little standoffish, I can't blame...well, Johnny Rotten, he talked to me. I like him. But everybody's a little bit different—he's a little bit frantic, y'know? But for Chris to be that level-headed and have that kind of stature, it was pretty amazing.

How does Soundgarden's music hold up?
Oh, it's always going to be classic. Now it does actually—sadly— fit into the "classic rock" category. But the songs were incredibly accessible. And how they did it, with these odd time signatures...it was crazy.

How would you like Chris to be remembered?
I think he should be remembered as the best rock singer of all-time. If he's not, then he's close. I mean, saying that about him to people who know their music and like him kind of go, "Yeah, he was incredible." But the rock writers or the public is going to say, "Oh, Freddie Mercury or Robert Plant." But I think he was more listenable than those guys. I think that he is the best of all-time— as far as rock vocals. I mean, maybe as far as rockabilly or blues there are other guys. Jazz or whatever, there are other guys. But as far as that goes, he was hard to beat. Night after night, hitting those notes, and then the overall creativity. He was a nice, mild-mannered guy...but nobody cares about that, we want somebody who is fucking crazy. [Laughs]

INTERVIEW

TRAVIS STEVER
Coheed and Cambria guitarist,
toured with Soundgarden in 2011

When did you first hear Soundgarden?
The first time I heard them and saw them was videos on television. I actually got to see them live in concert—it was one of the best concerts I've ever seen, still—Blind Melon, Soundgarden, and Neil Young with Booker T & the MG's. It was such a cool mix of music, because you had Blind Melon doing their thing, then Soundgarden came up with their more raw power. And we toured with Soundgarden years later, and I was able to get all the band members to sign the ticket from that concert. I still have it. And one day, I'll get the guys from Blind Melon to sign it, and...I can get Neil Young! You never know.

But I was a big fan—"Fell on Black Days" is one of my favorite songs. And that record, I would imagine that would be considered their most popular record. And I have a great memory of that record—when we were young, trying to find ways to "elevate the brain," one of the things that we would do is huff Glade, by putting a towel over the Glade and huffing. It's the same as doing a whippit. We were fourteen/fifteen, and I just remember "Black Hole Sun" being on in the background, and being like, "*Yeah*!" This is when it first came out. That's a Soundgarden memory.

I have on vinyl *Ultramega OK,* and I grew to love that record, and the early stuff. They were one of those bands that I was turned on to by friends. Just like Pearl Jam or any of them from that whole world—before it kind of came into the mainstream. I remember "the mainstream" was seeing Chris Cornell in *Singles.* That was like, "Alright, there you go. The band is now completely on the map." But touring with them was huge—just because every memory of growing up with them as the background music. Even *Singles,* seeing them live in front of you, I loved the movie when I was 15. I was like, "I remember seeing them at that concert, in that movie, and here we are, *touring with them.*" And they were all super, super sweet guys. Which made it really sad, because we were able to do that before he passed away.

Which venue was the Blind Melon/Soundgarden/Neil Young show at, that you saw?
It's PNC Bank Arts Center now, but I think it was the Garden State Arts Center. And every time we've been there since, it's a dream come true to be able to be playing that place, because it was a mile-marker. It was such a huge part of my youth.

Does anything else stick out about that Soundgarden performance in 1993?
The guitar playing is really what struck me and was very influential. Because we were coming listening to Blind Melon, and they were sandwiched with Neil Young, and Soundgarden brought that heaviness. That's why it was the perfect show. You can't call them metal, but I don't think you can pigeonhole them as just straight up "grunge." I always thought that was kind of like what people pigeonhole something like "emo," "emo prog," or "prog rock." It's all under the umbrella of rock, and they just combined different aspects within their umbrella. One of the things that really struck me was the heaviness—with a certain pop sensibility that I really loved about them.

And his vocals. To the day he died, he was one of those vocalists that...I think that one time, we discussed how Dio was one of those, who just had all the vocal abilities that they basically had from the get-go. So that was one of the things that struck me too, in watching Blind Melon—Shannon Hoon sounded great, but it wasn't the projection of how Chris Cornell sounded. It was just like a real *force.* It sounded like he could probably hold the mic ten feet from him, and it still would catch that.

That's a band that gets name-checked—Claudio [Sanchez] was working on a song a couple of years ago for this newest record ["Black Sunday" from 2018's *Vaxis—Act I: The Unheavenly Creatures*], and he would say, "Think '4th of July' by Soundgarden. Think that vibe." They're a band that you drop for a vibe, because they had their straight-up own sound—with Kim's guitar playing and just everything. And Chris Cornell's guitar playing. The band was super-nice too, so it really helped to fulfill the dream of when you meet somebody that you admire that much, and then they actually are so down to earth. But it still made it harder to understand—the dude seemed pretty happy. But, we're all complicated.

So Soundgarden was a musical influence on Coheed and Cambria?
Absolutely. Zach [Cooper], our bass player, is a huge fan, too. So is our drummer [Josh Eppard]—he likes them a lot. Soundgarden was definitely an influence on all of us—since we were younger.

Do you agree Chris was one of the greatest rock singers and songwriters of all-time?
That voice never went away. Songwriting-wise, the only album I never really dove into was the one with Timbaland. And I would not talk anything bad about it—I just never listened to it, really. But everything else he did, I really loved. Songwriting-wise, he was always killing it.

What else sticks out about Coheed's 2011 tour with Soundgarden?
We didn't have the best ending to that tour. That was when our original bass player, Mike [Todd], went off to Walgreens and got arrested. It was the last show—literally, the last show of the tour. And how they treated us, and just comforted us during that. They were surprised we were still going to do it, but we were like, "No. We're professional. We're still going to do the show." We had a guitar tech cover for the night—which in itself was fun. But they were very comforting and super-sweet to us, which was very appreciated. I think they were like, *"What the fuck?!"*

So, that's a memory, for sure. Not the best memory, but the better stuff was before that—being able to pass them every day, and see them do their thing. And be like, "Wow. We're out with *these guys.*" It was one of those tours where it was surreal that it flew by very fast. Every night you're listening to this band that had such a huge influence, and that you enjoyed your whole life. We're on a tour like that right now—with Mastodon. But I remember Soundgarden, every night, hearing that, and the songs didn't get old. And you loved watching it.

How much of a shock was Chris' death?
Oh, a big one. But you can't tell something from just touring with somebody. They were used to the road after all these years, so they kind of had their way that they did things. They'd show up, do their soundcheck...it's not like we had heart-to-hearts all the time, but he seemed genuinely happy. And he seemed to be doing well. His family would be around a lot. But like I said, it's complicated. I don't know what was fully going on inside. But it was a big shock—for all of us. I remember we were playing the night we found out, and Claudio dedicated the show to him.

Personally, the two deaths of rock singers that affected me the most were Shannon and Chris.
Yeah. Shannon Hoon was the hardest one for me growing up, too—because I found a singer that I had attached to. And I think being older made it a little easier with the Chris Cornell thing, because even though it was somebody that all of us had such memories attached to this voice and his presence, you're older. The Shannon Hoon one hit me when I was younger, and I was like, "Damn it. This was just starting." Because *Soup* had just come out. I would put it up there with it, though. But yeah, that one definitely hit me the hardest when I was younger. If he was still alive, I might be following that band or something—I might not be doing this, I might be in a minivan, following Blind Melon. [Laughs]

How do you think Soundgarden's music holds up?
It's going to stand the test of time forever. It's going to be one of those bands that's never going to be dated. They belong...they're not in the Rock and Roll Hall of Fame, right?

No. But I think they should have been the first grunge band in—before Nirvana and Pearl Jam.
Well, there's still time. We'll see. But they definitely should be.

Did you get to speak to Chris during that tour at all?
Yeah. Very light. He seemed like a very calm kind of person. Deep. When we talked, it seemed like he had a lot going on up there. That's why I say it's complicated. You say, "It's so surprising because it seemed like he was doing so well." But what do we know? We all have our own internal struggles, constantly. And that whole tour, he might have been struggling. It didn't seem like it, but he might have been.

How would you like Chris to be remembered?
The strongest vocals. Seemed like an amazing personality. And one of the best songwriters.

INTERVIEW

KAREN MASON-BLAIR
Photographer

How did you begin photographing Soundgarden?
I think I had already taken pictures of them live. When they decided to have Ben join the band, I drove down to Portland to take these pictures—at the Melody Ballroom [on July 25, 1990]. The venue was so different, because it was a ballroom—so they had a little practice stage, and then they had theater curtains. I wound up doing this one shoot—sort of a tribute to the Beatles, where it was all black...actually, the curtain was green. It was just really cool to use these curtains. [Note: One of the photos from this session was used for this book's cover]

And then I had them lay on the stage, that shot ended up being the cover of the Sub Pop Single of the Month Club ["Room a Thousand Years Wide"]. The thing about Ben is when Ben performs, he gives high energy. It's so cool—he's jumping up in the air, and everybody's rocking out. To see Ben play for the first time, you're just like, "OK. This is a really good fit." You could tell the energy matched. And he's tall, and Chris Cornell is tall, so it was cool—they looked really good together. So, we had gone down to Portland—me and my writer friend, who was doing this interview with Soundgarden, to announce that Ben had joined the band. I just remember during this interview, Chris said, "Anyone can play bass. *But it was all about the chemistry.*" That to him was why they chose Ben.

When I look back at those pictures, Chris' hair was just so long and curly and fuzzy, and he had it up in a ponytail, which honestly, a lot of guys at that time were wearing ponytails—like Stone Gossard from Pearl Jam—because their hair was so long. Sometimes, I know what I'm going to do, and other times, the set just kind of speaks to me. I was like, "I'm going to do this lighting"—because I had brought my lights down. And like I said, it was kind of a nod to the Beatles—it's really cool how it's on the black, or the dark green.

And then I saw this stage, and I was like, "Hey, why don't I do this forced view? You guys all lay on the stage." And then I could get down below them, so I'm shooting up at them. And then Kim turns all the way up—he was laying on his back, and his eyes...you could see the total whites of his eyes. [Laughs] The whole shot was about the eyes. And then I did a couple of other sets within that. They were really playful and happy that Ben was in the band. Everybody drove to Portland that day. Matt Cameron, his personality is unstoppable.

And what's the story behind the photo of Chris wearing the Pearl Jam shirt with the band, and the one of him solo, standing in the window?

I think that was like, a year later. They came to my studio—my studio was right in Pioneer Square, it was right down the street from Susan Silver's office. I can't remember what that was for, but maybe I was just shooting for A&M. Chris comes in, and he's wearing a Pearl Jam shirt. I was like, "It's better if you don't wear band t-shirts of local bands. Like, I don't mind if you are wearing a Ramones shirt or a Sex Pistols shirt. But no one has heard of this band." He was like, "Karen, *I don't care.* They're my friends and I have to help them out."

And the other thing about that session, Kim Thayil comes walking in, and he's like, "You guys, you've got to listen to this. It's Nirvana, *Nevermind*." He had the first copy—it hadn't even been pressed yet. So, he puts in the cassette, and we played it the whole time. We kept listening to it. Everybody was genuinely happy for them. And it was mind-blowing—that was the first time we all heard it, together. Soundgarden was recording their album in '91, and I did not know Soundgarden had a song called "Jesus Christ Pose." We're doing the shoot, and Chris just gets up in my windowsill in my studio, and stands in my window. I'm like, "Uh...*what's going on here*?" So, I took three frames.

How would you describe the personalities of the members of Soundgarden when you worked with them?

Kim is such a gentle soul. He's always been really calm. We were drinking beer. And Ben has great energy. And Chris...the thing is they were all so funny—even though they'd come off kind of stoic. And then Matt was super-fun, super-high energy. They all just totally balanced each other out. Like I said, we were just having a really good time.

How much of a surprise was Chris' passing?
Honestly, it was the worst one for me. I'm still not over it. I started to cry at the movie [a screening of *Live from the Artists Den* in 2019], and I did not want to. My friend was like, "Karen, you've got to keep it together." It was a total shock. We're not surprised that he was depressed—that we knew. But we had really thought that he had managed that. For me, if he really was that sad, then I want him to be in heaven. If that really was the depth of his pain that I had no idea about, then I wouldn't selfishly want him here anyways.

If that is how much he suffered and he just wanted out...because he's got a beautiful wife and kids, and was well-loved, if that is not enough for him, and that did not make him happy...I mean, the guy was on five pills. That is already not good. Your body can't go up, down, sideways one way, sideways the other way, and then you add a fifth pill—it doesn't know what to do. It's a fact. Five pills is dangerous. A lot of my friends that have done this, it's always five pills. I don't know what that cocktail is—I don't take anything—but there is something about five pills.

The thing is, Chris was the one that would be the first to give you a hand up when you're down. This doesn't even make sense to me. And it doesn't make sense that the minute you come off stage—that's your highest point and you're feeling the best. The next day or when you're on your tour bus, driving to the next city, *that's* when you're not. It just does not make sense. At all. And I don't even know if you're that high, how you can functionally, physically hang yourself. When you're drunk or when you're high, that is not when you've got mad skills. It's beyond me.

I was just hanging out with Mike McCready and Jeff Ament, and we would just look at each other deep into our eyes, and we were like, "*This doesn't make sense.*" We're super-sad. It's like my counselor said, you don't want to put them all together, but dear God, how can you not? Andrew Wood, Kurt Cobain...and then you're like, "I really don't know if I can take this. It's getting too much." Even Shannon Hoon, Scott Weiland, Chester Bennington...*I don't know.*

It's becoming very clear that these poor people that are prescribed all these meds, it's not really helping.
100%. Thank you. And then it says, "You can have suicidal tendencies." It's like you're taking this one pill to keep this one chemical balance down, well, so you're keeping that down, but you're taking it so far down that now, the guy physically, mentally, or physiologically can't come back up. You've tipped him with your pills.

I would like to have more conversation—if needed—about how you're feeling. I want to know *before* Kurt wanted to kill himself, "What's going on with you?" I want to have open dialogue, and not such a shame about it. And that's what I'm saying—I didn't know Chris felt that terrible. I had no idea. That's shocking—that you're feeling that shitty, and you're going on tour with your band. If you think about it, towards the end of his life, he did sing with his daughter, he got Temple of the Dog back together, he re-started Soundgarden...I mean, he kind of got his checklist going.

INTERVIEW

MARKY RAMONE
Ramones drummer,
toured with Soundgarden on Lollapalooza '96

Soundgarden were big Ramones fans.
We met them on the tour [Lollapalooza 1996], and they were always fans. So were the other grunge bands—Nirvana, Pearl Jam, etcetera. But Soundgarden—to me—was the more forceful, with a singer that definitely had more of an operatic voice. He was *a real singer*—he wasn't just a screamer. I thought Chris was great. And he looked great. And Matt Cameron was definitely a great drummer, and Kim, what a guitar player.

It's funny—they all wanted to come into the van. [Laughs] They had this great tour bus, and we had a 15-passenger Ford Econoline, and they wanted to drive with us in the van. That was one thing I remembered on the Lollapalooza tour. *They* were one of the headliners. And at that moment, they were huge. They kept humming songs when they were around us that they knew of the Ramones—as if to let us know that they really were fans. We always waited for them to play. A lot of the times, we would just leave, but most of the times, we would wait until they came on stage—and they kicked ass. For their genre, they were the best band.

Did Soundgarden ever invite the Ramones to ride on their tour bus?
I don't think so. I didn't hear it, but they might have asked one of us. Obviously, there were three other Ramones. But the thing is, I think we would have just stuck to our van, because we all had our assigned rows, and we were used to it. But, to have somebody else ride in the van with us, I think there would have been too many people in it to be comfortable.

From what I remember, Joey was a Soundgarden fan, as I've seen pictures of him wearing a *Badmotorfinger* shirt.
He obviously liked them if he was wearing a t-shirt. The last time I saw them was in New York City [in 1996], and they had a big

fight backstage. Ben and Chris had an argument. I think Joey was with me, and we were amazed, because we thought we were the only band that ever fought. [Laughs] That was the last time I saw them as a unit.

And then, a couple of years ago, I was on a plane going to Spain, and Chris was sitting in business. I guess he grew his beard out at that time, and I didn't recognize him, until he came up to me, and said, "*Marky*!" Then I knew close up that it was Chris. He was getting a little melancholy about the tour, when we toured together. And then the next thing I knew...what happened to him. I couldn't believe it. That was just so unexpected. What a waste. What a voice. On tour, when we were on Lollapalooza—which was around 20 shows we were on—the time differences were different, but we would wait around for them to play, and then go right to the hotel. That's how much we liked them. We rarely did that for anyone.

Before, when you said you witnessed a fight between Ben and Chris, do you recall what it was about?
No. No idea. You never know. I mean, Johnny and Joey never got along—but there was never any fisticuffs amongst us. Never. But there was a push and shove thing, and I said to myself, "Well, I guess we're not the only ones." Joey and Johnny never attacked each other or hit each other—it was more quiet, where nobody would talk. *That's even worse.* That stuff is feeding inside of you, and you don't let it out, and it can come to a head...and you just go crazy.

Wasn't Chris good friends with Johnny?
Yeah, they were friends—for sure. Johnny moved to California, and I stayed in New York. So, I don't know what they really did. I guess they went out to eat or went out to each other's houses—I don't have any idea about that. But I just know that they became friends.

Any other memories of Lollapalooza?

I remember me and Matt backstage, drumming around on the drum pads, trading licks and doing things together. Because I usually had a drum pad set up. We would do about six or seven songs to warm up, before we played. A lot of times, people would knock at the door, we'd let them in, and we'd just play around on the drum pads—Ramones stuff, this stuff, that stuff. I have a photo of him backstage doing that. Also, Kim was a very unique guitar player. I always liked the way he played.

Chris was at the final Ramones show.

He didn't sing—he egged the audience on, like, "*You want to hear more*?!" The usual histrionics. And Eddie Vedder was there—they represented "the grunge part of it." Lemmy was there, and two guys from Rancid. It was a "genre night"—you had Rancid who were punks, you had Lemmy who was a metal-punk, and then you had the grunge guys...and Steve Jones from the Sex Pistols, and Henry Rollins was there. It was a pretty good send-off.

What did you think of the grunge movement of the '90s?

Thank God it came along, because that whole hair metal/'80s rock was the worst. They all sounded the same, they all looked the same. You could tell they were definitely manufactured—most of them. And then grunge came along, and it just blew them away—especially Nirvana and Soundgarden. Because it was more realistic—it was more from the street. It wasn't so manufactured. We appreciated that. The same thing with a lot of the newer punk bands—some of them were good, but a lot of them were very gentrified. Gentrification. To me, Guns N' Roses is definitely a gentrified band. That's just my opinion. They have a lot of fans, but I never liked them, and I always thought they were a gentrified, LA hair band.

I saw a lot of similarities between the grunge movement and the punk movement of the mid-late '70s. Did you?

A lot of them liked the punk scene—of CBGB's and England. So, they incorporated their own style. And then the grunge movement started. I can equate both things, like you said—we started in the '70s and they started later on, and it was like the punk scene in New York City.

You could say that bands like Nirvana finally helped break punk through to the mainstream in the US.
I never considered grunge "punk." It was slow. Punk to me was fast, and very energetic. I'm not saying they weren't, but it was totally different music. I would never put Pearl Jam or Soundgarden in the punk genre. They had their own genre—they didn't need to be called a punk band.

How would you describe Soundgarden as a live band?
Very tight. Great musicians. And they knew how to play with the time signatures and the accents—which I really liked, because I was into jazz, I was in one of the first heavy metal bands in America [called Dust]. So, I was doing all these accents, too—when I was in this band. I understood exactly how they were finding different time changes and off-beats. They knew how to be off-time, but they knew exactly when to come back on time.

Now that I think about it, some of Dust's music does sound a bit like Soundgarden—the song "Suicide."
Yeah—we were playing 5/4, 6/4. We incorporated a lot of accents in the songs, itself. And I found that Soundgarden was way ahead of the other bands in that respect.

What do you think of Matt Cameron as a drummer?
To be able to play that stuff, you have to be really good. And to me, on that tour, he was the best drummer. Listen to "Black Hole Sun."

Do you have a favorite Soundgarden song?
"Black Hole Sun" is my favorite. It was just a perfect, great song.

Chris discussed in interviews that he battled addiction and alcoholism, and you're a recovering alcoholic. Did you ever speak to him about your experiences?
When I meet somebody that does have problems, I don't bring it up, because I was taught in the AA program that the person should bring it up first. Because you don't want to start becoming a preacher. You have to live and let live. And to bring a subject up like that, you get the other person paranoid. My thing is if they want to talk to me about it, fine. Like, "Hey, Marky...is everything alright? Are you still sober?" Fine. And then I would get the information out of them. But I never approached a person on their problems.
        The same thing with Lemmy. I was with Lemmy a lot of times, and I knew exactly what he was doing. When he went to the bathroom and when he came back—I knew what he was on, I knew what he was drinking. But I never brought it up to him. Because when you start preaching to somebody or telling them...they might shy away from you as a friend, or as an acquaintance, because you know what they're doing, but they might feel uncomfortable that you know. I try to stay away from that subject.

You mentioned before that Chris' death came as a shock.
The guy was still great, and then this happens. In my opinion, it could have been mental illness.

Now that I'm going back and reading past interviews with Chris, he referenced suicide several times, as well as in his song lyrics. It made me wonder if he had these thoughts for some time beforehand.
A lot of people think about suicide, but obviously, you don't go through with it. They wonder what it's like or what leads a person to do that. So, what do you do? You do drugs and you drink—to keep away from those inner-demons. But a lot of that stuff can bring it on, and if you're taking any kind of prescribed medication and you mix it with drink or other drugs, you can die from that—

you either get a stroke or a heart attack. There are always warnings on labels—"Don't do this." "Don't mix with that."

The guy had a very successful career, everything going for him, and then all of a sudden, he's gone. I just couldn't believe it. That could have been the reason—of everything together, which cancels out reality. And then, if you want to come back, you might not be able to. And then you say to yourself, "I can't take it anymore," and then you just end it. If you mix medication that helps control your depression—with say, alcohol or another drug—it could put you in a coma, or it could heighten the suicidal thoughts a lot more. We'll never know what went on in his mind at that moment—when he decided to end his life.

There was an interview that Chris did with Howard Stern a while back, in which they discussed Kurt Cobain's suicide, and it was sad to hear Chris say, "If he would have just hung on for six months, who knows? Six months later he would have been a completely different guy."
Addiction definitely takes time—you get addicted, and then you have to live with it. But the moment you decide to end your life, it's right at that moment. Somebody can the night before go, "Everything will be OK. You'll be fine." "Yeah, you're right." And then, when you're alone, it's a different story.

From what I understand, Chris' grave is near Johnny's grave.
I think so—in the same graveyard, in Hollywood Forever.

How do you think the music of Soundgarden holds up?
It holds up. If you're a musician that wants to learn something, they were the pinnacle of a band that really worked together as a unit—as one. That would be Soundgarden.

I think what makes such classic bands as Led Zeppelin, the Ramones, and Soundgarden stand the test of time is that their albums sound live—like a band playing together. Which seems to be the complete opposite of most rock bands today.

You can always tell. "Hey Bobby, did you get the bass riff?" "No, I've got to re-send it." That's how they do it now, and you can tell it's very sterile. You're not in the same room, you're not a unit, you're not playing together, you're not feeding off each other. There's no feeling. Thank God for analog, or at least thank God that it was there.

How would you like Chris to be remembered?
As the perfect histrionic singer. He could hold those notes, his vibrato kicked ass. What more can I say?

INTERVIEW

MATT PINFIELD
DJ and VJ, former host of MTV's **120 Minutes**

When did you first hear Soundgarden?
I first heard Soundgarden when they did their cover of the Ohio Players' "Fopp." I thought, "This is pretty cool." So I went back and bought *Screaming Life,* and I kept following the band from that time on. And as far as meeting the guys, when I saw them play—they were touring for *Louder Than Love*—when that record came out, I was a really early supporter of those guys. Not only on rock radio in New Jersey, on WHTG, but also, college radio. So, I was still doing shows at the Rutgers radio station [WRSU]— just because it was fun to do. I was always a fan of those guys.

And I knew Chris was a superstar. I just felt like, "Man, something is going to happen"—because of his vocal range. And I certainly love songs on that record—"Get on the Snake," "Big Dumb Sex" I thought was very cool. I really appreciate their sense of humor in "Big Dumb Sex," because I thought it was a reaction to all the hair metal bands at the time. It was them saying, "We're really different from all of this. We're *seriously* different. We don't want to be associated with that." It was more "do your own thing"—that's how it was for me.

And then *Badmotorfinger,* when that came out, that just blew me away. And I really thought the addition of Ben Shepherd was the thing that *really* brought the band to where they needed to be. Because once Ben was in the pocket with Matt Cameron playing, there was just something about them. Before, it didn't have the same kind of groove that put things right in the pocket, that they could do the kind of things they could do, and it freed Matt Cameron up to play. It was really interesting with all the weird time signatures and stuff they would do. In turn, it opened up things for Kim Thayil, and playing Chris' songs and everything.

I just thought they all came together on *Badmotorfinger.* It was just such a brilliant record. And it was very in-your-face. And I felt it was another one of those things where you would see it on *Headbangers Ball,* and you would see "Rusty Cage" and

"Jesus Christ Pose" and things like that...and "Outshined" of course being one of the greatest rock songs ever written—in my opinion. But, really, once again, there was something different, there was something darker, and it was a different approach that they were doing. Just incredible stuff. And some of the tours they started doing at that period of time, whether it be Metallica or Guns N' Roses, that were bigger and that were actually fans of the band. They were on their way, because *Badmotorfinger* was such a masterpiece.

And then the next record, when *Superunknown* came out, that was one of the most perfect rock records of all-time. To me, it's one of the greatest albums *ever*. Certainly, one of my favorite records ever recorded. Everything just came together at that period of time—I kind of feel that a lot of the reasons was that when Chris had the opportunity to write those songs on that EP that he did [*Poncier*]. Which is basically those demos that he recorded for the *Singles* soundtrack—and "Spoonman" was on there.

What was amazing about it is if you listen to the demo version of "Spoonman" that Chris had done on a solo EP, it was so fully-realized already—the time changes and those chords. It wasn't like he didn't already have those chords that were in that intro. I found that really amazing that Chris had fully-realized what was happening in "Spoonman" that early. I think it was one of those things that opened him up to do more introspective songwriting as things went on.

Not to say that he wasn't talking about how he was feeling in some of those earlier songs—in "Rusty Cage" and things like that—but I think when he did "Seasons" for the soundtrack to *Singles,* that was a point where Chris got more comfortable writing songs and taking that introspective approach, that ended up becoming parts of things on the next record, with things like "Fell on Black Days." It opened the door for "Fell on Black Days," and even songs like "Black Hole Sun." But at the time, I think Chris came from an honest place, anyway. I mean, he had "The Day I Tried to Live" on that record, which was absolutely brilliant, as well—lyrically. Chris was always expressive with deeper, darker feelings in a lot of his songs. And I found that people could really relate to it—including myself. So, I absolutely thought *Superunknown* was a masterpiece. I saw so many of those tour dates. I saw them in Canada, I saw them in New York. They played the Armory—this big show on a hot summer night. There were so many different shows.

I remember one of the ways that we started becoming close friends started really when I was over there and they were playing the Reading Festival in '95. Somebody was interviewing Chris, and they were getting things wrong. And I could tell, the band felt like if a journalist or somebody interviewing them was way off point or didn't really listen to music or do their research, they weren't afraid to show some attitude toward the journalist! And I remember somebody saying that *Ultramega OK* was on Sub Pop, and they were like, "No...*it was on SST.*" They were kind of pissed off. And then Chris and I just started talking about the acoustic version of "Like Suicide." We were hanging out, and we became closer and closer.

And then, I was doing *120 Minutes*. One of the things that was cool was that Chris was high-fiving me on the air, because it was his way to show people that they were really happy to be there, because there was a guy interviewing them—myself—that really loved the music and knew the music. I think that was one of the reasons why so many bands were really happy that I had taken over *120 Minutes*. And then we just did a lot of things together. I remember taking my oldest daughter—when she was really young—out to dinner with the band. We would meet up in New York City, and hang out. I remember Kim Thayil and his girlfriend buying my daughter a jacket, because it was so cold out. It was so cool. So, they became like family to me, and we were really close.

But when it came time to promote *Down on the Upside,* they flew me out to Seattle—to do the album radio special there. It was at a place called Bad Animals, that the people from Heart owned. And it used to be the studio for Muzak, believe it not. We had a blast. I remember going out with those guys and guys from other bands—like Steve Turner from Mudhoney—to eat or to drink. We were just having a blast. It was very much a long-term friendship.

So I did that special, and I remember one of the funny things was I was joking around, and we were talking about "Burden in My Hand"—we weren't recording at that time—and I said, "'Burden in My Hand'...I always thought that was about masturbating!" They were laughing so hard—that was a really funny moment. They invited me—but I couldn't go, because I was working—to when they played *Saturday Night Live,* that Jim Carrey hosted, when they were doing *Down on the Upside.* I loved that album. But the day they decided to break up, I was very, very upset. But at that period of time, I guess Chris was getting ready to do *Euphoria Morning,* and I also did that album special for Chris.

But nothing made me happier when 16 years later, they decided that they were going to get back together. They called me, and I was so excited. They only did a couple of shows that first time around, but I didn't get to see those first few shows that they did. But what I did do—and I thought was a wonderful, amazing thing—was when *King Animal* came out, they called me to do the radio album special. We did that in New York City. And I just thought how cool it was, and talked about the fact that here we were, 17 years later, because I was their "go-to guy" when it came to that radio stuff, and even the TV thing, and they called me again to do it.

Something that you and I discussed in an earlier book, *Long Live Queen*—the similarity between Queen and Soundgarden, in so much that all four members of Queen wrote great songs, and all four members of Soundgarden wrote great songs.
When a band is so versatile or talented enough to do writing, that's something that's really strong. That's one of the things Soundgarden had in common with Queen, absolutely—in both bands, all four people wrote their own songs. And one of the other bands from that era, who also had four members that wrote all different songs was Stone Temple Pilots—including Eric [Kretz] the drummer, he wrote "Trippin' on a Hole in a Paper Heart." But I loved that about Soundgarden.

And another reason Soundgarden has more in common with Queen is because I think Chris Cornell—and I told Chris this—was one of the greatest vocalists of all-time. And I know, I remember I was talking about this on a VH1 special, where they were talking about the greatest singers of all-time. And Chris *and* Freddie Mercury were up there in the top-3. The thing is, not only did all four members write, but he was one of greatest singers of all-time—in my opinion. The most versatile, the most range. Although their vocal styles were very different, they were incredible singers.

I have heard people compare Chris to Ronnie James Dio, and I never thought of that before until I listened back to the first two studio albums Dio did with Black Sabbath. What do you think of that comparison?
I remember Chris listening to *everything*. I remember Chris telling me about being a kid, and finding his next store neighbor's record collection, all downstairs in the basement, after they moved. And one of the reasons how he learned to sing was he would sing the third or fourth harmony of a Beatles song. So, he started creating his own harmony, and different ranges—by singing along with Beatles records. That's an interesting way, if you think about it. But I can see some of that. I can see him being compared to somebody different. People compare him to Robert Plant, people compare him to Jim Morrison. The thing that was amazing about Chris was he had an incredible scream, he had an amazing growl, he had incredible range that so many people couldn't sing.

Which is why the Chris tribute night, I thought was a great and beautiful thing to do—yet, it is so hard for people to sing those songs. People who do their own interpretation and make it their own, I appreciate that. It's like the way Johnny Cash did "Rusty Cage." The idea was Chris was a guy who could do a scream or a growl like Jim Morrison, he could sing high notes like Ronnie James Dio, Robert Plant, or Freddie Mercury. There were so many things. Chris listened to *everything*. But I just thought it was a really interesting thing—finding those Beatles records in that basement, and singing along with those, and doing that extra harmony with George, John, and Paul...so it was like, fourth place.

What do you recall about Soundgarden's music videos, and which are your favorites?
The thing that was really cool about Soundgarden videos was when they would do alternate versions—like "Fell on Black Days," where the vocal is a different vocal, completely. But I think "Black Hole Sun" remains one of the best, because it was creepy, dark, it was innovative—especially for its time. When you think about what they were doing, and the animated effects. I don't think anybody who saw "Black Hole Sun" ever forgot that video...no one would *ever* forget it. I'm sure it gives nightmares to some people. [Laughs] I think it was freaky, but beautiful at the same time. So, that's my favorite of them all. And I do love the "Rusty Cage" video. Those were some of my favorites.

They were honestly one of my favorite bands of all-time. I love those guys. I'm so glad I had a great relationship with them. Just them being such great guys...it was like a lot of Seattle bands, I was trusted by them, so a lot of those guys wouldn't let a lot of people in their circle. But I was really happy that Soundgarden did, and that just added to the fact that I was already such an incredible fan, and they were one of my favorite bands. That's one of the things I look back on and it's a great memory. And I wrote some of the liner notes in the *Telephantasm* box set. There are three versions—the short version, the deluxe edition, and the super deluxe edition. I was honored to do that for the super deluxe edition.

Losing Chris was truly one of the most heartbreaking moments of my life. I can be honest with you and say that. Even one of the last times I saw the band live—on the Nine Inch Nails tour—Chris wasn't really seeing a lot of people. It was when there was a stalker after him, and she was nuts—this woman was breaking into his properties. He was a little freaked out. But I went backstage, sat, and talked. We talked about movies and we talked about life. I loved him for a lot reasons. Losing him was devastating. And we were close—even through the Audioslave years. And I love Ben, Kim, and Matt, too.

As far as being friends with Chris, were you close enough that you would text and call him?
We would stay in touch. He loved to do emails and phone calls. So, he would talk to me on the phone. When he got clean and sober while he was on tour with Audioslave during Lollapalooza [in 2003], every night he got off stage, he would call me. We would talk all the time. And then over the years, there were periods where we wouldn't talk for three or four months, but then there were periods where we would talk all the time. It varied. If a lot was going on with his life at the time. It was one of those situations, where even when he did that album with Timbaland, which met with mixed reviews, he came and debuted it on my New York morning show, because I was always trusted.

Before, you mentioned Chris going to rehab, and I know you have admitted going to rehab, too. Did you ever talk about your experiences?
Yeah, we did talk a lot about it. I don't want to go too deeply into it, because it's a very personal thing. We were both open about saving our lives and the struggles that we've had, so we filmed that so it would help other people. But yes, we did talk in detail about it, and about being supportive.

How would you describe the personalities of Chris, Kim, Ben, and Matt?
All four of them different. Chris' personality was he loved people, and he was very open. Over the years, he definitely gave more of himself to people—where before, he would keep to himself. And then Kim I always loved, because even though he played incredibly heavy guitar, he was also a big punk rock fan. So, he and I would hang out, and Kim and I were very close, too. Kim is the guy who had a major attention to detail. He had an analytic personality.

Ben was kind of like the guy who was a great guy but very sarcastic, and really funny at times. He had a very dry sense of humor—but he was hilarious. And he also had that background of hard rock and punk. And then you had Matt Cameron, who always had this really outgoing, positive personality. There were interesting stories about his dad turning him on to Buddy Rich and all that stuff when he was a kid. He always had a very upbeat and positive attitude. It was amazing—his drumming and the things that he'd create with Soundgarden. He said once to me, "I feel lucky to be in two of the greatest bands of all-time." And he was of course talking about Pearl Jam and Soundgarden.

In another one of my earlier books, *100 Things Pearl Jam Fans Should Know & Do Before They Die*, you told me a cool story about Eddie Vedder mentioning you and Soundgarden backstage in the '90s.
What he said to me was, "Matt, I've been wanting to meet you," as he came off stage at the Tibetan Freedom Concert [in 1997]. He goes, "I love what you do on the air, but I'm sorry, we're not going to be making any videos for you to play. But the Soundgarden guys said you were really cool." Soundgarden gave me the stamp of approval—which was cool.

What did you think of *King Animal*?
I loved it. I thought it was a great comeback record. I thought it was very, very strong. I loved "Been Away Too Long"—I thought it was such a great, draw-a-line-in-the-sand single. And I also thought—even though it was new and modern—it even brought back really interesting signature changes, that were really apparent on albums like *Badmotorfinger*.

It was so strange and sad that in such a short span, we lost Scott Weiland, Chris, and Chester Bennington.
For me, it was really depressing and sad. Because all three of those artists were a big part of my life in music. I was friends with all three of them. And I loved Chester—he left me messages shortly before he died. Like a week before, he texted me. And I loved

Scott, and I was really sad because I was so worried that was going to happen with Scott...and then it did. But I was closest of all three to Chris. But I was friends with them all. It devastated me because you've got three incredible singers, and not a lot of great singers come along in our lifetime like these three guys. It was such a loss to music and rock n' roll. All three of those guys were different personalities, but they were all really amazing people. Talented, beautiful guys.

When would have been the last time you corresponded with Chris, and do you recall what you discussed?
My last correspondence was we were talking about film noir, and which movies we watched. Because Chris and I really loved film noir—from the '40s and '50s, black and white. *Incredible films.* Chris and I were really into that stuff, and I found that out when I was sitting with him for an hour backstage during the Nine Inch Nails/Soundgarden tour. And from that moment on, he and I would just correspond and talk about movies. But I did not see his death coming.

How do you think Soundgarden's music holds up today?
I think it holds up incredibly. I think Soundgarden didn't sound like anybody else, and I think their music still is as powerful and amazing as it's always been. I think their music is going to stand the test of time, and will always be considered great, powerful, and beautiful.

How would you like Chris to be remembered?
As one of the greatest vocalists of all-time. An incredible songwriter. And a beautiful human being. And a great father. That's how I'd want Chris to be remembered.

SOURCES

CHAPTER 01
Cornell: "It was bound...the wrong audience." (*Melody Maker*—March 28, 1992), **Thayil:** "From Metallica to...the audience wants." (*Melody Maker*—March 28, 1992), **Cornell:** "And believe me...anchors around them." (*Melody Maker*—March 28, 1992), **Shepherd:** "I always saw...it was music." (*Grunge Is Dead: The Oral History of Seattle Rock Music*—2009), **Cameron:** "We've worked very...into that situation." (*Rolling Stone*—July 9, 1992)

CHAPTER 02
Cornell: "I'm Bobby in *The Brady Bunch.*" (*Rolling Stone*—January 12, 1995), **Cornell:** "Very Seattle-ish. For...definitive Seattle neighborhood." (*Rolling Stone*—January 12, 1995), **Cornell:** "I would just...the whole day." (*Rolling Stone*—June 16, 1994), **Cornell:** "We all got...lived near me." (*Rolling Stone*—January 12, 1995), **Cornell:** "From eleven to...mind with drugs'." (*Rip*—July 1992), **Cornell:** "From auto theft...burning down buildings." (*Details*—April 1994), **Cornell:** "I was a...were true friends." (*Kerrang!*—August 13, 1994), **Cornell:** "It made me...to these records." (*The Los Angeles Times*—August 25, 1991), **Cornell:** "Most of my...to Black Sabbath." (*Q Magazine*—October 1994), **Cornell:** "I had a...time to run." (*Spin*—September 2006), **Cornell:** "I never went...waste of time." (*Rolling Stone*—January 12, 1995), **Cornell:** "I still regret...I had continued." (*Spin*—July 1996), **Cornell:** "I started playing...to do it." (*Us Magazine*—July 1996), **Cornell:** "There was no...me feel good." (*The Los Angeles Times*—August 25, 1991), **Cornell:** "I was in...to do anything." (*Reflex*—December 1991), **Cornell:** "We rehearsed in...into the Police." (*Rolling Stone*—January 12, 1995), **Cornell:** "The first time...going to happen." (*The Howard Stern Show*—June 12, 2007), **Cornell:** "I always liked...in fried food." (*Details*—April 1994), **Cornell:** "When I was...sacred than that." (*Pulse*—March 1994), **Cornell:** "Didn't allow its...it did creatively." (*Rolling Stone*—June 16, 1994)

CHAPTER 03

Thayil: "A somewhat suburban...Hispanic, white, Jewish." (*India Abroad*—December 2, 1994), **Thayil:** "My dad was...tendencies towards stoicism!" (*Kerrang!*—August 31, 1991), **Thayil:** "She's classically trained...music and English." (*Guitar for the Practicing Musician*—September 1990), **Thayil:** "Kiss: *Alive!* That...as a genre." (*Rock Power*—May 1992), **Thayil:** "In reading interviews...meant to play." (*Guitar One*—November 1996), **Thayil:** "I would say...my big influences." (*Guitar One*—November 1996), **Thayil:** "My first electric...like they should." (*Guitar One*—November 1996), **Thayil:** "It was 1978...a fucking Ramone!" (*Guitar World*—March 1991), **Thayil:** "I started playing...I could play." (*Guitar for the Practicing Musician*—September 1990), **Yamamoto:** "I listened to...in fifth grade." (*Soundgarden: New Metal Crown*—1995), **Yamamoto:** "It affirmed the...me go, 'Yeah'!" *Soundgarden: New Metal Crown*—1995), **Yamamoto:** "Back then he...all the time." (*Grunge Is Dead*—2009), **Thayil:** "I said, 'Hey...with his fingers." (*Guitar For The Practicing Musician*, September 1990), **Thayil:** "It seemed like...nothing going on." (*Grunge Is Dead*—2009)

CHAPTER 04

Thayil: "Initially, when I...different, artier elements." (*Kerrang!*—April 8, 1989), **Thayil:** "Not too many...the California bands." (*Punk! Hardcore! Reggae! PMA! Bad Brains!*—2014), **Thayil:** "Around '83/'84...guys on SST?" (*Too High to Die: Meet the Meat Puppets*—2012), **Yamamoto:** "A friend of...for a singer." (*Grunge Is Dead*—2009), **Thayil:** "Matt Dentino was...period of time." (*Grunge Is Dead*—2009), **Cornell:** "I always figured...attitude pretty quick." (*Select*—July 1992), **Thayil:** "When I met...doing shitty material." (*Select*—July 1992), **Dentino:** "When he came...to be sung." (*Grunge Is Dead*—2009), **Thayil:** "Chris at some...in this picture." (*Grunge Is Dead*—2009), **Cameron:** "They were playing...was still incredible." (*Grunge Is Dead*—2009), **Thayil:** "I was friends...Mark and me." (*Grunge Is Dead*—2009), **Yamamoto:** "Chris was living...in that house." (*Grunge Is Dead*—2009), **Thayil:** "Immediately everything clicked...University of Washington." (*Grunge Is Dead*—2009), **Thayil:** "They wanted me...with these jerks." (*Grunge Is Dead*—2009), **Thayil:** "At one point...do with it." (*Kerrang!*—April 8, 1989), **Thayil:** "Just a few...then head home." (*Too High to Die: Meet the Meat Puppets*—2012), **Thayil:** "'Ocean Fronts,' 'Open...is another title." (*Rolling Stone*—2009), **Thayil:** "In our early...cool way again." (*Too High to Die: Meet the Meat Puppets*—2012), **Dentino:** "I saw their...golfing or baseball." (*Grunge Is Dead*—2009), **Ament:** "I remember seeing...pretty frickin' cool." (*Grunge Is Dead*—2009), **Channing:** "I went to...long since gone." (*Grunge Is Dead*—2009), **Shepherd:** "The very first...disturbing and huge." (*Grunge Is Dead*—2009), **Endino:** "Scott was an...really pretty amazing." (*Classic Rock*—Summer 2005), **Thayil:** "Believe it or...restaurant, Ray's Boathouse." (*Grunge Is Dead*—2009), **Yamamoto:** "That's basically the...times of Soundgarden." (*Grunge Is Dead*—2009)

CHAPTER 05
Cameron: "My neighbors up...for the role." (*Westworld*—July 2011), **Cameron:** "I was playing...other earlier songs." (*Grunge Is Dead*—2009), **Cameron:** "I auditioned for...it,' I replied" (*Instagram*—May 2018), **Cameron:** "My first Soundgarden...Too fast!' etcetera." (*Pearl Jam Twenty*—2011), **Cameron:** "Opening for Love...own with anyone." (*Pearl Jam Twenty*—2011), **Thayil:** "It got a...to the songwriting." (*Grunge Is Dead*—2009), **Endino:** "After they got...be reckoned with." (*Grunge Is Dead*—2009), **Thayil:** "I think he...in the band." (*Livewire*—November 1992), **Thayil:** "We didn't even...important to us." (*The Faith No More & Mr. Bungle Companion*—2013), **Gould:** "Soundgarden opened up...a musical connection." (*Classic Rock*—October 2006)

CHAPTER 06
Thayil: "Both Jonathan and...you work together?" (*Grunge Is Dead*—2009), **Endino:** "They borrowed a...first few years." (*Grunge Is Dead*—2009), **Thayil:** "I had the...how that worked." (*Songfacts*—April 8, 2014), **Thayil:** "It was the...on the S-100."

(*Guitar Player*—July 1996), **Cornell:** "The first guitar...missed those tones." (*Guitar World*—March 30, 2011), **Endino:** "I got some...the real thing..." (*Unofficial SG Homepage*—date unknown), **Cameron:** "We only had...stage of development." (*Grunge Is Dead*—2009), **Thayil:** "'Tears to Forget'...and 'Little Joe'." (*Grunge Is Dead*—2009), **Shepherd:** "*Screaming Life* is...days of Seattle." (*Grunge Is Dead*—2009), **Thayil:** "I think it...sunshiny to me." (*Grunge Is Dead*—2009), **Thayil:** "Oh it was...at it. Wow!" (*Metal Hammer*—January 1998), **Cornell:** "It was just...even came out." (*Rolling Stone*—January 12, 1995), **Silver:** "I'd met Chris...help them out." (*Grunge Is Dead*—2009), **Cornell:** "Initially, I didn't...the complete turnaround." (*Rolling Stone*—January 12, 1995), **Silver:** "I didn't want...that worked out." (*Grunge Is Dead*—2009), **Thayil:** "We were generating...to be Susan." (*Grunge Is Dead*—2009)

CHAPTER 07
Thayil: "That's an Ohio...kick-ass rock song!" (*Guitar School*—May 1994), **Fisk:** "It was Bruce...the same time." (*Grunge Is Dead*—2009), **Cameron:** "We were playing...at his studio." (*Grunge Is Dead*—2009), **Fisk:** "At one point...to be cool." (*Grunge Is Dead*—2009), **Thayil:** "The *Fopp* EP...for humor's sake." (*Songfacts*—April 8, 2014), **Cantrell:** "Those early EP's...was very inspiring." (*Grunge Is Dead*—2009), **Thayil:** "They [Nirvana] had...He didn't move." (*Grunge Is Dead*—2009), **Hallerman:** "I stepped away...for being nice." (*Grunge Is Dead*—2009), **Shepherd:** "They were playing...the true Soundgarden." (*Grunge Is Dead*—2009), **Hallerman:** "After the show...he'd be into." (*Grunge Is Dead*—2009), **Arm:** "They were pretty...act of narcissism." (*Grunge Is Dead*—2009), **Pickerel:** "It was hard...rock n' roll." (*Grunge Is Dead*—2009), **Thayil:** "I didn't have...the same time." (*Pit*—Spring 1990), **Thayil:** "Before Ben joined...the Zig-Zag man." (*Guitar World*—July 1996), **Thayil:** "We wrote that...Pop Rock City'." (*Guitar School*—May 1994), **Silver:** "There was a...up with it'." (*Grunge Is Dead*—2009)

CHAPTER 08
Endino: "By the time...more indie record'." (*Grunge Is Dead*—
2009), **Thayil:** "When it came...and the distribution..." (*Raw*—?
1989), **Thayil:** "The cool thing...by SST Records." (*Punk!
Hardcore! Reggae! PMA! Bad Brains!*—2014), **Pickerel:** "I was
instrumental...SST signed them." (*Grunge Is Dead*—2009),
Cornell: "Initially, when Soundgarden...Nirvana were heard."
(*Spin*—September 1992), **Cornell or Thayil:** "absolutely,
amazingly not bad" (*Sounds*—February 11, 1989), **Cornell:** "It's
about a...burns out quick." (Sounds—May 13, 1989), **Thayil:**
"That chorus part...ever got recorded." (*Songfacts*—April 8,
2014), **Cornell:** "The alternative is...better that way." (*Sounds*—
February 11, 1989), **Thayil:** "Some people might...go beyond
666." (*Sounds*—February 11, 1989), **Cornell:** "It was about...shit
about you." (Concert stage rap—April 29, 2017), **Thayil:** "That
song is...best Soundgarden solos." (*Guitar School*—May 1994),
Cornell: "We learnt the...stage with you." (*Sounds*—May 13,
1989), **Yamamoto:** "I did and...stage with you." (*Sounds*—May
13, 1989), **Cornell:** "We couldn't do...are non-teutonic, non-
aryan." (*Sounds*—February 11, 1989), **Thayil:** "The song is...be
an anthem!" (*Sounds*—February 11, 1989), **Cornell:** "We wrote
one...doing that more." (*Rolling Stone*—January 12, 1995),
Thayil: "By the time...use that session." (*Guitar For The
Practicing Musician*—September 1990), **Cornell:** "We were
trying...a whole minute." (*Sounds*—February 11, 1989), **Thayil:**
"No, it's the...up to eleven." (*Sounds*—February 11, 1989),
Cameron: "We went down...rest in Newberg." (*Grunge Is
Dead*—2009), **Thayil:** "Production-wise we left...happening in
Seattle." (*Raw*—? 1989), **Cameron:** "I think some...it in there."
(*Modern Drummer*—June 1994), **Cornell:** "I think we...sound
like us." (*Kerrang!*—August 19, 1995), **Cornell:** "It was
Ultramega Alright." (*Select*—June 1996), **Yamamoto:** "That was
exciting...and dining started." (*Grunge Is Dead*—2009), **Thayil:**
"We'd do ten-week...perspective about ourselves." (*Grunge Is
Dead*—2009), **Thayil:** "The stuff in...'the SST tour'." (*Too High
to Die: Meet the Meat Puppets*—2012), **McKagan:** "I remember
hearing...the whole thing." (*Grunge Is Dead*—2009), **Cornell:**

"When we first...a good thing." (*The Rocket*—December 21, 1994), **Cameron:** "On one of...gram of pot." (*High Times*—July 1992), **Thayil:** "We'd sold like...in Washington State!" (*Pit*—Spring 1990)

CHAPTER 09
Cornell: "Actually, we'd been...providing major distribution." (*Raw*—? 1989), **Silver:** "A&M—as its...bands and managers." (*Grunge Is Dead*—2009), **Yamamoto:** "Faith No More...everybody was interested." (*Grunge Is Dead*—2009), **Thayil:** "A&M haven't worked...the company's affection." (*Kerrang!*—April 8, 1989), **Cornell:** "You gotta keep...worried about something." (*Pit*—Spring 1990), **Thayil:** "We recorded *Louder*...creeps at night." (*Loud*—? 1990), **Thayil:** "The people there...are engineering students." (*Rockpool*—October 1, 1989), **Cameron:** "It was a...a composition tool." (*Grunge Is Dead*—2009), **Date:** "There's a lot...I can imagine." (*Grunge Is Dead*—2009), **Date:** "They all got...got pissed off." (*Grunge Is Dead*—2009), **Yamamoto:** "Terry Date could...a metal band'?" (*Grunge Is Dead*—2009), **Cornell:** "It's not a...Neo-metal maybe." (*Sounds*—October 21, 1989), **Endino:** "I was pretty...exciting-sounding record." (*Grunge Is Dead*—2009), **Cornell:** "Magic, it was...what we want." (*Rockpool*—October 1, 1989), **Thayil:** "Yeah it's heavy...drums, bigger everything." (*Rockpool*—October 1, 1989), **Cameron:** "The songs are...choppy, more hypnotic." (*Rockpool*—October 1, 1989), **Cornell:** "I heard the...very late '80s." (*Sounds*—October 21, 1989), **Thayil:** "What I liked...'Hands All Over'." (*Guitar School*—May 1994), **Cornell:** "We're having problems...in the store'!" (*Pit*—Spring 1990), **Thayil:** "It can be...with the resistance." (*Pit*—Spring 1990), **Thayil:** "I think there...your fucking mother'!" (*Rolling Stone*—September 28, 2010), **Thayil:** "The thing about...we can play." (*Guitar School*—May 1994), **Cornell:** "If you believe...make it happen." (*Live at the Paramount Theatre*—1992), **Cornell:** "We're not a...and his reason." (*Faces*—December 1989), **Thayil:** "In 'Get on...on you anyway." (*Unofficial SG Homepage*—date unknown), **Thayil:** "Many people think...feedback with it."

(*Guitar School*—May 1994), **Alden:** "Yamamoto came in...a songwriting credit." (*Guitar World*—July 1997), **Cornell:** "The lyrics don't...crazy. It's hypocrisy." (*Sounds*—July 28, 1990), **Thayil:** "Hiro, our bass...of butt rock." (*Guitar School*—May 1994), **Thayil:** "Irritated Jerry Moss...were up to." (*Chicago Tribune*—October 18, 1989), **Cornell:** "'Big Dumb Sex'...of music, really." (*Spin*—September 1992), **Thayil:** "We're not interested...Soundgarden has theirs." (*Chicago Tribune*—October 18, 1989), **Chantry:** "They didn't have...*Love* came from." (*Grunge Is Dead*—2009), **Cornell:** "It's sort of...*Louder Than Love*?" (*Sounds*—October 21, 1989), **Kot:** "Even Soundgarden's hardest...(Elektra) in 1986." (*Chicago Tribune*—October 18, 1989), **Kaye:** "I've been championing...*Louder Than Love*." (Rip—May 1990), **Rose:** "I enjoy Sound...sings so great." (*Rolling Stone*—August 10, 1989), **Cornell:** "When we released...made the impression." (*Melody Maker*—March 19, 1994), **Hammett:** "I have a...came that riff." (*The Toucher and Rich Show*—September 13, 2017)

CHAPTER 10
Cornell: "He got tired...van rides anymore." (*Sounds*—October 21, 1989), **Thayil:** "He left about...kinds of temptations." (*Loud*—? 1990), **Cornell:** "He was losing...his own songs." (*Alternative Press*—March 1994), **Hiro:** "I guess the...been released yet." (*Grunge Is Dead*—2009), **Thayil:** "It was certainly...of seven relationships." (*Grunge Is Dead*—2009), **Yamamoto:** "Some of the...kind of sound." (*Grunge Is Dead*—2009), **Marander:** "[Kurt Cobain] loved...them that much." (*Grunge Is Dead*—2009), **Tillman:** "I played with...went bowling instead." (*Grunge Is Dead*—2009), **Shepherd:** "They were crunched...on-beat with it." (*Grunge Is Dead*—2009), **Cornell:** "Jason knew the...we were doing." (*Guitar World*—July 1997), **Cornell:** "Making the video...that killed Soundgarden." (*Headbangers Ball*—January 28, 1990), **Thayil:** "The video for...It really sucked." (*Guitar School*—May 1994), **Arm:** "I remember talking...about both camps." (*Survival of the Fittest: Heavy Metal in The 1990's*—2015), **Thayil:** "The first time...talk to them." (*Primus, Over the*

Electric Grapevine: Insight into Primus and the World of Les Claypool—2014), **Thayil:** "'Heretic' was the...the picked notes." (*Guitar Player*—July 1996), **Yamamoto:** "The only 'demonic'...refers to them." (*Sounds*—May 13, 1989), **Thayil:** "We played three...past five weeks." (*Loud*—? 1990), **Cornell:** "Detroit is always...audience and security!" (*Metal Hammer*—May 7-20, 1990), **Thayil:** "That tour was...Mechanix/MCA, their label." (*Metaverse.com*—1994), **Gilbert:** "Voivod play 'Loud...plays or not." (*The Rocket*—March 1990), **Cameron:** "I think Patton...from the lights." (*Classic Rock*—Summer 2005), **Thayil:** "When we started...stuff he's done." (*The Faith No More & Mr. Bungle Companion*—2013), **Thayil:** "If there was...had a history." (*The Faith No More & Mr. Bungle Companion*—2013), **Thayil:** "I think we...that from Patton." (*The Faith No More & Mr. Bungle Companion*—2013), **Silver:** "We were in...the whole screen." (*Grunge Is Dead*—2009), **Silver:** "We came back...off the machines." (*Grunge Is Dead*—2009), **Cornell:** "I felt alone...experiencing him squirming." (*Rip*—July 1992), **Thayil:** "Bruce Fairweather is...list keeps growing." (*Rip*—July 1992), **Cornell:** "When I went...this other space." (*Kerrang!*—October 17, 1992), **Cornell:** "The same as...didn't do it." (*Melody Maker*—August 26, 1995), **Wilding:** "'Loud Love' is...was simply jumping." (*Kerrang!*—April 14, 1990), **Thayil:** "He certainly could...personally and creatively." (*Grunge Is Dead*—2009), **Shepherd:** "I was born...had music going." (*Grunge Is Dead*—2009), **Thayil:** "Ben's mom has...with our moms." (*Kerrang!*—August 31, 1991), **Shepherd:** "My brothers were...the same way." (*Kerrang!*—February 12, 1994), **Shepherd:** "Hiro Yamamoto was...and he's one." (*Seconds*—#38, 1996), **Cameron:** "So after Jason...Luckily, he was." (*Grunge Is Dead*—2009), **Shepherd:** "It belonged to...to the neck." (*Bass Player*—March 12, 2013), **Shepherd:** "I met the...and smoked cigarettes." (*Grunge Is Dead*—2009), **Thayil:** "Actually, that lyric...in a song'." (*Songfacts*—April 8, 2014), **Thayil:** "I wrote the...total HIV baby'!" (*Guitar School*—May 1994), **Thayil:** "Our major label...what to expect." (*Hit Parader*—May 1997), **Brown:** "They had their...going on before." (*Survival of the Fittest: Heavy*

Metal in The 1990's—2015), **Hammett:** "It was about...came that riff." (*Toucher & Rich Radio Show*—September 13, 2017)

CHAPTER 11

Ament: "Not long after...wasn't anything else." (*Grunge Is Dead*—2009), **Silver:** "They went in...big, powerful record." (*Grunge Is Dead*—2009), **Vedder:** "It was during...onto that track." (*Grunge Is Dead*—2009), **Rachman:** "I'd been to...to collaborate with." (*Songfacts*—June 2, 2017), **Cornell:** "It didn't affect...kind of person." (*Reflex*—December 1991), **Cornell:** "A lot of...Cornell solo project." (*Kerrang!*—October 17, 1992), **Ament:** "I remember when...and they refused." (*Guitar World*—July 1997), **Cornell:** "Not really. Most...support both projects." (*Riff Raff*—November 1991), **Vedder:** "After the show...really strong impression." (*Grunge Is Dead*—2009), **Silver:** "[Alice in Chains]...your guy now." (*Grunge Is Dead*—2009)

CHAPTER 12

Cornell: "There was a...change their perspective." (*Reflex*—December 1991), **Cornell:** "In almost every...of influences whatsoever." (*Kerrang!*—December 7, 1991), **Cornell:** "Most all the...started recording it." (*Reflex*—December 1991), **Cameron:** "There's definitely more...on two songs." (*Circus*—January 31, 1992), **Ament:** "You could see...apart even more." (*Spin*—June 5, 2014), **Cornell:** "We'd developed a...someone else's personality." (*Riff Raff*—November 1991), **Cameron:** "We rehearsed our...quick and efficient." (*Grunge Is Dead*—2009), **Date:** "It was spring...good or not." (*Grunge Is Dead*—2009), **Date:** "They felt *Louder*...a good record." (*Grunge Is Dead*—2009), **Cameron:** "[*Badmotorfinger*] was a...*Louder Than Love*." (*Grunge Is Dead*—2009), **Thayil:** "It's the heavy...idea of heaviness." (*Kerrang!*—August 31, 1991), **Thayil:** "But it sounds...it on 11!" (*Kerrang!*—August 31, 1991), **Thayil:** "I was trying...good for vibrato." (*Guitar World*—May 1996), **Cornell:** "I think you...that on us." (*Raw*—October 30-November 12, 1991), **Thayil:** "It was sort...way it looked." (*The Music Paper*—February 1992), **Thayil:** "The tuning on...almost sounds backward." (*Guitar School*—May 1994), **Thayil:** "What I love...heavy, undanceable riff." (*Rolling Stone*—September 28, 2010), **Cornell:** "One of the...pushed that button." (*Details*—December 1996), **Cornell:** "After Andy had...of that feeling." (Matt Pinfield and Chris Cornell interview on 101.9 RXP—2008), **Thayil:** "It captures everything...during the verses." (*Kerrang!*—May 18, 2019), **Thayil:** "That's the second...making a wish!" (*Guitar School*—May 1994), **Thayil:** "Every solo of...the goal there." (*Shredders! The Oral History of Speed Guitar (And More)*—2017), **Cornell:** "The idea of...look really good." (*Seconds*—? 1991), **Thayil:** "We were at...'Jesus Christ Pose'." (*Classic Rock*—March 3, 2010), **Cornell:** "A lot of...music should be." (*Rock Power*—March 1992), **Cornell:** "In America, they...they're getting pushed." (*Raw*—October 30-November 12, 1991), **Cornell:** "The beauty of...of a sermon." (*Kerrang!*—December 7, 1991), **Tomashoff:** "It isn't for...front of you." (*People*—November 26, 1991), **Considine:** "Don't make the...Hear and believe." (*Musician*—December 1991), **Cameron:** "The first time...twice about them." (*Kerrang!*—December 7, 1991), **Thayil:** "I liked the...for some reason." (*Classic Rock*—March 3, 2010)

CHAPTER 13
Thayil: "We were the...much going on." (*Grunge Is Dead*—2009), **Thayil:** "We're not these...into contact with." (*Melody Maker*—March 19, 1994), **Endino:** "Those ['80s era metal] albums...hard rock records'?" (*Survival of the Fittest: Heavy Metal in The 1990's*—2015), **Thayil:** "There's always someone...the music scene." (*Guitar World*—May 1994), **Cornell:** "You see, I...perception of grunge." (*Raw*—September 15-28, 1993), **Thayil:** "We get a...money than us!" (*The Guitar Magazine*—December 1996), **Vedder:** "I think with...control real quick." (*Grunge Is Dead*—2009), **Cornell:** "I've already had...something you'd like." (*Raw*—September 15-28, 1993), **Cornell:** "It's hard not...It's that bad." (*Rolling Stone*—January 12, 1995), **Thayil:** "Yes, things have...adapt in it." (*Metaverse.com*—? 1994), **Shepherd:** "A lot of...stupider they

are." (*Kerrang!*—February 12, 1994), **Thayil:** "To begin with...which is good." (*Kerrang!*—March 1996), **Cornell:** "Celebrity is odd...it bugs him." (*Musician*—April 1994), **Cornell:** "The fantasy is...for thinking that." (*Spin*—September 1992), **Thayil:** "Chris was walking...he's now arrived!" (The Rocket—December 21, 1994), **Cameron:** "The only time...band from Seattle." (*Rolling Stone*—July 9, 1992), **Channing:** "My first impression...was pretty stoked." (*Survival of the Fittest: Heavy Metal in The 1990's*—2015), **Cornell:** "When we were...animosity between bands." (*Spin*—September 1992), **Cornell:** "Mark Arm once...Rush of Seattle." (*Musician*—April 1994), **Keifer:** "That look, which...not their eyes." (*Survival of the Fittest: Heavy Metal in The 1990's*—2015), **Wartell:** "Grunge is just...they're just metal." (*Survival of the Fittest: Heavy Metal in The 1990's*—2015), **Clarke:** "I remember in...Alice in Chains." (*Survival of the Fittest: Heavy Metal in The 1990's*—2015), **Halfin:** "Pearl Jam, with...were totally fine." (*Grunge Is Dead*—2009), **Cornell:** "It's never been...or San Francisco." (*Kerrang!*—March 1, 1997), **Shepherd:** "In the same...to this one." (*Waves*—? 1992), **Cornell:** "I can't look...me about grunge'." (*Rolling Stone*—May 19, 2017)

CHAPTER 14
Thayil: "We got to...the helicopter crash." (*The Faith No More & Mr. Bungle Companion*—2013), **Cornell:** "It's more of...would otherwise like." (*Kerrang!*—December 7, 1991), **Silver:** "The management company...to be around." (*A Devil on One Shoulder and an Angel on the Other: The Story of Shannon Hoon and Blind Melon*—2008), **Graham:** "The first show...fun of you." (*A Devil on One Shoulder and an Angel on the Other: The Story of Shannon Hoon and Blind Melon*—2008), **Eaves:** "Shannon and Chris...too, I think." (*A Devil on One Shoulder and an Angel on the Other: The Story of Shannon Hoon and Blind Melon*—2008), **Cornell:** "I really liked...really it's him." (*Kerrang!*—March 1, 1997), **Silver:** "[The Guns N'...dubbed them 'Frowngarden'." (*Grunge Is Dead*—2009), **Cornell:** "I think that...a bizarre thing." (*Raw*—September 15-28, 1993), **Cameron:** "We were going...to be

heard." (*Circus*—January 31, 1992), **Cameron:** "The first Guns...back on it." (*High Times*—July 1992), **Cornell:** "I think people...half empty arena." (*Kerrang!*—August 12, 1995), **Cornell:** "It's the same...party. That's fun." (*Select*—July 1992), **Cornell:** "The had this...was pretty crazy." (*Raw*—September 15-28, 1993), **Shepherd:** "We had a...have a chance." (*Grunge Is Dead*—2009), **Thayil:** "When we toured...taking that tour." (*Grunge Is Dead*—2009), **Thayil:** "That was our...to kill ourselves." (*Guitar For The Practicing Musician*—December 1992), **Cornell:** "The unseen version...hard rock video." (*Musician*—April 1994), **Thayil:** "We kind of...in a hotel." (*Grunge Is Dead*—2009), **Cornell:** "Our biggest single...song we've written." (*Spin*—September 1992), **Silver:** "That was the...it promoted properly." (*Grunge Is Dead*—2009), **Cameron:** "We were in...act for '91-'92." (*Grunge Is Dead*—2009), **Cornell:** "Playing with Skid...established new ones." (*Seconds*—#38, 1996), **Cornell:** "We were up...the party going." (*Spin*—April 1994), **Shepherd:** "It made me...too much TV." (*Rolling Stone*—July 9, 1992), **Cornell:** "That's what happens...you let it." (*Rolling Stone*—July 9, 1992), **Thayil:** "Sometimes, I can...just got 'Mud-hon-ey'." (*Melody Maker*—March 21, 1992), **Thayil:** "This was weird...more than anybody." (*The Faith No More & Mr. Bungle Companion*—2013), **Cameron:** "That's when Faith...in my life." (*The Faith No More & Mr. Bungle Companion*—2013), **Cornell:** "I'd rather not...capable of doing." (*Raw*—September 15-28, 1993), **Cameron:** "It was very...theatres and clubs." (*Modern Drummer*—June 1994), **Cornell:** "Spending time with...band ever has." (*Rip*—July 1992), **Cornell:** "Without saying anything...most. It's sad." (*Vulture*—November 13, 2012), **Cameron:** "That was our...with our friends." (*Grunge Is Dead*—2009), **Author unknown:** "Penned by Cornell...bottle-throwing political argument'." (*Reflex*—December 1991), **Cornell:** "If you ever...on and off." (*Guitar World*—July 1997), **Cornell:** "Because it was...his independent movie." (*Pulse!*—March 1994), **Cornell:** "No, I think...that's about it." (*Kerrang!*—March 1, 1997), **Cornell:** "We weren't planning...something like that." (*Kerrang!*—October 17, 1992),

Cornell: "Here's a song...the wrong things." (*Kerrang!*—October 17, 1992), **Pinnick:** "I loved Chris...an album together]." (*King's X: The Oral History*—2019), **Thayil:** "Chris spoke highly...friendly, amiable people." (*King's X: The Oral History*—2019), **Kirkwood:** "So everybody goes...*you're* wrecking things." (*Too High to Die: Meet the Meat Puppets*—2012), **Thayil:** "Guns N' Roses...true around here." (*Guitar For The Practicing Musician*—December 1992), **Cornell:** "I think it...an alternative audience." (*Kerrang!*—October 17, 1992), **Shepherd:** "That first [Lollapalooza...play another show'!" (*Grunge Is Dead*—2009), **Shepherd:** "That whole year...going for it." (*Grunge Is Dead*—2009)

CHAPTER 15
Cornell: "Susan was really...why they cared." (*Details*—December 1996), **Cornell:** "The funny thing...why they cared." (*Details*—December 1996), **Cornell:** "Every single person...and facial hair." (*Pulse*—March 1994), **Cornell:** "I never liked...shave your head." (*Select*—June 1996), **Thayil:** "I don't have...aren't far off." (*Musician*—April 1994), **Cornell:** "We were happy...to the limit." (*Hit Parader*—August 1994), **Cornell:** "It was good...where we were." (*Melody Maker*—November 27, 1993), **Shepherd:** "One reason why...like we sound." (*M.E.A.T. Magazine*—March/April 1994), **Cornell:** "This was the...back in there." (*Raw*—September 15-28, 1993), **Cornell:** "It seemed like...thought I'd feel." (*Kerrang!*—September 11, 1993), **Cornell:** "To be honest...again by ourselves." (*Kerrang!*—September 11, 1993), **Cornell:** "It's so much...it back out!" (*Kerrang!*—September 11, 1993), **Cornell:** "I have a...on Black Days'." (*Guitar World*—March 30, 2011), **Thayil:** "He ordered it...wait for delivery!" (*Kerrang!*—September 11, 1993), **Silver:** "They called it...that with them." (*A Devil on One Shoulder and an Angel on the Other: The Story of Shannon Hoon and Blind Melon*—2008), **Thayil:** "I remember Chris...the light show'." (*A Devil on One Shoulder and an Angel on the Other: The Story of Shannon Hoon and Blind Melon*—2008), **Cornell:** "It's sort of...on the record." (*Raw*—September 15-28, 1993), **Cornell:** "I

guess the...surprising so far." (*Raw*—September 15-28, 1993), **Thayil:** "There's gonna be...the performances translated." (*Kerrang!*—September 11, 1993), **Cornell:** "We did things...sounds in general." (*Melody Maker*—November 27, 1993), **Cameron:** "The way the...on some songs." (*Musician*—April 1994), **Cornell:** "We changed our...didn't know how." (*Guitar World*—May 1994), **Cornell:** "We have eight...like thirteen guitars." (*Rip*—April 1994), **Cornell:** "We're tending to...the last day!" (*Hard Music*—January 1994), **Shepherd:** "I personally don't...wanted to record." (*M.E.A.T. Magazine*—March/April 1994), **Shepherd:** "We recorded four...at a time." (*Headbangers Ball UK*—1994), **Cornell:** "It was cool...whole new door." (*Headbangers Ball UK*—1994), **Shepherd:** "Everybody was involved...the whole record." (*Headbangers Ball UK*—1994), **Cornell:** "When we were...friends again now." (*Metal Hammer*—June 1996), **Thayil:** "We had a...Chris play *Doom.*" (*Spin*—June 5, 2014), **Cornell:** "We almost got...lose his job." (*Spin*—June 5, 2014), **Cameron:** "We knew we...really good record." (*Grunge Is Dead*—2009), **Cameron:** "Hater came about...don't normally go." (*Modern Drummer*—June 1994), **Shepherd:** "The song 'Down...finished recording it." (*M.E.A.T. Magazine*—March/April 1994), **Cornell:** "The drums on...is so revered." (*Guitar World*—May 1994), **Shepherd:** "I thought that...heckled us more." (*Details*—April 1994), **Cornell:** "I think they...step was us." (*Pulse*—March 1994), **Shepherd:** "Because [Kiss'] fans...beat me up." (*Alternative Press*—March 1994), **Thayil:** "We got to...with that song." (*Long Live Queen: Rock Royalty Discuss Freddie, Brian, John & Roger*—2018), **Cornell:** "*Superunknown* is dyslexia...it inspired me." (*Pulse*—March 1994), **Cameron:** "We made an...what we did." (*Superunknown press release*—1993), **Vedder:** "They'd just finished...cylinders were firing." (*Grunge Is Dead*—2009), **Shepherd:** "[1993] was a...all really connected." (*Grunge Is Dead*—2009)

CHAPTER 16
Cornell: "I'd always thought...record some stuff." (*Guitar World*—June 1997), **Cornell:** "More or less...dishes for

somebody." (*Headbangers Ball*—1994), **Thayil:** "Because that song...terms of key." (*Shredders! The Oral History of Speed Guitar (And More)*—2017), **Shepherd:** "There was a...little bit further'." (*M.E.A.T. Magazine*—March/April 1994), **Cornell:** "I think we...for some people." (*Hit Parader*—October 1994), **Cornell:** "'Let Me Drown'...do that too." (*Rip*—April 1994), **Beinhorn:** "Take the end...completely hit it." (*Musician*—April 1994), **Thayil:** "Whenever we start...That loses everybody." (*Rolling Stone*—September 28, 2010), **Cornell:** "Tolerance, provided that...house on fire." (Fox Theatre, May 17, 2017), **Cornell:** "'Fell On Black...life is FUCKED!" (*Melody Maker*—March 19, 1994), **Cornell:** "That's where I...lot of words." (*Rip*—June 1996), **Cornell:** "I think that...with different stuff." (*Melody Maker*—November 27, 1993), **Cameron:** "We weren't really...tracks were down." (*Modern Drummer*—June 1994), **Thayil:** "On *Superunknown* I...one big instrument." (*Guitar Player*—July 1996), **Cameron:** "I've written a...what he'd done." (*Modern Drummer*—June 1994), **Cornell:** "'Superunknown' relates to...know nothing about." (*Melody Maker*—November 27, 1993), **Cornell:** "[Kim] had a...a couple more." (*Impact*—May 1994), **Cornell:** "There's a song...might sound like." *Melody Maker*—November 27, 1993), **Thayil:** "I think a...slips in there." (*Guitar World*—May 1994), **Cameron:** "Gregg and Ben...went for it." (*Modern Drummer*—June 1994), **Shepherd:** "I had people...show those guys." (*The Music Paper*—July 1994), **Shepherd:** "'Head Down' is...just doesn't work." (*Headbangers Ball*—March 12, 1994), **Shepherd:** "I went for...actually more experimental." (*Mesa Boogie*—1996), **Beinhorn:** "I was noticing...anything like it." (*Black Hole Sun: Inside the Song with Michael Beinhorn—Warren Huart: Produce Like A Pro*—April 1, 2019), **Cornell:** "I write songs...which is ridiculous." (*Melody Maker*—March 19, 1994), **Cornell:** "Yeah, I do...we were lucky." (*Rolling Stone*—January 12, 1995), **Thayil:** "It's a Leslie...the song completely." (*Guitar World*—May 1994), **Cornell:** "There's a Leslie...they all did." (*Rolling Stone*—May 19, 2017), **Pinnick:** "One time, we...we accomplished that." (*King's X: The Oral History*—2019), **Thayil:** "'Black Hole Sun'...'Astronomy

Domine' weirdness." (*Shredders! The Oral History of Speed Guitar (And More)*—2017), **Cameron:** "If you ask...the new album." (*Musician*—April 1994), **Cornell:** "*Superunknown* is a...can't explain why." (*Spin*—April 1994), **Cornell:** "It's a shame...but it worked." (*Melody Maker*—November 27, 1993), **Thayil:** "It's a riff...powerful and angry." (*Guitar School*—May 1994), **Cornell:** "We were on...and drive-by shootings." (*Pulse*—March 1994), **Cornell:** "It's about trying...in a cave." (*Rolling Stone*—January 12, 1995), **Beinhorn:** "The very first...track a song." (*Spin*—June 5, 2014), **Ament:** "A song I...personal for me." (*Spin*—June 5, 2014), **Cornell:** "It does remind...that period, really." (*Spin*—June 5, 2014), **Thayil:** "We always had...that's no joke." (*Spin*—June 5, 2014), **Cameron:** "I'm proud to...it every time." (*Modern Drummer*—June 1994), **Cameron:** "I replaced all...Gregg [Keplinger] invented." (*Modern Drummer*—June 1994), **Cornell:** "One time I...I'm hearing voices'." (*Rip*—April 1994), **Cornell:** "No, but '4th...the Indian reservation'." (*Rip*—April 1994), **Cornell:** "'4th of July...something they didn't." (*Kerrang!*—March 1, 1997), **Cornell:** "I remember having...never done before." (*Rolling Stone*—May 19, 2017), **Considine:** "As for bassist...of a b-side." (*Rolling Stone*—March 10, 1994), **Cameron:** "The drums were...little too obvious." (*Modern Drummer*—June 1994), **Cornell:** "It's a big...it was literal." (*Rolling Stone*—May 19, 2017), **Cornell:** "Yeah, the lyrics...sure specifically where." (*Rolling Stone*—May 19, 2017), **Shepherd:** "The cover kind...you go—*Superunknown*." (*M.E.A.T. Magazine*—March/April 1994), **Ashare:** "Soundgarden have always...promising new directions." (*The Boston Phoenix*—March 4, 1994), **Browne:** "On a purely...does Soundgarden justice." (*Entertainment Weekly*—March 11, 1994), **Considine:** "On the whole...so unfairly consigned." (*Rolling Stone*—March 10, 1994), **Masters:** "*SUPERUNKNOWN*—the title...win this time)." (*M.E.A.T. Magazine*—March/April 1994), **Poneman:** "There's a perspective...kick his ass." (*Spin*—April 1994), **Thayil:** "I think I...kicking your ass." (*Rolling Stone*—July 21, 2009), **Thayil:** "I think [*Superunknown*]...been done before'." (*Grunge Is Dead*—2009), **Cornell:** "I think the...we were successful."

(*Kerrang!*—August 12, 1995), **Thayil:** "We were in...interviews and touring!" (*Metal Hammer*—January 1998), **Thayil:** "The CD booklet...for some reason." (*Headbangers Ball UK*—1994), **Silver:** "All the managers...a good record!" (*Grunge Is Dead*—2009), **Thayil:** "I was at...through the roof'." (*Grunge Is Dead*—2009), **Cornell:** "I think Michael...his biggest moment." (*Entertainment Weekly*—June 3, 2014), **Cross:** "People have talked...is amazingly healthy." (*USA Today*—March 11, 1994)

CHAPTER 17
Cornell: "We wanted to...it live yet." (*Hard Music*—January 1994), **Cornell:** "We've had the...the opposite feeling." (*Kerrang!*—February 12, 1994), **Cameron:** "The first time...lyrics and stuff." (*Kerrang!*—February 12, 1994), **Gold:** "In the lobby...song or something." (*Spin*—April 1994), **Cornell:** "We went to...mind all along." (*Hit Parader*—September 1996), **True:** "The lecture hall...back in Seattle." (*Melody Maker*—March 19, 1994), **Shepherd:** "In Australia it...knew the record." (*The Music Paper*—July 1994), **Thayil:** "We heard rumors...was very credible." (*Grunge Is Dead*—2009), **Silver:** "Layne had been...went very well." (*Grunge Is Dead*—2009), **Ament:** "Unless you've been...sorts of actions." (*Grunge Is Dead*—2009), **Danielson:** "I heard this...room was sealed." (*Grunge Is Dead*—2009), **Thayil:** "I never saw...sitting around crying." (*Grunge Is Dead*—2009), **Silver:** "It put a...need to do'." (*Grunge Is Dead*—2009), **Neely:** "The following day...at one point." (*Rolling Stone*—June 16, 1994), **Silver:** "And then I...and walked away." (*Grunge Is Dead*—2009), **Cornell:** "I wasn't one...it fell off." (*Rolling Stone*—May 19, 2017), **Cornell:** "Yeah. The tragedy...able to resolve." (*Rolling Stone*—May 19, 2017), **Shepherd:** "They like to...and kicking back." (*Grunge Is Dead*—2009), **Cornell:** "It might not...of other people." (*Kerrang!*—August 13, 1994), **Cornell:** "That's one reason...Black Hole Summer'." (*Rolling Stone*—June 16, 1994), **Thayil:** "When Hiro heard...Like Teen Spirit'." (*Grunge Is Dead*—2009), **Cornell:** "['Black Hole Sun']...song like that." (*Grunge Is Dead*—2009), **Cornell:** "When the director...kind of grim." (*Headbangers Ball*

UK—1994), **Honda:** "We thought it...New Orleans way." (*Spin*—July 1996), **Cornell:** "I was glad...a hit song." (*Rolling Stone*—May 19, 2017), **Cornell:** "I wish it...little bit thick." (*CNN*—1994), **Thayil:** "I think we'd...for the forty-nothings." (*Rolling Stone*—June 16, 1994), **Cameron:** "Then towards the...a little bit." (*Grunge Is Dead*—2009), **Thayil:** "It started off...and took off." (*Grunge Is Dead*—2009), **Cornell:** "I think we...already knew that!" (*Kerrang!*—August 12, 1995), **Cornell:** "I don't know...I'll take this." (*MTV Video Music Awards*—September 8, 1994), **Benante:** "I'll never forget...change your stripes'?" (*Survival of the Fittest: Heavy Metal in the 1990's*—2015), **Thayil:** "The first time...a cool gig'!" (*Too High to Die: Meet the Meat Puppets*—2012), **Thayil:** "Around the time...good or bad?" (*The Rocket*—December 21, 1994)

CHAPTER 18
Cameron: "I just want...is for you!" (*The 37ᵗʰ Annual Grammy Awards*—March 1, 1995), **Cornell:** "Being given credit...cool and smart." (*Hit Parader*—September 1995), **Cornell:** "These bands have...marketing, all package." (*Melody Maker*—August 26, 1995), **Cornell:** "Shut up! We're talking now!" (*MTV Europe*—1995), **Turner:** "We did some...really nasty parents." (*Grunge Is Dead*—2009), **Silver:** "That was the...another significant blow." (*A Devil on One Shoulder and an Angel on the Other: The Story of Shannon Hoon and Blind Melon*—2008), **Cornell:** "Most of the...of time off." (*Metal Edge*—July 1996), **Silver:** "I think Chris...to do that." (*Grunge Is Dead*—2009), **Thayil:** "Came back, Chris...your guitars...now'!" (*Grunge Is Dead*—2009), **Cornell:** "We've always done...and way easier." (*Kerrang!*—August 12, 1995), **Cornell:** "Something about the...sound of Soundgarden." (*Hit Parader*—December 1996), **Cameron:** "Litho is a...room sound goes." (*Drum!*—September 1996), **Thayil:** "I used a...there for color." (*Guitar*—July 1996), **Cornell:** "When I was...just the demo." (*Rip*—June 1996), **Kasper:** "It was a...songs. Particularly Cornell." (*Grunge Is Dead*—2009), **Cameron:** "It was my...our buddy, Adam." (*Grunge Is Dead*—2009), **Thayil:** "I ended up...participation was diminishing."

(*Grunge Is Dead*—2009), **Shepherd:** "For me, it...but never did."
(*Grunge Is Dead*—2009), **Kasper:** "I don't remember...than a
drummer." (*Grunge Is Dead*—2009), **Cornell:** "The last
night...another beer then'!" (*Kerrang!*—September 7, 1996),
Morat: "Cornell is much...helmet with dust." (*Kerrang!*—
February 12, 1994), **Cornell:** "We wrote that...'Finger' was
better." (*Metal Hammer*—October 1996), **Kasper:** "I think
[Kim]...Chris the other." (*Grunge Is Dead*—2009), **Thayil:**
"Overall, I don't...have worked out." (*Grunge Is Dead*—2009),
Cameron: "It was good...we had been." (*Grunge Is Dead*—2009)

CHAPTER 19
Cornell: "An attractively packaged...to bite you." (*MTV News*—
1996), **Kozik:** "They got a...understand their problem." (*Toronto
Sun*—May 10, 1996), **Cornell:** "We had two...so we relented."
(*Rolling Stone*—May 30, 1996), **Thayil:** "I wanted to...problem
with it." (*Guitar World*—July 1996), **Shepherd:** "It was
basically...and didn't like." (*Kerrang!*—March 1, 1997), **Thayil:**
"People said there...reminiscent of AC/DC." (*Metal Hammer*—
January 1998), **Cornell:** "It's not the...on the melody." (*Rip*—June
1996), **Thayil:** "Even though there's...solos for that." (*Rolling
Stone*—September 28, 2010), **Thayil:** "I thought of...'Hey Joe'
elicited." (*Rolling Stone*—September 28, 2010), **Cornell:** "Out of
my...would do that." (*Rip*—June 1996), **Cameron:** "'Applebite,'
for example...riff-based tunes." (*Drum!*—September 1996),
Cornell: "Yeah, I loved...on the record." (*Guitar*—July 1996),
Thayil: "It's in 9/8...couple of days." (*Guitar*—July 1996),
Thayil: "The inspiration was...that time signature." (*Songfacts*—
April 8, 2014), **Thayil:** "It's about a...on personal experience."
(*Kerrang!*—March 16, 1996), **Shepherd:** "As we were...into the
mixing." (*Rip*—June 1996), **O'Connor:** "Chalk up a...to the
challenge." (*Rolling Stone*—May 30, 1996), **Browne:** "Upside has
its...purging of genres." (*US*—June 1996), **Thayil:** "Nirvana were
a...and housewives like!" (*Kerrang!*—March 1996), **Cornell:**
"Now there's this...actually gonna like." (*Guitar World*—May
1994), **Cameron:** "The sessions were...not about music." (*Grunge
Is Dead*—2009), **Silver:** "As far as...the same time." (*Grunge Is*

Dead—2009), **Gilbert:** "[Ben] was horribly...supposed to happen." (*Grunge Is Dead*—2009), **Farrell:** "I was very...and Ice-T." (*Rolling Stone*—May 21, 1995), **Cornell:** "Have you noticed...was entirely white." (*Rolling Stone*—May 30, 1996), **Thayil:** "I had my...gone to Detroit." (*Spin*—July 1996), **Cornell:** "Metal-sexist-apalooza...people feel better." (Hypno—V15/I4 1996), **Cornell:** "There were too...be really fun." (*Metal Hammer*—October 1996), **Cornell:** "There was a...figure it out." (*Metal Hammer*—October 1996), **Cornell:** "It's all just...without getting recognized." (*Metal Hammer*—October 1996), **Cameron:** "We'd done the...Kind of embarrassing." (*Grunge Is Dead*—2009), **Cornell:** "It's an issue...survive or not." (*Metal Hammer*—October 1996), **Cornell:** "Following a formula...that already exist." (*Livewire*—May 1996), **Halfin:** "I was in...you can't fight." (*Grunge Is Dead*—2009), **Cornell:** "I was simply...I've ever had." (*Spin*—November 22, 2011), **Chun:** "What made the...from this Soundgarden." (*Honolulu Advertiser*—February 10, 1997), **Shepherd:** "That last show...The final magic." (*Grunge Is Dead*—2009), **Cornell:** "Yeah. For the...that real soon." (*MTV*—February 26, 1997), **Thayil:** "On tour, Chris...little, too late." (*Grunge Is Dead*—2009)

CHAPTER 20
Cameron: "At the time...leaving the band." (*Grunge Is Dead*—2009), **Shepherd:** "Chris Cornell shows...fitting for me." (*Grunge Is Dead*—2009), **Thayil:** "One of the...people's employment periods." (*Grunge Is Dead*—2009), **Cornell:** "We started out...Soundgarden had become..." (*Spin*—November 2, 2012), **Cafaro:** "I was shocked...a shared vision." (*Rolling Stone*—May 29, 1997), **Silver:** "Chris kept it...home absolutely distraught." (*Grunge Is Dead*—2009), **A&M Records:** "After 12 years...members' future plans (press release—April 8, 1997), **Duda:** "Would only characterize...into the unknown'." (*The Rocket*—April 23-May 14, 1997), **Silver:** "There wasn't any...getting more depressed." (*Grunge Is Dead*—2009), **Wylde:** "I remember my...supply and demand." (*Survival of the Fittest: Heavy Metal in The 1990's*—2015), **Cameron:** "We recorded

it...lot of fun." (*Drum!*—September 1996), **Thayil:** "The break-up isn't...be Soundgarden anymore." (*Guitar World*—February 1998), **Thayil:** "No. I was...your desire is." (*Guitar World*—February 1998), **Thayil:** "If we ever...We had fun." (*Guitar World*—February 1998), **Cornell:** "Unfortunately, being a...and didn't care." (*Spin*—September 2006), **Cornell:** "At first to...like everybody else." (*Spin*—September 2006), **Commerford:** "We got together...period of time." (*Alternative Nation*—May 19, 2016), **Cornell:** "Realizing how I...bad it was." (*Spin*—September 2006), **Patrick:** "On September 28...never forget you." (*Instagram*—May 19, 2017), **Shepherd:** "My whole life...n' roll cliché." (*Spin*—September 2010), **Shepherd:** "It was just...*Hater Sessions Two*." (*Classic Rock*—May 2005), **Shepherd:** "Well, Chris' voice...song right there." (*Classic Rock*—May 2005), **Shepherd:** "I slipped into...a carpenter's grunt." (*Bass Player*—March 12, 2013), **Shepherd:** "Kim would be...the Mariners games." (*Classic Rock*—Summer 2005), **Halfin:** "The thing about...when they drank." (*Classic Rock*—Summer 2005), **Halfin:** "One of the...'Keep everyone away'." (*Classic Rock*—Summer 2005), **Kurtz:** "I realized...like...through my forehead." (*Apocalypse Now*—1979), **Ament:** "I don't think...a long time." (*Grunge Is Dead*—2009), **Thayil:** "Tom Morello was... the Crocodile Cafe]." (*Rolling Stone*—July 21, 2009)

CHAPTER 21
Thayil: "We're not the...to the idea." (*Spin*—September 2010), **Cameron:** "We got together...to put out." (*Spin*—September 2010), **Hay:** "I was lucky...I remember Soundgarden." (*Seattle PI*—April 17, 2010), **Shepherd:** "It was boring...The antiques are moving?'!" (*Spin*—September 2010), **Shepherd:** "Nowhere. Literally. I've...I'm totally broke." (*Spin*—September 2010), **Peisner:** "Shepherd is part...slightly gamey overcoat." (*Spin*—September 2010), **Thayil:** "Either a ghost...at a distance." (*CNN Entertainment*—October 26, 2010), **Soundgarden:** "Over the past...*Ben, Chris, Kim and Matt* (*soundgardenworld.com*—February 15, 2011), **Kasper:** "I'd gone on...like 'Helter Skelter'." (*Grunge Is Dead*—2009), **Prato:** "It's funny that...sounds like it."

(*Rolling Stone*—February 18, 2011), **Thayil:** "Ben and I...and collective performances." (*Rolling Stone*—February 18, 2011), **Thayil:** "What's unusual about...or a cathedral." (*Rolling Stone*—February 18, 2011), **Thayil:** "I think Matt's...talking about that." (*Rolling Stone*—February 18, 2011)

CHAPTER 22

Thayil: "We are jamming...to know that." (*Rolling Stone*—February 18, 2011), **Thayil:** "Now, we are...for that purpose." (*Rolling Stone*—February 18, 2011, **Shepherd:** "I think we...we were, actually." (*Grunge Is Dead*—2009), **Cameron:** "Ultimately, we took...in my life." (*Grunge Is Dead*—2009), **Thayil:** "The main riff...song that is." (*Songfacts*—April 8, 2014), **Thayil:** "Jokingly referred to...of the world." (*King Animal Commentary*—2012), **Thayil:** "This riff that...thing to it." (*King Animal Commentary*—2012), **Cornell:** "Lyrically kind of...going to happen." (*King Animal Commentary*—2012), **Shepherd:** "It was a...crap going on." (*King Animal Commentary*—2012), **Cornell:** "It's like one...a wood chipper." (*Live from the Artists Den*—2019), **Dolan:** "Now, there isn't...a Melvins t-shirt." (*Rolling Stone*—November 13, 2012), **Berman:** "And in the...out in 1998." (*Pitchfork*—November 16, 2012), **Ouellette:** "In music, it's...firmly in place." (*Loudwire*—November 12, 2012), **Prato:** "Although Soundgarden has...early next year." (*Rolling Stone*—November 14, 2012), **Shepherd:** "That's an old...I hang out." (*Bass Player*—March 12, 2013), **Cornell:** "'Limo Wreck' is...as important there." (*Rolling Stone*—May 19, 2017), **Thayil:** "We were asked...around to that." (*Rolling Stone*—February 18, 2011), **Silver:** "You have to...to this day." (*Grunge Is Dead*—2009), **Shepherd:** "Every record we...songs and stuff." (*Classic Rock*—Summer 2005), **Cornell:** "There's always a...what happened before." (*Rolling Stone*—September 30, 2016), **Cornell:** "#Detroit finally back to Rock City!!!!" (*Twitter*—May 17, 2017)

CHAPTER 23

Cornell: ""To my @vickycornell...Happy #MothersDay2017" (*Twitter*—May 14, 2017), **Cornell:** "I'm just tired." (*The Detroit*

News—May 19, 2017), **Michigan's Wayne County assistant medical examiner:** "Drugs did not...cause of death." (*Rolling Stone*—June 2, 2017), **Vicky Cornell:** "Many of us...type of tragedy." (*Rolling Stone*—June 2, 2017), **Vicky Cornell:** "Approximately a year...keeping him up." (*ABC News*—February 21, 2018), **Vicky Cornell:** "He had really...He was forgetful." (*ABC News*—February 21, 2018), **Cornell:** "___ is in...talk, had relapse." (email—March 22, 2017), **Recovery Village:** "Some of the...walking or talking." (*Recovery Village*—no date given), **Pinsky:** "Benzos over a...history of addiction." (*drdrew.com*—May 22, 2017), **Pinsky:** "This man should...End of story." (*drdrew.com*—May 22, 2017), **Croff:** "We stand by...cause of death" (*The Detroit News*—July 10, 2017), **Woody:** "We investigated all...but a suicide." (*The Detroit News*—July 10, 2017), **Vedder:** "About two days...love him forever." (*Rolling Stone*—June 7, 2017), **Vicky Cornell:** "Chris was dying...of Timmy C." (*Alternative Nation*—May 19, 2016), **Miller:** "Many people who...or planning it." (*Harvard Health Publishing*—September 24, 2012), **Cornell:** "I had friends...completely different guy." (*The Howard Stern Show*—June 12, 2007)

CHAPTER 24
Thayil: "There were two...vs. Black Sabbath'." (*Pit*—Spring 1990), **Thayil:** "An alternative underground...rock metal band." (*Melody Maker*—March 28, 1992), **Thayil:** "We were typed...Andrew Dice Clay." (*USA Today*—March 11, 1994), **Thayil:** "At the beginning...had told them." (*Alternative Press*—March 1994), **Thayil:** "We weren't influenced...was probably happenstance." (*Guitar Magazine*—July 1996), **Thayil:** "I think in...identified with them." (*Punk! Hardcore! Reggae! PMA! Bad Brains!*—2014), **Endino:** "Chrome, which was...on to Chrome." (*Survival of the Fittest: Heavy Metal in The 1990's*—2015), **Cornell:** "It includes some...afraid of crowds." (*Classic Rock*—July 6, 2016), **Thayil:** "When Soundgarden formed...of all time." (*Too High to Die: Meet the Meat Puppets*—2012), **Thayil:** Top-5 Album List (*Rock Power*—May 1992), **Lanham:** "Cornell is heavily...author Sylvia Plath." (*Pulse!*—March 1994), **Cameron:**

"Chris' lyrics deal...relate to them." (*Rolling Stone*—June 16, 1994), **Cornell:** "Lyrical ideas happen...the right feel." (*Metal Edge*—July 1996), **Cornell:** "Smoke a lot...it's paid off." (*Making Music*—May 1994), **Cornell:** "I always used...got my ranger." (*Musician*—April 1994), **Thayil:** "I'd say the...in drop-D." (*Guitar World*—July 1996), **Thayil:** "I smoke pot...is about beer..." (*Kerrang!*—April 4, 1992), **Cameron:** "On long drives...on the road." (*High Times*—July 1992), **Cameron:** "Sometimes. I think...always been helpful." (*High Times*—July 1992), **Thayil:** "That happened naturally...rest of us." (*Guitar One*—November 1996), **Thayil:** "I have the...like you'd expect." (*Guitar Player*—July 1996), **Thayil:** "Mine is East...a kid, perhaps." (*Guitar Magazine*—July 1996), **Thayil:** "Just the idea...other that way." (*Guitar Magazine*—July 1996), **Thayil:** "One of my...should be easy!" (*The Guitar Magazine*—December 1996), **Thayil:** "Don't take lessons...something you explore." (*Guitar World*—July 1996), **Thayil:** "I got an...trippy element too'." (*Guitar Player*—July 1996), **Shepherd:** "I played pretty...dirty, weird shit." (*Bass Player*—March 12, 2013), **Shepherd:** "Sometimes I would...gap. Rookie mistake!" (*Bass Player*—March 12, 2013), **Cameron:** "I think a...I already have." (*Modern Drummer*—July 1999), **Cornell:** "I'm influenced by...me into music." (*Metal Hammer*—October 1996), **Thayil:** "Chris had very...beautiful Beatles melody." (*Long Live Queen: Rock Royalty Discuss Freddie, Brian, John & Roger*—2018), **Cornell:** "If I didn't...anything he wants." (*Los Angeles Times*—August 25, 1991), **Townsend:** "Chris Cornell was...build some chops." (*Survival of the Fittest: Heavy Metal in The 1990's*—2015), **Tracy G:** "When I was...single like that." (*Long Live Queen: Rock Royalty Discuss Freddie, Brian, John & Roger*—2018), **Friend:** "This is what...he's always exploring." *Survival of the Fittest: Heavy Metal in The 1990's*—2015), **Dio:** "Soundgarden was a...their own 'independence'." *Survival of the Fittest: Heavy Metal in The 1990's*—2015), **Endino:** "I kind of...and it's accidental." *Survival of the Fittest: Heavy Metal in The 1990's*—2015), **Shepherd:** "Kim's a flake...as I am." (*Details*—April 1994), **Thayil:** "Chris is a...pull it off." (*The*

Rocket—December 21, 1994), **Cornell:** "I'm not the...way of working." (*Hit Parader*—September 1995), **Halfin:** "Soundgarden were probably...downhill from there." (*Grunge Is Dead*—2009)

PHOTO CREDITS

OTHER BOOKS
BY GREG PRATO

Music:

A Devil on One Shoulder and an Angel on the Other: The Story of Shannon Hoon and Blind Melon

Touched by Magic: The Tommy Bolin Story

Grunge Is Dead: The Oral History of Seattle Rock Music

No Schlock...Just Rock! (A Journalistic Journey: 2003-2008)

MTV Ruled the World: The Early Years of Music Video

The Eric Carr Story

Too High to Die: Meet the Meat Puppets

The Faith No More & Mr. Bungle Companion

Overlooked/Underappreciated: 354 Recordings That Demand Your Attention

Over the Electric Grapevine: Insight into Primus and the World of Les Claypool

Punk! Hardcore! Reggae! PMA! Bad Brains!

Iron Maiden: '80 '81

Survival of the Fittest: Heavy Metal in the 1990s

Scott Weiland: Memories of a Rock Star

German Metal Machine: Scorpions in the '70s

The Other Side of Rainbow

Shredders!: The Oral History of Speed Guitar (And More)

The Yacht Rock Book: The Oral History of the Soft, Smooth Sounds of the 60s, 70s, and 80s

100 Things Pearl Jam Fans Should Know & Do Before They Die

The 100 Greatest Rock Bassists

Long Live Queen: Rock Royalty Discuss Freddie, Brian, John & Roger

King's X: The Oral History

Facts on Tracks: Stories Behind 100 Rock Classics

Take It Off: Kiss Truly Unmasked

Sports:

Sack Exchange: The Definitive Oral History of the 1980s New York Jets

Dynasty: The Oral History of the New York Islanders, 1972- 1984

Just Out of Reach: The 1980s New York Yankees

The Seventh Year Stretch: New York Mets, 1977-1983

Printed in Great Britain
by Amazon